01/03

British Elections & Parties
VOLUME 7

BRITISH
ELECTIONS
& PARTIES
VOLUME 7

EDITED BY
Charles Pattie • David Denver
Justin Fisher • Steve Ludlam

FRANK CASS
LONDON • PORTLAND, OR

First published in 1997 in Great Britain by
FRANK CASS PUBLISHERS
Newbury House, 900 Eastern Avenue
London IG2 7HH

and in the United States by
FRANK CASS PUBLISHERS
c/o ISBS, 5804 N.E. Hassalo Street, Portland, Oregon 97213-3644

ISBN 0 7146 4860 4 (cloth)
ISBN 0 7146 4417 X (paper)
ISSN 1368-9886

Printed in Great Britain by
Bookcraft (Bath) Ltd, Midsomer Norton, Avon

CONTENTS

For details of past and future contents of this and our other journals please visit our website at *http://www.frankcass.com/jnls*

PREFACE

This is the seventh volume in a series published under the auspices of the Elections, Public Opinion and Parties (EPOP) specialist group of the Political Studies Association. As always, the book contains the best papers from the annual EPOP conference, hosted in this instance by the University of Sheffield in September 1996. The conference was sponsored by the Economic and Social Research Council, the International Political Science Association Research Committee on Comparative Representative and Electoral Systems, and UK-ELECT: we gratefully acknowledge their support. We are indebted to the conference participants who once again made EPOP a lively and stimulating experience, and to the authors of the articles published here, who coped admirably with tight deadlines. We also wish to express our thanks to Cathy Jennings of Frank Cass who has been a continuing source of support, encouragement, ideas and advice.

As in past years, the volume includes a comprehensive reference section containing information of interest to elections and parties specialists.

EPOP continues as one of the liveliest study groups in the PSA. As this volume testifies, the group's interests range widely. In large part, its dynamism is due to its membership, which includes academics, pollsters and journalists. Further details about EPOP can be obtained from any of the editors, or the EPOP web site at http://www.lgu.ac.uk/psa/epop.html.

Charles Pattie   David Denver   Justin Fisher   Steve Ludlam

April 1997

NOTES ON CONTRIBUTORS

Agnès Alexandre is completing a PhD at the *Institut d'Etudes Politiques* in Paris and at the *Centre d'Etudes de la Vie Politique Française* (CEVIPOF). Her main research interest is in French and British right-wing political parties and their attitudes to European integration.

John Bartle is a PhD student at the University of Essex. His research interests include voting behaviour, political marketing and political knowledge. He has forthcoming articles in the *British Journal of Political Science* and in *Readings in Political Marketing*, edited by N.J. O'Shaughnessy and S. Henneberg (New York: Praeger). He was awarded the David Butler prize at the 1996 EPOP conference for the article contained in this volume.

Harold D. Clarke is Regents Professor of Political Science, University of North Texas. His research focuses on voting, elections and the political economy of party support in Anglo-American democracies. His articles have appeared in journals such as the *American Political Science Review, American Journal of Political Science, British Journal of Political Scienc,* and *Journal of Politics*. Current projects include studies of voting behaviour in the 1995 Quebec sovereignty referendum and the dynamics of party support in Britain.

James Cornford is a Senior Research Associate in the Centre for Urban and Regional Development Studies (CURDS) at Newcastle University. In the field of electoral studies, he is the joint author (with Daniel Dorling and Bruce Tether) of 'Historical Precedent and British Electoral Prospects' (*Electoral Studies*, 1995, 14(2): 123–42). His other research interests include the implications of information and communications technologies for urban and regional development and the development of the UK housing market.

John Curtice is Deputy Director of the ESRC Centre for Research into Elections and Social Trends (CREST) and Reader in Politics at the University of Strathclyde. Co-Director of the British Election Study since 1983 he is co-author/editor of *How Britain Votes, Understanding Political Change, Labour's Last Chance?* and a number of reports in the British Social Attitudes series. He was a member of the Market Research Society's Inquiry team into the performance of the polls in the 1992 election.

Daniel Dorling is lecturer in Geography at Bristol University and formerly British Academy Fellow at Newcastle University. With James Cornford he has analysed the effects of the housing market crash for Her Majesty's Treasury. Recent books include *A New Social Atlas of Britain* (Wiley, 1995), *The Population of Britain* (Champion *et al.*, OUP, 1996) and *Mapping: Ways of Representing the World'* (with Fairbairn, Longman, 1997). He is currently studying the 1997 general election and inequalities in health for the ESRC.

Neil T. Gavin is a lecturer in the School of Politics and Communication Studies at the University of Liverpool. He has published in *Parliamentary Affairs, Representation* and *Media, Culture and Society*.

Nan Dirk de Graaf teaches at Nijmegen University, the Netherlands, and is an Associate Member of Nuffield College, Oxford. His main research interests are the political and cultural aspects of social stratification and marriage patterns. His recent (joint) publications include 'Class Mobility and Political Preference' (*American Journal of Sociology* 1995); 'Educational Heterogamy and Cultural Participation' (*Acta Sociologica* 1995); 'Why Are the Young More Postmaterialist?' (*Comparative Political Studies* 1996); 'Married Women's Economic Dependency' (*British Journal of Sociology* 1997); 'National Context, Parental Socialization and Religious Belief' (*American Sociological Review* 1997).

Anthony Heath is Professor of Sociology at the University of Oxford and, with Roger Jowell, is Co-Director of CREST (the ESRC-funded Centre for Research into Elections and Social Trends). His publications (with Roger Jowell and John Curtice) include *How Britain Votes* (Pergamon, 1985), *Understanding Political Change* (Pergamon, 1991) and *Labour's Last Chance* (Dartmouth, 1994). He is currently working on a study of the 1997 General Election.

Richard Heffernan teaches British politics in the Department of Government at the London School of Economics. Co-author of *Defeat from the Jaws of Victory: Inside Kinnock's Labour Party*, he is presently working on a study of political change in the UK since 1975, mapping out the ideological consequences of 'Thatcherism'.

Xavier Jardin is completing a PhD at the *Institut d'Etudes Politiques* in Paris and at the *Centre d'Etudes de la Vie Politique Française* (CEVIPOF). His main research interest is in the French Gaullist party and the connection between the RPR's national office and local party organizations.

Ron Johnston is Professor of Geography at the University of Bristol. His main research interests are in electoral and political geography, and he is currently involved in studies of the Boundary commission, of local campaign spending and fund-raising, and of the influence of perceptions of the health of regional economies on voting.

Michael Kenny is a lecturer in the Department of Politics, University of Sheffield. His principal research interests are the New Left, contemporary political theory, theories of British decline, and modernization in the Labour Party. His publications include *The First New Left* (Lawrence and Wishart, 1995).

Ariana Need is a graduate student at Nijmegen University, where she is completing her doctorate on the effects of religious and social mobility on political behaviour. She has been a Visiting Student at Nuffield College where she began the research on which the current article is based. Her publications include 'Losing my religion' (*European Sociological Review* 1996).

Charles Pattie is Senior Lecturer in Geography at the University of Sheffield. His primary research interests are in electoral geography. Recent publications include work on local economic conditions and voting, and political campaigning. He is currently working on local campaign fund-raising.

Andrew Russell is a lecturer in Government at the University of Manchester. His research interests centre around the impact of geography and economic attitudes on electoral behaviour. He is due to convene the EPOP conference at the University of Manchester in 1998.

Martin J. Smith is Senior Lecturer in Politics at the University of Sheffield. His principal research interests are British politics, public policy and pressure groups. He is currently directing an ESRC project on the changing role of government departments in the policy process. His publications include *Contemporary British Conservatism* (co-edited with S. Ludlam: Macmillan, 1996)

Nick Sparrow is Director of ICM Research, the company he and two other former directors of Marplan founded in 1989. He has conducted opinion polls regularly for *The Guardian* since 1980 and currently also works for *The Observer*, *The Scotsman* and the Mirror Group. Together with John Turner he won the 1995 Market Research Society prize for the best article in the society's journal. He was also a member of the Market Research Society's Inquiry team into the performance of the polls in the 1992 election.

James Stanyer is researching into news media reportage of the British party conferences in the 1990s. He teaches at Queen Mary and Westfield College, University of London and at City University.

Marianne C. Stewart is Professor, School of Social Sciences, University of Texas at Dallas. Her research interests concern the impact of economic evaluations and party leader images on voting behaviour and party identification in Canada, Great Britain and the United States. She has published in journals such as the *American Political Science Review, American Journal of Political Science, European Journal of Political Research, Journal of Politics,* and *Political Research Quarterly.*

Andrew Taylor is Professor of Politics at the University of Huddersfield. He has published several books on British politics, including *The Politics of the Yorkshire Miners, From Salisbury to Major: Continuity and Change in Conservative Politics,* and *The Trade Unions and the Labour Party.*

John Turner is Principal Lecturer in Politics in the School of Social Science and Law at Oxford Brookes University. A former journalist, he is a regular commentator on local and national elections for BBC Radio. Together with Nick Sparrow he won the 1995 Market Research Society prize for the best article in the society's journal.

Paul Whiteley is Professor of Politics at the University of Sheffield. He has published several books and his articles have appeared in journals such as the *British Journal of Political Science, European Journal of Political Research, Journal of Politics, Political Research Quarterly,* and *Political Studies.* His research interests include the causes and consequences of party activism, political participation in Britain and other mature democracies, and the political economy of party support.

ABSTRACTS OF ARTICLES

Political Awareness and Heterogeneity in Models of Voting:
Some Evidence from the British Election Studies
John Bartle

Voters appear to differ in both their interest in politics and ability to understand it. Formal models of voting behaviour have tended to assume, however, that the effect of any given variable is *homogeneous* – fixed with respect to other variables such as political knowledge. Relaxing this assumption enables an exploration of *heterogeneity*. It is easier to predict the attitudes of highly aware voters from knowledge of related attitudes as compared with those of less aware voters. More aware voters place greater weight on their general predispositions when deciding how to vote and in forming preferences about specific policy issues.

The Missing Tories in Opinion Polls: Silent, Forgetful or Lost?
John Curtice, Nick Sparrow and John Turner

Two principal methodological problems were identified after the polls failed to anticipate the Conservatives' victory in the 1992 general election. First, Conservative voters were less willing to say how they would vote. Second, the samples tended to be too downmarket. Since 1992, quota polls have persistently found that Labour 'won' the 1992 election when they ask their respondents to recall their 1992 vote. This discrepancy cannot be adequately accounted for by the tendency for voters to align their past behaviour with their current preference, a tendency which has in any case diminished. Rather, Conservative voters clearly continued to be less willing to participate in polls while quota controls still failed to ensure that those approached for interview were fully representative. Both problems may be addressed by 'adjustment' techniques, but these may not be adequate and are not always given sufficient prominence.

Anchors Aweigh: Variations in Strength of Party Identification and in Socio-political Attitudes among the British Electorate, 1991–94
Ron Johnston and Charles Pattie

Traditional accounts of the British electorate present a picture of long-term stability. Individual voters may be influenced at any particular election by short-term factors. But their basic loyalties are long term and fixed: party identification and political ideologies provide the anchors which hold voters' loyalties steady against short-term fluctuations. The traditional account has been increasingly questioned, however. Longitudinal data from the British Household Panel Survey allows an analysis of the stability of these anchors annually for a four-year period in the early 1990s. Contrary to the traditional account, the results reveal substantial short-term fluctuations in individual voters' party identifications and political attitudes. If party identification and political attitudes are voters' anchors, they are embedded in very shallow sediments.

Class and Nation in England and Scotland

Anthony Heath, Nan Dirk de Graaf and Ariana Need

Studies of electoral cleavages tend to agree that class is important only in the absence of other major political cleavages such as language, national identity and religion. Where these are present, the class cleavage is generally less important. British elections, however, have often been seen as an exception, with class playing a much more important role than either religion or national identity. But the rise of nationalist voting in Scotland and Wales gives grounds for re-examining the situation. A comparison of voting in Scotland and England reveals the importance of religion, national identity and ethnicity as voting cleavages, in addition to class. While religion and national identity play a part, they do not necessarily replace class, but there are grounds to suspect that class has been overtaken by national identity as an influence on the vote in Scotland.

Crooked Margins and Marginal Seats

James Cornford and Daniel Dorling

The next election will be substantively fought and won in a relatively small number of 'marginal' seats. The traditional concept of a marginal seat is not particularly helpful in studying the electoral landscape of today, as it is based on a rough rule of thumb established in the days when electoral competition in Britain was dominated by just two parties. Then, if the gap between the two parties' votes was less than 10 per cent of the total vote, the seat was considered to be vulnerable to change. The constituency results for every general election since 1955 have been examined here to determine more precisely, using probabilities based on previous general elections, the gap that is required for a seat to become vulnerable. In many cases it is found that the size of that gap is related to the performance of the third party.

A Question of Interaction: Using Logistic Regression to Examine Geographic Effects on British Voting Behaviour
Andrew Russell

Individual level data from 1990–92 is analyzed in order to assess the role played by social class, geography and economic attitudes in producing variations in reported vote intention during the long campaign leading to the 1992 British general election. Using logistic regression techniques all three independent variables are shown to be significant, but the crucial advantage of the logistic model is that it allows the detailed analysis of interaction effects between independent variables. The interaction effects between economic and geographic variables show that although how an individual decided to vote was largely shaped by what they thought of the economy – through personal economic expectations – the extent to which optimism or pessimism could be discounted was spatially variable. Crucially under certain conditions the geographic considerations were likely to dominate economic considerations, illustrating that an autonomous regional cleavage was an important part of the socialization milieux that framed an individuals' partisanship in the early 1990s.

Discourses of Modernization: Gaitskell, Blair and the Reform of Clause IV
Michael Kenny and Martin J. Smith

This contribution examines the debates surrounding both Gaitskell's and Blair's attempts to reform the party (and in particular Clause IV), and argues that while the 'Old Labour' versus 'New Labour' dichotomy is a simplification – and is unconvincing as an account of Blair's political trajectory – some important changes to party thinking and culture have taken place under Blair. Indeed it is argued that while Gaitskell did attempt to reshape social democracy, particularly through his distinction between the ends of socialism and the appropriate means for its realization, he still framed reform very much within the socialist and social democratic agendas that dominated the party until the 1980s and persisted in certain forms into the 1990s.

Voting Behaviour, the Economy and the Mass Media: Dependency, Consonance and Priming as a Route to Theoretical and Empirical Integration
Neil T. Gavin

This study looks at three areas of theoretical and empirical development in mass media research (Dependency Theory; Priming Theory; and Noelle-Neumann's concept of Consonance) and at their relevance to some outstanding theoretical issues in the modelling of voting behaviour and public opinion. The author examines aggregate and individual level models (with a predominant, though not exclusive, focus on the economy, and economic issue and perceptions). The object is to explore the potential contribution that a media dimension can make to the explanatory underpinning of models of voting behaviour and public opinion.

Error Correction Models of Party Support: The Case of New Labour

Harold Clarke, Marianne C. Stewart and Paul Whiteley

This study uses econometric methods for the analysis of nonstationary, cointegrated variables to specify and analyze an error-correction model of interrelationships among Labour vote intentions, best prime minister judgements and party identification since the beginning of 1992. These three series have varied over this time period, and analyses reveal that both best prime minister judgements and party identification have had important influences on the short- and long-term dynamics of Labour-vote intentions. The analyses also show that subjective economic evaluations have exerted direct and indirect effects on Labour support.

The Enhancement of Leadership Power: The Labour Party and the Impact of Political Communications

Richard Heffernan and James Stanyer

Political leaders use political communications to enhance their power and autonomy. Using Labour as a case study, this contribution explores how far modern media communications permit party leaders to set agendas within their parties and in the wider world. The Labour Party's communications strategies enable an 'inner core élite' to project a 'party identity' through the news media in order to manage the party's public profile. Distinguishing between the impact of media on parties as 'producers' and its effects on electors as 'consumers' is important in understanding and explaining the chronology, causes and consequences of political communications.

From the Europe of Nations to the European Nation?: Attitudes of French Gaullist and Centrist Parliamentarians

Agnès Alexandre and Xavier Jardin

This study analyzes the initial results of a survey of attitudes of French Gaullist and Centrist parliamentarians towards European integration, following the University of Sheffield/ESRC *Conservative Parliamentarians and European Integration* survey. Based on the same hypotheses, the survey observes the extent of potential Gaullist Euro-rebellion and confirms the strength of confederal attitudes within the Centrist party, in spite of both leaders' efforts to smooth out divergent attitudes. The results are examined here in respect to the questions of national sovereignty, economic and social issues, and institutional issues. The results stress the divisions on Europe within the governing majority and suggest future difficulties for the French government.

The Conservative Party, Electoral Strategy and Public Opinion Polling, 1945–1964

Andrew Taylor

The article looks at the Conservative Party's approach to opinion polling in the aftermath of defeat in 1945 and in the context of the electoral politics up to 1964. It considers how polling was related to electoral strategy in a period in which the Conservatives won three consecutive elections and then experienced decay and defeat in 1964. A key theme of the contribution is the party's attempts to understand the political consequences of mass affluence. The article also relates Conservative thinking on electoral strategy to the emerging academic analysis of mass electoral behaviour.

Political Awareness and Heterogeneity in Models of Voting: Some Evidence from the British Election Studies

John Bartle

In constructing general models of voting behaviour, analysts have traditionally treated the electorate as *homogeneous*. It is assumed that the impact of any given variable on vote is the same for all voters, so that regression coefficient represents a sort of 'average effect' for the electorate as a whole (see Rivers, 1991). While general models of voting behaviour are highly desirable, they should not ignore the possibility that the effect of any given variable depends upon the context and that there is considerable *heterogeneity*. The effect of continuous variables (such as age or years of education) may vary over their range, so that the constant marginal effect implied by a single regression slope is misleading. The effect of some variables may also depend upon the value of others (the effect of trade union membership might differ between the salariat and the working class, for example). It has been argued that one particularly important source of heterogeneity arises from differences in political awareness (Bartels, 1996).

The many uses of the phrase 'political awareness' has muddied research in this area. It has been used, for example, to refer to voters' awareness of their 'real' material interests. It has also been used to refer to interest in politics. As used in this article, however, it refers to the 'extent to which an individual pays attention to politics *and* understands what he or she has encountered (Zaller, 1992: 21; emphasis in the original). It 'denotes' intellectual or cognitive engagement with public affairs as against emotional or affective engagement or no engagement at all' (Zaller, 1992: 21). The measure of political awareness used in this article, is therefore based on what voters actually know about the machinery of government and elections.

Previous Research on Political Awareness

The earliest studies of voting behaviour in the United States set out to examine how voters' preferences shaped their choices between the parties and provided the vital link between the public interest and government activity (see Berelson *et al.*, 1954). Somewhat disturbingly for supporters of liberal democracy, these studies found that voters were only vaguely aware of the issues in any given election. Moreover, the attitudes that voters did have appeared to be highly unstable over time, so that what purported to be a 'true' political attitude seemed to be little more than a guess, a response to hide ignorance, or an attempt to please the interviewer. In addition, the electorate was said to be largely incapable of conceiving of the political world in abstract ideological terms. The only attitude which appeared to be meaningful and stable was party identification which was said to structure the political world for voters, providing cues about what was good, what was bad and what was to be desired (see Converse, 1964: 211; Miller, 1976: 24).

The authors of *The American Voter* recognized that such a generalization was much too sweeping to be applied without qualification. They identified various types of voters according to their 'levels of conceptualization', defined in terms of 'a priori judgements about the breadth of contextual grasp of the political system that each seemed to represent' (Converse, 1964: 215). The most sophisticated of these types were labelled group A. This comprised both 'ideologues', whose view of politics suggested an understanding of abstract terms, and 'near ideologues' who applied ideological terms with less consistency. The next group in terms of sophistication, group B, were called 'group benefits voters' since they evaluated politics 'in terms of their response to interests of visible groupings in the population' (Campbell *et al.*, 1960: 234). They were followed by group C, those who made some reference, 'however nebulous or fragmentary, to a subject of controversy over public policy' (Campbell *et al.*, 1960: 240). Often such references were limited to just one issue. The behaviour of the final group, D, either seemed to lack any issue basis at all or merely involved some form of 'mud-slinging' against the other side.

Embedded within these different groups were very different assumptions about the causal relationships among explanatory variables. Group A voters were most able to structure their attitudes by reference to a few simple beliefs about the world. Group B voters, on the other hand, established which party generally supported people like themselves and proceeded to support that party. While it might have been possible to suggest that this constitutes 'ideology by proxy' (see Campbell *et al.*, 1960: 234; Downs, 1957: 100), these voters had little knowledge of the day-to-day complexities of politics and there was little evidence that they were able to relate specific issues to their general beliefs without cues from their parties. They were linked to a party as a result of their identity with a group, rather than a correspondence between their issue preferences and the platforms of the parties. Group C was a highly heterogeneous group in itself, ranging from those who voted according to the 'goodness and badness' of the times to others who associated a particular party with some benevolent deed such as providing welfare payments. The final group, D, seemed to defy analysis and consisted of party identifiers who knew nothing other than to which party they 'belonged'. For these voters with 'impoverished attitudes' it was suggested that the sense of party identification would have a direct effect on voting, unmediated by specific attitudes towards issues (Campbell *et al.*, 1960: 136).

While *The American Voter* showed a commendable interest in heterogeneity, more recent research within the Michigan tradition has largely neglected the issue of voter awareness. Typically it is assumed that a single regression coefficient can summarize the effect of any given variable for all voters (compare Shanks and Miller, 1991: 184–188). That is, it is assumed that two voters with identical social and psychological characteristics behave in exactly the same way. However, variations in the causal processes across groups are clearly plausible if there are variations in voter awareness. Consider, for example, the case of two voters A and B, who have exactly the same characteristics: they are black, council house tenants, score -0.4 on a left–right scale and +1 on a scale of economic evaluations. If we assume that only these characteristics are relevant to the vote decision; that there are two parties X and Y; that the effect coefficients for A are 0.7. for race, -0.4 for tenure, 3 for left–right position and 1.2 for economic evaluations; and that the effect coefficients are exactly the same in the case of B, except that he places less weight on his left–right position, so that the effect coefficient is 2, then voters will support party X if their predicted probability is 0.5 or greater and the predicted votes of A and B are given by the equations:

(A) Vote = $(0.7 * 1) + (-0.4 * 1) + (3 * -0.4) + (1.2 * 1) = 0.3$ (Vote for Y)
(B) Vote = $(0.7 * 1) + (-0.4 * 1) + (2 * -0.4) + (1.2 * 1) = 0.7$ (Vote for X)

Thus, because voter A gives more weight to his ideological position, he is predicted to vote for Y rather than X. Even if B places less weight on economic evaluations (so that the effect coefficient is 0.8, for example), and thus has the same predicted probability of voting for X and Y (0.3), the processes *underlying* the vote are very different.

The difference between A and B may represent an important distinction between voter types. Voter A is analogous to a Group A voter in *The American Voter*. He is able to generalize from a few general beliefs to his specific preferences. He makes greater use of his general ideological position when responding to issues as diverse as the poll-tax, privatization and defence spending. His attitudes may be integrated into something approaching an 'ideational whole' or 'belief system', so that knowledge of his position on one issue can predict those on another (see Scarbrough, 1984: 24). His attitudes are also likely to be more consistent over time and he is unlikely to be confused in interviews by subtle variations in question wording and order. Voter B on the other hand, can make little overall sense of what appears to him to be a series of unrelated issues. He is confused by minor differences in question wording and question order and his responses vary rapidly. It could be argued that these differences are of little importance when the aim is to predict behaviour. If it is to characterize the causal processes underlying voting behaviour, however, heterogeneity cannot be ignored. This is particularly the case for variables located further back in the *funnel of causality*, such as ideological position or party identification, which can have large indirect effects by shaping variables located between them and the vote. A failure to recognize such heterogeneity would generate misleading estimates of their effects.

The authors of *The American Voter* also examined the effect of party identification on political awareness and found that 'independent' voters, who declined to accept a party identification, were *less* aware than party identifiers (Campbell *et al.*, 1960: 143). The typical 'independent', far from being the dispassionate juror weighing one issue against another, was ill-informed, disinterested and apathetic. By contrast, stronger identifiers were found to be much more aware of issues and more concerned about the outcome of the election.

The years since *The American Voter* and its British counterpart *Political Change in Britain* have witnessed a reappraisal of the basic assumptions about party identification and the virtual irrelevance of ideological positions. It now appears that party identification, far from being an *exogenous* variable which responds only to idiosyncratic changes in social characteristics, is actually *endogenous,* responsive to some of the political forces it was hitherto assumed to shape (see Fiorina, 1981; Franklin, 1992; Green and Palmquist, 1990, 1994). Improvements in survey design and measurement techniques have demonstrated that much of what the authors of *The American Voter* had taken to be random response was in fact attributable to measurement error – the problems which respondents encounter when faced with ambiguous questions and limited response categories (see Achen, 1975). Paralleling these improvements in methodology there has been a thoroughgoing reappraisal of the notion of ideology at the heart of the Michigan approach. It has been argued that the Michigan treatment of ideology in terms of 'a particularly elaborate, close-woven, and far reaching structure of attitudes' (Campbell *et al.*, 1960: 192) is a peculiarly narrow definition (Scarbrough, 1984). Heath *et al.* have argued that people hold:

> fundamental and *enduring attitudes* towards general moral and political principles like equality, and that these enduring core beliefs can account in part for the individual's attitudes towards the *more transient political issues* of the day. (1994: 115; emphasis added)

Scarbrough (1984) has also suggested that the recognition of 'abstract terms' – such as 'left' and 'right' – is also a poor measure of underlying fundamental attitudes as are single items (see, however, Evans *et al.*, 1996). Empirical and theoretical advances have been much kinder, therefore, to theories of voting behaviour based upon notions of instrumental choices (see Pierce and Sullivan, 1980). However, the homogeneity assumption has remained unchallenged until recently. This situation is now changing. Analysts such as John Zaller in his work *The Nature and Origins of Mass Opinion* and in collaboration with Stanley Feldman (Zaller and Feldman, 1992) have reopened the issues relating to political awareness and heterogeneity. Zaller's theory of survey response treads a middle course between the early Michigan analyses, which took temporal instability as an indication that voters did not have true attitudes, and later work which suggested that much of this instability was attributable to measurement error. For Zaller it is not enough to rely on convenient assumptions about measurement error. There does appear to be genuine ambivalence on many issues, which causes measurement error and this in itself requires explanation.

Axioms of Zaller's Theory of Survey Response

Zaller's theory of survey response is based on a few simple but powerful axioms about respondent behaviour. Like all general theories, these axioms simplify reality a great deal, but the resulting deductions are well supported by the data, suggesting that the theory has considerable leverage over a number of issues in survey response (see King *et al.*, 1994: 30).

There are two basic units of analysis in the model. The first is 'considerations', defined as 'any reason that might induce someone to decide a political issue one way or another'. The second is 'predispositions', defined as: 'stable individual traits that regulate the acceptance or non-acceptance of the political communications the person receives' (Zaller, 1992: 22). Zaller suggests that such predispositions are rooted in the respondent's enduring characteristics, their socialization and lifetime experiences. Analysts schooled in the Michigan assumptions would interpret predispositions as party identification, but more recent research on this subject has cast doubt on the stability of that variable and its centrality in the voter's mind. In this article predispositions are represented by positions on ideological dimensions.

The first axiom (the *reception* axiom) suggests that 'The greater a person's level of cognitive engagement with an issue, the more likely he or she is to be exposed and to comprehend (i.e., receive) political messages concerning that issue' (Zaller, 1992: 42). The second (the *resistance* axiom), is that 'People tend to resist arguments that are inconsistent with their political predispositions, but they do *so only to the extent that they possess the contextual information necessary to perceive a relationship between the message and their predispositions*' (Zaller, 1992: 44; emphasis added). The

third (the *accessibility* axiom) is that 'The more recently a consideration has
been called to mind or thought about, the less time it takes to retrieve that
consideration or related considerations from memory and brings them to the
top of the head for use' (Zaller, 1992: 48). The final axiom (the *response*
axiom) states that 'individuals answer survey questions by averaging across
the considerations that are immediately salient or accessible to them' (Zaller,
1992: 49).

For Zaller the vital point is that most people are genuinely ambivalent
about many issues. They have a series of considerations which they bring to
bear when responding to any survey item and responses are affected most by
those considerations that are immediately salient. Zaller agrees with the
authors of *The American Voter* that voters do not necessarily have 'true'
attitudes which simply await discovery. If asked similar questions in a variety
of contexts (using different question wording and order, for example) their
responses would fluctuate around a mean. Which one of the voter's multiple
potential opinions is expressed depends on the immediate context in which
the question is placed. So, for example, apparently minor variations in
question wording, the race of the interviewer and the order in which questions
are asked can prompt apparently contradictory responses over time, simply
because they bring differing considerations to mind (see Schuman and
Presser, 1981).

Zaller's axioms generate a series of deductions about the nature of public
opinion. Like Campbell *et al.* and Converse before him, he assumes that the
chief source of attitude constraint (that is, the extent to which attitudes on one
issue can be used to predict those on another) is sociological. He believes that
ideologies and belief systems are formulated by a minuscule segment of the
population – the political elites. These are communicated to the population as
a whole, but because levels of political awareness are generally low only the
most aware voters receive such messages. It follows that voters with higher
levels of awareness are more likely to learn 'what goes with what' and reject
considerations that conflict with their predispositions. Their attitudes are
therefore highly correlated along any particular ideological dimension
(Deduction 1).

It is possible to go beyond this somewhat intuitive proposition by noting
that, among the elites, positions on two or more dimensions are often
correlated *as if* they were underpinned by a few core beliefs about the world.
Among the British party elites, for example, attitudes towards economic,
political and social equality (positions on the left–right scale) are often
correlated with attitudes towards individual freedom (positions on the
liberal–authoritarian scale). Conservative ideology traditionally combines
right-wing, laissez-faire economics and authoritarian attitudes; while Labour
ideology traditionally combines left-wing economics and liberal attitudes. It

follows that attitudes across these dimensions should be more highly correlated for politically aware voters but, since it is difficult to make the more abstract links across dimensions, these correlations are low (Deduction 2) (Zaller, 1992: 48). It follows that there should be less variation with political awareness among those issues that are 'closer to home' (such as economic evaluations) (Deduction 3).

A further deduction (not made specifically by Zaller himself, but very much within the spirit of his model) is that more politically aware voters should place more weight on ideological predispositions when deciding how to vote (Deduction 4). They should also place more weight on their general ideological positions when evaluating specific policy proposals (Deduction 5).

Political Awareness and the British Voter

All of these deductions can be tested using evidence from the 1992 British Election Study. This survey contained ten 'true or false' questions, which are listed in the appendix, designed to measure political awareness. Correct responses were summed to create an index of political awareness which ranges from 0 (for the least aware) to 10 (for the most aware).

This index is, of course an imperfect measure of knowledge. It may well be that a voter fully understands where the parties stand on issues and is able to recognize prominent politicians, but is unable to answer the questions that are used to make up the index. However, one can assume that political awareness is rather like intelligence. Just as there is a reasonable correlation between those who are good at maths and those who are good at language, so those who have some knowledge about government ought also, on the whole, to be those most intellectually engaged in politics. All theories and models depend upon assumptions and, as they go, this seems to be quite plausible.[1]

The mean score for respondents across the ten questions was 5.4, so that voters did slightly better on average than they would have, had they simply made random guesses. Before examining the four deductions from Section 1 above, it is useful to consider briefly variables which are associated with political awareness. Table 1 shows the results of an ordinary least squares regression in which the dependent variable is the respondent's score on the index of political awareness.

Age is entered twice as an explanatory variable – as simple chronological age and as age squared. Both coefficients are significant but, while age has a positive coefficient, age squared is negative. This suggests that initially increasing age has a positive effect on political awareness but that after a certain age political awareness falls. This makes intuitive sense and underlines the importance of testing for non-linearities. Given that all the other characteristics are represented by dummy variables, it is possible to

TABLE 1

THE SOURCES OF POLITICAL AWARENESS

Variable	B Coeff	Std. error
Father Petty Bourgeoisie	-0.110*	0.162
Father Salariat	+0.249*	0.150
Father Foreman	-0.108*	0.184
Father Working Class	-0.239*	0.138
Age	+0.122	0.013
Age (Squared)	-0.001	0.001
Black	-1.272	0.218
Male	+1.179	0.083
Catholic	-0.235*	0.133
Church of England	-0.111*	0.082
Degree	+1.326	0.158
Further Ed. (Not Degree)	-0.333*	0.312
A Level	+0.741	0.133
O Level	+0.263	0.107
CSE	+0.053*	0.126
Petty Bourgeoisie	-0.135*	0.169
Salariat	+0.497	0.115
Foremen	-0.371	0.193
Working Class	-0.691	0.107
Home Owners (outright)	+0.287	0.110
Home Owners (mortgage)	+0.128*	0.103
Public Sector	+0.132*	0.090
Shares	+0.198	0.098
Private Health Insurance	+0.309	0.093
Benefits Main income source	-0.501	0.138
Trade Union Member	+0.171*	0.110
Former Union Member	+0.112*	0.091
Cared about outcome	+0.691	0.092
Read quality paper	+0.679	0.179
Constant	0.975	

Adj-R^2 = 0.35123 $p < 0.05$ (two-tailed test) * Not significant at 0.05 level.

Source: For this and all subsequent tables and figures, the source is the BES 1992 survey.

gauge their relative effects by simply comparing the regression coefficients. First, black voters are 1.27 points less aware than white voters, controlling for all other factors.[2] This may reflect some combination of language difficulties, cultural barriers to participation and alienation. Second, men are 1.18 points more aware than women. Third, as could have been expected, education has particularly strong effects on awareness. Those with degrees as their highest qualification are 1.33 points more aware than those without any formal qualifications. Those with A levels are 0.74 points more aware and those with O levels 0.26 points more aware. Fourth, social class also seems to have important effects. Members of the salariat are 0.49 points more aware than the base category (routine non-manual workers), while both foremen and technicians and the working class are 0.37 and 0.69 points respectively less aware. Fifth, home owners are 0.29 points more aware than council tenants, though housing tenure may be picking up the effect of other variables (in particular, income) that are not included in this model.[3] This suggestion is supported by the apparent importance of share ownership. Finally, although both present and past members of trade unions are more aware, these effects are not statistically significant.

The remaining two explanatory variables measure the respondents' interest in the campaign and their exposure to quality newspapers. Those voters who cared a great deal about the election result were 0.69 points more aware than those who did not, controlling for all other factors, while readers of the quality press were 0.68 points more aware than readers of other newspapers.

If the deductions made above are correct, then these results suggest the kinds of voter who approximate to group A voters. Male, white, university-educated, home owners, who care about the election outcome and read a quality newspaper, have a high predicted score on the index of political awareness. They ought to exhibit the sort of attitude constraint suggested in Deductions 1 and 2. Following Deductions 4 and 5, they should also place greater weight on their ideological positions when deciding how to vote or how to evaluate a specific policy proposal. Other groups such as female, black, poorly educated council tenants, who care little about the outcome and do not read a quality newspaper have a lower predicted score. Their attitudes should exhibit less evidence of constraint and they may place less weight on their ideological positions. They may approximate to group D voters.

Voter Awareness and Ideological Constraint

Deduction 1

Are attitudes on any underlying ideological dimension subject to greater attitude constraint for more aware voters? The BES survey contains a series of 'agree/disagree' items which enable the construction of a series of scales tapping general attitudes towards change in the direction of greater political, social and economic equality (that is, positions on a left–right scale) and general attitudes relating to matters of individual freedom and conscience (positions on a liberal–authoritarian scale).[4] There is a further left–right scale, based on voters' self-placement on four issue proximity scales which can also be used to test this deduction. The wording of these items are set out in the appendix. Analyses reported in Bartle (1996) suggest that these scales are both reliable and valid measures of the underlying constructs.

If Zaller's deductions are correct, then more aware voters should have a higher average inter-item correlation. Table 2 sets out the Cronbach's alpha (which summarizes the inter-item correlations for the items making up the scales) for each of the three ideological scales by levels of political awareness. In all three cases there is a positive relationship between political awareness and the alpha. For example, the alpha in the first column (for the 6-item left–right scale) falls with political awareness. To be sure, the pattern is not linear, but Figure 1 shows that the trend is undeniable. Moreover, where the alphas rise when they are expected to fall, this may be the result of the small numbers involved (thus, N=40 for those with a score of 10). A similar pattern occurs in Column 2 of Table 2 for the 8 -item liberal–authoritarian scale. However, the average alpha for this scale is generally lower compared with the left–right scale, suggesting that voters may have some difficulty in generalizing from their ideological positions to the specific items. Finally, the second left–right ideological scale, which uses respondent's self-placement on a scale with paired alternatives at the poles demonstrates a similar relationship between awareness and the alpha. However, the alpha falls somewhat more rapidly, suggesting that less aware voters may have particular problems with such items. On the whole, however, Zaller's first deduction is supported by the data.

TABLE 2

THE INTER-CORRELATIONS WITHIN VARIOUS IDEOLOGICAL SCALES AND
POLITICAL AWARENESS

Cell entries represent Cronbach's alpha for items making up scale

Quiz	L-R	L-A	L-P
10	0.62	0.79	0.71
9	0.81	0.78	0.86
8	0.76	0.68	0.77
7	0.76	0.67	0.72
6	0.75	0.66	0.64
5	0.69	0.45	0.65
4	0.56	0.52	0.36
3	0.63	0.52	0.46
2	0.44	0.29	0.44
1	0.55	0.43	0.44
0	0.54	0.48	0.65

Notes: 'Quiz' refers to score on index of political awareness; 'L-R' to the 6-item left–right scale; 'L-A' to the 8-item liberal–authoritarian scale and 'L-P' to the 4-item left–right scale based upon spatial measures.

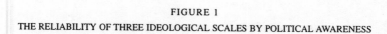

FIGURE 1

THE RELIABILITY OF THREE IDEOLOGICAL SCALES BY POLITICAL AWARENESS

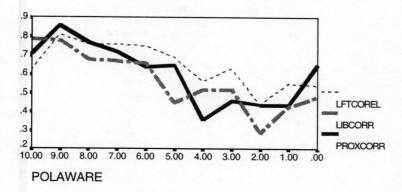

POLAWARE

Note: 'LFTCOREL' represents the 6-item left–right scale, 'LIBCORR' the liberal–authoritarian
scale and 'PROXCORR' the 4-item left–right scale.

Deduction 2

Zaller's second deduction implies that respondents' positions on the left–right
and liberal–authoritarian scales should be more highly correlated for the most
aware voters, because they are more likely to receive the messages from the
elites about 'what goes with what'. Their attitudes ought therefore to be bound
together into something approaching the structured belief system which the
authors of *The American Voter* and *Political Change in Britain* took as their
measures of 'ideological thinking' among the electorate. Column 1 of Table 3
sets out the correlation between the 6-item left–right scale and the 8-item
liberal–authoritarian scale. This information is also shown diagramatically in
Figure 2. Generally speaking, the correlations are quite modest, suggesting
that people do not, on the whole, relate their positions on one dimension to the
other. To a large extent therefore, these dimensions cut across each other.
Again, the pattern of correlations is not neatly linear – those who score 6 on
the index have a higher average correlations than those who score 7.
However, there is a fairly clear positive relationship: the higher the level of
political awareness, the higher the correlation between the two dimensions.

Column 2 in Table 3 shows the correlation between respondents' scores
from the 4 and 6-item left–right scales (also shown in Figure 2). The
relationship is again as predicted. More politically aware voters are more
consistent in their responses, no matter how positions on that particular
ideological dimension are measured.

TABLE 3

CORRELATIONS BETWEEN POSITIONS ON IDEOLOGICAL SCALES

Cell entries represent Pearson's R

Quiz	6-item LR & 8-item LP	6-item LR 4-item LR
10	0.28*	0.54*
9	0.27	0.83
8	0.24	0.78
7	0.14	0.67
6	0.19	0.57
5	0.11	0.53
4	0.13	0.44
3	0.04	0.31
2	0.14	-0.02
1	-0.15*	0.34
0	0.01	0.37

$p < 0.05$ * Not significant at 0.05 level.

Notes: See Table 2.

FIGURE 2

THE CORRELATIONS BETWEEN IDEOLOGICAL SCALES AND POLITICAL AWARENESS

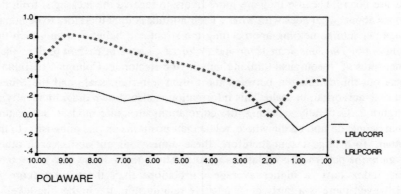

Notes: 'LRLACORR' represents the correlations between scores on the 6-item left–right scale and the 8-item liberal–authoritarian scale; 'LRLPCORR' represents the correlations between scores on the 4 and 6-item left–right scales.

Deduction 3

The third deduction made by Zaller is that there should be fewer differences in consistency at different levels of political awareness for questions which are 'closer to home' or involve less remote considerations than ideological values. Table 4 sets out the Cronbach's alpha for two economic evaluations scales made up of four items.

TABLE 4

CORRELATIONS BETWEEN ITEMS MAKING UP ECONOMIC EVALUATIONS SCALES

Cell entries represent Cronbach's alpha for items making up scale

Quiz	Econ1	Econ2
10	0.44	0.37
9	0.50	0.30
8	0.46	0.34
7	0.58	0.35
6	0.55	0.33
5	0.47	0.35
4	0.53	0.23
3	0.56	0.39
2	0.42	0.29
1	0.37	0.21
0	0.28	0.28

Notes: 'Quiz ' is score on index of political awareness; 'econ1' is a 4-item scale made up of respondent's evaluations of personal, national, regional and household standard of living and 'econ2' is a 4-item scale made up of respondent's evaluations of prices, unemployment, strikes and taxation.

The relationship between Cronbach's alpha and political awareness appears to be much weaker in these two cases. For example, for 'ECON1', made up of items measuring the respondent's, the general and the region's economic prosperity over the last five years, the alpha only really falls a great deal for those voters with a score of 2 or less on the index of political awareness. The same is true of 'ECON2' which is made up of evaluations of trends in unemployment, prices, strikes and taxation over the last five years. Here the relationship between political awareness and consistency is, if anything, rather weaker. This is clearly shown in Figure 3.

Of course, it could be argued that the most aware voters are *more* likely to distinguish between their personal standard of living and that of the nation as a whole, or to distinguish between trends in prices and unemployment. The responses of highly aware voters may be more firmly based in fact, while less aware voters may see the world in more black and white terms, according to their political predispositions or partisanship. The analysis in Table 4 only

FIGURE 3

THE RELIABILITY OF TWO ECONOMIC EVALUATIONS SCALES BY POLITICAL AWARENESS

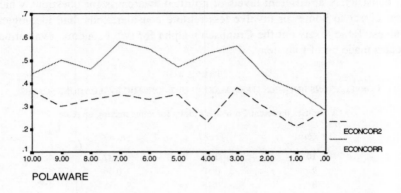

POLAWARE

Notes: 'ECONCORR' represents a 4-item scale of respondent's evaluations of personal, national, regional and household standard of living; 'ECONCOR2' represents a 4-item scale of respondent's evaluations of prices, unemployment, strikes and taxation.

really makes sense if one believes that the items are tapping some underlying economic evaluations dimension. Awareness of all these complications should caution against reliance on a single measure of economic evaluations. In particular, public opinion polls are likely to contain a lot of 'noise' from less aware respondents.

Political Awareness and Political Preference

Deduction 4

Deductions 4 and 5 are not specifically made by Zaller, but they are very much within the spirit of his model. Deduction 4 suggests that politically aware voters place greater weight on their general ideological beliefs when deciding how to vote. In order to test this proposition, it is necessary to construct a model of voter choice which contains interaction terms between political awareness and ideological positions. The first step, however, is to divide the electorate into high, medium and low awareness groups in order to produce a manageable number of interaction terms and to avoid the problem of multi-collinearity (which would occur if the political awareness variable entered the model many times). The sample was therefore divided into three groups of roughly equal size. The high awareness category consists of respondents who scored 7 or greater on the index of political awareness (N=1095), the medium category consists of those who scored either 5 or 6

(N=793) and the low category consists of those who scored 4 or less (N= 920).

The vote model in Table 5 sets out the results of a logistic regression in which the dependent variable is vote (scored 1 if Conservative and 0 if Labour).[5] In addition to the variables that are reported, this regression controlled for a wide variety of social characteristics.[6] The coefficients for these other variables are not reported here, in order to focus attention on ideological positions and political awareness. The variables reported in Table 5 are left–right and liberal–authoritarian ideological positions, dummy variables for those with high and low levels of awareness, together with interaction terms for highly aware voters and left–right position (Left–Right * High) and low awareness voters and left–right position (Left–Right * Low). Similar interaction terms are included for liberal–authoritarian positions.

TABLE 5

THE EFFECT OF POLITICAL AWARENESS AND IDEOLOGICAL POSITIONS ON
VOTING BEHAVIOUR

	B Coeff	Std. Error
Left–Right Position	+0.609	0.061
Liberal–Authoritarian Position	+0.133	0.042
High Awareness	-2.341*	1.451
Low Awareness	+2.297*	1.381
Left * High	-0.010*	0.086
Left * Low	-0.248	0.077
Liberal * High	+0.124	0.057
Liberal * Low	-0.004*	0.057

per cent predicted correct = 87.49%
p < 0.05 * indicates not significant at 0.05 level.

Note: Coefficients for social characteristics are not reported.

The positive coefficients for the left–right and liberal–authoritarian variables suggest that those who are right wing on matters of economic, political and social equality and those who are authoritarian on liberal–authoritarian issues are both more likely to vote Conservative. The higher value of the left–right coefficient suggests that this dimension is of rather more importance in determining voting behaviour, a finding that fits in well with a priori assumptions. The dummy variables for political awareness suggest that, controlling for all other factors, more aware voters are more likely to vote Labour and less aware voters are more likely to vote Conservative. It must be stressed, however, that both of these coefficients are only just significant at the 0.1 level, and that Table 5 controls for the effects of age, education and social class all of which have strong effects upon political awareness. As a result these coefficients must be interpreted with care.

The coefficients of greatest interest, however, are the four interaction terms. If the importance which voters attach to their general ideological positions varies with levels of political awareness, then the coefficients for the interaction terms will be significant. Moreover, the coefficients will be greater for those with higher levels of awareness. Since the original left–right variable is included in the model, the interaction coefficients indicate whether the effect of left–right position is greater or less than the base (excluded) category (those with medium levels of awareness). In Table 5, the interaction term High * Left–Right, is insignificant. This suggests that highly aware voters place no more weight on their ideological position than do those with medium levels of information. However, the interaction term Low * Left–Right is significant and, as expected, negative. This suggests that low awareness voters place less weight on their general ideological positions than those with medium (and logically those with high) levels of political awareness. Deduction 4 is thus supported. Moving on to the interaction terms for liberal–authoritarian positions and political awareness, it can be seen that the coefficient for High * Liberal is significant and positive, suggesting that highly aware voters place more weight on their position on this dimension, when deciding how to vote. However, the interaction term for those with low levels of awareness is insignificant, suggesting that there is no difference between this group and those with medium levels of information.

Both these results are intuitively plausible. In the case of the left–right dimension both those with high and medium levels of information place more weight on this general predisposition than do those with low levels of awareness. In the case of the liberal–authoritarian dimension, however, only those with high levels of awareness seem to place greater weight on their general liberal–authoritarian positions. In both cases, however, political awareness increases the apparent importance that voters attach to their general ideological positions.

Deduction 5

This deduction suggests that politically aware voters are likely to place more weight on their general ideological beliefs when forming preferences relating to specific issues. In order to test this proposition, it is necessary to construct a model of a specific policy preference which again contains interaction terms involving political awareness and ideological position. The specific policy proposal in this instance is the voter's attitude towards nationalization and privatization as measured by the following questions:

> Just to make sure about your views, are you generally in favour of more *nationalization* of companies by government, more *privatization* of companies by government, or, should things be left as they are?

A *lot* more nationalization/privatization or a *little* more?

Responses are coded from 0 (those who want a lot more companies nationalized) to 4 (those who want a lot more industries privatized), with those who want things to be left as they are coded as 2. Since the variable is not dichotomous, it is not possible to use logistic regression. Moreover, because the dependent variable is not unbounded, but is limited and ordered, unmodified ordinary least squares may generate predicted scores for the variable outside the natural range (0 to 4). For that reason the dependent variable is log-transformed. This is done by adding a very small value (0.01) for those respondents scored 0 and replacing the score 4 with the value 3.99. The logs of these scores are then regressed on the explanatory variables. The results are reported in Table 6.

Because attitudes towards nationalization and privatization should be based upon left–right ideological positions, on this occasion the interaction terms for liberal–authoritarian positions are omitted. Controls were again added for social characteristics. The results suggest that there is, as expected, a strong association between left–right positions and attitudes towards privatization and nationalization. More right-wing people tend to favour privatization, while left-wing people support further nationalization. In this case the dummy variable for high political awareness is insignificant. However, the dummy variable for low levels of awareness is almost significant at the 0.05 level (it is actually significant at 0.08) and positive. This suggests that, controlling for all other factors, less aware voters are more likely to support privatization. Again one must add the caveat that this is after controlling for many social characteristics that are associated with political awareness.

The interaction term for highly aware voters and left–right position (High * Left–Right) is statistically insignificant, suggesting that there is no difference between this group and those with medium levels of awareness. However, the interaction term for those with low levels of information and left–right position (Low * Left–Right) is statistically significant and negative, suggesting that the effect coefficient is smaller for less aware voters. Not only are more aware voters likely to make greater use of their general positions when deciding how to vote, they are more likely to use them when forming specific political preferences as well. Additional analyses suggest that attitudes towards the poll-tax and evaluations of the party leaders are associated with similar interactions between ideological positions and political awareness. Clearly, the effect of many variables appears to depend, at least in part, on the voter's level of political awareness. This is one source of heterogeneity that merits further research.[7]

TABLE 6

THE EFFECT OF POLITICAL AWARENESS AND IDEOLOGICAL POSITIONS ON ATTITUDES
TOWARDS PRIVATIZATION

	B Coeff	Std. Error
Left–Right Position	+0.498	0.046
High Awareness	+0.083*	0.055
Low Awareness	+0.102*	0.060
Left * High	-0.004*	0.005
Left * Low	-0.012	0.006

Adj-R^2= 0.165   p < 0.05   * indicates not significant at 0.05 level.

Note: Coefficients for social characteristics are not reported.

Conclusions and Implications for Research

This article began by suggesting that heterogeneity is an important but largely neglected feature of voting behaviour and that variations in political awareness are one important source of heterogeneity. The analyses reported in Tables 2 to 5 clearly demonstrated that voters appear to differ in their ability to integrate attitudes into some sort of 'belief system'. Politically aware voters appear to have the most consistent set of attitudes – a fact which both Converse and Zaller attribute to the fact that the most aware voters are more likely to receive the messages of the elite, telling them 'what goes with what' (so-called 'social constraint').

However, as Converse (1964: 211) himself noted, there is another source of constraint which is more psychological or cognitive in nature. More aware voters may be more likely to possess the cognitive skills that are required to refer each specific issue to a few core beliefs about the nature of the world. It is not necessary, therefore, to accept Converse and Zaller's 'elite-driven' account as the only possible explanation of the phenomenon of attitude constraint. Although there is much to commend Zaller's theory, it leaves open a number of questions. If the elite does create ideology for voters to absorb, then why did the British electorate apparently reject many of the basic tenets of the parties in recent decades (see Crewe et al., 1977)? What are the limits to the elite's ability to formulate and communicate ideologies? Is there really much connection between left–right, liberal–authoritarian issues and other value dimensions (like post-materialism) at the elite level? If there is not, then the findings in relation to deduction 2 should be less surprising: the party elites themselves may be divided and send contradictory messages to voters about the connections between issues.

The results in Tables 2 to 5 go some way to reconciling some opposing views on the nature of ideology. The first, associated with Converse suggests that voters do not have ideologies or underlying values because there is no evidence of constraint among attitudes, while the second, associated with Elinor Scarbrough, suggests that political issues are complex and voters find it difficult to fit values into specific choices. If one recognizes the importance of political awareness, it is possible to reconcile these two views. The results of improvements in question design and the observed coherence of the attitudes of highly aware voters, is evidence that Converse's general argument is too sweeping a generalization. However, for many voters with poor levels of awareness his characterization is still relevant. It may well be that poorly informed voters have some underlying values which they attempt to apply to any given proposal, but they are so confused by the complexity of the issues that in interviews they guess, hedge, equivocate and are apparently inconsistent. Analyses – particularly those using data from the mid-term, when political debate is less intense – should interpret public opinion with more caution (see Gelman and King, 1993). Pollsters might even consider discounting the responses of those respondents who are politically unaware and therefore sensitive to changes in context.

The results related to Deductions 4 and 5 suggest that the effect of any given explanatory variable is contextual and dependent upon the value taken by other explanatory variables. The models in Tables 5 and 6 suggest that a major source of contextual variation results from differences in political awareness. However, the importance of contextual effects is more general (see Achen, 1992: 197). The effect of unemployment on vote might vary with region. The effect of housing tenure may differ with class. To be sure, many of the possible interactions may turn out to be statistically insignificant but, if a model of increasingly fine grain that mimics the causal processes underlying voting behaviour is to be built, then they should be examined.

Heterogeneity is important, but has often been ignored. It should not be. The early Michigan studies emphasized that voters varied a great deal in their ability to understand issues and to make informed choices. This was emphasized by their extensive analysis of open ended questions which asked voters to describe in their own terms what they liked or disliked about the parties. The emphasis of the Michigan studies on such items served as a caution to analysts eager to believe that responses to every survey item was a measure of some true opinion. This article has also demonstrated that Zaller's theory of survey response represents a fruitful way of unifying many divergent areas of opinion research. Its appeal lies in the fact that it dispenses with the implausible assumption that voters possess a single opinion on any given issue. It reminds over-eager analysts that no survey item is perfect, because the context in which the interview takes place, or the issue is placed (by question wording or question order) can affect the response given. It is well to remind ourselves that some responses should be given more weight than others.

APPENDIX

Survey Items Used to Construct the Index of Political Awareness

 1. The number of members of Parliament is about 100.
 2. The longest time allowed between general elections is 4 years.
 3. Britain's electoral system is based on proportional representation.
 4. MPs from different parties are on parliamentary committees.
 5. No-one is allowed to be on the electoral register in two different places.
 6. Britain has separate elections for the European and the British parliament.
 7. Women are not allowed to sit in the House of Lords.
 8. British prime ministers are appointed by the Queen.
 9. No-one may stand for parliament unless they pay a deposit
10. Ministers of State are senior to Secretaries of State.

Survey Items Used to Construct Scales of Ideological Positions

Left–Right Positions (6-Item Scale)
 1. Ordinary working people get their fair share of the nation's wealth.
 2. There is one law for the rich and one for the poor.
 3. Private enterprise is the best way of solving Britain's economic problems.
 4. Major public services and industries ought to be in state ownership.
 5. There is no need for strong trade unions to protect employees working conditions and wages.
 6. It is the government's responsibility to provide a job for everyone who wants one.

Left–Right Positions (4-item scale)

Respondents are asked to place themselves on an 11-point scale, so that their selection represents their preference for the following series of paired statements.
 1. Getting people back to work should be the government's top priority/Keeping prices down should be the government's top priority.
 2. Government should put up taxes a lot and spend much more on health and social services/Government should cut taxes and spend much less on health and social services.
 3. Government should nationalize many more private companies/Government should sell off many more nationalized industries.
 4. Government should make much greater efforts to make people's incomes more equal/ Government should be much less concerned about how equal people's incomes are.

Liberal–Authoritarian Positions

 1. Young people today don't have enough respect for traditional British values.
 2. Censorship of films and magazines is necessary to uphold moral standards.
 3. People in Britain should be more tolerant of those who lead unconventional lives.
 4. Homosexual relations are always wrong.
 5. People should be allowed to organize public meetings to protest against the government.
 6. Even political parties that wish to overthrow democracy should not be banned.
 7. Britain should bring back the death penalty.
 8. People who break the law should be given stiffer sentences.

ACKNOWLEDGEMENTS

I would like to thank Sarah Birch, Tony Lyons, Elinor Scarbrough and Hugh Ward for comments on an earlier version of this article. I would also like to thank David Denver for advice given during the preparation of the article for this volume. All individuals concerned are absolved from any errors that remain.

NOTES

1. Zaller (1992: 333–45) contains a discussion of the various ways of measuring political awareness.
2. The estimated effects control for all other variables in the model. Strictly speaking therefore they are estimates of the direct effects and give variables no credit for the effect that they may have had on other explanatory variables.
3. The BES contains a lot of missing data on income. In the absence of any reliable method of estimating such missing data, the variable is omitted, in order to analyse as many respondents as possible.
4. Heath *et al.* (1994) construct a 6-item liberal–authoritarian scale. This proved to be unreliable in practice. Two additional items (relating to the death penalty and stiffer sentences) are added to improve the overall reliability of the scale.
5. The model is estimated for only Conservative and Labour voters. It is possible to model Conservative voters against all others or Labour voters against all others, but this might conceal some interesting differences in the effect of variables depending upon whether the 'choice' is between Conservative and Labour or Conservative and Liberal.
6. Other variables in the models include, age, ethnicity, gender, religion, education, social class, region, housing tenure, car ownership, share ownership, private health insurance, trade union membership, unemployment and self-assigned class.
7. Future research will test the proposition that more aware voters are more likely to engage in tactical voting.

BIBLIOGRAPHY

Achen, Christopher H. (1975) 'Mass Political Attitudes and Survey Response' *American Political Science Review* 69: 1218–31.
Achen, Christopher H. (1992) 'Social Psychology, Demographic Variables and Linear Regression: Breaking the Iron Triangle in Voting Research' *Political Behaviour* 12: 195–211.
Bartels, Larry (1996) 'Uninformed Votes: Information Effects in Presidential Elections' *American Journal of Political Science* 40: 194–230.
Bartle, John (1996) *Left–Right Position Matters, But Does Social Class? Causal Models of Voting Behaviour for the 1992 General Election* Paper presented at the Elections, Parties and Public Opinion (EPOP) Conference, University of Sheffield, September, 1996.
Berelson, Bernard; Paul Lazarsfeld, and William McPhee (1954) *Voting*. Chicago: Chicago University Press.
Breen, Richard and Anthony Heath (1993) *Rational Choice, Party Identification and Political Knowledge* Paper presented at the Elections, Public Opinion and Parties Annual Conference, University of Lancaster, 17–19 September.
Butler, David and Donald Stokes (1974) *Political Change in Britain: The Evolution of Electoral Choice*. London: Macmillan.
Butler, David and Dennis Kavanagh (1992) *The British General Election of 1992*. London: Macmillan.
Campbell, Angus, Philip Converse, Warren E. Miller and Donald Stokes (1960) *The American Voter*. New York: John Wiley.
Converse, Philip (1964) 'The Nature of Belief Systems in Mass Publics' in D. Apter, (ed.) *Ideology and Discontent*. New York: Free Press.
Crewe, Ivor; Bo Sarlvik and James Alt (1977) 'Partisan Dealignment in Britain, 1964–77' *British Journal of Political Science* 7: 129–190.
Downs, Anthony (1957) *An Economic Theory of Democracy*. New York: Harper & Row.
Elster, Jon (1989) *Nuts and Bolts for the Social Sciences*. Cambridge: Cambridge University Press.
Evans, Geoffrey, Anthony Heath and Mansur Lalljee (1996) 'Measuring Left–Right and Libertarian–Authoritarian Values in the British Electorate' *British Journal of Sociology* 47: 91–112.

Fiorina, Morris P. (1981) *Retrospective Voting in American National Elections*. New Haven: Yale University Press.

Franklin, Charles H. (1992) 'Measurement and the Dynamics of Party Identification' *Political Behaviour* 14: 297–309.

Gelman, Andrew and Gary King (1993) 'Why Are American Presidential Election Campaign Polls so Variable When Votes are So Predictable?' *British Journal of Political Science* 24: 409–451.

Green, Donald Philip and Bradley Palmquist (1990) 'Of Artifacts and Partisan Instability' *American Journal of Political Science* 34: 872–902.

Green, Donald Philip and Bradley Palmquist (1994) 'How Stable is Party Identification?' *Political Behaviour* 16: 437–466.

Heath, Anthony, Geoffrey Evans and Jean Martin (1994) 'The Measurement of Core Beliefs and Values: The Development of Balanced Socialist/Laissez Faire and Libertarian/Authoritarian Scales' *British Journal of Political Science* 24: 115–131.

Heath, Anthony, Roger Jowell and John Curtice (1985) *How Britain Votes*. Oxford: Pergamon Press.

Heath, Anthony, Roger Jowell, John Curtice, Geoff Evans, Julia Field and Sharon Witherspoon (1991) *Understanding Political Change: The British Voter 1964–1987*. Oxford: Pegammon Press.

King, Gary, Robert O. Keohane and Sidney Verba (1994) *Designing Social Inquiry: Scientific Inference in Qualitative Research*. Princeton: Princeton University Press.

Miller, Warren E. (1976) 'The Cross-National Use of Party Identification as a Stimulus to Political Inquiry' in I. Budge, I. Crewe and D. Farlie (eds) *Party Identification and Beyond*. London: John Wiley.

Palmer, Harvey D. (1995) 'Effects of authoritarian and libertarian values on Conservative and Labour Party Support in Great Britain' *European Journal of Political Research* 27: 273–292.

Pierce, John and John L. Sullivan (1980) (eds) *The Electorate Reconsidered*. Beverley Hills: Sage Publications.

Rivers, Douglas (1991) 'Heterogeneity in Models of Electoral Choice' *American Journal of Political Science*:737–757.

Scarbrough, Elinor (1984) *Ideology and Voting Behaviour: An Exploratory Study*. Oxford: Clarendon Press.

Schuman, Howard and Stanley Presser (1981) *Questions and Answers in Attitude Surveys: Experiments on Question Form, Wording and Context*. New York: Academic Press.

Shanks, J. Merrill and Warren E. Miller (1991) 'Partisanship, Policy and Performance: The Reagan Legacy in the 1988 Election' *British Journal of Political Science* 21: 129–197.

Zaller, John R. (1992) *The Nature and Origins of Mass Opinion*. Cambridge: Cambridge University Press.

Zaller, John R. and Stanley Feldman (1992) 'A Simple Theory of Survey Response: Answering Questions Versus Revealing Preferences', *American Journal of Political Science* 36: 579–616.

The Missing Tories in Opinion Polls: Silent, Forgetful or Lost?

John Curtice, Nick Sparrow and John Turner

In the 1992 general election the opinion polls seriously underestimated the Conservatives' strength. Four polls published on polling day, on average put the Labour Party one point ahead; but when the ballot boxes were opened just hours later the Conservatives proved to be as much as eight points ahead. The reasons for this debacle have been the subject of substantial debate (see particularly Jowell *et al.*, 1993; Worcester, 1996). The Market Research Society's own enquiry into the election polls found that part of the explanation lay in 'late swing'. But it also argued that there were two problems with the ways in which the polls had been conducted. First it stated that 'some inadequacies were found in the operation of the quota system' (Market Research Society, 1994) the effect of which was to render their samples too downmarket and thus pro-Labour. Second it also found that Conservative supporters were less 'likely to reveal their loyalties than Labour supporters', thus contributing to an underestimate of their number.

This article revisits this debate, not by looking once again at what happened in 1992, but by examining the performance of the polls since 1992. It argues that both problems were still apparent after the 1992 election. First, it suggests that Conservative supporters continued to be less willing to declare their party allegiance in line with the expectations of the theory of a 'spiral of silence' (Noelle-Neumann, 1986). Second, looking at the distribution of how people said they voted in 1992, it argues that quota polls in particular continued to interview too many Labour voters and that the discrepancy between these polls' 1992 vote and the actual outcome cannot be accounted for by people forgetting how they actually voted. Adjustment mechanisms introduced by some companies since 1992 may have helped to correct these problems, but they may still be inadequate and are certainly often given insufficient prominence by their media clients.

Recalling the 1992 Vote

By the 1980s quota sampling had become the norm in British public opinion polling. Under this method, each interviewer is given an area in which to work (usually either a local government ward or parliamentary constituency) and then is required to interview within that area a given number of persons with a particular set of social characteristics. The characteristics most commonly used in setting these quotas are sex, age, social class, work status and housing tenure. Although the sample may then be further weighted after interviewing by additional characteristics such as car ownership, the key assumption behind quota sampling is that the quota controls should be sufficient to ensure that a survey contacts a politically representative sample of the population.

The *prima facie* evidence that in practice the samples secured by quota surveys after the 1992 election continued to be unrepresentative lies in the results they obtained when they asked their respondents how they voted in the 1992 election. As Table 1 shows, all three companies which were still using quota sampling in their regular monthly opinion polls in spring 1996 found that according to their respondents, the Conservatives lost the 1992 election by a margin of between 5 and 7 per cent.[1] In reality, of course, they won by 8 per cent.

TABLE 1
RECALL OF 1992 VOTE (%)

	Con	Lab	Lib Dem	Other	Con Lead
Quota face-to-face. MORI	39	44	14	3	-5
Quota face-to-face. Gallup	38	45	14	3	-7
Quota face-to-face. NOP	38	44	13	5	-6
1992 result	43	35	18	3	7

Source: Aggregated Gallup, MORI and NOP polls, March–May 1996. We are grateful to Gallup, MORI and NOP for providing these data.

It might be thought that these figures were sufficient evidence that quota polls continued to suffer from an anti-Conservative bias. However, it has long been known that voters' recall of how they voted in a general election some years previously is liable to be faulty (Himmelweit *et al.*, 1978). Most importantly, the error is not random. Rather, voters tend to align their declared past votes with their present intentions, a kind of *post hoc* rationalization of how they now wished they had acted in the past. Moreover, those who voted for the Liberal Democrats (and their predecessors) appear to be particularly forgetful about how they previously voted. For example, an ICM poll in July 1990 found that only 9 per cent remembered having voted Alliance in 1987 when in reality they won 23 per cent of the vote.

We thus apparently have a ready rationalization for the discrepancy between how voters now say they voted in 1992 and the actual result. For in terms of current voting intentions these polls on average put Labour more than thirty points ahead of the Conservatives with the Liberal Democrats on just 15 per cent. We might then anticipate that some voters will indeed have forgotten having voted Conservative or Liberal Democrat and claim to have voted Labour instead. As a result any poll conducted in 1996 can be expected to have underestimated Conservative and Liberal Democrat support in 1992 and overestimated Labour's.

We are, however, able to test how far such rationalizations can account for the discrepancy between voters' recall of how they voted in 1992 and the actual outcome. The British Election Panel Study (BEPS) regularly interviewed throughout the 1992–97 parliament a sample of respondents who were first contacted immediately after the 1992 general election. These respondents were not only asked how they had voted immediately after the event, but they were also asked to recall their general election vote both in the summer of 1994 immediately after the European elections and in the spring of 1995 after the May local elections. We can therefore estimate the extent of the impact of misremembering on voters' reports of their 1992 vote during the middle of the 1992–97 parliament. And we find that although *post hoc* rationalization does account for some of the discrepancy between recall vote in the polls and the actual result, it is far from sufficient to account for all of it.

Recalled Past Vote and Voting Intentions: The British Election Panel Study

The British Election Panel Study, like the quota polls, found a significant swing from Conservative to Labour in voting intentions in the mid-term of the 1992–97 parliament. In the 1994 wave, respondents were asked how they would have voted if there had been a general election on the day of the European elections, while in 1995 they were asked the same question of a hypothetical general election held on the day of that May's local elections. As Table 2 shows, the results broadly confirm the message of the polls that Labour would indeed have won a general election comfortably on either occasion. So, if the reason why quota polls also found that Labour 'won' the 1992 election is because of *post hoc* rationalization, there is every reason to anticipate that this would be equally evident in BEPS.[2]

TABLE 2
ACTUAL AND INTENDED VOTE (%)

	1992	1994	1995
Con	46	28	26
Lab	34	45	51
Lib Dem	17	23	18
Other	3	4	4
Lead	+12	-17	-25

Source: British Election Panel Survey (BEPS) weighted data.

Table 3 meanwhile shows how members of the BEPS actually recalled how they voted in 1992 on the three occasions on which they were asked. (In each case those who either said they did not vote or could not recall how they voted have been excluded.) There was some decline in the proportion who remembered having voted Conservative, and a corresponding increase in the proportion saying they voted Labour. But, even so, the distribution of recall vote in both 1994 and 1995 is far closer to the actual election result than that in any of the quota polls. Moreover, there is not any evidence of a decline in reported Liberal Democrat voting.

TABLE 3
ACTUAL 1992 VOTE AND RECALLED VOTE (%)

	1992	1994	1995
Con	46	45	42
Lab	34	35	37
Lib Dem	17	17	18
Other	3	3	3
Lead	+12	+10	+5

Source: BEPS weighted data

There are two possible explanations for this outcome given the previous evidence that *post hoc* rationalization does occur. On the one hand the theory may no longer be as valid as it was. Perhaps British voters have become better able to remember how they actually voted at the last election. After all, unlike Alliance voters in the 1987–92 parliament, the party for which Liberal Democrat voters voted in 1992 has continued in existence. Perhaps this has reduced the potential for confusion. Or perhaps on the other hand, *post hoc* rationalization remains as widespread as before, but has simply never been strong enough to account for a discrepancy of the size found in Table 1.

Table 4 helps us to adjudicate between these two possible explanations. In the last two columns we show for each of the three main parties' 1992 supporters (and those who abstained), the proportion who gave the same report of their behaviour in 1994 and 1995 respectively. In order to establish whether the level of misremembering is different from earlier years we show in the first two columns the same information for previous panel studies in the British Election Study series. In the first column we show the proportion who in 1970 gave the same report of their behaviour in the 1966 election as they had given immediately after that election. Meanwhile in the second column we show the equivalent information for reports acquired in 1987 and 1992 of voting behaviour in the 1987 election.

TABLE 4
CORRECTLY RECALLING PAST VOTING

	of 1966 vote in 1970 (%)	of 1987 vote in 1992 (%)	of 1992 vote in 1994 (%)	of 1992 vote in 1995 (%)
Original Reported Vote				
Conservative	92	93	90	85
Labour	87	89	89	89
Lib/Alln/Lib Dem	45	54	76	73
Abstain	45	26	63	59

Source: 1966–70 and 1987–92: British Election Study as reported in MRS (1994); 1992–94 and 1992–95: British Election Panel Study.

Two points immediately stand out. First, despite the severe haemorrhaging of Conservative support after 1992, the proportion of 1992 Conservative voters still reporting the same behaviour two or three years later was almost as high as in previous panel studies. It would appear that about nine in ten Conservative and Labour voters can be relied upon to give consistent reports of their voting behaviour irrespective of the current popularity of the parties. So far as those two parties at least are concerned, the level of misremembering looks as though it has never been high enough to account for the kind of discrepancy we report in Table 1.

Second, however, both Liberal Democrats and abstainers were less forgetful of their previous behaviour than in the past. About two-thirds of 1992 Liberal Democrats gave the same report of their behaviour in 1994 and 1995, while around six in ten abstainers did the same. Although both groups were still more forgetful than Conservative and Labour supporters, the difference between them was much narrower than before. We can thus begin to see why the level of recalled Liberal Democrat vote did not show any evidence of falling in Table 3.

But how far were those who misremembered how they voted in 1992 aligning their reported past vote with their current preference? It should of course be borne in mind that some of the difference between the various reports of 1992 voting behaviour is the product of measurement error generated by, for example, mispunching, miscoding and so on. Our figures thus probably overestimate both the real level of instability in reported vote and the number of people actively aligning their past behaviour with their current preference. This aside, in the 1994 wave we find that as many as 59 per cent of those who gave an inconsistent report of their voting behaviour shifted their recalled 1992 vote to the party they also said they would have voted for in 1994. At 58 per cent, the equivalent figure for the 1995 wave is almost the same.

These figures are almost identical to those found in previous panel surveys. In 1992, 53 per cent of those who gave a different report of their

1987 behaviour in 1992 than they offered in 1987, aligned their past behaviour in line with their 1992 vote. The equivalent figure for the 1966–70 panel was 55 per cent. So although the proportion of those who misremember their vote may indeed have been lower in the 1992–97 parliament, thanks to the improved memory of Liberal Democrat voters (and abstainers), the degree to which those who did misremember were aligning their memory with their current preference does not appear to have changed.

However, the pattern of aligning past vote with current preference has in fact changed in one important respect. Previous panel surveys have found that not only were previous Liberal Democrat voters more forgetful of their past behaviour, but also that those voters who had subsequently switched their current preference to the Liberal Democrats were less likely to align their past behaviour with that current preference. For example, of those who said that they had voted Liberal Democrat in 1992 and who in 1992 misremembered their 1987 vote, just 22 per cent apparently aligned their past behaviour with their current preference. In contrast, the equivalent figure among 1992 Conservative and Labour voters was as high as 73 per cent.

But in the 1992–97 parliament that difference disappeared. In the 1994 wave of BEPS we find that among those currently preferring the Conservatives or Labour and who misremembered their 1992 vote, 66 per cent did so by aligning their 1992 vote with their current preference. This is similar to the figure in the 1987–92 panel. But in contrast to 1987–92, the equivalent figure among current Liberal Democrat voters, 60 per cent, is almost the same as among Conservative and Labour supporters. Similarly, in the 1995 wave the equivalent figures are 65 per cent and 70 per cent respectively.

Thus we can see why what has previously been a perennial feature of recall vote data, that is a tendency for it to underestimate the proportion of former Liberal Democrats, does not appear to have been present in the 1992–97 parliament. Although still a little more forgetful than their Conservative and Labour counterparts, 1992 Liberal Democrat voters were more consistent in their report of their voting behaviour than in the past. Additionally, and again in contrast to previous periods, after 1992 switching to the Liberal Democrats proved to be just as good a reason for aligning past behaviour with current vote as switching from Conservative to Labour.

We can see precisely what impact this new pattern of misremembering has had on the distribution of recall vote by looking at the full matrix of 1992 vote as reported in 1992 by 1992 vote as reported in 1994–95. This is shown in Tables 5 and 6. Some of those who said they voted Liberal Democrat in 1992 did indeed no longer report doing so in 1994 or 1995. They constituted 4 per cent of the panel in 1994 and 3 per cent in 1995. The 'losses' to Labour were twice as heavy as to the Conservatives, which, given Labour's popularity at the time, is precisely what we would expect if voters are aligning their past vote with current preference. But at the same time, in both 1994 and 1995, 4 per cent of the panel said they had voted Liberal Democrat in 1992 after reporting a different behaviour in 1992 itself. As we would expect, these gains came particularly from the Conservatives.

TABLE 5
1994 RECALL OF 1992 VOTE (%)

		Did not vote	Con	Lab	Lib Dem	Oth	'Losses'
1992	Did not vote	**8**	2	2	1	0	5
Recall	Con	1	**36**	1	2	0	4
of	Lab	1	1	**27**	1	0	3
1992	Lib Dem	1	1	2	**11**	0	4
Vote	Other	0	0	0	0	**2**	0
	'Gains'	3	4	5	4	0	

Notes: Percentages are based on all respondents included in the table. 'Gains': total number of respondents who reported that behaviour in 1994 after not having done so in 1992. 'Losses': total number of respondents who did not report that behaviour in 1994 after having done so in 1992.

Source: BEPS.

TABLE 6
1995 RECALL OF 1992 VOTE (%)

		Did not vote	Con	Lab	Lib Dem	Oth	'Losses'
1992	Did not vote	**8**	2	2	1	0	5
Recall	Con	1	**34**	2	3	0	6
of	Lab	1	1	**27**	1	0	3
1992	Lib Dem	0	1	2	**11**	0	3
Vote	Other	0	0	0	0	**2**	0
	'Gains'	2	4	6	4	0	

Notes: Percentages are based on all respondents included in the table. 'Gains': total number of respondents who reported that behaviour in 1995 after not having done so in 1992. 'Losses': total number of respondents who did not report that behaviour in 1995 after having done so in 1992.

Source: BEPS.

So part of the explanation why the discrepancy in Table 1 cannot be accounted for by *post hoc* rationalization is that there are some important differences between the pattern of rationalization in the 1992–97 parliament from what we have come to expect from previous parliaments. Voters became less forgetful about having voted Liberal Democrat in the past, while those switching to the Liberal Democrats became just as likely as those switching to the Conservatives or Labour to align their former behaviour with current preference. It is of course too early to say whether this change is permanent or temporary. In other respects, however, *post hoc* rationalization proved to be just as prevalent as before. But this 'normal' level of prevalence is simply not sufficient to account for the large 1992 Labour leads found by the quota polls in 1996.

So what distribution of recall vote does the BEPS data suggest should have been collected by the quota polls in Table 1? Perceptive readers will have noted that the Conservative lead over Labour recorded by BEPS in 1992 was a little higher than the actual lead (see Table 3). We need to correct for that bias. Our best estimate of the recall data that should have been generated by a truly representative poll can be calculated by applying the change in reported 1992 vote for each party between the 1992 and 1995 BEPS waves to the actual election result in 1992. This produces an expected recall vote of Conservative 40%, Labour 38 per cent and Liberal Democrat 19 per cent. In short, as can be seen from Table 7, *post hoc* rationalization can account for rather less than half of the discrepancy we found in Table 1.

TABLE 7
VOTES: QUOTA SAMPLE COMPARED TO BEPS SAMPLE

	Con	Labour	Lib Dem	Other	Con Lead
Quota face-to-face. MORI	39	44	14	3	-5
Quota face-to-face. Gallup	38	45	14	3	-7
Quota face-to-face. NOP	38	44	13	5	-6
BEPS 'estimate'	40	38	19	2	+3
1992 result	43	35	18	3	+8

Moreover, a virtually identical result is obtained if the same calculation is applied to similar data collected by the British Household Panel Survey which asked respondents how they voted in the 1992 election both in the autumn of 1992 and again in 1995–96. If we apply to this data set the same calculation as we have applied to the BEPS data presented here, this produces an estimate of correct recall of Conservative 40 per cent, Labour 39 per cent and Liberal Democrat 17 per cent (see also Kellner, 1996a). It looks unlikely indeed that the pattern of recall vote in the quota polls simply reflects recall rather than sample bias.

Can We Trust BEPS?

There are, however, objections that might still be made to our analysis. As a panel survey, BEPS is potentially subject to the effects of both attrition and conditioning. Perhaps those who were willing to be re-interviewed were more likely to be interested in politics and as a result more likely to remember accurately how they voted in the past. Or perhaps the fact that panel members were asked to recall how they had voted on no less than three occasions helped to improve the accuracy of their memory.

However, the conclusions we have drawn from BEPS are confirmed if we look at the result of polls of fresh samples of voters undertaken using random rather than quota sampling. In each case these random polls produced recall data similar to what we might expect from BEPS.

First, let us take a look at an ICM random poll conducted in September 1995 at exactly the same time as an ICM quota poll conducted using traditional methods. The two samples were matched exactly in terms of age, sex, class, region, work status, tenure, car ownership and foreign holidays taken in the last three years. Yet as Table 8 shows, whereas the quota poll produced results similar to those we saw earlier in Table 1, the random poll produced a result close to the actual outcome.

TABLE 8
RECALL OF 1992 VOTES: QUOTA SAMPLE COMPARED TO TELEPHONE SAMPLE

Declared past votes	Quota sample	Random by telephone
Conservative	38	46
Labour	43	36
Liberal Democrat	15	15
Other	4	3

Source: ICM.

Second, we can look at the recall vote recorded in random polls undertaken by ICM at the same time as the quota polls detailed in Table 1 (see Table 9). Again these random polls did not replicate the Labour lead found in the quota polls. Rather, they produced a result rather similar to what we would expect from the BEPS data.

TABLE 9
RECALL OF 1992 VOTE: QUOTA BEPS AND TELEPHONE SAMPLES (%)

	Con	Labour	Liberal	Other	Con Lead
Quota face-to-face. MORI	39	44	14	3	-5
Quota face-to-face. Gallup	38	45	14	3	-7
Quota face-to-face. NOP	38	44	13	5	-6
Random telephone. ICM	42	39	16	3	+3
BEPS 'estimate'	40	38	19	2	+3
1992 result	43	35	18	3	7

Third, we can examine the results of NOP's random omnibus polls conducted between August 1995 and July 1996. Although not as close to the BEPS estimate as the ICM polls, on average these only recorded a Labour lead of two points. It thus looks unlikely that the BEPS results are an artefact of conditioning or attrition. Rather, it appears that it is the results of the quota polls that are an artefact of their methodology.

But Can We Trust Telephone Samples?

The ICM random polls, however, differed from the quota polls not only in their sampling methodology, but also in conducting their interviews by telephone rather than face to face. Perhaps, as a result they were biased towards the Conservatives because Conservative voters are more likely to own telephones than Labour voters. Our evidence suggests this is unlikely.

The 1995 National Readership Survey showed that, following growth of 0.5 per cent a year, the proportion of adults that can be contacted by telephone had reached 93 per cent. Unsurprisingly, therefore, the survey indicated that the demographic profile of telephone owners closely matched that of the population as a whole. The largest difference was among the social grades D and E which comprised 28 per cent of the total population but only 25 per cent of telephone owners. All other differences in terms of social composition were 2 per cent or less.

Most importantly, there now appears to be little difference between the voting behaviour of those who can be contacted by telephone and the behaviour of the general population, at least after appropriate weights have been applied (see Husbands, 1987; Miller, 1987). To demonstrate this we have taken a year's worth of ICM quota poll data collected for the *Guardian* (N = 16,500) and identified those respondents that had a telephone. The whole sample was weighted to the demographic profile of the adult population aged 18+ and those contactable by telephone were separately weighted to that same profile. This means we represent what would have happened if ICM had only interviewed telephone owners using face-to-face quota methods and then matched them to the profile of all adults aged 18+.

Table 10 shows that once this procedure has been applied there was virtually no difference between the declared past vote of the whole sample and that of telephone owners. Similar results were obtained when we applied the same procedure to current voting intention. Thus, given that the figures for ICM's random polls in Table 9 were also weighted to the profile of all adults, it is highly unlikely that the difference between their declared past vote and that of the quota polls was the result of telephone rather than face-to-face interviewing.

TABLE 10
RECALL OF 1992 VOTE: TELEPHONE OWNERS COMPARED TO ALL RESPONDENTS (%)

	Total Sample	Telephone Owners	Gap
Conservative	28.4	28.6	+0.2
Labour	31.3	31.1	-0.2
Liberal	11.8	12.1	+0.3
Other	2.8	2.8	0
Did not vote	12.5	12.3	-0.2
Refused	4.4	4.2	-0.2
Can't recall	8.8	8.8	0

Source: ICM polls September 1994 to August 1995.

Why Might Quota Polls Be Missing Tory Voters?

We conclude that there is strong evidence that quota polls continued to identify too many Labour voters after the 1992 election. But why might this be the case?

Item Refusal and the Spiral of Silence

Perhaps the most important reason to consider is the possible impact of differential refusal and evasion. One possible form of this is item refusal. The MRS inquiry argued that there was considerable evidence that during the 1992 election Conservative voters had been more likely than Labour voters either to refuse to give or to evade giving details of their voting intention. One possible explanation of this is the 'spiral of silence' phenomenon which argues that voters who support a party whom they believe to be unpopular may be more reluctant to voice their preference in conversation (Noelle-Neumann, 1986). This thesis is consistent with a long tradition of research which suggests that individuals will refrain from expressing their views in the face of a hostile climate of opinion (Asche, 1955; Sherif, 1936). Given that the opinion polls, and following their lead the media, suggested that Labour might win the 1992 election, it is quite plausible that Conservative voters may have felt that their views lacked social acceptability.

Certainly there can be little doubt that after the pound fell out of the Exchange Rate Mechanism in September 1992, the weakness of the Conservative Party in the polls and the subsequent coverage of these polls in the media did not give Conservative voters any encouragement to express their views. And indeed across all of ICM's polls conducted between January 1994 and July 1996, we find that of those who said they did not know how they would vote but who declared how they had voted in 1992 no less than 65 per cent said that they had voted Conservative (N=3009). Not once did the figure drop below (or even come close to) 50 per cent. A similar pattern is also observable in BEPS.

Most importantly for our purposes here, there is no reason to believe that this reluctance of Conservatives to declare themselves will be confined to voting intention. It is just as likely that Conservatives were also more reluctant to say how they voted in 1992. Given that as many as one in eight survey respondents may refuse or be unable to say how they voted at the last election, the impact of such differential refusal could well be substantial. Indeed, one estimate suggests it could account for as much as 36 per cent of the discrepancy between recall vote and the actual outcome in 1992 (Sparrow and Turner, 1995).

All of this implies that quota polls may, in fact, have interviewed a rather more politically representative sample of the electorate than the pattern of their recall data implies, but that they then find it relatively difficult to secure the full cooperation of Conservative supporters in answering their questions. But if this were the only explanation for the apparent under-representation of Conservatives in those polls, the problem should have been just as apparent in random polls. As we have seen this does not appear to be the case.

Refusal to Participate

If Conservatives have been particularly reluctant to say how they have voted in the past or will do so in future, there is no reason why should we assume that their reluctance stopped at answering particular items in an opinion poll. They may also have been more reluctant to participate in an opinion poll at all. The effects of any spiral of silence may be even more pervasive than we have considered so far.

But if this were the sole explanation for the recall vote figures in quota polls we saw in Table 1, then there is no reason why there should be such a marked difference between the recall figures found in quota and random polls. If Conservatives were refusing to participate in quota polls, that reluctance should be equally marked in respect of random polls. In fact, there is reason to believe that quota polls may be more susceptible to the effects of a spiral of silence than random ones.

Quota polls provide interviewers with few incentives to minimize refusal rates. They are simply required to interview anyone who fits their specified quota. If someone refuses the interviewer can simply replace them with a more willing respondent who shares the same demographic (but possibly not political) characteristics. Interviewers tend to favour quota polls for this reason because it means they can always achieve a set number of productive interviews. But equally it means they have relatively little reason to expend energy on encouraging those whom they first approach to participate. Indeed two experiments found that refusals to participate in quota polls at all could be as high as 35 per cent, even before any allowance is made for persons who may succeed in avoiding being approached in the first place (MRS, 1994).

Such high overall refusal rates clearly leave plenty of potential for quota polls to produce biased samples in the presence of any spiral of silence phenomenon.

True, differential refusal to participate by Conservative voters should not be a problem if the quota controls used in such polls are strongly correlated with vote. This would ensure that those who eventually were interviewed were politically representative, even if a significant proportion of them were 'substitutes' for earlier refusals. However, this is not the case. Of the characteristics commonly used to set quotas, only social grade and housing tenure are at all closely correlated with voting behaviour. Moreover, the social grade schema is difficult for interviewers to code reliably and is open to manipulation. One study found that 40 per cent of respondents on a panel survey apparently changed their social grade within a period of a year. As many as half of the changes were errors attributed to misclassification by interviewers and a further 25 per cent were the result of inadequate probing (O'Brien and Ford, 1988).

Other Limitations

This limitation of quota controls means interviewers in effect have considerable discretion about whom to interview, a discretion which means that quota polls cannot be relied upon to produce representative samples even if a spiral of silence is not at work. The MRS inquiry into the 1992 election showed that other classification variables which did not form part of the quota controls displayed a downmarket bias. Polling companies found too many council tenants and too few people living in households with two or more cars. This is precisely what we would expect to happen if interviewers find it easier to interview less affluent (and thus more pro-Labour) people, and use the discretion which the social grade schema gives them by consciously or subconsciously up-grading such respondents. Moreover, even if this were not the case, each social grade is sufficiently heterogeneous that interviewers could still well favour certain types of people within each grade than others.

Interviewers also have considerable freedom about where to interview (Kellner, 1996b). Sampling points for quota polls are usually either parliamentary constituencies or local government wards. In both cases interviewers can go wherever they like within the sampling point to obtain their interviews. In some cases this may allow interviewers to choose areas where they are most likely to be able to fill their quota relatively easily, such as areas with a good mix of council and middle-class homes. They may prefer to avoid not only run-down areas but also affluent areas where houses are well spaced out. Yet we know that how people vote is associated not only with their own social characteristics, but also those of their neighbours (Butler and Stokes, 1974).

Even if interviewers did not have considerable discretion about whom to interview and even if refusal rates were lower, it still might be the case that interviewers find certain kinds of people to be more likely to be available for interview. Quota polls are commonly conducted over no more than a few days. They are thus inevitably more likely to interview those who are easily contactable than others. Some of the most obvious biases that could arise as a result are again in theory avoided by the quota controls which are used. Thus young people and those in employment are less likely to be at home than the retired but the potential impact of this should be removed by quota controls for employment, status and age. However, it has been argued that those who are easily available for interview are still relatively more likely to be Labour voters, even after such quota controls have been applied (Jowell *et al.*, 1993).

We have further evidence that suggests such an 'availability bias' may also have been present in polls conducted after 1992. Although only conducted over a relatively short three-day fieldwork period (Friday to Sunday) ICM's random telephone polls nevertheless attempt to contact each phone number on up to five occasions. We have analysed the recalled 1992 vote across seven of these polls conducted in 1996 (N = 8,400) comparing the recalled 1992 vote of those respondents who were successfully interviewed at the first attempt with that of those only interviewed after two or more calls. We find that the latter group are noticeably more Conservative than the former even after we weight both groups so that their demographic characteristics match those of the whole population. Among those who had to be contacted more than twice, the Conservatives have a lead in 1992 votes of 4 per cent whereas among those interviewed first time around the lead is just half a per cent.

If indeed those who are easily contactable are more likely to vote Labour even after we take into account their demographic characteristics, then of course even random polls conducted over a relatively short period of time will not be immune from the consequences. But they are at least better insulated than quota polls. Moreover, they can enable its impact to be estimated by assuming that those who are not contacted at all are likely to behave like those who could only be contacted after two or more attempts. In any event we clearly have another reason why quota polls apparently find too many Labour voters.

What Can Be Done?

This article suggests that many of the problems that afflicted the polling industry in the 1992 election were still present four years later. We have demonstrated that the pro-Labour bias in the 1992 recall data of quota polls conducted in 1996 cannot simply be accounted for by *post hoc* rationalization or forgetfulness. Rather, there was a continuing pro-Labour bias, as serious as at the time of the 1992 election and brought about both by the failure of pollsters to contact sufficient Conservatives and the preference of some of those that were to stay silent. Despite the efforts of the industry to learn from what went wrong in 1992, it would seem that little has been achieved.

In practice, there have been some important modifications to the analysis and reporting of opinion polls which could take account of the problems we have identified here. All of the regular polling companies now perform one or more 'adjustments' to their polls in order to correct for possible sources of anti-Conservative bias. But each company uses different methods of adjustment. They also vary in whether they chose to headline their 'adjusted' or their 'unadjusted' figures. What implications does the evidence of this article have for the apparent validity of these differing practices?

Let us consider first which figures should be highlighted by the pollsters. We would argue that this article adds significantly to the weight of evidence which suggests that unadjusted quota polls do not provide us with an accurate picture of the political preferences of the electorate. Given that is so there seems little reason why polling companies should continue to prefer to headline their unadjusted rather than their adjusted figures.

How, though, should the polls be adjusted? Broadly speaking, two strategies have been adopted. The first is primarily intended to deal with the impact of differential item refusal, that is the apparent reluctance of Conservative supporters to declare their voting intention. The consistent evidence from polls conducted since 1992 that those who say they do not know how they will vote now were more likely to have voted Conservative in 1992 suggests that this procedure is indeed a sensible one and needs to be used in random as well as quota polls. However, our evidence also suggests that such an adjustment procedure must not only take account of those who refuse to answer the voting intention question while indicating how they voted in 1992, but must also be capable of correcting the probable differential reluctance of Conservatives to say how they voted in 1992.

However we have also argued that differential item refusal is unlikely to be the only reason for the discrepancy between recall 1992 vote as recorded by the quota polls and the actual outcome of the election. Thus, such adjustments on their own are unlikely to be sufficient. If quota polling is to continue to be used, an additional mechanism needs to be deployed to ensure that their results are politically representative.

Some companies have indeed adopted such a second strategy. This has been to weight their results by recall 1992 vote. In some cases this weighting has been designed to result in a distribution of recall vote which matches the actual 1992 election result; in others it has been to estimate some of what the distribution of recall vote should be after allowing for the estimated impact of *post hoc* rationalization.

The evidence presented in this article provides considerable support for this strategy. It suggests that while the impact of *post hoc* rationalization still has to be considered, its influence was less in the 1992–97 parliament than we might have expected from previous experience. Even at the height of the Conservatives' unpopularity in 1995, weighting procedures which resulted in a distribution of recall vote which matched the 1992 vote were only likely to have been overcompensating mildly for the apparent absence of former Conservative voters in quota polls. In spring 1994, when Labour's lead was somewhat lower, our evidence suggests that such weighting introduced very little error at all.

Quota polls need, then, to do more than account for the effects of differential item refusal. Weighting by recall vote can provide a useful mechanism to achieve this. There is undoubtedly some difficulty and room for disagreement in determining exactly how much allowance should be made for such distorting effects as *post hoc* rationalization still continues to have. But the industry certainly needs to grapple with this problem rather than do nothing at all. Otherwise, the calls for a switch to random sampling, which thanks to the spread of telephone ownership is now significantly more feasible to achieve within the tight time constraints imposed by the media, and which has already been adopted by two companies, are only likely to grow.

Postscript: The 1997 Election

Superficially the 1997 election did much to restore the credibility of the polls. They consistently pointed to the prospect of a Labour landslide when most journalists and politicians remained sceptical that such an outcome was possible. The eventual result, a Labour majority of 179, apparently vindicated the former and made fools of the latter.

Yet it requires only a little more than a superficial analysis to appreciate that the performance of the polls in 1997 gives further reason to doubt whether quota polls do secure politically representative samples. Four such polls were undertaken within 48 hours of polling day; their published results are shown in Table A1.

All of these polls used one or more techniques to try and improve on their performance in 1992, including weighting by past vote and either estimating the likely behaviour of 'don't knows' or recontacting them closer to polling day. Even so, they all overestimated Labour's support while all but one underestimated the Conservative vote. In three out of the four cases the error on Labour's lead was greater than the conventional three-point margin of error, while the average error on the lead was as much as six points, only three points down on 1992.

TABLE A1
RESULTS OF FINAL QUOTA POLLS IN 1997 ELECTION

Co./Sponsor	F'work	Con %	Lab %	LDem %
Harris/*Indep.*	27–29/4/97	31	48	15
MORI/*Standard*	30/4/97*	29	47	19
MORI/*Times*	29–30/4/97	28	48	16
NOP/Reuters	29/4/97	28	50	14
Average		29	48	16
Outcome		31	44	17
Error		-2	+4	-1
1992 Error		-5	+4	+1

* *Note*: Reinterview of sample first contacted on 11–14/4/97.

In contrast two companies which used some variation of random or quasi-random telephone sampling (Curtice, 1997) were much closer to the final outcome (Table A2).

TABLE A2
RESULTS OF FINAL RANDOM POLLS IN 1997 ELECTION

Co./Sponsor	F'work	Con %	Lab %	LDem %
ICM/*Guardian*	29–30/4/97	33	43	18
Gallup/*Telegraph*	30/4/97	33	47	14
Average		33	45	16
Outcome		31	44	17
Error		+2	+1	-1

Both these polls actually overestimated Conservative support while ICM were the only company to underestimate (slightly) Labour support. On average the two polls underestimated Labour's lead by just one point while all of their estimates were within the conventional three point margin of error. As might have been anticipated from the evidence in this paper, random or quasi-random polls clearly outperformed face-to-face quota samples in 1997.

Moreover, not only did the two kinds of poll differ in their estimates of party strength in 1997, but their samples also differed in their distribution of 1992 recall vote. Among the quota polls, more people usually said that they had voted Labour in 1992 than said they had voted Conservative. In the two random polls in contrast, the Conservatives were in the lead. This difference was not only apparent in the final polls, but was consistently evident throughout the campaign (Table A3).

TABLE A3
RECALL 1992 VOTE IN FINAL CAMPAIGN POLLS

	Con %	Lab %	LDem %
Quota Polls			
Harris/*Indep.*	40	45	13
MORI/*Standard*	40	40	15
MORI/*Times*	40	44	13
NOP/*Reuters*	39	44	17*
Random Polls			
Gallup/*Telegraph*	45	41	11
ICM/*Guardian*	41	40	16

Notes: * includes Others.

Figures exclude those who said they did not vote in 1992, were too young to vote or were unable/unwilling to say how they had voted. These constituted 21–29% of all respondents.

Source: Calculated from figures provided by Gallup, Harris, ICM, MORI and NOP.

In short, the performance of the polls in the 1997 election adds significant further weight to the arguments in this article. Those interviewed by quota polls were more pro-Labour in their declared political history than were random polls. At the same time unlike random polls, quota polls still demonstrated a significant pro-Labour bias in their estimates of current party support. Despite the efforts made to improve the performance of quota polls between 1992 and 1997 and even bearing in mind that some people do indeed forget how they voted in the past, the evidence on recall voting strongly suggests that quota samples were still interviewing too many Labour voters in 1997.

ACKNOWLEDGEMENT

The British Election Panel Study is financed by the Economic and Social Research Council as part of its grant to the Centre for Research into Elections and Social Trends (CREST) as part of its research centres programme.

NOTES

1. Gallup subsequently switched to telephone random sampling in January 1997. ICM had already abandoned face-to-face quota sampling in 1995.
2. After weighting to account for oversampling in Scotland, the 1992 wave of BEPS consists of 2,855 respondents. After equivalent weighting, the 1994 wave comprises 1,859 respondents and the 1995 wave 1,654. In order to overcome the impact of differential attrition, the 1994 and 1995 waves have been further weighted so that the distribution of their 1992 vote (as reported in 1992) matches that of the original sample. For further details of the BEPS see Brook and Taylor (1996).

BIBLIOGRAPHY

Asche, S. (1955) 'Opinions and Social Pressure', *Scientific American* 193: 31–5.

Brook, L. and B. Taylor, 1996, The British Election Panel Study (BEPS) 1992–95: Interim Technical Notes', CREST Working Paper No. 41.

Butler, D. and D. Stokes (1974) *Political Change in Britain*. London: Macmillan.

Curtice, J. (1997) 'Are the Opinion Polls Ready for 1997?', *Journal of the Market Research Society* 39: 317–30.

Himmelweit, H., Biberian, M. and Stockdale, J. (1978) 'Memory for Past Vote: Implications of a Study in Recall', *British Journal of Political Science*, 8: 365–84.

Husbands, C. (1987) 'The Telephone Study of Voting Intentions in the June 1987 General Election', *Journal of the Market Research Society,* 29: 405–11.

Jowell, R., B. Hedges, P. Lynn, G. Farrant, and A. Heath (1993) 'The 1992 British Election: The Failure of the Polls', *Public Opinion Quarterly*, 57: 238–63.

Kellner, P. (1996a) 'Why the Polls still get it wrong', *The Observer*, 15 September.

Kellner, P. (1996b) 'Spiral of Truth', *British Journalism Review*, 7: 20–27.

Market Research Society (1994) *The Opinion Polls and the 1992 General Election*. London: Market Research Society.

Miller, W.L. (1987) 'The British Voter and the Telephone in the 1983 Election', *Journal of the Market Research Society* 29: 67–82.

Noelle-Neumann, E. (1986) *The Spiral of Silence*. Chicago: University of Chicago Press.

O'Brien, S. and R. Ford (1988) 'Can We At Last Say Goodbye to Social Class? An Examination of the Usefulness and Stability of Some Alternative Methods of Measurement', *Journal of the Market Research Society* 30: 289–332.

Sherif, M. (1936) *The Psychology of Social Norms*, New York: Harper & Row.

Sparrow, N. and J. Turner (1995) 'Messages from the Spiral of Silence: Developing More Accurate Market Information in a More Uncertain Political Climate', *Journal of the Market Research Society* 37: 357–83.

Worcester, R. (1996) 'Political Opinion Polling – 95 Percent Expertise and 5 Percent Luck', *Journal of the Royal Statistical Society Series A* 159: 5–20

Anchors Aweigh:
Variations in Strength of Party Identification and in Socio-Political Attitudes among the British Electorate, 1991–94

Ron Johnston and Charles Pattie

A number of models – some explicit, some implicit – underpin the study of electoral behaviour in Great Britain, but evaluation of their relative merits has been hindered by the paucity of relevant data, especially longitudinal data. The new availability of such a data set, albeit one that is far from perfect for the task having been designed to service a much wider community than electoral analysts alone, allows some tentative initial steps in the sort of evaluation needed.

The Model

The model to be evaluated is summarized in Figure 1. The dependent variable is the vote, incorporating not only the decision which party to support at an election but also, because voting is a relatively rare event, voting intentions. Traditional approaches focus on the central stream in the diagram. People are socialized in their compositional and contextual situations (Thrift, 1983; Johnston, 1986) into adopting certain political attitudes, which lead them to identify with a particular party (Himmelweit *et al.*, 1985, provide the clearest presentation). Thus both what people are (especially, in the British context, their class position) and where they are, plus the interaction of the two, strongly influence their core beliefs about economy, society and polity and the political programmes to which they are committed (Scarbrough, 1984).

In the 'purest' version of this model, voting behaviour was largely a foregone conclusion once attitudes and identification had been crystallized, hence the stability in voting patterns identified by Butler and Stokes (1969, 1974). But the campaign issues at any particular election can stimulate individuals to vote in a way contrary to predictions based on their attitudes and/or party identification. If such unexpected behaviour is temporary, it produces what American political scientists term a 'deviating election', after which the 'old order' is re-established. If short-term issues generate permanent change (a 'realigning election') they impact on the independent variables, as indicated on the left-hand side of Figure 1.

FIGURE 1
THE GENERALIZED MODEL OF VOTING BEHAVIOUR

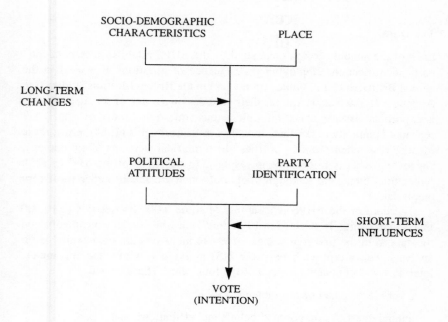

VOTE
(INTENTION)

British electoral behaviour has changed substantially over recent decades, with many analysts identifying a growing volatility in partisan choice. Some suggest that the decline of class through social mobility and of community influences through spatial mobility have eroded the key links in the model's central stream; they stress instead the importance of short-term influences, focusing in particular on the economic 'feel-good factor' in an 'embourgeoized' society (see Price and Sanders, 1995, and Sanders, 1996, for example). Others acknowledge the importance of those short-term influences, but argue that political attitudes and party identification continue to provide stability to voters' assessments of the choices before them (Heath *et al.*, 1985, 1991), while long-term changes in society – in its class composition, for example – and in general attitudes on a wide range of issues (such as sexual equality: Heath and McMahon, 1992) stimulate changes to the compositional and contextual variables.

If the latter argument is accepted, then political attitudes and party identification should remain as the anchors of voter choice around which the tides of short-term influences ebb and flow. In this article we use the longitudinal data produced by the British Household Panel Study (BHPS) at the University of Essex to explore the firmness with which those anchors are grounded.

The Data

Each of the annual surveys conducted by the BHPS establishes respondents' party identification, employing the sequence of questions also used in the annual British Social Attitudes survey and in the British Election Studies (see Appendix I). Each also explores their attitudes on a range of social, economic and political issues, using multiple choice questions, most of which are repeated biennially rather than annually: in Scarbrough's (1984) terms, these identify respondents' action profiles, the 'empirical elements of an ideology, suggesting what is to be done in response to questions of the day' (p.125), rather than their core ideologies/beliefs (which are much harder to discern empirically).

The core of the BHPS is a sample of some 5,000 households (c.10,000 individuals), initially selected in 1991. Interviews are conducted annually, and the data from the first four waves (1991–94 inclusive) are now available for analysis: we concentrate here on the 7131 individuals with whom a complete interview was conducted in each of the four years. These provide:

· a very large panel of respondents;

· annual questions on political beliefs and affiliations; and

· data collected in non-election as well as election years, thereby avoiding the 'chicken-and-egg' problem of whether the decision about which party to vote for precedes or follows that about which party to identify with.

These data allow exploration of themes and issues previously inaccessible to electoral analysts.

Party Identification

On average, some 80 per cent of the respondents identified with one of the three main British political parties (see Table 1) but the data suggest considerable instability in the strength of party identification which is not in line with party identification theory.

The clearest change over the four-year period is the declining percentage of respondents who identified with the Conservative Party, with corresponding increases in those identifying with Labour and the Liberal Democrats. These shifts parallel the general trends of voting intentions after the 1992 general election, and especially after the financial crisis of September 1992 (Sanders, 1996): the Liberal Democrats benefited most from the anti-Conservative shift in 1992–93, and the Labour Party made a very substantial gain in 1993–94 (after the election of Tony Blair to the party's leadership and the onset of his programme to modernize the party). Table 1 can be interpreted in one of two ways, therefore. Either

1. the party identification measure employed is not tapping stable identifications which transcend short-term political changes; or

2. a major shift was taking place within the British electorate (which can only be confirmed by the next general election, which might be a 'realigning' contest).

If the former conclusion is valid, then party identification may be a good indicator of current voting intentions, as Harrop and Miller (1987) argue, but no more.

TABLE 1
STRENGTH OF PARTY IDENTIFICATION 1991–94

1991 Conservative	1992 %	1993 %	1994 %	%
Identifier				
Very strong	2.8	2.8	1.6	1.3
Fairly strong	11.2	11.2	7.9	6.5
Not very strong	7.5	11.3	9.3	8.7
Feels closer to	11.2	9.0	9.2	7.9
Would vote for	4.3		2.5	2.1
TOTAL	37.0	34.3	30.5	26.5
Labour				
Identifier				
Very strong	3.4	3.1	3.6	3.7
Fairly strong	8.6	10.2	9.5	11.1
Not very strong	4.0	5.8	6.0	6.4
Feels closer to	9.7	9.8	8.9	11.0
Would vote for	5.3		5.3	7.2
TOTAL	31.0	28.9	33.3	39.4
Liberal Democrat				
Identifier				
Very strong	0.3	0.3	0.5	0.3
Fairly strong	1.6	2.2	2.9	1.7
Not very strong	1.3	2.0	2.5	2.1
Feels closer to	4.6	4.8	5.7	4.3
Would vote for	3.7		5.2	4.1
TOTAL	11.5	9.3	16.8	12.5
All Parties				
Identifiers				
Very strong	6.5	6.1	5.7	5.3
Fairly strong	21.4	23.6	20.2	19.4
Not very strong	12.9	19.2	17.8	17.2
Feels closer to	25.5	23.6	23.8	23.1
Would vote for	13.3		13.0	13.4
Independent	20.5	27.5	19.4	21.4

Notes: N=7131. The question 'which party would you vote for...' was not asked in 1992. Independents are those who identified with no party.

Further evidence that the party identification measures do not uncover permanent political affiliations (assuming that they exist) is provided by intra-party shifts in strength of identification. Table 2 cross-classifies respondents who reported an allegiance to the same party in both 1993 and 1994 according to the strength of allegiance at each date. (Those who reported an allegiance at one date but not the other and also those who shifted their allegiance between parties are excluded: 1993 and 1994 were the only adjacent years when the full suite of questions was asked.) Just over half of the 4451 respondents involved reported the same strength of allegiance to the same party at two dates only twelve months apart: this was the case for 53.1 per cent of the Conservative identifiers, 50.7 per cent of those associated with Labour, and 49.8 per cent of the Liberal Democrats.

Our provisional conclusion, backed by other analyses (Johnston and Pattie, 1996, 1997), is that these data do not identify an underlying stability in party identification during the ebb and flow of political events. On the assumption that some such stability does exist, then one of the assumed anchors is grounded in very shallow sediment only.

TABLE 2

CHANGING STRENGTH OF PARTY IDENTIFICATION (INTRA-PARTY ONLY)
BETWEEN 1993 AND 1994

(% of row totals)

1993	VS	FS	1994 NVS	C	WV	N
Conservative						
VS	43.6	39.1	13.6	3.6	0	110
FS	6.5	53.8	26.8	10.6	2.3	511
NVS	1.3	15.8	52.7	26.8	3.4	537
C	0.9	8.2	26.9	56.1	7.9	428
WV	0	5.4	17.4	28.3	48.9	92
Labour						
VS	57.6	30.6	5.6	4.8	1.2	248
FS	11.5	59.9	15.3	11.5	0.5	646
NVS	2.9	30.7	35.1	24.5	6.8	384
C	2.0	20.7	16.7	49.9	10.6	545
WV	2.2	7.6	12.7	31.3	46.2	275
Liberal Democrat						
VS	44.4	37.0	11.1	7.4	0	27
FS	3.4	39.6	26.8	24.8	5.4	149
NVS	1.6	18.8	37.5	31.3	10.9	128
C	0.5	8.2	16.8	55.0	19.5	220
WV	0	3.3	6.0	27.2	63.6	151

Note: Key to categories: VS – very strong identifier; FS – fairly strong identifier; NVS – not very strong identifier; C – closer to that party than any other; WV – would vote for that party if there were a general election tomorrow. N is the number of observations.

Socio-Political Attitudes

The BHPS explores a range of attitudes: we focus here on only two groups, which relate to the socio-economic-political domain. The first, involving four items used in the 1992 and 1994 surveys, covers views about government; the second, used in 1991 and 1993, involves six items concerned with what are often interpreted as left-right socio-political dimensions in British politics (see Appendix 1). We factor analysed each set of responses to isolate underlying attitude dimensions (including only those respondents who answered every item in each survey); two clearly-identifiable varimax-rotated dimensions were extracted in every case.

The main political attitudes dimension evaluated in 1992 and 1994 is a 'belief in democracy' factor, involving three of the four items. It was virtually the same in each survey (see Table 3): people who believed that government reflects the popular will also believed that it puts nation before party and disagreed with the statement that ordinary people can't influence government. The other item, which deals with a specific policy issue, is only weakly related to those three, and is excluded from further consideration.

The two analyses of the socio-political issues explored in 1991 and 1993 also produced almost identical findings. The first dimension links those items related to traditional policies of the 'left' in Britain: a belief in public ownership of key services, government obligations to ensure full employment, and the efficacy of trades unions. The second dimension taps a 'one nation' scale: people who thought that society is divided (one law for the rich...) disagreed with statements that ordinary people share the country's wealth and that private enterprise solves economic problems. (People who think that private enterprise is effective in such contexts oppose the traditional policies of the 'left', as indicated by the cross-loading on the first dimension.)

The factor loadings shown in Table 3 identify consistent attitude scales over the two-year periods in each case, but do not indicate whether individuals' attitudes also remained the same: the structure of opinions was the same on each occasion but were the same opinions held by the same people? To answer this question we regressed the individual respondents' scores on each factor at the second date on those at the first (excluding the second factor in the political attitudes analysis). If people held the same attitudes at each date, then the two sets of scores should be highly correlated. In fact, the resulting equations indicated considerable variation in individuals' attitudes over a short period. With score at the second date as the dependent variables, the results were:

	a	b	r^2	N
Political I	0.00	0.53	0.28	5388
Socio-political I	0.00	0.62	0.39	5560
Socio-political II	0.00	0.52	0.27	5560

It is the r^2 values which are of particular interest. In no case is even 40 per cent of the variation in scores at the second date accounted for by scores at the first. Thus, although the structure of attitudes was the same, the pattern of individual attitudes was extremely variable: the scales remained the same, but people moved rapidly along them over time.

TABLE 3

VARIMAX ROTATED FACTOR LOADINGS

Political attitudes	1992		1994	
	I	II	I	II
Government reflects the will of the people	0.81	-0.14	0.83	-0.11
Ordinary people can't influence government	-0.62	0.35	-0.62	0.41
Government ought to impose an earnings ceiling	-0.05	0.95	-0.01	0.94
Government puts nation before party	0.78	0.15	0.78	0.15
Socio-political attitudes	1991		1993	
	I	II	I	II
Ordinary people share the nation's wealth	-0.12	0.85	-0.11	0.86
There is one law for the rich and one for the poor	0.20	-0.79	0.20	-0.78
Private enterprise solves economic problems	-0.54	0.37	-0.52	0.41
Public services ought to be state owned	0.64	-0.16	0.67	-0.10
Government has an obligation to provide jobs	0.70	-0.14	0.71	-0.10
Strong trade unions protect employees	0.75	-0.07	0.70	-0.18

This point is emphasized by the differences in individuals' scores between the two dates. Table 4 shows frequency distributions of differences in scores in terms of standard deviation units. In each case, the average movement (irrespective of sign) is approximately 0.7 standard deviation units. Although a substantial proportion of all respondents fall into the central categories (a shift of less than 0.50 units in either direction), some changed their opinions very substantially over the two-year periods. On the second of the socio-political factors, for example, four per cent of respondents moved more than two standard deviation units in a negative direction: given the scoring on the relevant variables, this means that there was a shift towards the 'one law for the rich and another for the poor' opinion and away from the view that 'ordinary people share in the nation's wealth'.

Cross-classifications of the responses to the three individual variables loading heavily on the first factor in the political attitude analysis further illustrate this finding (see Table 5). A majority gave the same answer in 1994 as they had two years earlier in only four of the 15 response categories: the percentages on the main diagonal of the tables were 49, 57 and 47 respectively. Many shifted their positions quite substantially. On whether the government reflects the popular will, for example, more of those who agreed with this proposition in 1992 disagreed with it in 1994 rather than agreed again, and of those who disagreed with the statement that ordinary people can't influence government more agreed rather than disagreed with it two years later. Cross-classifications of the six socio-political attitude variables produce similar findings (not reproduced here); approximately half of the respondents changed their positions on the six scales over the two years.

TABLE 4

FREQUENCY DISTRIBUTIONS OF CHANGES IN INDIVIDUALS' SCORES ON THE POLITICAL
AND SOCIO-POLITICAL FACTORS

Difference	Political I	Socio-political I	II
Positive			
2.0<	2.9	1.2	2.7
1.75 – 1.99	1.5	1.1	1.4
1.50 – 1.74	2.3	1.5	2.2
1.25 – 1.49	3.4	3.1	3.1
1.00 – 1.24	3.7	4.4	4.9
0.75 – 0.99	6.9	6.4	5.4
0.50 – 0.74	6.4	8.4	7.7
0.25 – 0.49	11.1	11.9	9.0
0.00 – 0.24	7.5	12.0	11.7
Negative			
0.00 – 0.24	16.7	11.4	12.4
0.25 – 0.49	9.2	10.4	10.6
0.50 – 0.74	8.1	8.3	8.1
0.75 – 0.99	6.4	6.2	6.0
1.00 – 1.24	3.5	4.5	4.5
1.25 – 1.49	4.5	2.6	2.9
1.50 – 1.74	1.9	1.7	2.2
1.75 – 1.99	1.5	1.2	1.2
2.00<	2.4	3.6	4.0
Mean labsolutel	0.74	0.67	0.74
Standard deviation	0.62	0.55	0.63
N	5388	5560	5560

TABLE 5

CHANGING POSITIONS ON POLITICAL ATTITUDES, 1992–94

(% of row totals)

Government reflects the will of the people

1992	SA	A	1994 N	D	SD	Total
SA	8	32	13	39	8	38
A	1	37	23	34	5	1484
N	0	16	34	44	6	1330
D	1	8	14	63	15	3286
SD	1	4	6	50	40	790
Total	34	1059	1311	3266	958	

Ordinary people can't influence government

1992	SA	A	1994 N	D	SD	Total
SA	42	50	2	5	1	819
A	13	71	6	10	0	4213
N	4	49	24	22	1	560
D	6	45	10	38	1	1392
SD	33	30	0	26	10	69
Total	1013	4303	558	1124	55	

Government puts nation before party

1992	SA	A	1994 N	D	SD	Total
SA	6	40	12	22	20	50
A	2	31	16	42	9	1105
N	1	14	27	48	10	931
D	1	8	9	62	21	3569
SD	1	3	2	38	56	1269
Total	61	818	785	3602	1658	

Note: Key to rows and columns: SA – strongly agree; A – agree; N – neither agree nor disagree;
D – disagree; SD – strongly disagree

Some variation in people's responses to such items is likely (reflecting either or both of measurement error and random variation), but it is the scale of change that is surprising. It may reflect longer-term secular changes. The row and column totals in Table 5, for example, suggest a growing 'democratic deficit' which, despite the attempt in the question wording to stimulate normative responses, may indicate growing disaffection with the current British government during a period of increased publicity and concern over 'sleaze' (see Ridley and Doig, 1996). But similar shifts are reported in both sets of analyses (as well as in those of other attitude scales not reported here) and we conclude that either there is a great deal of randomness in people's attitudes over short periods or the items used in the BHPS and other surveys are unable to tap their relatively stable core beliefs.

Attitude/Identification Interactions

The substantial changes reported here in both people's socio-political attitudes and the strength of their party identifications over short periods suggest that neither – as measured here, at least – is a reliable anchor for studies of political behaviour (assuming that there are such attitudinal anchors). To test this conclusion further, we examine the relationship between variations in factor scores and changes in strength of party identification.

Political Attitudes 1992–94

Table 6 shows the average factor score for respondents in each cell in the 1992–94 intra-party cross-tabulations of party identification, using the first factor from the analysis of political attitudes. (Mean scores are shown only for those cells containing ten or more respondents.) For Conservative identifiers, the row and column means on each of the two factor scores are as expected: the more strongly an individual identified with the party in either year, the further his/her score on the government efficacy dimension was from the grand mean (0.0) – very strong Conservative identifiers were more likely to agree that government puts nation before party and reflects the will of the people than were fairly strong identifiers (that is, to have large negative scores), and so on. The pattern within the first two matrices is also as expected. In the first row of the first block, for example, the average value for

TABLE 6

MEAN SCORES ON FIRST POLITICAL ATTITUDES FACTOR BY CHANGE IN STRENGTH
OF PARTY IDENTIFICATION

Conservative

Mean Score 1992

1992	VS	FS	NVS	C	WV	All
VS	-1.20	-0.96	-0.55	*	*	-0.95
FS	-1.07	-0.98	-0.69	-0.72	-0.81	-0.78
NVS	*	-0.44	-0.53	-0.36	-0.37	-0.41
C	*	-0.24	-0.50	-0.26	-0.08	-0.21
All	-1.04	-0.86	-0.57	-0.37	-0.20	

Mean Score 1994

	VS	FS	NVS	C	WV	All
VS	-1.24	-0.86	-0.33	*	*	-0.68
FS	-1.25	-0.89	-0.47	-0.25	-0.24	-0.51
NVS	*	-0.68	-0.48	-0.32	-0.31	-0.29
C	*	-0.29	-0.39	-0.32	-0.39	-0.16
All	-1.15	-0.83	-0.46	-0.30	-0.31	

Mean Difference 1992–4

	VS	FS	NVS	C	WV	All
VS	-0.04	0.09	0.22	*	*	0.27
FS	-0.18	0.10	0.22	0.47	0.56	0.27
NVS	*	-0.25	0.05	0.04	0.06	0.11
C	*	-0.06	0.11	-0.07	-0.31	0.05
All	-0.11	0.03	0.11	0.07	-0.11	

TABLE 6 (contd.)

Labour

Mean Score1992

1992	VS	FS	NVS	C	WV	All
VS	0.58	0.34	0.66	*	*	0.50
FS	0.47	0.37	0.43	0.34	0.14	0.38
NVS	0.44	0.43	0.17	0.29	0.49	0.30
C	0.10	0.45	0.29	0.30	0.15	0.30
All	0.51	0.36	0.24	0.29	0.12	

Mean Score 1994

	VS	FS	NVS	C	WV	All
VS	0.44	0.39	0.53	*	*	0.39
FS	0.41	0.20	0.26	0.10	0.09	0.21
NVS	0.79	0.33	0.08	0.32	0.04	0.25
C	0.38	0.30	0.21	0.21	-0.10	0.21
All	0.47	0.25	0.16	0.24	0.12	

Mean Difference 1992–94

	VS	FS	NVS	C	WV	All
VS	-0.13	-0.01	-0.13	*	*	-0.12
FS	-0.07	-0.17	-0.17	-0.23	-0.05	-0.17
NVS	0.34	-0.10	-0.09	0.04	-0.45	-0.05
C	0.28	-0.15	-0.07	-0.09	-0.25	-0.10
All	-0.04	-0.11	-0.08	-0.05	-0.01	

Liberal Democrat

Mean Score 1992

1992	VS	FS	NVS	C	WV	All
VS	*	*	*	*	*	0.58
FS	*	0.22	0.15	0.65	*	0.41
NVS	*	0.00	0.10	-0.09	*	0.06
C	*	0.17	-0.11	0.40	0.27	0.27
All	0.75	0.14	0.08	0.23	0.08	

Mean Score 1994

	VS	FS	NVS	C	WV	All
VS	*	*	*	*	*	0.44
FS	*	0.26	0.06	0.31	*	0.34
NVS	*	0.29	0.01	0.15	*	0.15
C	*	0.17	-0.06	0.28	0.29	0.22
All	0.37	0.21	0.06	0.15	0.13	

Mean Difference 1992-4

	VS	FS	NVS	C	WV	All
VS	*	*	*	*	*	-0.13
FS	*	0.04	-0.09	-0.34	*	-0.07
NVS	*	0.29	-0.09	0.25	*	0.09
C	*	0.00	0.05	-0.12	0.01	-0.05
All	-0.38	0.08	-0.02	-0.08	0.05	

Notes: Key to rows and columns: VS – very strong identifier; FS – fairly strong identifier; NVS – not very strong identifier; C – closer to that party than any other; WV – would vote for that party if there were a general election tomorrow. * – less than ten individuals in the cell.

respondents who were very strong identifiers in both 1992 and 1994 (-1.20) is larger than that for those who shifted from very strong identification at the first date to fairly strong at the second, and so on.

The same general pattern occurs in the first two blocks of mean scores for Labour identifiers; positive values indicate agreement with the contention that ordinary people cannot influence the government and disagreement with the other two contentions loading on the factor. With Liberal Democrat identifiers too, the stronger their association with the party the stronger their belief, like Labour supporters, that government is partial and unresponsive to ordinary people's needs. (Indeed, in 1992 especially, Liberal Democrat identifiers were on average stronger in this belief than were their Labour counterparts.)

If the general hypothesis relating strength of party identification to strength of attitude is valid, then there should be a decline in the mean score values down the columns and across the rows within each matrix. For the Conservative Party, for example, this occurs 9 times out of 11 down the columns in the first matrix and 8 times out of 12 along the rows; in the second it occurs only 3 times out of 11 down the columns, however, although it is the case 10 times out of 12 along the rows. The reason for this latter discrepancy is indicated by the third block in each matrix, which gives the mean change in the two scores between 1992 and 1994 according to changing strength of party identification. The row totals for Conservatives show that the stronger the strength of identification in 1992 the further the movement on the attitude scale (with the positive mean indicating shifts towards the average Labour position). Similarly in the final block for Labour identifiers, the stronger the identification with the party in 1992 the further the shift over the next two years in attitudes to government efficacy, towards the Conservative position. (Given that identification with Labour strengthened over the period, this implies that its supporters became more convinced that government is undertaken in the interests of all.) Liberal Democrat identifiers, on the other hand, on average shifted substantially in the opposite direction, indicating increasing disillusion with the nature of British democracy. Within the matrices of average changes in score values, we anticipated least variability along the main diagonals: people whose strength of party identification remained constant should also have changed least in their attitudes. This is generally the case: in the Conservative matrix, for example, the average value in the four cells on the diagonal (irrespective of sign) is 0.07, compared to 0.18 in the off-diagonal cells, with the comparable figures for the Labour matrix being 0.12 and 0.15 and those for the Liberal Democrats 0.08 and 0.17. (Note that the figures in the final column – those who would have voted for the named party in 1994 – cannot be used in this exercise because that question was not asked in 1992.) Thus changes in the strength of party identification and in attitudes move together within all three parties.

Socio-Political Attitudes 1991–93

Similar patterns were identified in comparable matrices for the analyses of both socio-political factors in 1991 and 1993. (The tables are not reproduced here, but can be provided on request.) They show, for example, that the stronger an individual's identification with the Conservative Party in each year the more 'right wing' his or her views on public services, trades unions and the government's obligation to ensure full employment, whereas Labour identifiers display a strong correlation between strength of identification and commitment to 'left-wing' views on the traditional issues that divide the parties. Liberal Democrats are very much 'middle-of-the-road' on these issues. Very strong Conservative identifiers at both dates were the most 'right-wing' in their views; those similarly attached to the Labour Party were the most left wing. Those whose attachment to either party weakened over the two-year period were closer to the mean than those whose strength of identification remained constant: those whose strength of identification increased tended to have more 'extreme' views, on the other hand. Finally, the average change in factor score value for those whose strength of party identification remained constant over the two years was less than for those who changed their level of attachment.

Discussion

The BHPS longitudinal data provide the first opportunity to explore changes in individuals' political attitudes over relatively short periods, and produce intriguing findings. There was substantial year-on-year variability in both strength of party identification and position on the attitude scales, and these patterns of variability were interrelated: people whose strength of party identification was unchanged tended to be those whose positions on the attitude scales altered very little.The implications of such findings for the analysis of electoral behaviour are several; some are contradictory, and as yet their relative significance cannot be evaluated. For example, it may be that the changes we have identified are little more than random variation around individuals' true positions, to which they will return by the time of the next general election. If this is the case, then *no model should be able to account for the shifts in terms of other variables.* On the other hand, there may have been a substantial secular trend over the period linked to a decline in the Conservative Party's popularity and a shift in attitudes reflecting the insecurity generated by, and increased dissatisfaction with, Conservative government market-focused policies since 1979. If this is the case, then *these shifts should be predictable using a range of variables reflecting the short-term influences identified in Figure1.*

If the first interpretation is correct, then regular and repeated measurement of party identification and political attitudes offers little for those wanting to identify the stable aspects of British voting behaviour – the anchors are weakly grounded. If the second is true, however, then such measurements are clearly useful in charting not only the core characteristics of voters but also the secular trends in patterns of party support.

APPENDIX 1
PARTY IDENTIFICATION QUESTIONS

1. Generally speaking, do you think of yourself as a supporter of any one political party?
   If YES, go to 4

If NO
2. Do you think of yourself as a little closer to one political party than to the others?
   If YES, go to 4

If NO
3. If there were to be a General Election tomorrow, which political party do you think you would be most likely to support?
4. Which one?
5. Would you call yourself a very strong supporter of < party>, fairly strong or not very strong?

APPENDIX 2
QUESTIONS ON POLITICAL AND SOCIO-POLITICAL ATTITUDES

Political Attitudes

People have different views about the way governments work. I'm going to read out some things people have said about governments in Britain and I'd like you to tell me which answer off the card comes closest to how you feel about each statement [strongly agree; agree; neither agree nor disagree; disagree; strongly disagree; can't choose]:

> On the whole, what governments do in Britain reflects the will of the people.
> Ordinary people don't really have a chance to influence what governments do.
> The government should place an upper limit on the amount of money that any one person can make.
> Governments can be trusted to place the needs of the nation above the interests of their own party.

Socio-Political Attitudes

People have different views about society. I'm going to read out some things people have said about Britain today and I'd like you to tell me which answer off the card comes closest to how you feel about each statement [strongly agree; agree; neither agree nor disagree; disagree; strongly disagree; can't choose]:

> Ordinary people get their fair share of the nation's wealth.
> There is one law for the rich and one for the poor.
> Private enterprise is the best way to solve Britain's economic problems.
> Major public services and industries ought to be in state ownership.
> It is the government's responsibility to provide a job for everyone who wants one.
> Strong trade unions are needed to protect the working conditions and wages of employees.

ACKNOWLDGEMENT

The British Household Panel Study is conducted by the ESRC Research Centre in Micro-Social Change at the University of Essex, and the data have been obtained from the ESRC Data Archive, also at the University of Essex: the assistance of many people at those two centres in obtaining access to these data is much appreciated. Introductory material on the BHPS is obtainable from the Research Centre (bhpsug@essex.ac.uk).

BIBLIOGRAPHY

Butler, D. and D. Stokes (1969) *Political Change in Britain: Forces Shaping Electoral Choice.* London: Macmillan.
Butler, D. and D. Stokes (1974) *Political Change in Britain: The Evolution of Electoral Choice,* second edition. London: Macmillan.
Harrop, M. and W.L. Miller (1987) *Elections and Voters.* London: Macmillan.
Heath, A. and D. McMahon (1992) 'Changes in Values', in R. Jowell, L. Brook, G. Prior and B. Taylor (eds) *British Social Attitudes: The 9th Report,* pp.113–30. Aldershot: Dartmouth.
Heath, A., R. Jowell and J. Curtice (1985) *How Britain Votes.* Oxford: Pergamon.
Heath, A. , J. Curtice, R. Jowell, G. Evens, J. Field and S. Witherspoon (1991) *Understanding Political Change.* Oxford: Pergamon.
Himmelweit, H., P. Humphreys and M. Jaeger(1985) *How Voters Decide* (second edition). Milton Keynes: Open University Press.
Johnston, R.J. (1986) 'The Neighbourhood Effect Revisited: Spatial Science or Political Regionalism', *Environment and Planning D: Society and Space* 4: 41–56.
Johnston, R.J. and C.J. Pattie (1996) The Strength of Party Identification among the British Electorate: An Exploration, *Electoral Studies* 15, 295–310.
Johnston, R. J. and C.J. Pattie (1997) 'Fluctuating Party Identification in Great Britain: Patterns Revealed by Four Years of Longitudinal Study', *Politics* 17.
Price, S. and D. Sanders (1995) 'Economic Expectations and Voting Intentions in the UK 1979–87: A Pooled Cross-section Approach', *Political Studies* 43, 203–31.
Ridley, F.F. and A. Doig (eds) (1996) *Sleaze: Politicians, Private Interests & Public Reactions.* Oxford: Oxford University Press.
Sanders, D. (1996) 'Economic Performance, Management Competence and the Outcome of the Next General Election', *Political Studies* 44: 203–31.
Scarbrough, E. (1984) *Political Ideology and Voting: An Exploratory Study.* Cambridge: Cambridge University Press.
Thrift, N.J. (1983) 'On the Determination of Social Action in Space and Time', *Environment and Planning D: Society and Space* 1: 23–57.

Class and Nation in England and Scotland

Anthony Heath, Nan Dirk de Graaf and Ariana Need

It is widely held that class is a major basis of political cleavage only in the absence of other competing cleavages such as religion or ethnicity. Thus Sartori wrote that 'class is the major determinant of voting behaviour only if no other cleavage happens to be present' (1969, p.76). Similarly, in his four-country comparison Lijphart found that, 'where class, religion and language were all present as competing bases, religion turns out to be victorious, language is a strong runner up, and class finishes as a distant third' (1979: 52).

Lijphart's explanation for the success of religion and language is essentially that they involve 'primordial' communal loyalties. In the case of language he also emphasizes the link with nationalism: 'A shared language is regarded as one of the principal building blocks of nationalism ... Because language is a crucial differentiator among nations, it is bound to be a major cleavage and a strong source of partisan differences in "nations" that are not linguistically homogeneous' (p.453). In Lijphart's account, then, language appears to be a marker for national or ethnic differences (indeed in two of his countries he talks about the linguistic–ethnic cleavage). In essence, then, his theory appears to be that religious, national and ethnic cleavages will vanquish class cleavages because of the greater communal loyalties that they engender.

Britain is often thought to be a country[1] in which religion and language and ethnicity fail to provide competing bases of partisan choice, and hence class is able to exert a relatively powerful influence on party choice. It is not entirely clear that this is true even for England, where, as we shall see, there are both religious and ethnic influences on vote. Nor is it true for Wales where the linguistic basis for Welsh nationalism is clear (but little researched). Scotland, however, provides a particularly interesting test of Lijphart's thesis since the rise of nationalist sentiment in Scotland suggests that north of the border there is a potentially powerful competitor for class. Indeed, nationalism is often seen as one of the most potent bases of political cleavage. 'Nationalist passions are probably the strongest in the whole political spectrum, and are generally stronger today than those aroused by religion, class, individual or group interest' (Kellas, 1991: 1).

Despite its plausibility, there are two major ambiguities in the analysis provided by Sartori and Lijphart. First, they do not make it clear what should count as a 'competing basis' of partisan choice. It is, we suggest, useful to distinguish between the existence of a social cleavage and the politicization of that cleavage. Thus, on the social side, even in England, there are divisions between the religious and the irreligious in their attitudes towards, say, abortion and family values. Indeed, these cultural differences are probably as great as those found throughout continental Europe (see Heath *et al.* 1993). But on the political side there is no explicitly religious party that would provide a ready vehicle for religious voting in the way that Christian Democratic parties in continental Europe explicitly cater for the religious vote. Nor do the main parties in Britain take up different political stances on issues such as abortion, and these issues are usually left to 'free votes' in the House of Commons.

It seems plausible enough to suppose that a social cleavage needs to have a political vehicle if it is to have a major impact on party choice. This assumption is implicit in Lijphart's analysis, and the four countries that he considers – Belgium, Canada, Switzerland and South Africa – are all ones where there are clear political vehicles for religious or ethnic cleavages. We would not, therefore, expect religion to be as important a source of political cleavage either in England or Scotland as are class or national identity. But the reason, we suggest, is not because the social basis for a religious cleavage is absent but rather because the cleavage has not been politicized.[2]

In Scotland, however, national identity has a ready vehicle for political expression through the SNP (as of course does Welsh national identity through Plaid Cymru). Perhaps in reaction to the electoral threat posed by the nationalists the other parties in Scotland have also taken up distinctive stances on Scottish home rule. (See for example Brown *et al.* 1996.) So the conditions for nationalism to compete with class are surely in place in Scotland.

The second ambiguity concerns the criterion for deciding that a cleavage has been vanquished. Lijphart himself uses two sorts of measure. He first uses indices analogous to the Alford index of class voting (which as he points out can be interpreted as a regression coefficient when the relevant dependent and independent variables are dichotomized).[3] He then goes on to compare how much of the variance in vote is explained by class, religion and language. These two measures – the Alford index and variance explained – could in principle yield quite different answers, and they often do in practice. For example, in Britain the ethnic cleavage between whites and blacks shows a large regression coefficient (see Heath *et al.* 1991), and in that sense might well vanquish class, but because the proportion of blacks in Britain is so small, the variance in vote explained by ethnicity will be a great deal smaller than that explained by class.[4]

It is more useful, we suggest, to recognize that the two measures are in fact tapping two related but distinct concepts, which we have previously termed *absolute* and *relative* class voting (Heath, Jowell and Curtice 1985). Relative class (or religious or ethnic) voting is essentially a comparison of the voting propensities of two groups, and is usually measured by odds-ratios or the Alford index. In contrast, absolute class (or religious or ethnic) voting is the proportion of the total electorate who vote along class (or religious or ethnic) lines. In the case of class it is usually measured by summing the number of middle-class voters who supported the Conservatives and the number of working-class voters who supported Labour. This quantity is then expressed as a proportion of all voters.[5]

Relative class voting, whether measured by odds-ratios or by the Alford index, in essence deals with the extent to which differences between the social locations of voters translate into votes. They are an appropriate way (although not necessarily the only one) for investigating what impact social cleavages have on partisan choice. But from the point of view of the political parties, the aggregate impact of these differences on the number of votes may be of more interest.

The assumption implicit in the arguments of Sartori and Lijphart is that the presence of a primordial cleavage like religion or ethnicity will necessarily reduce the impact of the class cleavage. This may be true in absolute terms provided the two cleavages cross-cut: in the extreme case, if votes are cast wholly along ethnic lines they cannot at the same time be cast wholly along class lines.

But in relative terms a cross-cutting cleavage, and a new political party to give it political expression, can leave the effect of other social cleavages on party choice unchanged. Even if the established parties reorient their policies and take up distinctive stands on the new cleavage as well as on the old, this will not necessarily alter their relative appeal along the older cleavages.

For example, if class and national identity are cross-cutting cleavages, we might expect the SNP to draw the votes of working-class nationalists from Labour and of middle-class nationalists from the Conservatives. However, it can easily be seen that this kind of process could still leave the relative class basis of Conservative and Labour voting unchanged. Consider the simplified example in Table 1.

TABLE 1
IN THE ABSENCE OF A NATIONALIST PARTY

	Con	Lab	
Middle class	60	40	100
Working class	40	60	100

IN THE PRESENCE OF A NATIONALIST PARTY

	Con	Lab	SNP	
Middle class	48	32	20	100
Working class	32	48	20	100

In this example, the SNP takes votes equally from the two established parties, and absolute class voting promptly falls (from 120/200 to 96/200). The simple presence of a nationalist party and cross-cutting cleavages thus reduces the overall level of class voting, since by definition the nationalist party does not have a class base. But relative class voting remains unchanged, in our example with a Conservative:Labour odds-ratio of 2.25 (since $\{60/40\}/\{40/60\} = \{48/32\}/\{32/49\} = 2.25$).

An alternative scenario is one where the cleavages do not cross-cut but instead overlay each other. Thus, Scottish nationalism might be much more prevalent in the working class than elsewhere, and the nationalist party might thus capture votes primarily from Labour's working-class constituency. In the next example, then, the SNP only takes working-class votes (Table 2).

TABLE 2

	Con	Lab	SNP	
Middle class	60	40	0	100
Working class	32	48	20	100

In this example, Labour becomes more of a middle-class party, and absolute class voting once again falls (to 108/200) but, since the nationalists also take proportionately the same amount of working-class votes from the Conservatives, the Conservatives also become more middle class. Relative class voting for Conservative and Labour remains unchanged with an odds-ratio of 2.25 once more.

Finally, the most interesting scenario, and perhaps also the most plausible one, is where the presence of a nationalist competitor for votes leads the existing parties to reposition themselves on the second, nationalist dimension. The Conservatives, for example, might opt to take a unionist position (as indeed they have in practice), thus appealing to working-class unionists who would otherwise have voted Labour. Labour also might react to the competition from the SNP by adopting a more nationalist rhetoric, possibly gaining votes from middle-class nationalists and stemming the loss of working-class votes to the SNP.

Rather remarkably, even this scenario could leave the Conservative:Labour odds-ratio unchanged, as indeed it does in the final example with a figure of 2.25 once again (Table 3).

TABLE 3

	Con	Lab	SNP	
Middle class	48	32	20	100
Working class	36	54	10	100

In this example, as in the two previous ones, absolute class voting falls (to 102/200) but relative class voting for the two established parties remains unchanged. Even when the parties reorient themselves, therefore, and adopt distinct nationalist positions in addition to their class ones, relative class voting does not necessarily fall.

All three examples, then, suggest that absolute class voting will fall when a new cleavage is present and has a distinct political vehicle. In this respect, then, the proposition that religious or nationalist cleavages will reduce the aggregate impact of the class cleavage is true but unsurprising. Whether they actually vanquish the class cleavage (in the sense that absolute religious voting exceeds absolute class voting) will however be a contingent matter, depending on the strength of the cleavage, the sizes of the groups and the popularity of the parties concerned. Contra Lijphart, there is no reason to suppose that a cleavage such as the religious one is bound to vanquish class, even in absolute terms: a small religious group may overwhelmingly support a small religious party, as in Norway, but absolute religious voting could still fail to rival absolute class voting.

All three examples also suggest that the existence of a second cleavage, and the presence of a party to give it political expression, does not guarantee a decline in relative class voting for the established parties. While we have readily been able to construct examples where the odds-ratios remain unchanged, there is no necessary reason why they should in practice. It is an interesting empirical question whether, as Lijphart's analysis implies, they actually do or not.

In this article, therefore, we ask whether the nationalist cleavage in Scotland has reduced absolute and relative class voting and further whether it has made such inroads as to be hailed victorious. The comparison between England and Scotland also perhaps provides us with a fairer test than the comparisons that Lijphart used. Lijphart termed his comparison a 'crucial experiment' but there was of course no control group. The comparison between England and Scotland, however, provides us with something approaching a natural experiment: they are two countries with (more or less common) class, social and political structures but differing with regard to the crucial 'experimental' condition of having a nationalist cleavage in Scotland and a nationalist political vehicle to give it expression.[6]

As with all natural experiments, the assumption of 'other things being equal' will not strictly hold; to claim otherwise would be to ignore the many subtle and not-so-subtle ways in which the two countries differ in their culture, histories and economic situation. None the less, there will surely be more in common between the two countries, not least in the presence of common Conservative, Labour and Liberal Democrat political parties, than is normally the case in comparative research.[7]

Data

Our data come from the 1992 British and Scottish Election surveys. The Scottish Election Survey was made possible by a grant from the ESRC to Jack Brand and James Mitchell enabling a larger sample to be obtained in Scotland than would have been the case in the conventional election survey of Britain as a whole (Brand *et al.*, 1993, 1994a, 1994b).[8] The bulk of the questionnaire was identical in England and Scotland, but some additional questions were asked only of respondents resident in Scotland.

To obtain a representative sample of Britain as a whole, the Scottish respondents need to be down-weighted, but in the present article we treat England and Scotland as two separate countries and use unweighted data. The relatively small number of respondents resident in Wales have been omitted, although there are many interesting questions that could be addressed about social cleavages in Wales.

National Identity and Vote

We begin with our 'experimental' condition of the nationalist cleavage in Scotland. We use as our measure of national identity the question devised by Moreno (1988) and included in the SES:

> *We are interested in how people living in Scotland see themselves. Which of the statements on this card best describes how you see yourself?*
> *Scottish not British*
> *More Scottish than British*
> *Equally Scottish and British*
> *More British than Scottish*
> *British not Scottish*

Overall, only 2.9% said that they were British not Scottish. Because of the small numbers in this category, we have combined them with the 'more British than Scottish' category. To preserve symmetry we do the same with the first two categories as well. In our analysis we therefore distinguish three groups, namely those who saw themselves as more Scottish (including Scottish not British), those who saw themselves as equally Scottish and British (an important group with dual identity), and those who saw themselves as more British (including British not Scottish). The overall proportions in these three groups were 60%, 33% and 6% respectively.

 This question was not asked among the respondents resident in England. Moreover, although British nationalist sentiment is not an unimportant dimension among respondents in England (see Heath and Taylor, 1996), national identity *per se* does not seem to play a substantial role in English voting behaviour. (In the 1992 BES we asked respondents whether they thought of themselves as English or British, but the political differences between these two groups were slight.) We therefore restrict ourselves to an analysis of national identity and vote in Scotland on its own in Table 4.

TABLE 4
NATIONAL IDENTITY AND VOTE IN SCOTLAND

Vote in the 1992 general election

	Con	Lab	LD	SNP	Other	N
More Scottish	15.1	41.5	10.4	32.3	0.6	470
Both	39.6	35.4	11.6	12.7	0.7	268
More British	60.8	19.6	13.7	5.9	0.0	51
All	25.9	38.3	11.2	24.1	0.5	789

As previous researchers have shown from these data, there is a powerful relationship between national identity and support for the Conservatives and the SNP (Brand, *et al.*, 1994b; Brown, McCrone and Paterson, 1996). Thus 61% of voters who thought of themselves as 'more British than Scottish' supported the Conservatives but only 6% voted SNP. Conversely, 32% of voters who thought of themselves as more Scottish than British supported the SNP but only 15% voted Conservative. Comparing these two groups, then, we obtain a Conservative:SNP odds-ratio of 22.0, much larger, as we shall see, than any of the class or religious odds-ratios.

However, the SNP is not the only vehicle for Scottish identity, and as we can see the Labour Party is also more likely to win the support of voters with Scottish identity than it is to secure support from people who think of themselves as more British than Scottish. Comparing these two groups we find a Conservative:Labour odds-ratio of 8.5, again rivalling the class odds-ratios.

The nationalist cleavage, then, represents a powerful force in Scottish voting behaviour. What are the consequences for the other cleavages?

Class Voting

Table 5 begins to provide an answer to this question and compares class voting in England and Scotland. We distinguish six classes, defined in terms of their economic interests and market situation:[9]

Upper salariat: professionals plus managers and administrators in large enterprises.

Lower salariat: semi-professionals, plus managers and administrators in small enterprises.

Routine nonmanual: routine clerical, secretarial and sales workers.

Petty bourgeoisie: small employers, own account workers plus farmers.

Upper working class: foremen, technicians and skilled manual workers.

Lower working class: semi- and unskilled workers in agriculture and industry.

TABLE 5
CLASS AND VOTE IN ENGLAND AND SCOTLAND

England

Vote in the 1992 general election

	Con	Lab	LD	Other	N
Upper salariat	64.8	16.0	18.0	1.2	244
Lower salariat	51.2	18.2	29.5	1.2	346
Routine non-manual	54.7	27.5	17.6	0.2	494
Petty bourgeoisie	65.2	14.9	19.1	0.7	141
Upper working	38.8	48.6	12.0	0.6	317
Lower working	31.3	54.9	13.4	0.4	463
All	48.1	33.3	18.0	0.6	2069

Scotland

	Con	Lab	LD	SNP	Other	N
Upper salariat	42.6	13.1	23.0	21.3	0.0	61
Lower salariat	30.2	32.1	14.2	22.6	0.9	106
Routine non-manual	29.5	37.0	11.0	22.0	0.5	200
Petty bourgeoisie	50.0	19.6	8.9	21.4	0.0	56
Upper working	17.4	47.1	11.6	24.0	0.0	121
Lower working	15.3	48.5	7.2	28.1	0.9	235
All	25.9	38.3	11.2	24.1	0.5	789

There are of course some important differences between England and Scotland in the distribution of the vote, the Conservatives receiving a much smaller share of the vote in Scotland and the SNP having a major presence north of the border. However, the pattern of relative class voting is much the same in the two countries – at least as regards the parties they have in common. Thus as we move up the class structure, we see that in England support for the Conservatives rises from 31% in the lower working class to 65% in the petty bourgeoisie and the upper service class. In Scotland, support for the Conservatives is lower in every single class, but the gradient as we move up is much the same, moving up from 15% to 50% in the petty bourgeoisie.

The story for the Labour party is broadly the same in the two countries, but there are some differences of detail. Thus in Scotland, Labour fares slightly worse among the lower working class, and substantially better among the lower salariat and routine non-manual workers, than would be expected from the English pattern.

Labour's success among the lower salariat in Scotland in 1992 is mirrored by a lack of Liberal Democrat success in this class. With this exception, however, class support for the Liberal Democrats is much the same as in England, being somewhat stronger in the nonmanual classes than in the working class.

Relative class voting thus seems to be as strong in Scotland as it is south of the border – at least as regards the Conservatives, Liberal Democrats and Labour. For example, if we compare the upper salariat with the lower working class, we find that the Conservative:Labour odds-ratio is 7.1 in England but 10.3 in Scotland. And the Labour:Liberal Democrat odds-ratio is 4.6 and 11.8 respectively. On this criterion, the nationalist cleavage has had little impact on the class cleavage.[10]

The story with the SNP is rather different, however. As previous investigators have noted, there is a modest class basis to the SNP vote, with its support rising from 21% in the higher salariat to 28% in the lower working class (Brand et al., 1993; Brown, McCrone and Paterson 1996). But this is a rather modest class gradient, and in turn this means that a substantial proportion of the Scottish electorate is not voting along class lines.

If we calculate absolute class voting (the proportion of the electorate voting for the natural party of their class), we can readily see that absolute class voting is much lower in Scotland. In England, 55% of the electorate in 1992 voted for the natural party of their class, whereas in Scotland only 41% did so. As we suggested in the introduction, this is hardly surprising. Since the combined Conservative and Labour share of the vote is substantially lower in Scotland than it is in England, there would need to have been much stronger relative class voting in Scotland to have achieved the same level of absolute class voting. Clearly, the SNP changes the character of Scottish electoral competition. The presence of a political vehicle for national identity has indeed, in the absolute sense, made inroads into class voting while leaving relative class voting undiminished.

Religious Voting

The nature of the religious cleavage is highly variable between countries. Sometimes, as in Germany for example, the cleavage is essentially based on religiosity – regular church attenders, Protestant and Catholic alike, supporting Christian Democrat political parties while voters who have no religion tend to support left-wing parties such as the Greens or Socialists (Heath *et al.*, 1993). In other political systems, and Northern Ireland is an extreme example, denominational differences provide the basis of the cleavage, with Protestants opposing Catholics or, as in Bulgaria, the Orthodox opposing Muslims. These denominational cleavages are often surrogates for ethnic cleavages, and when they are they tend to be especially powerful.

In England and Scotland both sorts of religious cleavage are present, although it is the denominational one that tends to be stronger. In Table 6 we distinguish between the two established Churches of England and Scotland, Catholics, other Christians (largely non-Conformists), small numbers of non-Christian, and a large category of respondents with no religion.

TABLE 6
RELIGIOUS DENOMINATION AND VOTE IN ENGLAND AND SCOTLAND

England

Vote in the 1992 general election

	Con	Lab	LD	Other	N
C of England	55.1	26.8	17.6	0.5	951
C of Scotland	83.3	8.3	8.3	0.0	12
Catholic	37.0	47.0	15.5	0.5	200
Other Christian	47.4	31.1	21.1	0.4	228
Non-Christian	42.6	51.1	6.4	0.0	47
No religion	41.9	37.5	19.6	1.0	626
All	48.4	32.9	18.1	0.6	2064

Scotland

	Con	Lab	LD	SNP	Other	N
C of England	53.3	16.7	20.0	10.0	0.0	30
C of Scotland	33.6	31.8	10.2	23.7	0.8	384
Catholic	7.4	64.8	8.2	19.7	0.0	122
Other Christian	31.3	32.8	14.9	19.4	1.5	67
Non-Christian	14.3	42.9	28.6	14.3	0.0	7
No religion	19.4	38.7	11.8	29.6	0.5	186
All	26.6	38.1	11.2	23.5	0.6	796

Given the small numbers of Church of Scotland members resident in England and of Church of England members resident in Scotland, we should place little reliance on the estimates of their party support. However, some clear patterns do emerge among the members of the established Churches in their respective countries: in both countries they are clearly inclined towards the Conservative Party, giving the Conservatives 55% of their votes in England and 34% in Scotland (in both cases about 7 points higher than the Conservatives' overall percentage).

In both countries we also find the Catholics to be the group least likely to support the Conservatives and much more inclined to vote Labour. Comparing the established Church with the Catholics, then, we find a Conservative:Labour odds-ratio of 2.6 in England and 9.3 in Scotland.

In both countries, too, we find a modest link between non-Conformity (included within our Other Christian category) and support for the Liberal Democrats, while in Scotland there is a very modest difference between Catholic and Church of Scotland support for the SNP.

Finally, respondents with no religion exhibit the tendency found throughout Europe to support parties of the left. In both countries they are slightly less likely than the average voter to support the Conservatives and slightly more inclined than the average to support the left (if we include the SNP as a party of the left in Scotland).

None of this is especially surprising. Denominational differences have a long history in Britain, and the link between Catholicism and Labour is well known, almost certainly reflecting the parties' historical stances on home rule for Ireland (see for example Budge and Urwin, 1966; Bochel and Denver, 1970; Miller and Raab, 1977; Wald, 1983; Hornsby-Smith, 1987; Heath *et al.*, 1991). In Scotland in particular there was a powerful link between Protestantism and Unionism. There was, suggests McCrone, 'a complex of interrelated elements of Protestantism and Unionism welded together by a strong sense of British national and imperial identity ... given the powerful strand of militarism that ran through Scottish society in the late nineteenth and early twentieth centuries' (McCrone, 1992: 158).

While the disappearance of the religious factor from the political arena has often been predicted, its continued presence in England and Scotland demonstrates eloquently the force of Lipset and Rokkan's theory of cleavage structures frozen at the point when the contemporary political structure emerged. No doubt they are melting gradually, but the process is notable for its glacial character. Would that they melted rather faster in Northern Ireland.

Turning to absolute measures, it is not entirely clear how to proceed. With a multi-party system and a multi-category treatment of denomination, it is somewhat arbitrary how one computes a measure of absolute denominational voting. We could treat Labour as the natural party of Catholics and the Liberal Democrats as the natural party of non-Conformists, leaving the Conservatives as the natural party of the established church. If we follow this logic, then absolute denominational voting in England is 32.2% and 27.4% Scotland, well short in both cases of absolute class voting.

The assignment of parties as the 'natural' homes of religious groups is a somewhat arbitrary exercise in Britain, reflecting the absence of explicit politicization of the religious cleavage. Could we not argue that the SNP is the natural party of the non-religious, thus immediately increasing the measure of absolute denominational voting in Scotland?

An alternative measure, which takes account of the whole range of groups and parties but without making arbitrary assumptions, is the index of dissimilarity. In essence, this tells us what proportion of the electorate would have to change their votes in order to make the denominational (or class) profiles of the parties identical. In the multi-category case this can be calculated as

$$\{(F_i - E_i / 2) / N\} * 100$$

where F_i represents the frequency in cell i of the cross-tabulation and E_i represents the frequency expected if there were no association between denomination and vote.

We can readily calculate that the index of dissimilarity for denominational voting in England is 7.4 in England (compared with 14.8 for class voting) while in Scotland it amounts to 11.6, rivalling the 11.4 which the index of dissimilarity for class voting reaches in Scotland.[11] In this sense, then, as previous researchers have noted, religion seems to play a larger role in Scotland than it does in England (Budge and Urwin, 1966; Bochel and Denver, 1970).

Class, Religion and National Identity

The impression so far is that, in relative but not absolute terms, the three cleavages of class, denomination and national identity coexist. Large denominational and nationality odds-ratios in Scotland are not associated with any reduction in the class odds-ratios, although they are associated with a reduction in the absolute measures of class voting. In other words, the presence of the national cleavage in Scotland does not in itself seem to undermine the effect of class on support for the Labour and Conservative parties although it does reduce the total proportion of votes cast along class lines.

We can check this conclusion more rigorously by conducting a pooled analysis of the two countries and testing formally whether there are significant differences in the strengths of the class and denominational cleavages. We conduct a series of logistic regression analyses in which we regress party choices on class, denomination and national identity (Table 7). What we do is to run analyses in which we contrast each of the parties in turn with all the others (that is, Conservative vs non-Conservative, Labour vs non-Labour, Liberal Democrat vs non-LD, and finally SNP vs non-SNP).[12] The parameter estimates in these models are fitted log odds-ratios and are thus related to the odds-ratios reported in the previous sections.

We conduct a pooled analysis of both countries, except in the case of the SNP where we necessarily restrict ourselves to Scotland alone. We also include controls for age, which has been shown to be an important predictor of support for the SNP (Brand *et al.*, 1993), and, in England only (but not in Scotland because of the tiny numbers involved), ethnicity.

TABLE 7
LOGISTIC REGRESSION MODELS

	Con	Lab	LD	SNP
Country	-0.41	1.03*	0.50	–
Class				
Upper salariat	1.38**	-1.97**	0.50**	-0.12
Lower salariat	0.85**	-1.59**	0.90**	-0.24
Routine nonmanual	0.97**	-1.15**	0.30	-0.37
Petty bourgeoisie	1.57**	-1.92**	0.40	-0.51
Upper working	0.35*	-0.22**	0.03	-0.35
Country*lower salariat		-0.65**		
Denomination				
Church of England	0.46**	-0.50**	-0.08	-0.24
Church of Scotland	0.90**	-0.54**	0.18	-0.01
Catholic	-0.35*	0.60**	-0.38	-0.41
Other Christian	0.18	-0.24	0.13	-0.39
Non-Christian	0.06	0.16	-0.18	-0.52
Ethnicity				
White	0.19	-0.19	-0.16	
Black	-1.09*	2.01**	-4.81	
Asian	0.03	0.67	-2.04	
National identity				
More Scottish	-2.21**	0.83*	0.17	1.84**
Both	-0.91*	0.66	-0.08	0.77*
Age (*100)	0.69*	0.23	0.53	2.51**
Constant	-1.18**	-0.17	-2.90**	-0.83*
Model Chi²	444.1(17df)	381.3(18df)	87.1(17df)	73.3(13df)

Note: The omitted categories are England, the lower working class, no religion, other ethnic group, and more British than Scottish.

We tested whether significant improvements to fit could be achieved by including interaction effects between country and class, denomination, or age. But only one significant interaction was found – that between country and the lower salariat for the Labour party. In other words, with this one exception, the effects of class and denomination on support for the Conservative, Labour and Liberal Democrat parties are not significantly different in the two countries. The parameter estimates also confirm the story told by the simple cross-tabulations that class differences are in general larger than the denominational ones. It is perhaps worth noting that, once we control for class, age and national identity, the voting behaviour of Catholics is not significantly different in Scotland from that in England.

It is also striking that, out of class, denomination and national identity, only the latter has significant effects on SNP voting. Once we introduce controls, the modest class differences that we observed in Table 5 become nonsignificant. Moreover, the effect of national identity, although undoubtedly large, proves to be no larger than some of the class effects in this multivariate analysis.

At the other extreme, however, comes the Conservative Party. Here we find statistically significant multiple cleavages: class, denomination, ethnicity (in England), national identity (in Scotland) and age (in both countries) are all significant predictors of support for the Conservatives. And despite the presence of the additional nationalist cleavage in Scotland and the ethnic cleavage in England, the common cleavages have common effects on Conservative choice in the two countries.

Conclusions

These results, although somewhat paradoxical at first sight, are nevertheless readily explicable in terms of the simple numerical examples given in the introduction. The key point is that, when measured in relative terms, a cross-cutting cleavage such as national identity may not vanquish older cleavages such as class. The two may coexist. In Scotland, as we saw in Table 4, large effects for national identity, which have no direct equivalent in England, can coexist with class effects which are every bit as large as those found south of the border.

But in another sense class has been vanquished north of the border. If we calculate the index of dissimilarity for nationalist voting in Scotland, we obtain a value of 14.1, well in excess of the 11.4 for Scottish class voting. In aggregate, then, the parties in Scotland now differ more in the national identity of their supporters than they do in their class profiles and more votes are cast along national lines than class lines. This in turn may generate a new dynamic within Scottish politics which leads the older parties to play down their class appeals. In the long run, class could lose its impact, even in the relative sense, in Scotland, although this will surely depend on politically contingent events like the outcome of a referendum on a Scottish parliament. If nationalist goals are achieved in Scotland, support for the SNP might wane and class might reassert itself in absolute terms.

ACKNOWLEDGEMENTS

We are grateful for Jack Brand and James Mitchell and to the ESRC for making the Scottish Election Survey possible, and to the ESRC and the Sainsbury Family Charitable Trusts for their support of the 1992 British Election Survey. We also wish to thank our colleagues in CREST for their help and support.

NOTES

1. Britain (which we take to refer to England plus Wales plus Scotland) is not strictly a state (a term that correctly applies only to the UK). Nor is it a single nation. Certainly many citizens of Britain would regard themselves as belonging to English, Welsh or Scottish nations. We therefore use the lay term 'country' for convenience.
2. In the past, of course, the religious cleavage between the established Church and other denominations was to some degree politicized in Britain, and denominational differences in voting behaviour, as we shall see later, have persisted.
3. For a discussion of the Alford index and its limitations see Alford, 1962; Korpi, 1972; Heath *et al.* 1985; and Heath *et al.*, 1995.
4. There is also a third sense in which a cleavage such as ethnicity might vanquish class. Thus we might find an interaction effect between class, ethnicity and vote such that, among members of the ethnic minority, class differences are eliminated while among members of the majority class differences persist. We would regard this as the clearest case of one cleavage vanquishing another, and there are grounds for supposing that ethnicity sometimes has this character.
5. The variance in vote explained by class will tend to track this measure of absolute class voting, since variance explained depends on the distributions of the variables as well as on the size of the effect.
6. Ideally, in order to monitor the results of this 'natural experiment' we would have a 'before and after' design, comparing the changes in class and religious voting in the two countries before and after the rise of the SNP. While the SNP actually came into existence in 1934, it only really achieved electoral breakthrough in 1970, when it contested 65 seats in Scotland and achieved 11.4% of the vote. A comparison of patterns using the 1964 and 1992 British Election Surveys would be instructive, although it would be hampered by the very small size of the Scottish samples. It is unlikely with very small samples that we would be able to reject the null hypothesis that the trends in, say, class voting in Scotland had been the same as those in England. See Weakliem and Heath, 1995.
7. We recognize that, in a formal sense, there is a distinct Scottish Labour Party, etc. But for most practical purposes – its leadership, its programme – it can be thought of as a single political entity.
8. The Scottish Election survey was funded by the ESRC, award R000235290. It was based on a random sample of 957 electors stratified by region and clustered within 59 Scottish constituencies.
9. This is a slightly modified version of Goldthorpe's seven-class schema. Because of the small numbers involved in the Scottish sample, we combine the foremen with the skilled working class. See Goldthorpe, 1980 and Heath *et al.*,1995 for further details.

10. We must always be cautious in comparing odds ratios, especially those such as the Labour:Liberal Democrat one in Scotland where some of the cells involved will be very small. This odds ratio will therefore have quite a large standard error, and we need to do a formal test of significance. Formal tests are carried out as part of the pooled logistic regression analysis below.

11. The index of dissimilarity is sensitive to the number of categories used. As it happens, however, we have used six-category schemes both for class and for denomination.

12. An alternative would have been to conduct a multinomial logistic regression in which we simultaneously modelled the impact of the structural variables on the full array of partisan options. The parameters in such a model apply to contrasts between specific pairs of parties, e.g. Labour and Conservative. In our approach, however, the parameters apply to contrasts between one specific party and all the others. This better reflects the nature of the voting choice, since voters do of course decide to vote for one party rather than any of the others.

BIBLIOGRAPHY

Alford, R.R. (1962) 'A Suggested Index of the Association of Social Class and Voting', *Public Opinion Quarterly* 26: 417–25.

Bochel, J.M. and D.T. Denver (1970) 'Religion and Voting: A Critical Review and New Analysis', *Political Studies* 18: 205–19.

Brand, J., J. Mitchell and P. Surridge (1993) 'Identity and the Vote: Class and Nationality in Scotland', pp.143–57 in D. Denver, P. Norris, C. Rallings and D. Broughton (eds) *British Elections and Parties Yearbook 1993*. Hemel Hempstead: Harvester Wheatsheaf.

Brand, J., J. Mitchell and P. Surridge (1994a) 'Will Scotland Come to the Aid of the Party?' pp.213–228 in A. Heath, R. Jowell and J. Curtice (eds) *Labour's Last Chance?* Aldershot: Dartmouth.

Brand, J., J. Mitchell and P. Surridge (1994b) 'Social Constituency and Ideological Profile: Scottish Nationalism in the 1990s'. *Political Studies* 42, 616–29.

Brown, A., D. McCrone and L. Paterson (1996) *Politics and Society in Scotland*. Basingstoke: Macmillan.

Budge, I. and D. Urwin (1966) *Scottish Political Behaviour: A Case Study in British Homogeneity*. London: Longman.

Goldthorpe, J.H. (1980) *Social Mobility and Class Structure in Modern Britain*. Oxford: Clarendon.

Heath, A.F., R.M. Jowell and J.K.Curtice (1985) *How Britain Votes*. Oxford: Pergamon.

Heath, A.F., R.M. Jowell, J.K. Curtice, G. Evans, J. Field and S.Witherspoon (1991) *Understanding Political Change*. Oxford: Pergamon.

Heath, A.F, B. Taylor and G.Toka (1993) Religion, Morality and Politics, Pp 49–80 in R Jowell *et al.* (eds) *International Social Attitudes: the 10th BSA Report*. Aldershot: Dartmouth.

Heath, A.F., G. Evans and C. Payne (1995) 'Modelling the Class–Party Relationship in Britain, 1964–93, *Journal of the Royal Statistical Society, series A*, 158: 563–74.

Heath, A. F. and B. Taylor (1996) 'British National Sentiment', CREST working paper, No 50. Oxford and London: CREST.

Hornsby-Smith, M. (1987) *Roman Catholics in England: Studies in Social Structure Since the Second World War*, Cambridge: Cambridge University Press.

Kellas, J.G. (1991) *The Politics of Nationalism and Ethnicity*. London: Macmillan.

Korpi, W. (1972) 'Some Problems in the Measurement of Class Voting', *American Journal of Sociology* 78: 627–42.

Lijphart, A. (1979) 'Religious vs Linguistic vs Class Voting: The "Crucial Experiment" of Comparing Belgium, Canada, South Africa and Switzerland', *American Political Science Review* 73: 442–58.

McCrone, D. (1992) *Understanding Scotland: The Sociology of a Stateless Nation*. London: Routledge.

Miller, W.L. and G. Raab (1977) 'The Religious Alignment at English Elections between 1918 and 1970', *Political Studies* 25: 227–51.

Moreno, L. (1988) 'Scotland and Catalonia: The Path to Home Rule. In D. McCrone and A. Brown (eds), *The Scottish Government Yearbook*, 166–181. Edinburgh: The Unit for the Study of Government in Scotland.

Sartori, G. (1969) 'From the Sociology of Politics to Political Sociology', in S.M. Lipset (ed.), *Politics and the Social Sciences*, 65–100. New York: OUP.

Wald, K.D. (1983) *Crosses on the Ballot: Patterns of British Voter Alignment since 1885*. Princeton, NJ: Princeton University Press.

Weakliem, D. and A.F. Heath (1995) 'Regional Differences in Class Dealignment', *Political Geography* 14: 643–51.

Crooked Margins and Marginal Seats

James Cornford and Daniel Dorling

This article presents a new approach to the question of defining 'marginality' in a plurality electoral system with more than two parties, such as that found in Britain. The method described here has a significant advantage over more traditional definitions in that it is uses the probability that a seat will actually change hands (based on the historical precedent), rather than being simply based on the size of the gap between the two best performing parties. Although the new method requires a significant amount of computation, this is rendered fairly trivial by the use of computers.

The article is in three parts. The first part presents the traditional definition of marginality and sets out some of the problems which are encountered when using this approach. The second part introduces the new method and applies it to the current electoral situation in Britain. A final section briefly draws out a few of the implications from the findings in part two of the article.

Traditional Marginality

What is a marginal constituency? The concept of marginality is used to direct attention to those seats which are most likely to change hands at the next election. There is, of course, no guarantee that a marginal seat will change hands; that depends on the actual behaviour of the voters in the following election. However, the perception of a seat as marginal influences the nature of electoral competition in that seat. First, perceived marginals make the obvious target for the party organizations, which can therefore be expected to concentrate their resources in those seats. Second, a seat which is seen as being marginal offers voters more plausible opportunities for effective tactical voting. Marginals are, therefore, different and, in terms of electoral competition, particularly important seats.

Because they are so significant, especially at elections which are expected to be close, accurate identification of marginals is important. Already, lists of 'marginals' are being published in Britain in preparation for the next general election, taking into account the recent boundary changes (see for example, *New Statesman and Society*, 1995), both to identify key target seats to the party organizations and as a guide to tactical voting for the electorate.

If marginals are so important, then how can we identify them? As Norris and Crewe (1994: 216) point out, 'there is no consistent definition of a "marginal seat"'. The simple answer is that the margin between the parties which came first and second at the last election should be 'small'. A conventional definition of 'small' might be 'within ten percentage points in terms of the total number of votes cast for all parties'. Conversely, seats where the gap is large are defined as 'safe'. Of course, such a cut-off is arbitrary – we could choose another value. Equally, we can give a specific 'marginality' (or 'safeness') value for a given constituency in terms of the percentage point gap between the first and second parties. In its favour, this measure of marginality is extremely easy to calculate requiring only knowledge of the number of votes for the first and second parties.

However, let us note a key point about this definition of marginality – it is wholly arbitrary in terms of actual performance. By this we mean that it generates a definition which is rarely (if ever?) checked against reality. How often are 'safe' seats lost? How often are 'marginal' seats retained? This question is seldom explored; as Norris and Crewe (1994: 202) have noted, some authors 'mistakenly assume that the marginality of a seat is evidence of vulnerability to turnover' (see e.g., Curtice, 1992).

The traditional model of a marginal can best be illustrated by the use of a simple graphical device– the standard electoral triangle (Upton, 1976; 1994; Miller, 1977; Linton, 1987; Cornford et al., 1995; Dorling et al., 1996).

The Electoral Triangle

The electoral triangle allows us to plot the relative performance of three parties on a flat plane. For example, Figure 1 provides a graph upon which can be shown the distribution of votes by seat for the three main parties (Conservative, Labour and the Democrats or their forebears) at any given election. Readers who are unfamiliar with the electoral triangle may need some guidance in interpreting Figure 1. In the electoral triangle the share of the vote gained by each of the three main parties in each constituency is displayed graphically by a dot. A dot falling in the upper subsection of the triangle represents a seat won by the third party (in our case, that is the Liberal Party, Liberal/SDP Alliance, or Liberal Democrats – termed Democrats from now on). A dot in the lower right-hand subsection represents a seat won by the Conservative Party. Similarly, a dot in the lower left-hand subsection represents a seat won by the Labour Party.[1]

The closer the dots are to the boundaries between the subsections of the triangle, the more (conventionally) 'marginal' are the seats that they represent. The traditional definition of marginality (in terms of a difference between the two leading parties of ten percentage points or less) can thus be shown on the triangle by inserting a few straight lines (see Figure 2). The current numbers of seats thus defined are shown in Table 1. The obvious

question which arises concerns just how reasonable these ominously straight
lines actually are. Are seats which fall within the shaded area on Figure 2
really more marginal (in the sense of more likely to change hands) than those
which fall outside the shaded areas? The only way we can test this is by
examining the historical record.

FIGURE 1
THE ELECTORAL TRIANGLE

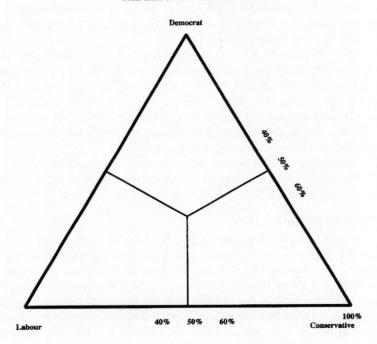

TABLE 1
CONVENTIONAL MARGINAL SEATS FOLLOWING THE 1992 GENERAL ELECTION

(after accounting for boundary changes, marginal = second party less than 10 percentage
points behind winner in terms of the total poll)

		Con	Runner up Lab	LDp	Nat	Total
	Con	–	72	18	3	93
	Lab	61	–	2	1	64
Winner	LDp	7	1	–	1	9
	Nat	4	0	1	–	5
	Total	72	73	21	5	171

FIGURE 2
THE ELECTORAL TRIANGLE WITH TRADITIONAL MARGINAL AREAS SHADED
(where marginal = second party is within 10 percentage points of the winner)

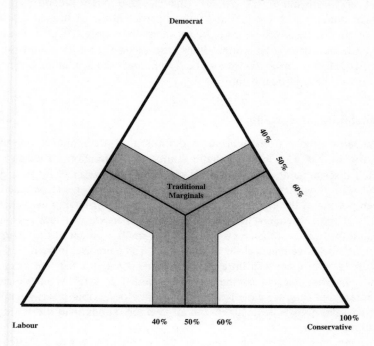

The Historical Record

Most constituencies tend to be primarily *contested* (in the sense of being fought with a reasonable chance of winning) by just two parties regardless of the number of parties which put up a candidate. A simple analysis of every one of the six hundred plus British mainland parliamentary seats at each of the twelve[2] general elections from 1955 and 1992 (inclusive) reinforces this point. According to this analysis, there were 6,799 constituency contests in which at least two parties' candidates stood in a given election *and* in the subsequent election. A total of 6,730 of these seats (or 99.0 per cent) were won by one of the three main parties at both elections (that is to say, only 69 seats out of 6,799 have ever been won by parties other than the main three). Of the 6,730 seats dominated by the three main parties, 8.3 per cent changed hands at the subsequent election (a total number of 560). Almost all of the 560 seats which changed hands were won by the party which was in second place at the previous election of the pair (533 or 95.2 per cent). In summary: in any one seat in a British post-war general election, it is almost certain that only two parties will be effectively contesting to win; in the vast majority of contests, just three parties – Conservative, Labour and Democrats (or their political forebears) – are significant 'players' (that is, come first or second).[3]

The concern with the first and second parties in the traditional definition of marginality therefore seems to be substantially correct. There still remains the issue of whether the straight lines (shown on Figure 2) are historically justified. Here we need to move to a different basis of calculation, once again looking to the historical record.

Probabilistic Marginality

How can we move from an arbitrary definition of marginality to one that is empirically based? The only reliable source of information for constructing such a discriminator is the historical precedent: for instance, if, for a given number of previous general elections, the proportion of seats represented in a given portion of the electoral triangle at each election t having ever changed hands at the subsequent election $t+1$, is low, then we can feel reasonably assured that any seat that is currently in that small segment of the triangle is unlikely to change hands at the next election. To be precise, in such a case we would say that there was little 'historical precedent' for the seat to change hands, and that that seat can therefore be regarded as 'safe'. While we cannot be sure about this, we can create a much more defensible discriminator for sorting seats into 'safe' and 'marginal' categorizations than the traditional arbitrary cut-off.

Using this method, we can set the distinction between 'safe' and 'marginal' seats at a given level of probability, based on a given set of previous elections. To create this more rigorous discriminator for distinguishing between 'safe' and 'marginal' seats based on precedence, every election result for every general election from 1955 to 1987 was plotted on the electoral triangle. A grid was then superimposed over the triangle at the one per cent level to create several thousand individual cells. For each cell that contained more than five election results, the probability of a seat in that position on the electoral triangle changing hands at the subsequent election (1959–92) was calculated. Because some of the probabilities were based on a sample of only a few seats, and because the imposition of any particular grid over the triangle is arbitrary, it is desirable to smooth these probabilities locally on the triangle. Therefore, a single pass, two-dimensional, binomial smoothing process was undertaken to incorporate the probabilities of contiguous cells and thus to create a more robust probability for each individual cell. For each cell on this grid, the probability of a seat which falls within that cell changing hands at the subsequent election was thus calculated (this process is fully described in Appendix 1).

The resulting probability surface can then be used to discriminate between different levels of marginality (which we will label as 'contestability' from now on to distinguish our probabilistic concept from the traditional concept of maginality). From this surface, 'probability contours' on the electoral triangle can be defined. The position on the triangle of each seat at each election, relative to the probability contours, defines its level of 'contestability'. In order to ease the following narrative, a cut-off point has been selected to group seats into just two categories ('safe' and 'contestable'). For the purposes of this article, a 'contestable' seat at any given election is defined as one which occupies a position in the triangle with a precedented probability of changing hands at a subsequent election which is 0.1 *or greater* (a one in ten or better chance). By contrast, if there was a less than one in ten probability (on past experience) of a seat in a given position changing hands, then that seat is classified as 'safe'. Lines showing these 'ten per cent probability of a seat changing hands' areas are shown in Figure 3.

FIGURE 3
THE ELECTORAL TRIANGLE WITH PRECEDENTED
'CONTESTABLE' AREAS SHADED
(where 'contestable' = a historical probability of 0.1 or greater that a seat in that position will change hands at the subsequent election)

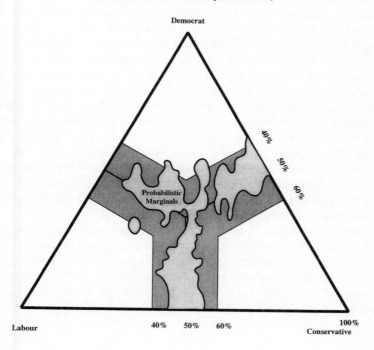

The 0.1 probability contour was selected in preference to some other level for a number of reasons. First, it creates a clear set of contiguous areas which appear intuitively meaningful when plotted on the electoral triangle. Such intuition is supported by the fact that 88 per cent of all seats which have changed were within the area delimited by the 0.1 contour, while 99 per cent of seats outside that area have not changed hands over the 1955–1992 period. By definition these figures compare favourably with those produced using the traditional concept of marginality. Further, the concept of a one in ten *or better* chance of a seat in that area having changed hand in the past is relatively easily comprehensible (the *average* chance of a seat defined as 'marginal' here changing hands at any election over the period is 28 per cent). Finally, and more whimsically, this one-in-ten cut-off contrasts nicely with the more traditional definition of a marginal seats as being one in which the second placed party is within, at most, ten percentage points of the winner. Other probability contours could, of course, be used to construct a number of bands of 'contestability'. This possibility was not explored here because it would unnecessarily complicate the following analysis.

As we can immediately see (Figure 3), the neat and tidy straight lines of the conventional definition have been replaced by a much more complex shape. A first point to note is the much larger area of the Liberal Democrat portion of the triangle which is defined as contestable when compared with the sections of the other two parties. A second point concerns the relatively straight line separating Conservative safe seats from those that are contestable with Labour when compared with the equivalent line within the Labour portion of the triangle. For Conservative seats, it appears that the proportion of the vote going to the Liberal Democrats makes little difference to Labour's chance of winning them. For Labour seats, by contrast, there is a greater probability of their being won by the Conservatives where the Liberal Democrats have a small but significant share of the vote. In Labour seats where the Liberal Democrat vote approaches 30 per cent, the Labour/Conservative contestable area narrows, as it does somewhat in seats where the Liberal Democrats have a very small share of the vote. It is where the Liberal Democrats have some 15 per cent of the vote that Labour seats appear to be most vulnerable.

Using the definition of a contestable seat as one which occupies an area of the triangle enclosed within the 0.1 probability contour, we can construct a table of safe and contested seats at a given election. Using the 1992 general election results, reallocated to take account of the new constituencies,[4] we can replicate Table 1 with the new definition of contestable seats (see Table 2).

TABLE 2
PRECEDENTED CONTESTABLE SEATS FOLLOWING
THE 1992 GENERAL ELECTION
(after accounting for boundary changes)

		Runner up			
		Con	Lab	LDp	Nat	Total
	Con	–	60	13	3	76
	Lab	73	–	1	1	75
Winner	LDp	8	1	–	1	10
	Nat	0	0	1	–	1
	Total	81	61	15	5	161

Note: Five marginal seats where nationalists came second have been defined by traditional means (within 10 percentage points of the total vote (or less) of the winner).

The only exception to the probabilistic approach in Table 2 is in the Scottish and Welsh seats where the Nationalist parties are estimated to have come first in 1992 on the new boundaries (6) or second (40). In these 46 seats we have used the traditional 10 percentage point cut-off to give just six marginals (three where the Nationalist parties challenge the Conservatives, one where they challenge Labour, one where they challenge the Liberal Democrats and one where the Nationalists are challenged by the Conservatives). This approach was chosen in preference to expanding the analysis to an extra dimension for three main reasons:

1. There is still a paucity of previous election results in which the Nationalists were a significant force, thereby limiting the available precedents on which to base the probabilities;
2. It would increase the complexity of the calculations required; and
3. It would entail losing the ability to visualize contestability on the two dimensional electoral triangle.

A full list of all seats which occupy areas of the triangle within the 0.1 probability contour in the run-up to the 1997 general election is given in Appendix 2.

There are a number of drawbacks with this approach. First, and most importantly, we take no account of the current political context. It is unlikely that very many of the Labour-held seats defined as contestable will change hands at the next election. However, this is also true of the traditional measure and an analyst, aware of the current situation, should simply concentrate on the Conservative seats which have been defined here as contestable. A second weakness, which derives from using the historical record to calculate the probabilities, is that it may be unduly influenced by atypical election results, such as the 1983 election when the emergence of the Social Democratic Party briefly bolstered the third party vote. Third, we do not take into account the changing nature of contestability over time. Finally, many other factors could be included in the model – for instance, the socio-economic characteristics of constituencies (for example, in- and out-migration levels), incumbency of candidates (which may make a seat less vulnerable) or the targeting of the seat by the national party organizations. All of these factors could be incorporated, to greater or less extent, in a more complex model. What we have done here is simply to make a first small step towards such a more complex model.

Implications

What are the implications of our findings? Four points emerge most strongly. The first is how well the arbitrary definition of marginality works in most cases. If we plot the relationship between the traditional measure of marginality (percentage point gap between the first and second parties) and our new probability based definition of marginality, we get a clear inverse relationship with relatively few outliers. Further, when we compare the results for individual seats, we can see that most of the discrepancies are minor.

A second point is the striking number of safe Conservative seats. The Conservatives seem to have had real 'strength in depth'. The impressive performance of Labour in the polls has led some to suggest that it would be possible for the Conservatives to suffer the same kind of defeat that was experienced by the Canadian Conservatives in the 1993 Federal Election. However, we should merely point out that such electoral 'meltdown' is precedented in the Canadian context – a Liberal Canadian government has undergone a similar collapse in the early 1980s (LeDuc, 1995: 163) – while such events are unprecedented in post-war British electoral history.

A further point that comes out of the analysis is the irrelevance of Labour/Democrat contests. With just one seat each in which the other party has a ten per cent or better probability of winning (Greenwich and Woolwich for Labour, Rochdale for the Democrats), there would appear to be little point in the two opposition parties attempting to win seats from each other (Crewe, 1993). Whether they are aware of this fact is another matter (see for example, Jones, 1994). For the same reasons, there seems to be little need for a formal electoral pact (as argued for by, for example, Dent, 1993) between the two opposition parties as they have little to win from competing with each other. Simple electoral calculation leading to the concentration of campaigning resources in each party's most winnable seats should generate the desired effect.

Most importantly, however, the analysis reinforces the huge mountain which the Labour Party have to climb if they are to form an administration after the next election. Even if we assume that the flow of the vote at the next election will be large and uniformly away from the Conservatives and towards Labour, the Democrats and the Nationalists (for example, that only the Conservatives will lose seats), and even if every Conservative seat with a historically precendented one in ten or better chance of changing hands actually does change hands, Labour would still be five seats short of an absolute majority.

Postscript (2 May 1997)

After the election we can see that 'New' Labour did not so much climb the mountain as demolish it. It seems almost traditional for stable relationships identified by social scientists to collapse the moment that they have been identified and the result is a salutary, if pleasing, reminder of the dangers of claiming too much for the predictive powers of simple extrapolation from the past.

The Labour landslide at the 1997 general election, although still falling short of the Conservative meltdown in Canada, will have dramatically changed the shape of the marginality surface shown in the article, penetrating far deeper into the Conservative portion of the triangle and dramatically reducing the Conservatives' 'safe' area. Indeed, the majority of the seats won by Labour were not even marginal under the traditional (10 per cent) definition. One advantage of using the probability definition is that it can be changed over time to incorporate landslides such as this. In the end, what the election shows clearly is the limits of any purely mathematical definition of marginality. Such methods work – until they don't.

NOTES

1. The advantage of the graphical triangle over more traditional statistical measures is that the relative fortunes of three parties can be shown while still displaying the variation between seats. In most cases in Britain this is adequate. However, in situations where there is a significant fourth party (for example, the Nationalist parties in Scotland and Wales) these seats will be incorrectly represented as having been won by one of the three main parties, but the relative share of the vote between the three main parties will still be correctly represented. In the analysis we have generally omitted the handful of seats which have been won or contested by the Nationalists or other parties. It is, however, possible to use further dimensions (which cannot, of course, be correctly represented on paper) to include the Scottish and Welsh nationalist parties and 'other' candidates. Between 1955 and 1992 there were two geographical re-districtings of seats. Cornford *et al.* (1993) discusses how these were dealt with and gives the data sources.
2. Of course, there have been only eleven general elections between 1955 and 1992. However, a further set of changes is included as a pseudo 1979 election (reaggregated to the 1983 seats – see BBC/ITN, 1983) to represent the major redistricting which took place between 1979 and 1983. The reason for this is to illustrate the possible magnitude of such major boundary changes. The dataset used in this analysis has been deposited in the ESRC Data Archive at

Essex so that other researchers can access it (Dorling *et al.*, 1993). It is based on many previous studies deposited at the archive including previous attempts to geographically link constituencies over time.

3. The only exception to this rule (accounting for almost all of the 69 seats in which any party other than the main three parties came first or second at successive general elections) is in Scotland or, to a lesser extent, Wales where Nationalist parties are significant contenders in a number of seats. Even in these non-English seats, although somewhat less clearly, the tendency is for a sustained pattern of two-party contests to emerge with the nationalists contesting with one of the three main parties.

4. Estimates for the 1992 election results, based on the current (1996) electoral boundaries were made by David Rossiter (see Pattie *et al.*, 1996).

BIBLIOGRAPHY

BBC/ITN (1983) *The BBC/ITN Guide to the New Parliamentary Constituencies.* Chichester: Parliamentary Research Services.

Brown, K. (1994) 'Lib Dems Target Urban Tory seats', *Financial Times*, 3 March .

COI (1991) *Parliamentary Elections* (Central Office of Information, *Aspects of Britain* Series). London: HMSO

Cornford, James, Dan Dorling and Bruce Tether, (1995) 'Historical Precedent and British Electoral Prospects', *Electoral Studies* 14(2): 123–42.

Crewe, Ivor (1993) 'Tories Could be Trounced Without Lib–Lab Pacts', *The Independent on Sunday*, 9 May.

Crewe, Ivor, Pippa Norris and Robert Waller, (1992) 'The 1992 General Election', in P. Norris *et al.* (eds) *British Elections and Parties Yearbook 1992*, pp.xv–xxxvi. New York: Harvester Wheatsheaf.

Curtice, J. (1992) 'The British Electoral System: Fixture Without Foundation' in Dennis Kavanagh (ed.), *Electoral Politics*. Oxford: Clarendon.

Dent, M. (1993) 'The Case for an Electoral Pact Between Labour and the Liberal Democrats', *Political Quarterly* 64(2): 243–51.

Dorling, Daniel, Charles Pattie and Ron Johnston, (1993) 'Measuring Electoral Change in Three Party Systems: An Alternative to Swing', *PS: Political Science and Politics* 26(4): 737–41.

Dorling, Danny, Ron Johnston and Charles Pattie, (1996) 'Using Triangular Graphs for Representing, Exploring and Analysing Electoral Change', *Environment and Planning A:*, 28: 979–8.

Jones, M. (1994) 'Hope for the Blue Gang as the Reds and Yellows Clash', *Sunday Times*, 12 June.

LeDuc, Larry (1995) 'The Canadian Federal Election of 1993', *Electoral Studies*, 13(2):163–8.

Linton, Martin (1987) 'Charting a Path through the Tactical Voting Forest', *The Guardian*, 25 May.

Miller, W.L. (1977) *Electoral Dynamics*. London: Macmillan.

New Statesman and Society (1995) 'Key Seats Next Time', 15 September, p.8.

Norris, Pippa and Ivor Crewe (1994), 'Did the British Marginals Vanish? Proportionality and Exaggeration in the British Electoral System Revisited', *Electoral Studies*, 13(3): 201–21.

Pattie, Charles, David Rossiter, Daniel Dorling and Ronald Johnston (1996) 'Missing Voters', in David Broughton *et al. EPOP Yearbook 1996*, pp.37–49. London: Frank Cass.

Upton, Graham (1976) 'The Diagrammatic Representation of Three Party Contests', *Political Studies* 24: 448–54.

Upton, Graham (1994) 'Picturing the 1992 General Election', *Journal of the Royal Statistical Society,* Series A, 157(2): 231–52.

APPENDIX 1
MEASURING THE CONTESTABILITY OF ELECTORAL POSITION BASED ON
HISTORICAL PRECEDENT

This appendix describes the technical details of defining parliamentary constituencies as contestable or safe based on the election results of all general elections since 1955 in Britain. Constituencies which are contestable are those in which a party, other than that holding the seat, has a reasonable chance of winning the seat. Contestability is defined here as a measure of how likely a seat is to be lost by the party holding that seat at an election.

The probability that a seat is lost is well known to depend most strongly on the 'closeness' of the votes for the various parties which had candidates standing at the previous election (Cornford *et al.*, 1995). More generally, the probability that a seat is lost at a subsequent election can be seen to be strongly influenced by the share of the votes of each contesting party at the general election immediately prior to the new election of interest. Other events, local- or by-elections, are not necessarily as good a guide to contestability.

The aim here is to be able to assign a probability to each constituency which quantifies the likelihood that that constituency could be lost by the incumbent party based on the prior votes of the parties contesting that seat at the previous general election. The context for this calculation is the results of all contests at all general elections in Britain since 1955. This context is used because past precedence is intuitively the best yardstick upon which to calibrate a model of probabilities which is itself aiming to quantify the precedent. The period from 1955 is chosen because the constituencies in which general elections are held have been relatively stable, the boundaries of some of them having being significantly altered only twice since then.

The following procedure is used to assign a probability of changing hands to each seat at each election. It is based upon the concept of the electoral triangle which is described in more detail in the main text. It can be shown that only the main three parties, Conservatives, Labour and Liberals (of various forms) have had a significant effect on the outcome of British general elections since 1955. With just these three parties to work with, each seat can be categorized by the proportion of the vote for the Conservatives and Labour (this in turn defines the proportion of the vote gained by the variously named third party). These two proportions locate a position on the electoral triangle and it is that position which is used to define the prior political position of each seat.

- A dataset is created of all election results by constituency between 1955 and 1992.

For each constituency at each election the votes for the Conservative Party, Labour Party and Liberal Party/Alliance/Liberal Democrats are recorded. Between 1955 and 1992 there were two major sets of boundary changes. Previous studies were used to decide whether a seat was substantially the same after the boundary changes, had ceased to exist, or was created – thus simplifying a generally more complex geographical process. The single boundary change prior to the 1992 election, in which an extra seat in Milton Keynes was created, is dealt with in a different way – by combining the new seat with the existing Milton Keynes seat.

The elections of 1955, 1959, 1964, 1966, 1970, 1974 (February and October), 1979, 1983, 1987 and 1992 are included along with the results of the 1979 election as they have been estimated if transferred to the seats defined for the 1983 election (BBC/ITN, 1983). Thus we have a data set of 705 seats for 12 elections and 3 parties – potentially over 25,000 counts of votes for all the individual candidates who represented the three main parties at general elections in this period.

- Each seat at each election is assigned to a 'cell', X,Y, on the electoral triangle defined by the ranges:

  $X\% <=$ Conservative share of the three party vote (%) $< X\% + 1\%$

  $Y\% <=$ Labour share of the three party vote (%) $< Y\% + 1\%$

  $0\% <= X\% + Y\% <= 100\%$

where X and Y are integers.

- For each cell, X,Y, in the resulting triangle the following four counts are made:

A: The number of times a seat has existed at two consecutive elections and in which candidates from at least two of the three main parties stood at each election. This is based on all the elections that have occurred between 1955 and 1992 and all the seats on the mainland of Britain.

B: The number of contests in A where the parties coming first and second at both pairs of elections were drawn from the three main parties.

C: The number of contests in B where the first-placed party at the first election was not first placed at the second election (that is, seats which changed hands).

D: The number of contests in C where the first-placed party at the second election was the second-placed party at the first election (that is, seats which changed hands and which were won by the party placed second at the preceding election).

•   For each cell in the triangle, the raw probability that seats which have occupied that cell were contestable is defined as:

The ratio D/B taken from the counts described above.

That is, the proportion of all the contests where the main parties played the leading roles and in which the second-placed party at the first election won at the second election – as the main text shows, these represent 99.0 per cent of all contests and 95.2 per cent of seats which have changed hands. The vast majority of contests and changes are thus covered by this definition. The result is a raw probability surface with each cell allocated a value between 0 (no seat occupying that position ever having passed from first-placed party to second-placed party) and 1 (every seat occupying that position having passed from the first party to the second party at successive elections).

•   For each cell in the triangle a smoothed probability that seats in that cell will pass to the second party at a successive election is calculated.

The choice of which grid to place over the triangle is arbitrary and has some influence on the resulting raw probability surface. To create a more robust measure of how likely a seat is to be won by the second-placed party at the next election, this raw probability surface is locally smoothed according to the following procedure:

a) The ratio for each cell is taken as D/B only if B is greater than or equal to five (that is, only if the probability is based on at least five previous contests occurring in that cell). If B is less than five, neighbouring cells are taken (beginning with the immediately contiguous cells and moving out in one per cent increments in all directions) until five contests are found. If five contests cannot be found within six one per cent cells of a particular cell on the triangle, then that cell is deemed not to have an estimable probability associated with it. The resulting estimates of probability for all cells which can be estimated are termed the 'robust probability' that a seat will change hands.

b) The smoothed probability is subsequently calculated for every cell on the triangle as a weighted average of the cell's robust probability and the robust probabilities of all its nearest neighbours through simple one-pass binomial smoothing. The cell's smoothed value is taken to be 1/4 of its robust value plus 1/8 of its immediate neighbours' values and 1/16 of its point-wise neighbours in the three-by-three neighbourhood of the cell. These fractions differ at the edges of the triangle and when probabilities could not be defined according to standard practice. The resulting probability for each cell is termed 'smoothed probability'.

•   Areas on the triangle were defined as contestable when their smoothed probability was equal to, or greater than, 0.1

To achieve a simple dichotomy between areas of the electoral triangle within which seats were thought to be contestable, and areas in which seats were thought to be 'safe', a cut-off contour had to be chosen on the smoothed probability surface. The level 0.1 was chosen partly to contrast with the different kind of 10 per cent cut-off which is traditionally used in these kinds of studies. More substantively, a 0.1 smoothed probability was found to result in largely contiguous areas being defined as contestable (see Figure 3). Further, the 0.1 contour was found to include 88 per cent of those seats which have ever changed hands at elections. The area outside this limit included 99 per cent of seats which did not change hands. This 0.1 probability level is obviously fairly arbitrary. Nevertheless it is thought that this process should result in a more reliable, and certainly a more explicit definition of what is, and what is not, likely to be a 'winnable' constituency.

APPENDIX 2
CONTESTABLE CONSTITUENCIES AT THE 0.1 OR BETTER PROBABILITY LEVEL
FOLLOWING THE 1992 GENERAL ELECTION
AND INCORPORATING THE MOST RECENT BOUNDARY CHANGES

Margin in terms of precedented probability of seat changing hands (%)	Winner 1992	Runner Up 1992	Constituency	Traditional margin (%)
Conservative/Labour Marginals				
50	Con	Lab	Vale of Glamorgan	0.12
44	Con	Lab	Dudley South	0.28
44	Con	Lab	Acton and Shepherds Bush	0.03
44	Con	Lab	Hayes and Harlington	0.08
35	Con	Lab	Batley and Spen	1.30
35	Con	Lab	Blackpool South	0.50
35	Con	Lab	Corby	0.60
35	Con	Lab	Lincoln	1.17
35	Con	Lab	North West Leicestershire	1.30
35	Con	Lab	Rossendale and Darwen	0.62
34	Con	Lab	Edmonton	1.22
34	Con	Lab	Slough	1.06
34	Con	Lab	Warrington South	2.45
34	Con	Lab	Regents Park and Kensington N	1.29
34	Con	Lab	Vale of Clwyd	2.10
33	Con	Lab	Eltham	1.72
33	Con	Lab	Kingswood	2.54
32	Con	Lab	Amber Valley	2.15
32	Con	Lab	Bury South	1.50
30	Con	Lab	City of Chester	3.87
29	Con	Lab	Southampton Itchen	2.67
29	Con	Lab	Preseli Pembrokeshire	2.99
27	Con	Lab	Brentford and Isleworth	2.00
27	Con	Lab	Croydon North	1.81
27	Con	Lab	Dover	1.44
27	Con	Lab	Middlesbrough S and E Cleveland	1.67
27	Con	Lab	Luton South	1.66
27	Con	Lab	Staffordshire Moorlands	3.57
26	Con	Lab	Ilford South	3.35
26	Con	Lab	Halesowen and Rowley Regis	3.85
25	Con	Lab	Mitcham and Morden	3.43
25	Con	Lab	Tynemouth	5.66
24	Con	Lab	Stevenage	7.17
23	Con	Lab	Norwich North	4.90
23	Con	Lab	Worcester	5.65
21	Con	Lab	Chorley	4.81
21	Con	Lab	South Derbyshire	5.78
19	Con	Lab	Harlow	3.87
18	Con	Lab	Birmingham Hall Green	7.80
18	Con	Lab	Bolton West	5.46
18	Con	Lab	High Peak	7.89
18	Con	Lab	Northampton North	7.65
17	Con	Lab	Exeter	4.92

Margin in terms of precedented probability of seat changing hands (%)	Winner 1992	Runner Up 1992	Constituency	Traditional margin (%)
Conservative/Labour Marginals (continued)				
16	Con	Lab	Calder Valley	7.99
16	Con	Lab	Gloucester	8.44
16	Con	Lab	Leeds North East	8.51
15	Con	Lab	Derby North	7.53
15	Con	Lab	Forest of Dean	6.17
14	Con	Lab	Loughborough	10.29
14	Con	Lab	Elmet	5.57
14	Con	Lab	Keighley	6.60
14	Con	Lab	Monmouth	6.32
13	Con	Lab	Bury North	8.03
13	Con	Lab	Stockton South	7.29
13	Con	Lab	Cardiff North	6.19
12	Con	Lab	Brighton Pavilion	6.79
11	Con	Lab	Plymouth Sutton	4.83
10	Con	Lab	Basildon	10.27
10	Con	Lab	Birmingham Edgbaston	8.12
10	Con	Lab	Swindon South	10.43
Conservative/Democrat Marginals				
28	Con	LDp	Hazel Grove	1.69
25	Con	LDp	W Aberdeenshire and Kincardine	6.41
24	Con	LDp	St Ives	2.87
24	Con	LDp	Torridge and West Devon	5.41
23	Con	LDp	Eastbourne	8.42
23	Con	LDp	Brecon and Radnorshire	0.27
19	Con	LDp	Portsmouth South	0.45
18	Con	LDp	Hereford	5.88
18	Con	LDp	Isle of Wight	2.28
18	Con	LDp	Southport	5.52
14	Con	LDp	Twickenham	10.85
12	Con	LDp	Torbay	10.08
11	Con	LDp	Somerton and Frome	7.10
Labour/Conservative Marginals				
60	Lab	Con	Thurrock	2.14
57	Lab	Con	Stirling	0.92
55	Lab	Con	Birmingham Northfield	1.11
51	Lab	Con	Ipswich	0.50
50	Lab	Con	Bolton North East	2.78
50	Lab	Con	Feltham and Heston	2.01
50	Lab	Con	Lewisham East	2.61
50	Lab	Con	North Warwickshire	2.50
44	Lab	Con	Coventry South	0.73
43	Lab	Con	Birmingham Selly Oak	3.70
43	Lab	Con	Halifax	0.77
42	Lab	Con	Ellesmere Port and Neston	5.34
42	Lab	Con	Hyndburn	4.42

Margin in terms of precedented probability of seat changing hands (%)	Winner 1992	Runner Up 1992	Constituency	Traditional margin (%)
Labour/Conservative Marginals (continued)				
42	Lab	Con	Lewisham West	4.17
42	Lab	Con	Sherwood	4.73
40	Lab	Con	West Lancashire	3.79
39	Lab	Con	Bristol North West	0.46
39	Lab	Con	Nuneaton	2.78
39	Lab	Con	Carmarthen W & S Pembrokeshire	2.93
36	Lab	Con	Barrow and Furness	6.49
36	Lab	Con	Copeland	5.19
36	Lab	Con	Darlington	5.08
36	Lab	Con	Nottingham South	5.94
36	Lab	Con	Wakefield	6.44
36	Lab	Con	Delyn	6.41
35	Lab	Con	Hampstead and Highgate	5.15
30	Lab	Con	Carlisle	2.13
29	Lab	Con	Cannock Chase	7.88
29	Lab	Con	Southampton Test	3.88
29	Lab	Con	Walsall South	6.29
29	Lab	Con	Ayr	4.89
27	Lab	Con	Pendle	4.02
27	Lab	Con	Weaver Vale	4.80
26	Lab	Con	Dewsbury	7.33
25	Lab	Con	Dudley North	9.19
25	Lab	Con	Dulwich and West Norwood	6.51
25	Lab	Con	Hornsey and Wood Green	9.39
25	Lab	Con	Stretford and Urmston	7.29
25	Lab	Con	Strathkelvin and Bearsden	8.01
23	Lab	Con	Streatham	9.94
23	Lab	Con	Wolverhampton North East	7.97
23	Lab	Con	City of York	9.82
22	Lab	Con	Derby South	10.56
22	Lab	Con	Wallasey	7.00
22	Lab	Con	Walthamstow	5.41
21	Lab	Con	Tooting	8.09
21	Lab	Con	Cunninghame North	6.82
20	Lab	Con	Plymouth Devonport	10.27
20	Lab	Con	Edinburgh South	9.40
19	Lab	Con	Blackburn	10.98
19	Lab	Con	Coventry North West	10.53
17	Lab	Con	North East Derbyshire	10.62
17	Lab	Con	Cambridge	1.08
17	Lab	Con	Edinburgh Central	5.94
15	Lab	Con	Morley and Rothwell	12.08
15	Lab	Con	Bradford South	9.29
15	Lab	Con	Bristol East	6.89
15	Lab	Con	Crewe and Nantwich	7.20
15	Lab	Con	Leicester West	8.21
15	Lab	Con	Norwich South	8.10
15	Lab	Con	Stockport	8.09

Margin in terms of precedented probability of seat changing hands (%)	Winner 1992	Runner Up 1992	Constituency	Traditional margin (%)
Labour/Conservative Marginals (continued)				
15	Lab	Con	Walsall North	7.34
15	Lab	Con	West Bromwich East	8.12
14	Lab	Con	Southall	10.60
12	Lab	Con	Great Grimsby	14.80
12	Lab	Con	Wythenshawe and Sale East	14.34
12	Lab	Con	Stoke South	13.07
11	Lab	Con	Birmingham Erdington l	6.70
11	Lab	Con	Wrexham	15.84
11	Lab	Con	West Renfrewshire	13.77
10	Lab	Con	Bassetlaw	18.19
10	Lab	Con	Leicester South	17.70
10	Lab	Con	Telford	13.45
Labour/Democrat Marginal				
20	Lab	LDp	Greenwich and Woolwich	6.80
Democrat/Conservative Marginals				
35	LDp	Con	Bath	3.85
28	LDp	Con	North East Fife	7.89
22	LDp	Con	Argyll and Bute	7.19
21	LDp	Con	Cheltenham	3.72
19	LDp	Con	North Cornwall	3.07
15	LDp	Con	Berwick upon Tweed	11.59
14	LDp	Con	North Devon	1.39
13	LDp	Con	Tweeddale Ettrick and Lauderdale	2.86
Democrat/Labour Marginal				
18	LDp	Lab	Rochdale	1.31
Democrat/Nationalist Marginal				
16	LDp	Nat	Inverness East Nairn and Lochaber	1.72
Nationalist/Democrat Marginal				
12	Nat	LDp	Ceredigion	6.92

A Question of Interaction: Using Logistic Regression to Examine Geographic Effects on British Voting Behaviour

Andrew Russell

The economic and political contexts of Britain in the early 1990s meant that several tenets of psephological conventional knowledge were put to the test at the 1992 general election. Economically, the Conservative government apparently owed their success in the 1983 and 1987 elections to real economic prosperity (see Sanders *et al.*, 1987; Sanders, 1991, 1993; Price and Sanders, 1993, 1995; Heath *et al.*, 1985, 1991). Geographically, the government were the beneficiaries of the supposed development of a two-nations identity with hostility to the Conservatives being concentrated in the old industrial heartlands of northern Britain and in inner cities (see Johnston *et al.*, 1988; Johnston and Pattie, 1989, 1990; Pattie and Johnston, 1990, Johnston *et al.*, 1992).

The 1992 election however, took place in the context of widely different circumstances. The economy was undergoing a severe recession, notable for its impact upon the hitherto protected sections of the economy in the service sector and the south of Britain (see Regional Trends, 1995; Martin, 1993; Pattie, *et al.*, 1995) which altered the prospect for personal economic optimism and threatened the orthodox north–south electoral divide.

Clearly then, the 1992 election requires some explanation since the Conservatives were returned with a clear majority of 21 in the House of Commons, presenting them with a fourth consecutive term of office – a feat unprecedented in this century. Moreover although the north–south divide narrowed significantly (see Pattie and Johnston, 1995), a remarkable feature of the geography of the vote was that the recession in the south of England failed to prompt enough of a revolt among Conservative voters to oust the government.

Many efforts have been made to explain the outcome of the 1992 election, but it is a major contention here that those studies which concentrate on the election event itself miss some of the vital inter-election swings in public opinion which contributed to the Conservative victory. Furthermore aggregate-level studies may not be the best method of assessing individual change over the longest of long campaigns, leading to the Conservatives victory in 1992.

Consequently this article concentrates at the individual level on the period from 1990–92, using the *NOP/Newsnight* 'New Decade' series of monthly opinion polls. Its primary focus is on the relationship between geography, economic attitudes, social class and reported vote intention during the period between mid-term and full-term in the life of the parliament. The analysis here uses a pooled data set of more than 31,000 respondents from every poll which asked respondents for their personal economic expectations (the period July 1990–February 1992 inclusive). The most appropriate statistical technique for this model of reported vote intention is logistic regression analysis.

The basic linear regression model makes a number of assumptions that are far from easy to satisfy. Not least among these assumptions is that the variance in the dependent variable is normally distributed. This assumption can only be safely made if the dependent variable is quantitative rather than qualitative. For a qualitative dependent variable, reflecting binary choices, yes–no responses, buy–no buy decisions, or choices between two alternatives (Conservative reported vote intention vs non-Conservative, for example), such an distribution cannot be safely assumed since responses would have to be categorized as either zero or one, on or off, Conservative or non-Conservative. The distribution between the values of a dichotomous qualitative dependent variable then, cannot be normally distributed.

Greene points out that the error terms in linear regression approaches are: 'heteroscedastic in a way that depends on β.' (1993: 637). Critically, it treats the variance for the dependent variable as normally distributed – an assumption which cannot be sustained for a dichotomous variable such as party support, where possible responses can only have the values of one (party supporter) or zero (non-supporter). A binary response does not run from zero to infinity and hence OLS estimates are likely to give biased and nonsensical estimates. To this end, and despite its widespread use in the modelling of party support, it is not a wholly satisfactory method for predicting levels of party support. A preferable method involves logistic regression which can be used for predicting values for dichotomous dependent variables. Moreover since this method is more robust it ought to enable the interaction effects between geography and economic attitudes to be modelled with greater confidence.

Furthermore, this type of regression analysis has the distinct advantage over least square variants of regression since it allows for the predictive values of the B coefficients to be expressed in terms of log odds-ratios which seem intuitively preferable. In least squares linear regression modelling it is common to predict that an individual could have a chance of greater than 1 (or less than 0) of following a certain outcome. This is clearly senseless for modelling government support, since an individual cannot have a chance of voting for a party that is equal to greater than one or less than zero (see also

Gujarati 1992). As Greene has it, the failure to constrain $\beta'x$ to the zero–one interval

> produces both nonsense probabilities and negative variances. In view of this, the linear model is becoming less frequently used except as a basis for comparison to some other more appropriate models (1993: 637).

Some authors have attempted to rescue the linear regression model, or have attempted to modify it, but even in studies where its shortcomings have been noted 'the resulting estimator may have no known sampling properties.' (1993: 637 footnote)

From logistic modelling it is possible to arrive at estimated probabilities of party support for individuals that are fairly robust and, as Paulson states, 'more sticky' than for least squares linear modelling (Paulson, 1994: 98), in that the probabilities it produces make more intuitive sense at the top and bottom of the scale, since in the linear model the predicted value of p can often be negative or larger than one – thus violating its interpretation as a relative frequency. (Gujarati, 1992; Maddala, 1987; Kennedy, 1992).

A classic account of the uses of logistic regression by Griliches (1957) demonstrated the advantages of logistic regression techniques for multi-layered relationships between independent variables. Griliches used logistic regression to estimate the parameters of corn growing in different regions of the USA – and critically – attempted to explain the differences in those parameters in terms of variable economic conditions (see Maddala, 1987 for further discussion of this point). The contention here is that a similar approach to reported vote intention ought to reveal interesting diversions from the national trend according to economic context.

The Dependent Variable: Reported Vote Intention

The *NOP/Newsnight* series of opinion polls asked respondents to state which party, if any, they would vote for if there were a general election the next day. Non-respondents and 'don't knows' were then prompted with a secondary question to ascertain which party, if any, they would be most likely to support in a general election the next day. Hence two different levels of intensity in party support were recorded. In this analysis, reported vote intention combines supporters from the primary and secondary question on vote intention.

Two separate but parallel, logistic regression models were built. Conservative reported vote intention measures those respondents who claimed to be likely to vote Conservative (from either measure of intensity) against all non-Conservatives (including the supporters of other parties, non-responses, refusals and don't knows). By the same token, Labour reported vote intention pits Labour supporters against non-Labour supporters.

Since this dependent variable is a dichotomous, qualitative one, the variance within the dependent variable cannot be normally distributed. Consequently the orthodox regression technique – ordinary least squares (or indeed any general linear regression model) – would be an inappropriate measure of analysis (Intriligator, 1978).

The analysis of interaction terms between independent variables is the next major advantage of using logistic regression. The relatively simple and clear presentation of interaction effects adds a practical advantage for the use of logistic regression over linear regression to the theoretical advantages it also holds. This practical advantage would be particularly useful in addressing the ordering of geographic effects on voting behaviour in Britain, and the debate on geographic milieux and composition (see for instance, Pattie and Johnston, 1995 versus Rose and McAllister, 1990 and McAllister and Studlar, 1992).

Model Diagnostics

The greatest drawback of the logistic regression method of analysis is its perceived inadequate goodness of fit statistics. As Kennedy has it there is no universally accepted goodness of fit measure for logistic estimation (Kennedy, 1992: 235).

The most common goodness of fit statistic reported with logistic regression is the likelihood ratio index, a version of the maximum likelihood estimates familiar from linear regression models. The –2 log likelihood statistic is reported here for reasons of consistency, and can provide a relative measure of best fit within a single data set but its meaning of itself is unclear.

The overall fit of the model is supposedly measured through a quantity known as the deviance, rather than through the residual sum of squares (as in linear regression). The deviance is a log likelihood statistic which has parallels in other forms of quantitative analyses. As Bailey and Gatrell (1995) state:

> if the model is an adequate explanation of variations in the response the deviance should theoretically be distributed as chi-squared, having degrees of freedom equal to the difference between the number of observations and the number of parameters in the model; if the model is poor the deviance will be significantly larger than this (Bailey and Gatrell, 1995: 312).

Although what constitutes 'significant' is left to the imagination by Bailey and Gatrell.

Supposedly the -2 log likelihood is a measure of how well the model fits the data. The smaller the value (the smaller the deviance) the better the fit. In stepwise models, the change in -2 log likelihood provides a test of the null hypothesis that the coefficients of the terms removed from the model are zero. In logistic models however, it must be remembered that in themselves -2 log likelihoods reveal little. They can provide relative measures within a single data set (so from the example used here, it is clear that the Conservative reported vote intention model performs better than the Labour reported vote intention model) but the raw statistic tells us nothing without some relative anchorage to other models drawn from the same data set.

Another convention with logistic regression and goodness of fit is to produce a statistic giving the number of $y = 1$ and $y = 0$ values correctly predicted by the model. Despite the initial attraction of this convention, it generates rather more heat than light. As Kennedy shows,

It is tempting to use the percentage of correct predictions as a measure of goodness of fit. This temptation should be resisted: a naive predictor, for example that every $y = 1$, could do well on this criterion. It should be noted that a feature of logit is that the number of $y = 1$ predictions it makes is equal to the number of $y = 1$ observations in the data' (1992: 236).

So, in summary then, logistic regression is the preferred model for categoric dichotomous dependent variables and is well equipped for the analysis of a multi-layered model, with *a priori* theoretical grounds for supposing that interaction effects may be significant. Its major drawback however centres on the production of goodness of fit statistics, which, for the most part, can only be meaningful when directly compared to statistics produced by a different model from the same data set.

The goodness of fit statistics reported in Table 1 can interpreted in this light. Clearly the Conservative reported vote intention model, performs better than the Labour reported vote intention model (the -2 log likelihood statistic is lower) for both the original model and the improved model (after the interaction effects are added). Further if, as Bailey and Gatrell suggest, the goodness of fit statistics are treated in the same way as chi-squared, what becomes important is the significance of the statistic rather than the statistic itself. For both Conservative and Labour reported vote intention models, a high level of statistical significance is reported in both the original and the improved states.

Economic Optimism in the Long Campaign

Regional variations in personal optimism and pessimism throughout the long campaign leading to the 1992 general election revealed an apparently trendless pattern of regional differences (Russell *et al.*, 1996). Throughout the period from July, 1990 to November 1991, the south and areas typified by employment in the service sector failed to turn on the government despite the

TABLE 1

THE IMPACT OF MONTH, REGION, CONSTITUENCY TYPE, CLASS AND ECONOMIC ATTITUDES
(WITH INTERACTION EFFECTS) ON CONSERVATIVE AND LABOUR REPORTED VOTE INTENTION
JULY 1990–FEBRUARY 1992 (LOGISTIC REGRESSION)

VARIABLE	CONID			LBRID		
	B	S E	EXP (B)	B	S E	EXP (B)
Jul 1990 (vs Feb 1992)	*	*	*	0.19	0.079	1.21
Aug 1990 (vs Feb 1992)	*	*	*	0.13	0.079	1.14
Sep 1990 (vs Feb 1992)	*	*	*	*	*	*
Oct 1990 (vs Feb 1992)	*	*	*	*	*	*
Nov 1990 (vs Feb 1992)	0.16	0.081	1.18	*	*	*
Dec 1991 (vs Feb 1992)	0.39	0.080	1.48	*	*	*
Jan 1991 (vs Feb 1992)	0.36	0.081	1.45	*	*	*
Feb 1991 (vs Feb 1992)	0.42	0.081	1.53	*	*	*
Mar 1991 (vs Feb 1992)	*	*	*	-0.18	0.080	0.84
Apr 1991 (vs Feb 1992)	*	*	*	*	*	*
May 1991 (vs Feb 1992)	*	*	*	*	*	*
Jun 1991 (vs Feb 1992)	*	*	*	*	*	*
Jul 1991 (vs Feb 1992)	*	*	*	*	*	*
Aug 1991 (vs Feb 1992)	*	*	*	*	*	*
Sep 1991 (vs Feb 1992)	*	*	*	*	*	*
Oct 1991 (vs Feb 1992)	-0.19	0.083	0.83	0.22	0.081	1.25
Nov 1991 (vs Feb 1992)	0.15	0.082	1.16	-0.22	0.081	0.80
Jan 1992 (vs Feb 1992)	*	*	*	*	*	*
CELT (vs South)	-0.57	0.091	0.57	0.44	0.069	1.55
NORTH (vs South)	-0.22	0.082	0.80	0.62	0.067	1.86
MIDS (vs South)	*	*	*	0.24	0.070	1.27
LDON (vs South)	*	*	*	0.15	0.072	1.16
DEPLA (vs Affluent)	-0.18	0.072	0.84	0.19	0.056	1.21
SERVICE (vs Affluent)	*	*	*	*	*	*
CLASSAB (vs ClassDE)	1.22	0.079	3.37	-0.98	0.073	0.38
CLASSC1 (vs ClassDE)	0.74	0.069	2.10	-0.64	0.056	0.53
CLASSC2 (vs ClassDE)	0.26	0.068	1.30	-0.18	0.050	0.84
OPTIM (vs Pessim)	1.45	0.091	4.26	-0.78	0.088	0.46
NEUTRAL (vs Pessim)	0.89	0.085	2.44	-0.36	0.074	0.70
CELT BY OPTIM	*	*	*	0.23	0.111	1.26
NORTH BY OPTIM	*	*	*	*	*	*
MIDS BY OPTIM	*	*	*	*	*	*
LDON BY OPTIM	*	*	*	*	*	*
DEPLA BY OPTIM	-0.22	0.095	0.80	*	*	*
SERVICE BY OPTIM	-0.21	0.094	0.81	*	*	*
CLASSAB BY OPTIM	-0.24	0.106	0.79	-0.20	0.111	0.82
CLASSC1 BY OPTIM	*	*	*	-0.26	0.089	0.77
CLASSC2 BY OPTIM	*	*	*	-0.20	0.083	0.82
CELT BY NEUTRAL	*	*	*	*	*	*

TABLE 1 (Continued)

Interactions

VARIABLE	CONID			LBRID		
	B	S E	EXP (B)	B	S E	EXP (B)
NORTH BY NEUTRAL	*	*	*	*	*	*
MIDS BY NEUTRAL	*	*	*	*	*	*
LDON BY NEUTRAL	*	*	*	*	*	*
DEPLA BY NEUTRAL	*	*	*	*	*	*
SERVICE BY NEUTRAL	*	*	*	*	*	*
CLASSAB BY NEUTRAL	*	*	*	-0.25	0.099	0.78
CLASSC1 BY NEUTRAL	*	*	*	-0.15	0.078	0.86
CLASSC2 BY NEUTRAL	*	*	*	-0.13	0.071	0.88
CONSTANT	-1.75	0.089		-0.22	0.077	

	ORIG − 2 L L	NEW − 2 L L	DF	SIG	IMPROVEMENT	SIG
CONID	38777.1	35263.8	30075	0.000	3513.3	0.000
LBRID	39587.7	36834.7	30075	0.000	2753.0	0.000

new recession. However, a critical feature of geographic variation was discernible at the end of the poll series (November 1991 to February 1992). In two measurements of geography (region and constituency type), the orthodox geographic variation of the 1980s was reasserted as the election drew close. There was an upturn in optimism in the run-up to the election in the southern regions which was absent further north, and a similar pro-optimistic shift was discernible in voters residing in areas typified by service sector employment. The evidence is amassing to show that the Major government was able to convince potential waverers where it mattered. Just as the Thatcher governments benefited from the tergiversating Tories of the 1980s (Russell, 1995), the Conservatives won in 1992 not least because of a widening spatial divide in economic optimism just when it mattered; moreover a divide which reflected the spatial divisions of the 1980s, recession and recovery rather than the new recession of the early 1990s. Underpinned by the long-term belief in the south of England that the recession there was temporary (see Russell, 1995; Russell et al., 1996), voters in critical regions and in crucial types of seats were persuaded not to turn against the government in the run-up to the 1992 general election.

Data Presentation

The logistic regression tables used here report the regression coefficients, standard error and the exponent of B (the odds-ratio) of the independent variables. As a general rule of thumb, a B coefficient which is twice the size of its own standard error is statistically significant. Only those variables which assumed statistical significance at or below the 0.1 level are reported. An asterisk denotes an insignificant variable. Each table also reports the appropriate diagnostic statistics: original and improved 2 log likelihoods, improvement figures and significance tests for the logistic regression model.

The odds-ratios produced by logistic modelling represents the multiplier by which the constant can be combined in order to produce the final impact of the variable. An odds-ratio of less than one means that an event is less likely to happen; a ratio of more than one means that the event is more likely to happen. So for example, Table 1 which shows the logistic models for Conservative and Labour reported vote intention can be interpreted in the following manner. The exponents of the B coefficients (the odds-ratio) for those living in Scotland or Wales (the CELT group) was 0.57. This can be interpreted that CELT respondents were only 0.57 times as likely (and therefore less likely) to favour the Conservatives than respondents from the comparator group (the SOUTH); on the other hand CELTS were 1.55 times as likely (and thus more likely) to be Labour supporters than respondents from the comparator group.

The Variables

The following variables were used in this analysis. The dependent variables Conservative and Labour reported vote intention were dichotomized so that a score of 1 equalled a reported vote intention for that party, a score of zero denoted some other outcome (including reported vote intentions for other parties, and don't knows and refusals). Categoric independent variables were taken and each of their categories was expressed as a binary dummy variable. This enabled the fitting of categoric data in an unambiguous fashion.

When dichotomies or dummy variables were used, one category for each of the independent variables is left out of the model. The reported coefficients for the other categories of each variable should be seen in relation to this comparator category. The comparator categories were February 1992, the south of England, affluent areas, Class DE and personal economic pessimism. In all cases, the comparator category was the most populous category of the independent variable from which it was constructed. The B coefficient for Conservative reported vote intention presented in Table 1 for respondents from the CELT region (Scotland and Wales) was -0.57. The direction of the coefficient shows that these respondents were less likely than southern respondents to express an intention of voting for the Conservative Party. The magnitude of the coefficient shows the intensity of this likelihood; so for instance the B coefficient of -0.57 for the CELT category and of -0.22 for the

NORTH category illustrated that both groups of respondents were less likely to express a reported vote intention for the Conservatives than the SOUTH comparator category, but northern respondents were less hostile to record a Conservative reported vote intention, than Scots or Welsh respondents, other things being equal.

Month: divides the 19 separate months in which the personal economic expectations question was asked in the *NOP/Newsnight* series of Opinion Polls. The 18 monthly dummies were compared to the last poll – FEBRUARY 1992 – which serves as the base month against which the impact of each poll is compared. This permitted the testing for particular 'period' effects in the poll series upon levels of party support and economic attitudes.

Region: divides the five geographic regions of mainland Britain into discrete regions. Four regional dummies, CELT (respondents from Scotland and Wales), NORTH, MIDLANDS and LONDON were compared to SOUTH the 'baseline' group. This was especially useful for testing the extent of the 'Major effect' on Conservative and Labour fortunes.

Constituency Type: is a measure of the functional use of space which divided the British electorate into three categoric groups (for a fuller discussion of classification of constituencies by functional space, see Crewe and Fox, 1984; Webber, 1978; CACI Inc., 1988; and Russell, 1995). Two constituency type dummies, DEPLA (respondents from constituencies typified by industrial depression and local authority housing), and SERVICE (respondents from areas characterized by service sector employment) were set against AFFLUENT (respondents from high status economically prosperous areas) which serves as the default comparator category.

Class: is the respondent's occupational class as measured by the *NOP/Newsnight* pollsters. The schema used is the ABC1 scale leaving four class dummies CLASS AB, CLASS C1, and CLASS C2 and a comparator category CLASS DE.

Personal Economic Expectations: divides the three combinations of economic outlooks of respondents for the next twelve months. This allows two economic expectation dummies OPTIMISM and NEUTRALITY to be compared to a baseline variable called PESSIMISM. (This is, of course the classic personal economic expectations variable used by Sanders *et al.*, 1987, and their followers.)

Logistic Regression Model: The Monthly Model of Conservative and Labour Reported Vote Intention

Month

The results of the logistic modelling of Conservative support by month during the period July 1990 – February 1992, presented in Table 1, confirm that the Major honeymoon period in Conservative electoral fortunes was brief. Conservative support was first swelled by Margaret Thatcher's departure and was built on by the new regime as the Major premiership was positively associated with levels of Conservative reported vote intention for the next three months. The Major honeymoon period, however, was a transient feature of British electoral politics, decaying after only three months. Nevertheless it should be remembered that throughout the run-up to the 1992 election, support for the Major-led Conservatives was always higher than during the nadir of Conservative support under Margaret Thatcher, and that the change of personnel in Downing Street may have been vital to electoral fortunes of the Conservative Party.

Conservative support during the four months between November 1990 and February 1992 was significantly different from the level of Conservative support in February 1992. Thereafter only two other polls (October and November 1991) were substantially different from the comparator poll in February 1992 and their effects were contradictory.

The parallel model of Labour reported vote intention presented in Table 1 also suggests that although the Major succession had helped to revive the electoral fortunes of the Conservatives, it did not have the reverse effect of dampening Labour support significantly. At best, Major's leadership helped to neutralize Labour's electoral base. Indeed the only trend in the monthly dummies appears to be the benefit Labour accrued at the beginning of the series in July and August 1990 which coincided with the height of Margaret Thatcher's unpopularity, when respondents were 1.21 and 1.14 times more likely to express an intention to vote Labour than in February 1992. The rest of the monthly dummies which achieve statistical significance to the 0.1 level were sporadic in their incidence and have contradictory effects – two acted as relative drags on Labour support, one boosted the relative Labour advantage.

Region

The logistic modelling of Conservative support presented in Table 1, supported the classic north–south divide in British voting behaviour. Other things being equal, respondents from the Celtic regions and from the north of England were less likely to express support for the Conservatives than the comparator category which covers respondents in the south of England. The odds-ratios of 0.57 and 0.80 for the CELT and NORTH dichotomous variables illustrate the extent to which the propensity to support the Conservatives is hampered by living in Scotland or Wales and the north. The failure of the MIDS and LDON dummy variables to produce statistically significant coefficients or odds-ratios showed that for the purposes of recruiting potential Conservative voters, the Midlands and the capital were just as fertile for the governing Party as the default SOUTH category.

Variations in Labour reported vote intention could be explained to a considerable degree by regional differences. Not only was the classical north–south divide in evidence, with the north being relatively more predisposed to Labour than Scotland and Wales, the Midlands and London also represented more fertile territory for Labour than the south of England.

The differences in the odds-ratios for the four regional dummies confirmed many of the findings of other studies into modern British voting behaviour (see for instance, Johnston *et al.*; 1988; Pattie and Johnston, 1995; Fieldhouse, 1995). Respondents from the north of England were, *ceteris paribus*, 1.86 times more likely to express a reported vote intention for Labour than their counterparts in the south of England. At the same time, Scots and Welsh were 1.55 times more likely, Midlanders 1.27 times more likely and Londoners 1.21 times more likely to express a preference for Labour than respondents from the comparator group in the south of England, taking all the other effects in the model into account.

It is interesting to note that the pattern of Conservative support meant that the Midlands and London were no different from the south, while they both provided Labour with a relative advantage over the south of England. This may well reflect the differences in the state of the anti-Conservative vote in different parts of the country. With the Liberal Democrats providing the effective opposition to the Conservatives in parts of the south, but remaining firmly in third place in much of the Midlands, the nuances of the anti-Conservative vote in the run-up to the 1992 election were not altogether surprising.

Constituency Type

Constituencies characterized by industrial depression and local authority housing proved to be difficult recruiting territory for the Conservatives throughout the period July 1990 – February 1992. Table 1 showed that respondents from depressed areas were only 0.84 times as likely as respondents from affluent areas to express an intention to vote Conservative.

Meanwhile if it can be seen that DEPLA constituencies were relatively disinclined to support the Conservatives, those in SERVICE areas were no different from AFFLUENT areas in their propensity to support the Conservatives. The parallel model of Labour reported vote intention showed that the type of constituency in which a respondent resided did affect his or her likelihood to support the Labour Party. Constituencies characterized by industrial depression and council housing provision were relative hotbeds of Labour support; individuals from these constituencies were 1.21 times more likely to support Labour than those from AFFLUENT constituencies. At the same time, those in SERVICE areas appeared no different from AFFLUENT areas in their propensity to express an intention to vote Labour.

Class

The expected relationship between class and Conservative Party voting – that the Conservatives pull support disproportionately from the highest social classes – proved to be a reasonable explanation of the variation in levels of Conservative reported vote intention. The comparator class, Class DE appeared to be the most hostile of all social classes to Conservative support, while respondents from classes C2, C1 and AB were 1.30 times, 2.10 times and 3.37 times more likely to express an intention to vote for the Conservatives than respondents from Class DE. Conversely Labour fared best among voters from the lower social classes and worst in the higher social strata.

Economic Attitudes

One of the major themes of the thesis that economic attitudes have a clear effect on levels of party support was supported by this regression analysis (Table 1). Put simply, economic optimists were – after considering the effects of the other variables in the model – more prone to express an affinity to Conservative reported vote intention than those who feel pessimistic about their personal economic futures. The odds-ratio presented in Table 1 reveals that they were in fact 4.26 times more likely to support the Conservatives than pessimists *ceteris paribus*. The fact that this was the largest single odds-ratio in the model revealed the comprehensive explanatory power of personal economic expectations for the level of Conservative support.

Those expressing neutral forecasts about their economic circumstances were also relatively likely to favour Conservative reported vote intention when compared to economic pessimists. The odds-ratios revealed that neutrals were nearly two and a half times more likely to favour the Conservatives than personal economic pessimists.

The original thrust behind much of this research was that those who felt well disposed towards their own economic fortunes were likely to reward the government at election times (the reward-punishment axiom of electoral politics probably goes back to VO Key 1966). By implication, opposition parties needed to capitalize on hostility to personal economic fortunes among the electorate. In short while the government could claim the votes of those who 'felt good' about their economic conditions, those who did not would form part of the Opposition's natural electoral community.

The logistic model of Labour support revealed this to be the case; those who felt optimistic about their economic future were less than half as likely to support Labour than those who felt pessimistic (Table 1). Those who expressed neutrality in their economic future were also less prone to Labour support than those who felt their economic position would worsen over the coming year.

Interactions

The most interesting aspects of the logistic modelling of Conservative and Labour support in Table 1 were the interaction effects between geography and economic attitudes. In effect they provide evidence for an autonomous geographic cleavage in the reported vote intentions of the British electorate. For while the economy seems to be the key electoral battleground in the 1990–92 period and geographic impact on reported vote intention was less dramatic, the analysis of interaction effects shows that geography assumes the primary role in the relationship between itself and economic attitudes. As far as the effect of geography on reported vote intention is concerned – and as the logistic regression analysis makes clear – the devil is in the detail.

While there were no significant interaction effects for the regional schema and economic attitudes in the model of Conservative reported vote intention, there was a significant interaction term between constituency type and economic optimism (see Table 1). These interactions are the crux of this article because they illustrate how the geographic context in which economic attitudes are formed can remain important despite the necessary restructuring of the original model. They show how geography can act as the filter through which economic attitudes are viewed, diluting or exacerbating the trends in reported vote intention associated with views about the economy. The importance of these interactions terms requires a full explanation of how they may be interpreted.

Each interaction effect has an independent B coefficient and associated log odds-ratio. Where these effects are statistically significant to the 0.1 level, they are reported in Table 1. However, it is important to acknowledge that these independent effects are additive, and must be integrated into the main effects of the model. This integration gives three comparator combinations against which to judge the effect of the interaction.

To show how interaction terms are interpreted, an interaction from Table 1 will be analysed in detail. Economic Optimists were much more likely to express Conservative support than those who were pessimistic about their personal economic future. The B coefficient for the OPTIM group of respondents was 1.45, the associated odds-ratio 4.26; hence those who were optimistic about their personal economic future were 4.26 times more likely to express government support than those who felt pessimistic about their personal economic prospects. On the other hand, those respondents who resided in depressed areas with high intensity local authority housing were relatively disinclined to support the Conservative government. The B coefficient for the DEPLA group was -0.18, the associated odds-ratio 0.84; that is the DEPLA group of respondents were only 0.84 times as likely (and therefore less likely) to support the Conservative government than respondents from AFFLUENT areas of Britain. The interaction effect for the combination of economic optimism and residence in depressed constituencies had an independent effect upon the dynamic of party support, – illustrated by a coefficient of -0.22. These statistics can be interpreted in the following manner.

The analysis of the interaction effect of economic optimism and residence in a depressed constituency provided three comparator groups – pessimists living in affluent regions, optimists living in affluent regions and pessimists living in depressed areas. These coefficients provided the following matrix and the addition of these coefficients provided a new set of coefficients with associated odds-ratios (Table 2).

TABLE 2

INTERACTION MATRIX FOR ECONOMIC OPTIMISTS LIVING IN DEPRESSED AREAS
(CONSERVATIVE REPORTED VOTE INTENTION)

	Economic Pessimism	Economic Optimism	
Affluent Areas	0.00	1.45	
Depressed Areas	-0.18	-0.22	
COMPARATOR GROUP	Coefficients to add	Cumulative B	Exp. (B)
Pessimists in Affluent Areas	-0.22 +1.45 -0.18	1.05	2.86
Optimists in Affluent Areas	-0.22 -0.18 +0.0	-0.40	0.67
Pessimists in Depressed areas	-0.22 +1.45 +0.0	1.23	3.42

The addition of the coefficients provided the following comparisons. Economic optimists in depressed areas were 2.86 times more likely to express Conservative support than pessimists in affluent areas (the addition of the coefficients (-0.22 + -0.18 + 1.45 = 1.05) has an associated odds-ratio of 2.86); they were less likely (0.67 times as likely) to support the government than optimists in affluent areas (-0.22 + -0.18 = -0.40 [Exp. = 0.67]); and they were 3.42 times more likely to express Conservative support than pessimists in depressed areas (-0.22 + 1.45 = 1.23 [Exp. = 3.42]).

Meanwhile optimists in constituencies characterized by service employment were 3.46 times more likely to support the Conservative government than pessimists from affluent areas, and pessimists from service areas but were only 0.81 times as likely to support the Conservatives as optimists from affluent areas. If the interaction between optimism and service areas had been insignificant, these ratios would have been 4.26 and 1 respectively.

A similar interaction effect occurred with the coincidence of economic optimism and residence in an area typified by SERVICE sector employment. From Table 1 the following matrix of Conservative reported vote intention was constructed (Table 3).

TABLE 3

INTERACTION MATRIX FOR ECONOMIC OPTIMISTS LIVING IN SERVICE AREAS
(CONSERVATIVE REPORTED VOTE INTENTION)

	Economic Pessimism	Economic Optimism	
Affluent Areas	0.00	1.45	
Service Areas	0.00	-0.21	
COMPARATOR GROUP	Coefficients to add	Cumulative B	Exp. (B)
Pessimists in Affluent Areas	1.45 -0.21 +0.0	1.24	3.46
Optimists in Affluent Areas	-0.21 +0.00 + 0.0	-0.21	0.81
Pessimists in Service Areas	1.45 -0.21 +0.0	1.24	3.46

As a result of the interaction between economic optimism and residence in areas typified by service sector employment, respondents were 3.46 times more likely to support the government than pessimists in either AFFLUENT or SERVICE areas, but were less likely (0.81 times as likely) to be Conservatives than optimists in AFFLUENT regions. The geographic interactions in the Conservative model have begun to illustrate that when economic attitudes contradicted the general outlook of the surrounding area, the effect of the local environment tended to dilute personal economic attitudes. The economic optimism of these respondents should have made them pro-government, but the overriding local context tempered their Conservatism.

There was a signification interaction term between aspects of region and economic optimism. The following interaction matrix was constructed (Table 4).

TABLE 4

INTERACTION MATRIX FOR ECONOMIC OPTIMISTS LIVING IN CELTIC REGIONS
(LABOUR REPORTED VOTE INTENTION)

	Economic Pessimism	Economic Optimism	
Southern Region	0.00	-0.78	
Celtic Regions	0.44	0.23	
COMPARATOR GROUP	Coefficients to add	Cumulative B	Exp. (B)
Pessimists in Southern Region	-0.78 +0.23 +.44	-0.11	0.90
Optimists in Southern Region	0.23 +0.44 +0.00	0.67	1.95
Pessimists in Celtic Regions	0.23 -0.78 +0.00	-0.55	0.58

Economic optimists who lived in the Celtic regions of Scotland and Wales were 0.90 times as likely to report an intention to vote Labour as southern pessimists (+.23 +.44 -0.78 = -0.11 [Exp 0.90]). In other words, the Celtic identity of these Labour supporters was almost as important as their personal economic outlook. The interaction term provides evidence for the existence of an autonomous regional cleavage, as individuals who felt optimistic about their personal economic circumstances but who lived in Scotland and Wales were nearly as inclined – *ceteris paribus* – to support Labour than those economic pessimists living in the south. Incidentally, they were also nearly twice as likely to support Labour than southern optimists (+.23 +.44 + 0 = 0.67 [Exp = 1.95]), but only little more than half as likely as likely to support the Labour Party than Celtic pessimists (1.23 -0.78 + 0 = 0.55 [Exp = 0.58]). It seems that whenever personal circumstances and spatial location provided voters with contradictory cues for reported vote intention, the geographic criteria took precedence.

If no interaction terms were significant, the effects of coincidental independent variables could be estimated by adding their respective B coefficients. Hence, an individual from the CELT region has a B coefficient of .44, and thus as the odds-ratio shows was – other things being equal – 1.55 times more likely to express support for Labour than a southern respondent. At the same time an economic neutral – who had a coefficient of -0.36 – was only 0.70 times as likely to support Labour as an economic pessimist. The absence of significant interaction terms allowed the simple addition of coefficients to predict the likelihood of Labour support among Celts who also happened to be neutral about their personal economic future. By combining these coefficients it could be ascertained that Celtic Neutrals had an associated B coefficient of (.44 -0.36 = 0.8). The odds-ratio derived from this coefficient shows that Celtic Neutrals would be only 2.23 times as likely to support Labour than their southern Pessimist counterparts, whereas it is clear from the interaction of CELT and OPTIM, that optimists who resided in Scotland and Wales were almost as likely (0.94 times as likely) to support Labour as pessimists from the south. The dynamics of the relationship between Celtic residence and personal economic attitudes were altered by the interaction terms. In short, residence in Scotland and Wales was an advantage for Labour in the construction of – and to some extent regardless of – personal economic attitudes.

Despite the apparent primacy of economic attitudes over geographic criteria, the interaction terms gained from logistic modelling revealed that being optimistic about one's personal economic future was watered down for Scottish and Welsh electors in favour of the local context in which their optimism was formed. The coincidence of two features which had opposite effects on the likelihood of Labour support in fact increased the relative chances that individuals would express an intention to vote Labour; the regional criteria fought against the natural instinct otherwise associated with economic optimism.

Summary and Conclusions

The logistic regression modelling confirmed that class, economic attitudes and geography all played significant roles in explaining variations in reported vote intentions in the 1990s. They also showed that temporal considerations were important, clearly identifying John Major's electoral honeymoon period and the subsequent steady decay in Conservative support thereafter – although Conservative support never returned to the level experienced under the last months of Margaret Thatcher's premiership. There was no evidence for a significant bandwagon effect, since knowing the level of party support for one month was of little assistance in predicting an individual's reported vote intention in the next.

For the most part Conservative support was apparently based on egocentric values. Labour Party support tended to be determined by sociotropism. The 'ownership' of these issues was confirmed. Moreover while Conservatives seemed to think that what was good for them was also good for the country, significant numbers of Labour supporters were intending to vote Labour in spite of the economic self-interest. How egocentric and sociotropic issues mixed was largely a matter of socialization and geographic milieux.

A key finding in this article was provided by the regression modelling which revealed the spatial variation in levels of economic optimism and pessimism. The detail of the regional analysis rather than the general schema was important here. Hence living in Scotland or Wales proved a significant drag on levels of personal economic optimism. This relationship became even clearer when the interaction terms between geography and economic attitudes were considered.

The exploration of interaction effects between independent variables showed how geographic variation may have influenced economic attitudes in the 1990s. Hence the Celtic regions, the north and depressed areas were associated with a reluctance to express support for the Conservative government, while economic optimists were typically pro-Conservative in their reported vote intentions. However, when these factors coincided the most likely outcome was that the regional characteristics would overcome individual economic evaluations in predicting how an individual would behave. Thus Scots and Welsh optimists were significantly less likely to support the Conservatives than southern pessimists; respondents from depressed areas who were personally optimistic about their economic future were still more prone to support Labour than pessimists who live in AFFLUENT areas. In short under certain conditions the regional cleavage defeated the challenge from the economic cleavage.

The geographic–economic interaction effects highlighted here were the most revealing aspect. They showed that how an individual decided to vote was largely shaped by what they thought of the economy – through personal economic expectations, Labour support through sociotropic issues. However, the extent to which optimism or pessimism could be discounted was spatially variable. Northerners who approved of the government's economic policies were less likely to back the government than their southern counterparts; Scots and Welsh voters who felt the government were not culpable for the British recession were less inclined to express support for the government as a result of their local context; individuals from areas typified by service sector employment who were pessimistic about their personal economic future were less likely to turn on the government than their counterparts in the north. The economy–geography interactions illustrated that an autonomous regional cleavage was an important part of the socialization milieux that framed an individuals' partisanship in the early 1990s.

The logistic regression model has two key advantages; the first theoretical, the second empirical. Theoretically it solves some of the problems associated with linear models which assume normally distributed variance in dichotomous dependent variables (and provides at the same time a more logical interpretation of relative frequency predictions). Empirically it enables the relatively straightforward dissection of interaction terms between independent variables in a multi-layered model of that dichotomous dependent variable. The major research findings here are in the detail; and detail only emerges from logistic modelling.

ACKNOWLEDGEMENT

The assistance of NOP in providing the *NOP/Newsnight* 'New Decade' series of polls is gratefully acknowledged.

BIBLIOGRAPHY

Bailey, T. and A. Gatrell, A. (1995) *Interactive Spatial Analysis.* Harlow, Longman.
Crewe, I. and A. Fox (1984) *British Parliamentary Constituencies: A Statistical Compendium.* London: Wiley.
Fieldhouse, E. (1995) 'Thatcherism and the Changing Geography of Political Attitudes, 1964–87', *Political Geography* 14: 3–30.
Greene, W. (1993) *Econometric Analysis,* second edition. New York: Macmillan.
Griliches, Z. (1957) 'Hybrid Corn: An Exploration of Technological Change' *Econometrica 1957*: 501–22.
Gujarati, D. (1992) *Essentials of Econometrics.* New York: McGraw Hill.

Heath, A., R. Jowell and J. Curtice (1985) *How Britain Votes*. Oxford: Pergamon.
Heath, A., R. Jowell, J. Curtice, G. Evans, G., J. Field and S. Witherspoon (1991) *Understanding Political Change*. Oxford: Pergammon.
Intriligator, M. (1978) *Econometric Models, Techniques and Applications*. New Jersey: Prentice-Hall.
Johnston, R. and C. Pattie (1989) 'A Growing North–South Divide in British Voting Patterns, 1979–87', *Geoforum* 20: 93–106.
Johnston, R. and C. Pattie (1990) 'The Changing Geography of Unemployment in Great Britain', *Social Studies Review* 5: 205–8.
Johnston, R., C. Pattie and G. Allsopp (1988) *A Nation Dividing*. London: Longman.
Johnston, R., C. Pattie and A. Russell (1992) 'Dealignment, Spatial Polarisation and Economic Voting: An Exploration of Recent Trends in British Voting Behaviour', *European Journal of Political Research* 23: 67–90.
Kennedy, P. (1992) *A Guide to Econometrics*. Oxford: Blackwell.
Key, V.O. (1966) *The Responsible Electorate*. Cambridge Mass: Harvard University Press.
McAllister, I. and D. Studlar (1992) 'Region and Voting in Britain, 1979–87 – Territorial Polarisation or Artefact?', *American Journal of Political Science* 36: 168–99.
Maddala, G. (1987) *Econometrics*. London: McGraw-Hill.
Martin, R. (1993) 'Remapping British Regional Policy: The End of the North–South Divide?' *Regional Studies*, 27 (8): 797–805.
Pattie, C. and R. Johnston (1990) 'One Nation or Two? The Changing Geography of Unemployment in Great Britain 1983–1988', *The Professional Geographer* 42: 288–98.
Pattie, C. and R. Johnston (1995) 'It's Not Like That Around Here: Region, Economic Evaluations and Voting at the 1992 British General Election', *European Journal of Political Research*, 28: 1–32.
Pattie, C., D. Dorling and R. Johnston (1995) 'A Debt-Owning Democracy: The Political Impact of Housing Market Recession at the British General Election of 1992' *Urban Studies*, 32: 1293–315.
Paulson, B. (1994) 'The Economy and the 1992 Election: Was 1992 Labour's Golden Chance?' in A Heath, R. Jowell and J. Curtice (eds), *Labour's Last Chance? The 1992 Election and Beyond*, 85–106. Aldershot: Dartmouth.
Price, S. and D. Sanders (1993) 'Modelling Government Popularity in Postwar Britain: A Methodological Example', *American Journal of Political Science* 37: 317–34.
Price, S. and D. Sanders (1995) 'Economic Expectations and Voting Intentions in the United Kingdom, 1979–87: a Pooled Cross-Section Approach', *Political Studies* 43: 451–70.
Regional Trends (1995) Vol.30. London: HMSO.
Rose, R. and I. McAllister (1990) *The Loyalties of Voters: A Lifetime Learning Model* .London: Sage.
Russell, A. (1995) *Spatial Variation in Economic Attitudes and Voting Behaviour in Britain, 1983–92*. PhD, University of Sheffield.
Russell, A., R. Johnston and C. Pattie (1996) 'Partisan Preferences, Regional Patterns and the 1992 and 1997 General Elections in Great Britain', *Environment and Planning A*.
Sanders, D. (1991) 'Government Popularity and the Next General Election', *Political Quarterly* 62: 235–61.
Sanders, D. (1993) 'Forecasting the 1992 British General Election Outcome: The Performance of an "Economic" Model' in D. Denver, P. Norris, D. Broughton and C. Rallings (eds) *British Elections and Parties Yearbook 1993*, 100–115. Hemel Hempstead: Harvester Wheatsheaf.
Sanders, D., H. Ward and D. Marsh (1987) 'Government Popularity and the Falklands War: a Reassessment' *British Journal of Political Science* 17: 281–313.
Webber, R. (1978) *Parliamentary Constituencies: A Socio–Economic Classification*. London: OPCS.

Discourses of Modernization: Gaitskell, Blair and the Reform of Clause IV

Michael Kenny and Martin J. Smith

Tony Blair's symbolic reform of Clause IV may be seen as the defining moment of his 'New Labour' project and has led to comparison with Hugh Gaitskell's previous attempt at reform in 1959/60. The parallel is often deployed to illustrate that 'New Labour' is in many respects not as different to 'Old Labour' as it likes to think, but more generally reflects the difficulties which party members, political pundits and academic interpreters alike have encountered in placing the contemporary Labour Party within a particular historical tradition or ideological category. The terms New Labour and Old Labour have been deployed by the leadership to advance a strategy which separates the party under Blair from some of its older traditions and beliefs. A variety of commentators have used it either as a means of supporting or deriding the party under Blair. However, as Eric Shaw (1996) has pointed out, the distinction between Old and New Labour is generally misleading.

In this article we examine the debates surrounding both Gaitskell's and Blair's attempts to reform the party (and in particular Clause IV), and argue that while this dichotomy is a simplification – and is unconvincing as an account of Blair's political trajectory – some important changes to party thinking and culture have taken place under Blair. Indeed we will argue that while Gaitskell did attempt to reshape social democracy particularly through his distinction between the ends of socialism and the appropriate means for its realization, he still framed reform very much within the socialist and social democratic agendas that dominated the party until the 1980s and persisted in certain forms into the 1990s. As Brian Brivati (1996) argues, Gaitskell was an ethical collectivist and therefore closer to Aneurin Bevan than Tony Blair. In the case of Tony Blair's leadership, the party has witnessed a significant change in terms of its policy discourse, and this amounts to a break from the traditions of socialism and social democracy. Blair is an 'ethical individualist' who sees collectivism as a means of improving the conditions of individuals. While the contexts in which constitutional reform were attempted differ, we argue that the solutions offered to pressing economic problems by Gaitskell were collectivist and state-centred; under Blair they reflect a different ethical outlook and are generally market based. Our analysis is limited to a survey of the party elites in both these periods, and should not be read as an argument about ideological change throughout the party. Nevertheless, drawing upon the extensive social movement literature which highlights the importance of ideological frame-setting by leaders, one might also argue that ideological leadership plays a crucial role in wider attitudinal change within political parties. We begin by looking at the reform debate under Gaitskell.

Revisionism in the 1950s

A reconsideration of the debates which took place at the Labour Party conferences of 1958, 1959 and 1960 as well as arguments in party organs like *Tribune* and contemporary pamphlets and journals reveals one of the greatest differences between the Blair and Gaitskell reforms – the degree of opposition faced by the latter. Undoubtedly, there was some opposition to Blair's change but most senior figures kept quiet and dissent was registered by relatively marginalized groups (although perhaps the most significant opposition was from a group of MEPs). In contrast Gaitskell's proposals elicited considerable hostility throughout the party. In certain respects this was the result of tactical errors on his part. Whereas Blair chose his moment carefully and manoeuvred skilfully, Gaitskell failed to make the necessary compromises (until 1960 when he was forced to accept the commitment to common ownership would remain within the party's lexicon of aims) in order to achieve his goal. Neil Kinnock, for instance, argues that Gaitskell failed because he was badly advised by supporters who had insufficient contact with the unions and the rest of the party, he was too ideological in his approach and he failed to communicate his desire to reform Clause IV, not abolish it (Interview 9 September 1996). Patrick Wintour (1995) sees the attempt at reform as resulting directly from the 1959 electoral defeat, suggesting that it came as a complete surprise to the party. For Blair the assault on the Clause came at a time when the left was marginalized and leaderless, the unions were greatly weakened and much of the groundwork for reform (in terms of *de facto* changes in policy) had been undertaken by Kinnock.

The most important backdrop to the debate which took place in 1959 was the third election defeat to the Conservatives, despite a relatively successful campaign and a strongly optimistic mood within the party. The Clause IV debate has to be set in the context of the fall-out from this event as a range of arguments diagnosing Labour's ills appeared in the months after the election. Yet, the issues which surfaced in the Clause IV debate were not solely immediate responses to defeat but had been elaborated throughout the 1950s by key figures in preparation for the reform of the party. Consequently, it is difficult to see Gaitskell's problems as arising solely from tactical naïveté in 1959.

A number of intra-party arguments took place in the early 1950s about which economic sectors were appropriate for nationalization. Sceptical voices were raised, in some cases by influential figures, from an early stage over the issue of nationalization leading to the publication in 1957 of *Industry and Society*, which was the first official questioning of existing policy. Socialist Union, founded in 1951 as a grouping committed to the critical reassessment of core features of party policy, began to question the conflation of public ownership and the nationalized industries (for a review, see *Socialist Commentary* October 1957). Nevertheless, throughout the decade, the party officially supported the renationalization of steel and road haulage, and the nationalization of sections of the chemical and machine tool industries. Its literature also confidently called for the creation of new public enterprises. Despite the rhetoric, the commitments to nationalization in the 1959 manifesto were extremely limited. Steel and long-distance road haulage were to be denationalized but the manifesto (Labour Party, 1959) stated: 'We have no further plans for nationalization'.

In 1956 Gaitskell made a fairly explicit and far-reaching restatement of his views on public ownership in *Socialism and Nationalisation*. He did not reject nationalization outright but argued that the case for further nationalization could not be taken as given but had to be argued for, on an industry by industry basis. He concluded (1956: 31) that: 'the most vital question is how far greater social and economic equality can be achieved without more nationalisation and public ownership'. He also suggested (1956: 34) that greater social equality had been secured by the welfare state and progressive taxation but argued strongly that the extension of public ownership, rather than nationalization, 'is almost certainly necessary if we are to have a much more equal distribution of wealth'. While rejecting wholesale nationalization, he maintained (1956: 36) that different forms of public ownership constituted important means for his goal of greater equality and social justice:

> The point is that we need not conceive of public ownership as always a matter of taking over a whole industry, making structural change within that one industry and setting up a single large organisation, but as embracing also many other types of change: in some of these the State will be a passive and in others an active participant; in some, completely new public or semi-public enterprises will be launched; in others, existing firms may come into public ownership and management.

Like others, Gaitskell came to these conclusions in the wake of Tony Crosland's (1956) highly influential reassessment of Labour's historic mission – *The Future of Socialism*. Crosland provided one of the most concise statements of the anxieties felt by many about party policy. Significantly he connected these concerns with an analysis of the deep-seated social and economic changes which had taken place since 1945. In fact, as Noel Thompson (1996) illustrates, Crosland's ideas emerged within a particular 'climate of feeling' which was prevalent in the early 1950s; within this a number of critical ideas about Labour policy were aired.

In July 1957, the party issued two pamphlets on public ownership which revealed the influence of some of this rethinking. The first was *Public Enterprise*, a fairly sober and balanced review of the achievements and faults of the nationalized industries. The second was the much higher profile *Industry and Society*, 'an enquiry into the wider question of the place, character and purpose of public ownership in the kind of society the Labour Party wishes to bring about in Britain' (Robson, 1960: 476). The pamphlet set out the five main reasons why socialists have attached so much importance to public ownership. It then switched attention to the realities of the contemporary mixed economy, arguing that it was unrealistic to lump together all the privately owned firms regardless of their size and irrespective of whether they were public or private companies. Attention should be shifted to the relatively small number of large firms who earn nearly half of the total profits generated by private industry. They were directly responsible for about half of the total investment in the private sector and indirectly for a good deal more. It was the sector constituted by these enterprises which dominated the economy. But these concerns differed greatly from the classic model of capitalist enterprise which socialism has traditionally opposed. Ownership had become separated from control and management, and large shareholders were largely powerless to shape the development of these companies. While *Industry and Society* reasserted the party's determination to renationalize the road haulage and iron and steel industries, it also suggested different possible ways of extending the public sector and increasing the state's involvement with profitable private businesses – for instance through the state purchase of a majority of equity shares in key enterprises – without resorting to full-scale nationalization.

The central argument offered by Gaitskell and his supporters involved the disaggregation of the notion of public ownership. This had been interpreted almost universally to mean nationalization in the style of the Attlee government, when in fact a variety of different forms of public ownership were available – for instance co-operative ownership, or local authority control. The commitment to nationalization had become totemic, it was argued – a matter of faith rather than a useful programmatic commitment. A constant motif within the debate was the concern of the Gaitskellites to present their opponents as 'conservatives' allied to a now archaic symbolic commitment. This line of argument was underpinned by the repeated assertion that nationalization was not one of the party's ethical goals, merely a means towards its ultimate ends: 'public ownership is not itself the ultimate objective; it is only a means for achieving the objective' (Gaitskell, 1959: 112). While Gaitskell carefully sought to present the party's aims as those to which all reasonable socialists must be committed, they in fact constituted a redefinition of the core values of many socialists. Increasingly Gaitskell's ends–means distinction allowed for a distinction between nationalization and public ownership. At the 1959 conference, he defined socialism as:

> first of all equality and social justice – and I make no apologies for saying that to me that has always been the core of my own socialist faith. It has very far-reaching implications. This feeling of ours, the instinct which surely unites all socialists, that there is no room in the world today for first and second-class people ... Secondly, we believe in co-operation. It is not always easy to find the right words exactly to express what is in our minds. But we want to see a state of society, and we want to see established in industry, people working together more in a sense of true fraternity ... Thirdly, we believe in the principle of accountability: that those who wield the weapons of economic power, whichever they may be, shall be accountable to the community for their actions. Fourthly, we believe in planning for full employment. And fifthly, we believe that through public ownership and control we can achieve higher productivity.

These goals – social justice and equality, co-operation, accountability, planning for full employment, and higher productivity – were reiterated by Gaitskell and his supporters throughout the debates over Clause IV. They reveal his belief that full employment and economic growth were in some ways as important as more conventional ethical principles – social justice and co-operation. In one sense Gaitskell was extremely prescient, and perhaps more influential than he has been given credit for: his coupling of social justice with economic efficiency and competitiveness foreshadowed the far more explicit linkages offered by later Labour leaders, including Blair, between social justice and economic strength. The Marxist critic Perry Anderson believed that Gaitskell went much further: 'For the first time in the history of the Labour Party, capitalist industry was formally legitimated as socially useful and responsible' and the state was to be subordinated to market demands (1965: 5).

Anderson's argument exaggerated the extent of the ideological break which Gaitskell sought. The latter continued to adhere to the belief that statist regimes possess great advantages when it came to organizing and managing economic life. As Macintyre (1996) acknowledges, 'Gaitskell was a collectivist, a Keynesian believer in economic planning rather than markets'. Within the mixed economy, authority and control had to reside with public powers. The emphasis that developed from Crosland's work was on control rather than ownership, and planning was seen as a way of retaining public control in an economy dominated by private ownership.

The central problem for the revisionists was not only that the economic circumstances changed but there was now a new social context which meant the visions of the 1940s and early 1950s were losing their relevance. Changes to the internal structures of large firms, as well as the spread of a consumer-based affluence which had supposedly eroded traditional forms of class antagonism and cultural aspiration, figured prominently in the discourse of revisionist disseminators like Roy Jenkins. Crosland (1960) was the most explicit and far-reaching in his social analysis, drawing very painful implications for Labour from the 1959 defeat:

> Labour is badly placed to take advantage of these trends, since its sectional one-class image positively repels the more fluid, less class-oriented new voter. But if it can acquire a broader appeal and a relatively classless image, it surely stands an equal chance with the Conservatives of winning his support.

This argument was supported by psephological evidence which suggested that nationalization was electorally unpopular and that social and economic changes were making it harder for Labour to win (Abrams, 1957, 1960; Crosland, 1960). As early as 1955 Gaitskell (1955) observed that that the Tories would not dismantle the welfare state and affluence was making it increasingly difficult for Labour to regain office.

Opposition to Gaitskell's reform came not only from the trade unions but from senior party figures and many constituency parties. He was opposed by Richard Crossman, Anthony Greenwood, Michael Foot, Barbara Castle and in a more constrained way by Aneurin Bevan. Even Harold Wilson argued that the party should not scrap its principles and policies for electoral purposes (*The Times* 11 February 1960). Gaitskell's main support came from Crosland, Douglas Jay, Roy Jenkins and Bill Rodgers, though Jenkins and Crosland had not made it to the most senior post in the party and Rodgers carried very little weight. The opposition from the constituency parties was represented in nearly every speech from the floor at the party conference of 1959.

Disagreement centred upon four main points: first the degree or extent of nationalization which was desirable; second, whether the means–ends rhetoric employed by the leader was appropriate; third, the nature of the modern economy, and fourth, the respective roles of state and market in economic management. Crossman (1960: 9), for instance, was convinced that the apparent success of capitalism in the 1950s was due entirely to the contingent conditions of the temporary economic boom and argued that, despite prosperity:

in terms of military power, of industrial development, of technological advance, of mass literacy and eventually, of mass consumption too, the planned Socialist economy, as exemplified in the Communist States, is proving its capacity to outpace and overtake the wealthy and comfortable Western economies.

For Crossman and others, nationalization not only represented a means of improving economic efficiency but it was also the only way of controlling economic power within a Western political system. Nationalization was commonly referred to as a 'success' by defenders of Clause IV. Pride in the achievements of the 1945–48 period in government mingled with the recognition that the party had made a fundamental alteration to the political economy of post-war Britain. Thus nationalization was an integral element of Labour's political identity which could not be jettisoned for short-term electoral gain. This commitment recurs throughout conference speeches in the late 1950s and a number of articles defending Labour's traditional position (for example see *The Times* 29 July 1957; *Tribune*, Hughes, 1960). The critic Norman Birnbaum pointed to the continued existence of a ruling elite and the degree of penetration of the British economy by foreign capital to demonstrate that ownership and control had not in any meaningful way been separated. William Thomas (1956: 29–30) defended public ownership in a moral context:

> Even if public ownership as an instrument of economic planning and of raising efficiency were shown to be very little superior to other techniques this would not be an adequate reason why socialists should abandon it. For the success of the party of change in democratic politics depends upon it presenting clear alternatives ... The second reason is the crux of the matter for it involves the moral case for socialism. The socialist is concerned that industry should serve the community ... But those who are concerned in private industry are concerned with profits.

A frequent argument from the left was that the right had given up the idea of transforming capitalism and now wished to manage it (Crossman, 1960: 2). A retreat from the extension of the public sector represented a retreat from socialism. As Bevan argued in *Tribune* (11 December 1959), to abandon the goal of public ownership would mean that Labour was no different from the Conservative Party: 'the only conflict would be over nuances'.

An examination of these debates also shows that the clear line between so-called 'modernizers' in favour of reform, and 'traditionalists' opposed to it was in fact a mythical construction. Several themes which emerged throughout these exchanges transcended such a simple divide and illustrate the number of shared assumptions which continued to underpin many of the arguments. Most importantly, extending public ownership remained a core commitment of nearly all involved in the debate. Indeed Gaitskell (*The Times*, 12 March 1960) told a meeting in 1960 that:

> If we are to have full employment and an advancing economy with a classless society, then I think that you have to have a substantial degree of common ownership in various forms: some proportion in the form we know it best – State monopolies, some in corporative organizations; some under municipal ownership: and some in Government participation and ownership of shares in private concerns.

Undoubtedly some of this was an attempt to assuage the party after the hostile response at the 1959 conference. But it is clear that most revisionists still accepted the need for public ownership, and *Industry and Society* was produced by a working group that included prominent figures from across the party. Despite disagreement about what form this should take, a general consensus about the possibility and desirability of the state's management of economic life persisted. It was widely accepted that there were problems with nationalization and the relationship between the state and the economy had to be reconsidered. Only at the fringes of the debate was this (implicitly) challenged. Increasingly the notion of planning came to dominate Labour Party thinking about the relationship between state and economy.

Nevertheless, planning carried a multitude of meanings and resonances. For the Labour left it provided a new expression for the long-held goal of extending the public sphere of the economy, and taking some of the remaining private sector giants into state control. For some on the revisionist right, planning came to stand for the state manipulation of the macroeconomic levers available to it. Long-standing socialist goals such as full employment and social justice were achievable through these policies, and did not therefore involve further nationalization. But the stress on planning, articulated almost routinely after 1961, worked to provide an apparent unity of focus, if not of commitment. Significantly this was one of the strands of policy thinking that Wilson was able pick up after 1962 in his bid to reunite the party's different factions and divert its gaze on to questions other than those which sustained the divisions of this period.

What we can see from Gaitskell's attempt at reform was that while he was undoubtedly attempting to change the party's approach to meet new economic and social conditions, he was operating within a value set familiar to most party members. The debate did not essentially turn on whether public ownership should be extended or not, but whether, on a case-by-case basis, it was the best mechanism for achieving equality, social justice, redistribution, economic efficiency and full employment. Gaitskell still accepted the need for public ownership, planning and progressive taxation. What we see in Blair's reform of Clause IV is a qualitative shift in the debate which distinguishes 'New Labour' from Gaitskellite revisionism.

Modernization under Tony Blair

We lack the space here for a full examination of the complex of political and social circumstances in which he has been operating as party leader since 1994 and the particular blend of different traditions and ideas which underpin his policy shifts (see Kenny and Smith, 1996 and Thompson, 1996). Yet several themes within the debates which occurred within the party in 1994 are of particular significance in the light of these earlier arguments. Here we show that while Blair shared some of the same normative goals as Gaitskell, the way in which he has attempted to change the party is to make a significant break with the framework within which policy was developed by revisionists and other members of the party elite in the late 1950s.

Nevertheless, a clear distinction between Old and New Labour is clearly an oversimplification. When contextual and linguistic differences are taken into consideration, there are some clear and important parallels between the two modernization cases. Like Gaitskell, and other Labour leaders such as Wilson and Kinnock, Blair (1996: 4) repeatedly deploys the notion of an unfriendly and hostile public opinion with which the party has lost touch: 'The Tories didn't win four elections. We lost them. And we lost them because we lost touch with the people.' In the context of several electoral defeats, this line of argument proved powerful in both cases. Blair also framed the ethical argument for a revised Clause in terms of the clear-cut means–ends distinction favoured by Gaitskell. For Blair (1995a), the values of socialism remain as relevant now as when the party was formed, allowing him to journey (if selectively) into Labour's past and to connect current programmatic change with the achievements of earlier eras. As he said in 1995 (1996: 4): 'I have no hesitation whatsoever in describing the 1945 Labour government as the greatest peacetime government this century'.

But he too adopts a rigid distinction between these values and their programmatic embodiment: thus, while eulogizing the post-war Labour administration, he is able (1996: 18) to distance himself from the top-down public corporation model which shaped the party's nationalization programme: 'Our values do not change ... But the ways of achieving that vision must change'. Such a line of argument gave both leaders a much greater degree of programmatic flexibility, and allowed them to seize the initiative against opponents who were presented as clinging to nationalization, with all its flaws, as the embodiment of socialist principle. In both cases, the ends–means distinction represented a simplification of the arguments of opponents, none of whom advocated nationalization as a socialist goal in itself. Other comparable elements within their rhetorical strategies stand out, for instance their stress upon social and cultural change and the moral arguments embodied in the 'new realism' offered by them, notably the idea that winning the next election and the compromises this entailed should 'trump' doctrinal purity. Like Blair, Gaitskell (*The Times* 30 November 1959) explicitly stated the need in his 1959 conference speech for the party to revise its statement of values in order to meet the requirements of the modern age: 'The only official documents which embodies such an attempt is the party constitution written over 40 years ago. It seems to me that it needs to be brought up to date'. He told the 1959 (1959: 113) conference:

> I am sure that the Webbs and Arthur Henderson who largely drafted this Constitution, would have been amazed and horrified had they thought that their words were to be treated as sacrosanct 40 years later in utterly changed conditions. Let us remember that we are the Party of the future, not the past; that we must appeal to the young as well as the old.

This line of argument was echoed fairly directly by Blair in 1994. Similarities can be found too between the arguments of those who opposed these proposed constitutional revisions. In both cases, a key argument concerned the dangers of jettisoning principles because they appeared to be electorally unpopular. Underlying this view was a much stronger belief in the continued relevance of core aspects of the socialist tradition. Of course in both cases there were all sorts of variants of this basic commitment: in 1994, for instance, a group of Labour MPs and a body of party opinion were clearly supportive of the rewriting of the Clause in a more modern and up-to-date idiom, yet were unhappy about the attempt to jettison common ownership (see Seyd and Whiteley, 1994). Likewise, the means–ends distinction deployed by modernizers in both instances was attacked as a smoke-screen for the real intentions of the party leadership, namely to remove common ownership from the lexicon of Labour's values. There are other important similarities, for instance: the suspicion of the leadership's intentions throughout the party's ranks; the perception that alien influences, especially intellectual ones, had come to hold too much sway at the top of the party; and the belief that social change was being overstated and misinterpreted by the proposers of constitutional change.

Behind these similarities lie certain parallels between the 'projects' pursued by these respective leaders. Both faced electoral defeats and changing social situations and tried to reform the party's constitutions to win electoral support. As Rita Hinden pointed out (1956: 4), the 1950s constituted a rich period of, '"new thinking" among socialists', with a whole range of writers beginning to 'define the outline of [a] new approach to socialism'. Similarly, Blair (1996: 221–2) has developed 'New Labour' for a 'New Britain' arguing that he is adapting socialism for the Britain of the 1990s:

The process of what is called 'modernization' is in reality, therefore, the application of enduring lasting principles for a new generation – creating not just a modern party and organization but a programme for a modern society, economy and constitution. It is not destroying the Left's essential ideology: on the contrary, it is retrieving it from an intellectual and political muddle.

Blair and Gaitskell: Different Paths?

While there may be similarities in what Gaitskell and Blair were trying to achieve in the broadest terms, these debates were framed in very different ways. In terms of Blair's ethical beliefs, some obvious differences with his predecessor cannot be ignored. Even before he became party leader, Blair (1991) was clear in his own mind that Labour's normative platform needed reconstruction. The party had to steer a course between 'old-style' collectivism and the aggressive individualism of the New Right in its approach to social and moral issues. While this emphasis does not particularly demarcate him as a new or original ethical thinker, it does point to the unease he feels with many aspects of the party's cultural and philosophical heritage. A comparison with Crosland's definition of socialism in 1960 reveals the extent to which Blair has changed the terms of party discourse. For Crosland, the arguments did not amount to being in favour or against public ownership, but concerned its form and extent. In addition (1960: 2), socialism included:

> An overriding concern with social welfare ... (2) A much more equal distribution of wealth ... (3) A socially classless society ... (4) The primacy of social over private interests and an allocation of resources ... determined by public need and not solely by profit considerations. (5) The diffusion of economic power, and in particular a transfer of power from the large corporations both to workers and consumers. (6) Generally the substitution of co-operative for competitive ... economic and social relations and on to economic growth and racial equality.

Gaitskell, as much as Nye Bevan or Frank Cousins, deployed certain kinds of collectivist moral arguments, though he was also attuned to the ethical and social significance of the 'new individualism' of the 1950s. But Blair is not a collectivist in the same sense. His constant refrain about the need for a new moral reconciliation of community ties and interests with individual freedom and autonomy sets him on a different ethical course and arguably underwrote the different kind of political economy which he has favoured.

For Blair, the individualism unleashed during the 1980s was not the sole product of Thatcherite policies, but represented an important and undeniable social advance. For Blair (1996: 216–17) collectivism is not an end but a means for 'individuals to advance'. Simultaneously, though, he remains acutely aware of the crisis of social cohesion and the disruption to established cultural patterns engendered by the market-oriented policies of the Conservatives since 1979. Similarly, his ambivalence towards aspects of Labour's traditionally collectivist culture is manifest also in his marked hostility to statist approaches to social issues and economic management more generally. Blair (1996: 261) believes that , 'The era of big, centralized government is over'. Solutions to economic and social problems should be found regionally, locally and within the community. While there are arguments over whether this is a 'genuine' or electorally opportunist intellectual stance, it is nevertheless one of the most pronounced characteristics of his political thinking. This too has important consequences for the political economy at the heart of Labour's current policy thinking.

Moreover, Blair is less committed to the view that social interests have primacy over private ones, and is committed to reducing the role of the state in certain areas. A Blair government is unlikely to deliver the redistributive measures necessary to produce greater equality of wealth, while the goal of co-operation is no longer seen as a substitute for competitive economic relations. Whereas Gaitskell thought state intervention could increase competitiveness, for Blair the role of the state is to help create the right market conditions in which the economy can succeed, hence the stress upon improving the 'supply-side' conditions which affect labour productivity. For both, economic growth is necessary for social justice but the mechanisms for achieving competitiveness and social justice differ greatly. Indeed, one of Blair's most commonly repeated aims is to make the economy competitive enough to compete more successfully abroad (Blair, 1995b). This is the context within which macroeconomic policy has to be framed. Blair's discourse is framed by different boundaries to the debates of the 1950s and even to the political economy which predominated in Labour circles in the 1980s (Thompson, 1996). He and his closest associates are primarily concerned with regulating the economy without resorting to public ownership and regard social justice as the outcome of a broadly free and competitive market.

While Gaitskell retained a powerful faith in the state's ability to co-ordinate the economy to sustain a level of demand to match steady productive growth, contemporary Labour thinking has moved away from such ideas. Blair and his leading supporters, notably Gordon Brown, operate with a model driven by the notion of market regulation where it will advance the public interest, but assume that the private sector will power the economy's next phase of growth. To this end, both remain highly fiscally 'correct', prioritizing inflation over all other goals, especially full employment (Brown, 1995). Even a rise in economic productivity ('the dash for growth' as Blair unflatteringly puts it) may have to be forestalled in pursuit of a cap on inflation; meanwhile the financial markets and City investment fund managers have been repeatedly reassured about the caution that would govern an incoming Labour government's economic policy making. As he told business leaders, 'New Labour is increasingly seen as a party with whom you can do business' (*The Guardian* 5 September 1996). Increasingly, New Labour devotees suggest that 'old' debates about planning, Keynesianism and public ownership are simply irrelevant in the current socio-economic context. Meanwhile, Blair and his advisers have begun to distance themselves from the goal of achieving full employment within a finite period. This objective remains an ideological touchstone connecting the contemporary party to the past in the minds of many activists and leaders. The indications are that it may well become the key site on which the tensions arising from the Blairite break from Keynesianism are played out.

Admittedly none of these elements are in themselves entirely new within the repertoire of the party's leaders: previous Labour prime ministers have consistently had to meet the demands of the market (see Coates 1980). Contemporary Labour thinking has not broken entirely from the past. Yet while this sketch barely does justice to contemporary debates about macro and micro-level economic issues within the party, it does point to the different agendas around which Gaitskellite 'revisionism' and Blairite thinking have revolved. It is clear that the belief in nationalization as the centrepiece of a socialist macroeconomic strategy has become a minority commitment. More positively, alternative conceptions of the role and nature of public sector institutions and partnerships with private interests have become influential throughout the party.

The Clause IV debate of 1994 was hardly a 'debate' at all: key points of difference within the party leadership and beyond have in fact shifted away from the question of common ownership, though related issues such as the party's strategy for the privatized utilities continue to figure high on its policy agenda. In fact Blair did not actually mention public ownership in either his conference speech in 1994, where the reform was announced, or in his speech at the special conference to change the clause. In crucial respects ideological conflict within the party now turns on a different axis from that which structured political arguments and affiliations in the early 1960s. Yet perhaps significantly New Labour devotees remain reluctant to push this argument very far. Despite the relentless rhetoric of newness and of a clean break from the past, the Blairite camp remain enthusiastic about their social democratic mantle. As Mandelson and Liddle (1996: 4) put it:

New Labour is fundamentally different from old Labour in its economic, social and political approach. It goes well beyond the battles of the past between public and private, and about the role of the unions and the relevance of public expenditure, to the achievement of a more equal society. Nevertheless, New Labour's concept of One Nation socialism still stands firmly in the social-democratic tradition – but with a new hard edge to its economic thinking.

It would be easier to accept this claim to have forged a new, 'toughened' social democracy if it was clear exactly which aspects of this 'tradition' the authors had in mind. In substantive terms, there is a gulf between New Labour's political economy and that espoused by different generations of social democrats since the second world war: hence the criticisms articulated by Roy Hattersley who has always been associated with the revisionist wing of the party.

What Blair and his social democratic predecessors do share is the primary normative commitment to social justice and equality which are inextricably blended in with economic success. While this may establish a family resemblance between contemporary Labour thinking and social democratic ancestry, it says little about priorities and trade-offs. It is not clear that Blair's economic priorities are compatible with social justice and greater equality.

Whereas for Crosland and Gaitskell, the pursuit of equality remained a key criterion for determining policy, it is less clear what Blair (or Mandelson and Liddle) mean by equality, let alone social justice. The suspicion is raised that these goals have been so 'hollowed out' by seventeen years of Conservative rule, that they can only be advanced in the most tepid fashion, as window dressing which will rapidly be discarded once the harsh realities of office close in. Certainly there is precious little substance to Mandelson and Liddle's (1996: 30) elaboration of this position:

> This is a socialism based on a set of beliefs and values, and is similar to the social democracy found in other European countries. It is founded on the simple notion that human beings are socially interdependent and cannot be divorced from the society they live in.

This is a fairly odd definition of the core of social democracy: this kind of commitment to social interdependence can be found within a broad range of ideological traditions outside neo-liberalism. Blair's ethical base is derived as much from Christianity as socialism and in certain respects his views sit more comfortably within a Christian, rather than social, democratic tradition. Most significantly, this approach detaches the social democratic heritage from any vestige of a redistributive ethic. While defining the 'essence' of social democracy is actually a difficult enterprise, given the range of arguments and schools which have historically lived under its roof, it is hard to imagine social democrats who did not place either justice or equality very high on their list of normative priorities.

Finally, it is worth considering the extent to which it is possible to compare the ideological belief-system forged by the party's leadership in the late 1950s with that which pertains now. New Labour advocates like Mandelson and Liddle claim that the degree and nature of the social and economic changes which have occurred since the late 1970s have made many traditional political labels and divisions largely redundant. Clearly they did not invent this kind of argument: a range of intellectual currents have emerged in recent years around this idea. Certainly there are some important arguments to be considered about the impact of the changes associated with the intensified and expanded globalization of economic life which has taken place in the last two decades. Whatever the nature of these developments, they have been perceived by many socialists as far-reaching in their consequences – inhibiting the room for manoeuvre of the nation-state and obviating a strategy based upon exchange controls and high tariffs. Most importantly, this kind of thinking has lent greater credence to the argument that Britain's economic survival lies in the context of co-operation with her European partners, and, for some, in European Monetary Union.

In other words, the contexts against which 'modernizing' arguments in both the late 1950s and the mid-1990s were advanced have changed enormously, making easy comparisons along an imaginary ideological scale difficult, though perhaps not impossible. In some important respects Gaitskell helped legitimate a set of arguments within the party which have considerably advanced the ideological repertoire available to subsequent party leaders. He also pointed the way for Blair in sensing the symbolic as well as doctrinal hold of Clause IV of the party's constitution on the imagination and thinking of many of its members.

Conclusion

A comparison between the reform attempts of both Gaitskell and Blair highlights some of the most important lines of change within the thinking of the party elite. While the Old/New Labour divide is a simplification, it is apparent that Blair is now operating within a very different ideological universe. In part this is the result of a very different socio-economic context. In the 1950s the left had a coherent alternative which was not marginalized and the party's collective memory still invoked the post-war administrations. By the 1990s the left was marginalized and discredited, Communism had collapsed, Labour's electoral problems were even more acute and the replacement of public provision by private competition held ideological sway. Public ownership was no longer really an issue for debate and few even on the left saw it as an important policy option.

Yet these policy changes cannot be read as flowing 'naturally' from a shift in circumstances: such a reading is too redolent of crude structuralist ideas. In some ways Blair has seized the opportunities provided by the political defeats of the 1980s and accompanying social change to orchestrate a break with many of the traditions particular to Labour, but also to realign the party away from social democratic bearings. In many ways he is challenging the ethos and traditions of the party in a way no previous leader has attempted: he is sceptical about collectivism and an overextended role for the state and has been critical of the close link with the trade unions. In this sense the meaning of 'modernization' has shifted qualitatively since the late 1950s, and that the new ideological trajectory which Blair is now charting poses tough challenges for analysts of the Labour Party.

ACKNOWLEDGEMENTS

We would like to thank the Nuffield Foundation for funding the research for this article and Francesca Gains for her tireless assistance with the research.

BIBLIOGRAPHY

Abrams, Mark (1957) 'Disturbing Thoughts for the Next Election', *Socialist Commentary*, October.
Abrams, Mark (1960) 'Why Labour Lost the Election', *Socialist Commentary*, July and August.
Birnbaum, Norman (1959) 'Ideals or Reality', *Socialist Commentary*, September.
Blair, Tony (1991) 'Forging a New Agenda', *Marxism Today*, October.
Blair, Tony (1995a) *Let Us Face the Future: The 1945 Aniversary Lecture.* London: Fabian Society.
Blair, Tony (1995b) 'Left with No Option', *The Guardian*, 27 July.
Blair, Tony (1996) *New Britain: My Vision of a Young Country.* London: Fourth Estate.
Brivati, Brian (1996) *Hugh Gaitskell: A Biography.* London: Richard Cohen Books.
Brown, Gordon (1995) 'Speech to the Labour Party Annual Conference', 2 October.
Coates, David (1980) *Labour in Power?.* London: Longman.
Crosland, Anthony (1956) *The Future of Socialism.* London: Cape.
Crosland, Anthony (1960) *Can Labour Win?.* London: Fabian Society.
Crossman, Richard (1960) *Labour in the Affluent Society.* London: Fabian Society.
Gaitskell, Hugh (1956) *Socialism and Nationalisation.* London: Fabian Society.
Gaitskell, Hugh (1959) Speech to Labour Party Annual Conference, Labour Party Annual Conference Report, 1959, London: Labour Party.
Greenleaf, W.H. (1983) *The British Political Tradition Vol I: the Rise of Collectivism.* London: Methuen
Hinden, Rita (1956) 'The New Socialism', *Socialist Commentary*, November.
Hughes, John (1960) *Nationalised Industries in the Mixed Economy.* London: Fabian Society.
Kenny, Michael and Smith, Martin J. (1996) 'Understanding Tony Blair; towards a Multidimensional Analysis of the Labour Party'. *Paper presented at the Annual Conference of the PSA*, University of Glasgow, April.
Labour Party (1959) *Britain Belongs to You.* London, Labour Party.
Macintyre, Donald. (1996) 'Hugh Gaitskell – But without the Dancing', *The Independent*, 12 September.
Mandelson, Peter and Roger Liddle, (1996) *The Blair Revolution: Can New Labour Deliver?.* London: Faber.

Robson, W.A.(1960) *Nationalised Industry and Public Ownership*. London: George Allen and Unwin.

Seyd, Patrick and Paul Whiteley (1994) 'Red in Tooth and Clause', *New Statesman and Society*, 9 December.

Shaw, Eric (1996) 'From Old to New Labour', *Renewal*, 4: 51–9.

Thompson, Noel (1996) *Political Economy and the Labour Party*. London: UCL Press.

Wintour, Patrick (1995) 'How Gaitskell got a Bloody Nose', *The Guardian*, 24 January.

Voting Behaviour, the Economy and the Mass Media: Dependency, Consonance and Priming as a Route to Theoretical and Empirical Integration

Neil T. Gavin

In the United Kingdom there has been a recent surge in interest in the relationship between the media, public opinion and voting behaviour at general elections. This would include studies by Dunleavy and Husbands (1985) and Miller (1991) on of the role and impact of the media at the 1983 and 1987 elections, as well as the work of Newton (1992) and Webber (1993) on the role of the press in 1992. It would also encompass the work of Curtice and Semetko (1994) and Semetko *et al.* (1994). Interest in the role of the media between elections is a relatively recent development and there are few studies from within the political science community. There has been some work on press and public opinion (Sanders *et al.*, 1993) and, recently, some exploration of the impact of television (Gavin and Sanders, 1995, 1996a and 1996b). This follows work by Mosley (1984) who analysed the impact of press coverage on public opinion, and Miller *et al.* (1990) who looked at the impact of newspapers and television in the run-up to the 1987 election. To this short list might be added Harrop's (1987) deductive exploration of the case for media influence. The limited empirical attention to the role of the media is reflected in the literature on elections and psephology generally (Heath *et al.*, 1985 and 1990; Denver, 1989; and Denver and Hands, 1992).

With such limited attention to the media, it is not surprising that there has been little sustained attention to *theoretical* integration across the sub-disciplines of media and psephology, or investigation of the potential for theoretical cross-fertilization. The recent work has not been explicitly articulated to media theory. Newton's study looks at press exposure in the context of issue voting models rather than media theory. Webber's work pays limited attention to media theory but relates aggregate readership patterns to constituency voting. Curtice and Semetko's study deployed raw poll data to explore the relationship between press exposure, voting behaviour and public opinion. The work of Semetko *et al.* describes the nature of media output at the last election, although it can be located within the general context of agenda-setting theory and research. Aggregate-level analysis between elections also tends to focus more attention on data exploration than on theoretical elaboration, although Gavin and Sanders (1996b) look at the implications of their results for the integrity of the classical Downsian thesis. Overall, the existing work on media and voting behaviour is not greatly informed by the prevailing and emerging theoretical developments in the field of media research.

This is a great pity. There are some interesting theoretical developments within media studies (and even some long-standing theoretical propositions) that are of particular relevance to the analysis of voting behaviour and public opinion modelling. The aim of this article is to look at three of these theories (models of Dependency, Consonance and Priming) and assess their relevance to contemporary debates within psephology. Particular emphasis will be placed on the economy and economic models of public opinion and voting behaviour, although it will be argued that the theoretical cross-fertilization may extend beyond this particular sphere.

Dependency, the Economy and Economic Voting

Early empirical explorations of media and political attitudes tended to suggest that the impact of the media was relatively modest and that the immediate effect of media coverage was the reinforcement of voters' existing partisan preconceptions (Lazarsfeld et al., 1944; Klapper, 1960). Even the most ardent 'limited effects' theorists did accept, however, that there were specific circumstances in which the media had some potential to mould public opinion. This could be realised in a context where the public lacked intimate knowledge or personal experience. This was scarcely the case in relation to domestic policy and politics, but might be the case with regard to foreign policy and political developments abroad (Klapper, 1968). Here the public use the media as their main, indeed perhaps their only source of information, and as a result are more vulnerable to influence. This thesis was developed by Ball-Rokeach and DeFleur (1976) in the mid-1970s and refined subsequently by Ball-Rokeach (1985). These authors maintain that there are a wide range of 'dependencies' that include some aspects of domestic politics. They maintained that,

> when people do not have social realities that provide adequate frameworks for understanding, acting and escaping, and when audiences are depending in these ways on media information received, such messages may have a number of alteration effects...Thus, both the

relative adequacy of the audience's social realities and the relative degree of audience dependency on media information resources must be taken into account to explain and predict the effect of media messages (Ball-Rokeach and DeFleur, 1976: 19).

It has to be conceded that the notion of dependency is much more fully developed as a *theory* than as a platform for sustained empirical demonstration of particular effects (although see Becker and Whitney, 1980). However, the concept of dependency is useful in relation to some important aspects of economic voting. Early attempts to model the relationship between the economy and public opinion took 'objective' measurements of economic turbulence (essentially government statistics) and looked at their connection with government support (Paldam, 1981; Nannestad and Paldam, 1994). This approach has (by and large) been superseded by models that use poll-based measures of the public's *perception* of economy (Sanders *et al.*, 1987; Sanders, 1991) and by a focus on attitudes towards the national economy – so-called sociotropic voting (Kinder and Kiewiet, 1981, among a great many others). However, there has been a tendency to assume that the 'feel good factor' and sociotropic perceptions are rooted (directly or indirectly) in the public's personal experience of the economy. Downsian rational utility maximisers are rarely absent from the wings, even in the new models of economic opinion formation (Downs, 1957).

There is growing evidence, however, that this assumption is rather less well founded than was originally thought. Kinder and Kiewiet (1981: 139,157) point out that sociotropic perceptions are *not* strongly related to (and hence not derived from) personal experience, a point also noted by Alt (1979) and, elsewhere, by Conover *et al.* (1987). Others have noted that the public hold two *separate* levels of perception concerning the economy: one concerning bread-and-butter issues with tangible implications for the individual, and another concerning preoccupations with more abstract and general economic conditions (Blumler *et al.*, 1975). In this kind of context the notion that voters extrapolate their perceptions of the national economy from intimate knowledge of their own financial position (the so-called 'extrapolative model' Lockerbie, 1991) is rather unconvincing. Further evidence of this may be gleaned from *inter-election* data (in this case Gallup Political Index data from October 1981) as well as from comparable *electoral* survey figures (BES, 1992). The data are presented in Tables 1 and 2 where personal retrospective attitudes (presumably drawn from the public's direct and intimate experience of economic turbulence) are cross-tabulated with attitudes towards national economic conditions.[1]

TABLE 1
PERSONAL RETROSPECTIVE EVALUATIONS AGAINST GENERAL RETROSPECTIVE
PERCEPTIONS

General Retrospective Perceptions

		Got Better	Stay Same	Got Worse	DK
Personal	Better	12	14	87	7
Retrospect.					
Perceptions	Same	31	45	258	10
	Worse	21	37	531	10
	DK	1	2	15	1

Source: Gallup Political Index, October 1981, n = 1082.

TABLE 2
PERSONAL RETROSPECTIVE EVALUATIONS AGAINST GENERAL RETROSPECTIVE
PERCEPTIONS

General Retrospective Perceptions

		Got Stronger	Stay Same	Got Weaker
Personal	Up More	62	141	204
Retrospect.	Than Prices			
Perceptions				
	Kept Up	210	507	638
	With Prices			
	Fallen	130	414	991
	Behind			
	Prices			

Source: British Election Survey, 1992, n = 3297.

It is clear that the two levels of perception are not strongly related. Indeed, even where the two levels of perceptions coincide this only suggests the *possibility* of an extrapolative dynamic – it does *not* establish that this is the case.

Of course, an alternative explanation is that sociotropic perceptions are derived from sources other than personal experience. Individuals may take cue from their *local* economic environment to gauge the national situation. If this is the case it would, indeed, be a mistake to suggest that people were in any way dependent on the media for information about the national economy. While data addressing this issue are not readily available, again there is evidence from inter-election questionnaires *and* election surveys suggesting that personal experience is *not* intimately related to views about the local economy (and, moreover, that people do not extrapolate from the local to the national context). Tables 3 and 4 are drawn from the 1992 BES survey and the 1989 BSA respectively.

TABLE 3
PERCEPTIONS OF CHANGE IN HOUSEHOLD INCOME AGAINST ATTITUDES TOWARDS LOCAL ECONOMIC PROSPERITY

Relative Change in Prosperity of Region

		More Prosper.	Same	Less Prosper.
Change in Household Income	Above Average	200	164	176
	About Average	318	486	518
	Below Average	119	227	416

Source: Johnston And Pattie, 1995, n = 2624.

TABLE 4
PERCEPTIONS OF LOCAL ECONOMIC CONDITIONS AGAINST ATTITUDES TOWARDS NATIONAL INDUSTRIAL PERFORMANCE

National Industrial Performance

		Improv.	Same	Decline
Economy In Own Area	Better	161	179	59
	Same	538	967	302
	Worse	143	207	106

Source: British Social Attitude Survey, 1989, n = 2662.

It seems clear that not only are local and personal perceptions capable of diverging – so too are attitudes towards the local and national environments. Finally, we can return to Gallup's inter-election data from 1981 shown in Table 5.

TABLE 5

PERSONAL RETROSPECTIVE EVALUATIONS AGAINST PERSONAL PROSPECTIVE
PERCEPTIONS

Personal Prospective Perceptions

		Will Get Better	Will Stay Same	Will Get Weak	DK
Personal	Better	47	52	17	4
Retrospect.					
Perceptions	Same	41	208	81	15
	Worse	53	176	345	25
	DK	3	1	1	14

Source: Gallup Political Index, October 1981, n = 1082.

It is clear that personal 'prospections' (the 'feel good factor' that was at the heart of the work of David Sanders' Essex team in the 1980s and early 1990s) is only weakly related to people's direct experience of financial turbulence.

In the context in which a range of election and inter-election sources tell a similar story, it is legitimate to enquire from whence people derive the information that informs their perceptions of the national economy and, indeed, of their families' future prospects. In the absence of obvious alternative information sources it is important to ask how far the public are dependent on the mass media for such information. Recent research on the role of television certainly supports the notion of public sensitivity to media coverage of the national economy (Gavin and Sanders, 1996a, 1996b). This study suggest that television's economic news has an important role in cuing the public's economic perceptions (and, through this, political support for the government). The model deployed in this analysis also suggests that, by comparison, the public's *personal* economic experiences and perceptions play a minimal role.

Clearly there is a need to explore the extent of dependency on the mass media for economic cues and to determine whether the dependent elements of the community have any distinctive characteristics. The cross-tabulation method used in Tables 1 through 5 may be a way of isolating those who are most likely to exhibit dependency on the media (that is, where alternative sources of information – such as personal or local circumstances – can be identified and discounted). This technique offers the potential to explore dependency and media effects more fully through aggregate modelling. In the past there have been some attempts to disaggregate time-series data –

although the emphasis has been on how economic turbulence affects different *social class* strata (Hibbs, 1982). However, access to individual-level codes for Gallup's time series on the economic perceptions would make it possible to deploy the cross-tabulation technique used in Tables 1 to 5 to isolate those most likely to be dependent on the media for information about the national situation or family prospects. It should then be possible to re-aggregate the survey data to give an assessment of the dependent element's sensitivity to media coverage of the economy (using measures of media content and conventional time-series techniques). This would give us more of an empirical test of the dependency thesis than has, so far, been offered by its advocates.

Finally, there is one other aspect of dependency that deserves consideration. It still relates to media cues about the economy, but not to information about its vitality or ill-health. The issue of concern is the ascription of responsibility or blame for economic turbulence. In the United States the formal division of powers complicates the issue of who is to blame for bad economic news and who to be applauded for delivering the good times (see Weaver, 1986 for a broad analysis of the rhetoric and politics of blame and blame-avoidance). There is a growing literature that deals with the impact of these contingencies on economic voting (Peffley, 1984; Peffley and Williams, 1985; Petrocik and Steeper, 1986; and Abramowitz et al., 1988, among others). In Britain this issue is given much less prominence, perhaps on the assumption that with parliamentary sovereignty as an established fact of political life, notions of who is to blame are less controversial. Only a few studies of the economy and political support have dealt with this issue directly (among them Lewis-Beck, 1986 and Johnston and Pattie, 1995), although some have touched on the more general aspects of regime responsibility for the economy (Paulson, 1994).

In communication studies there is a relatively poorly developed body of literature in the area of media coverage of the economy. Nowhere is this more apparent than in the analysis of the coverage of causal attribution and impact this may have on public opinion concerning the causes and consequences of economic policies. The topic of attribution is thought to be of considerable importance (Gamson and Modigliani, 1989; Entman, 1993), yet empirical exploration is very limited. However, the limits of media dependency are an important consideration here too. It is certainly plausible to suggest that the public assess economic news against their own economic financial experiences (a partisan press may have difficulty in convincing the unemployed worker or individual in mortgage arrears that the economy is performing well). However, the same home-grown informational resources necessary to counterbalance or counteract partisan media coverage are not as readily available when the issue concerns the more abstract issues of blame for unemployment or for problems in the housing market (or responsibility for other, equally abstract, aspects of the economy). Economic explanations, in the abstract, are not the sorts of things that are easily grounded in the experiences of everyday life. Here again it is important to address the issue of the source of attitudes towards ascription of blame and to consider the public's degree of dependency on the mass media for relevant information. This is particularly relevant where the government avoids punishment at the polls at least partly as a function of evading responsibility for recessionary ills (Newton, 1993). What little empirical evidence there is on this topic suggests that the media does influence the public agenda on the causes and cures for economic ills (Benton and Frazier, 1976). As such, an assessment of the sorts of attributions the media make with respect to the economy ought to be an important part of an integrated explanation of economic voting behaviour (a point to which I will return to in the next section).

The Theory of Consonance

Noelle-Neumann's (1981) thesis concerning 'consonance' in the media's political coverage can be seen as another offshoot of the classical 'weak effects' paradigm. The minimal influence thesis maintained that the mechanisms of selective perception, exposure and retention protected the individual from blandishments of partisan media (Severin, 1988). In this view, people misperceive media coverage that threatens their political opinions and they actively direct their attention towards coverage they feel comfortable with. These cognitive strategies allow the voter to filter out messages that are at odds with their partisan predispositions. Noelle-Neumann has, however, pointed out that selectivity options are narrowed in the context of *consonant* coverage of political issues (defined as the 'unanimous illumination, unanimous argumentation with regard to events, people and problems': (Noelle-Neumann, 1981: 81). As we approach consonant coverage across a range of media, viewers and readers are less able to select the sort of political material they find most congenial. Here the mass media gain leverage on public opinion (Neolle-Neumann and Mathes, 1987).[2]

Given the number of broadcast channels in Britain and the range of newspapers on sale, it might be assumed that the public are unlikely to encounter consonance in the coverage of political issues. However, there is evidence to suggest that this is not always the case (Halloran et al., 1970). Moreover, a recent study suggests there is a degree of consonance in television's handling of the economy. Table 6 shows the range of causal factors offered by BBC and ITN as an explanation of fluctuations in inflation.[3]

TABLE 6
THE RANGE OF CAUSAL FACTORS AFFECTING INFLATION AND PRICES,
NOVEMBER 1993–NOVEMBER 1994
(Figures are percentages; number of instances in parentheses)

	BBC1		ITN	
Interest Rates	12.2	(22)	10.0	(12)
Growth	6.1	(11)	1.6	(2)
Gatt	3.3	(6)	3.3	(4)
Seasonal Sales	3.3	(6)	3.3	(4)
Devaluation	1.1	(2)	0.0	(0)
Supply and Demand	2.7	(5)	0.0	(0)
Government Actions	14.5	(26)	21.6	(26)
Businesses	46.3	(83)	39.1	(47)
Suppliers and Materials	1.6	(3)	5.8	(7)
Wages	5.0	(9)	2.5	(3)
Competition	1.1	(2)	3.3	(4)
Customers	2.2	(4)	4.1	(5)
Milk Supply Reorganization	0.0	(0)	5.0	(6)

With one or two exceptions, the same range of factors are represented on both stations. And in terms of prominence (if, by prominence, we mean the frequency of occurrences) the weight given to each is roughly comparable across BBC and ITN. Some of the elements identified have an underlying political dimension. Wage-led inflation has its own ideological history (Glasgow University Media Group, 1980), but is also important in the context of Labour's plans for minimum wage legislation. Of greater potential importance are the references to direct government responsibility – an issue touched upon in the previous section. Not only is this issue of attribution significant in itself, but it is important to note that the agenda exposed in this analysis is approaching the degree of 'consonance' across broadcasting channels that Noelle-Neumann sees as maximizing the potential for powerful influence.

The issue of consonance also has a bearing on the study of public attitudes towards the general health of the economy. While numerous studies have dealt with economic attitudes and political support, relatively few (as already noted) have explored the role of economic news. The studies that have dealt with this have tended to look *either* at television (Gavin and Sanders, 1995, 1996a and 1996b) *or* at the press (Sanders et al., 1993). Some have narrowed their focus even further to one particular newspaper (Mosley, 1984). As yet no study has looked at the *combined* influence of press and television. This is significant if we consider four hypothetical situations concerning media coverage – Figure 1.[4]

FIGURE 1
THE CONTINGENCIES OF MEDIA COVERAGE OF THE ECONOMY

Economic News on Television

		Good News	Bad News
Economic News in the Press	Good News	A) Increased support for the Government	B)
	Bad News	C) ?	D) Decreased support for the Government

Although this figure obviously simplifies the range of possibilities, the columns and rows are a hypothetical representation of the broad sweep of coverage by the television and press respectively. Current research tends to suggest that both press and television have an indirect effect on government popularity. In this light, we may presume that when television and press are consonant in their content (that is, where both press and television present a favourable or negative view of the economy – contingencies A and D), their conjoined influence will increase or decrease government support accordingly. A plausible example of a case that might fit contingency A is the period prior to the 1987 general election, where Britain's apparent economic buoyancy will have been covered by television, as well as celebrated in the Conservative press. Given the traditional loyalties of the bulk of the press, it is difficult to venture examples that fit contingency D, although the worst days of the first Thatcher recession or Britain's embarrassing exit from the ERM are possible candidates.

While recent independent studies suggest that press and television are influential, as yet we have no clear indication of whether the impact of the two sources is cumulative or multiplicative (or, indeed, whether output of one media is capable of counterbalancing or cancelling out the coverage of another – contingencies B and C in Figure 1). It is also impossible to determine whether the power to move public opinion is *contingent* on consonant coverage of the economy across the respective media. By their very nature, separate studies of press and television are incapable of addressing this issue (especially if they are undertaken in different time periods). Models based on one or other media are particularly vulnerable on this count.

Even those among the public who report not watching television or not reading a paper there may be awareness of what the media report about the economy through contact with those who *have* been exposed. Those who *are* exposed to a variety of media may receive different stories from different sources. We are, in this sense, dealing with highly variegated patterns of informational diffusion. This requires that we appreciate much more fully than has been the case in the past, the sort of consonant or divergent *content* that both the major sources of political information convey to the public. This is relevant not only to the general balance of coverage on the health or otherwise of the economy, but also concerning the sorts of attributions that are made about the causes and consequences of economic turbulence. We also need to examine the degree of consonance that pertains in any given time period if time-series models are going to iron out the potentially confounding problems of overlapping coverage.

Priming and the Economy

The final theoretical element I want to examine revolves around the concept of 'priming' (Iyengar and Kinder, 1987; Iyengar and Simon, 1993), a relatively new development in media theory. Given this novelty (and the fact that evidential sources relating 'priming' to the topic of economic voting are relatively scarce and scattered), the argument here is, of necessity more speculative and provisional than was the case with dependency theory and notions of consonance. Caveats aside, the priming thesis is based on a mix of experimental techniques and contends that television news does more than simply set the political agenda for the viewers. Iyengar and Kinder have shown that when news covers a particular topic, viewers, perceptions of that issue increase in salience in their political evaluations. In other words, when a topic is covered, the viewing public's perceptions on that issue are counted more heavily in the political balance than those which are not covered. By 'political balance' Iyengar and Kinder mean they are more strongly related (statistically) to a range of dependent measures that include candidate evaluations and voting decisions. Iyengar and Kinder note that:

> By calling attention to some matters while ignoring others, television news influences the standards by which governments, presidents, policies and candidates for public office are judged.

so

> should television news become preoccupied with, say, the prospects of nuclear annihilation, then citizens would judge the president primarily by his success, as they see it, in reducing the risk of war. Should television news shift its attention to the economy, citizens would follow suit, now evaluating the president largely by his success, as they see it, in maintaining prosperity... (Iyengar and Kinder, 1987: 63).

Although priming stops short of attitudinal manipulation, it is a mechanism which offers the tantalizing prospect of an explanation for one of the anomalies in modelling the economy and political support. It has been noted that there is a great deal of instability in aggregate models of public opinion that deploy 'objective' economic measures (Paldam, 1981; Sanders, 1991; Nannestad and Paldam, 1994). These models notionally reflect the relationship between 'real economy' and government support (although, in effect, the former is measured through official, government-produced statistics). These models tend to perform well in the short-term, but have a tendency to break down in the longer term. Hence, for instance, a measure of inflation may figure prominently and significantly as a correlate of government support at one point, although subsequently that relationship may break down altogether; unemployment may offers a significant parameter over one period, but not over another. This leaves the analyst with a perplexing explanatory problem and some of the attempts to explain away the instability of the models have occasionally seemed rather strained and implausible (Husbands, 1985).

The role of priming in unravelling this conundrum hinges on how we conceptualize the observational measures that are used in these models (government economic statistics). Traditionally, the statistical indicators deployed are thought to reflect the lived experience of economic turbulence – the 'objective economy' as represented by official economic statistics. However, it is clear that economic news (on television at least) is often a *catalogue* of such statistics (Gavin and Goddard, forthcoming). Coverage often hinges on the periodic release of these figures – which are subsequently presented and interpreted by economic journalists. Television economic news is often *about* the 'objective economy' of official statistics. However, recent work suggests that it is this *televisual* representation of statistics (rather than the statistics themselves or personal experience of economic turbulence) that has an important influence of public perceptions of the government's handling of the economy (Gavin and Sanders, 1996b).

This leaves open the possibility that the traditional way of conceptualizing what the official figures represent in these models, may be misconceived, and that the relationship between official statistics and government support is at least partly a function of their *televisual* presentation. However, in the light of priming theory, it is very important to note that the attention of the *media* is not fixed on one cluster of all-important economic issues or indicators. The topics that are covered (and the emphasis they are given) change significantly over short periods of time and markedly in a longer time frame. The economy *is* a consistent feature of television and press coverage. But others have remarked on how the news agenda has changed markedly over the decades (Parsons, 1987). This is partly due to the fact that economic theorists such as

Keynes, Galbraith, Friedman or Samuelson (and even the journalistic literati such as Samuel Brittan and Peter Jay) were also effective self-publicists who were anxious to have their ideas aired prominently in public debates. The economic debate is, therefore, fluid and today's important economic indicator is tomorrow's redundant side-issue. In Britain in the 1960s, the journalistic preoccupations were the balance of trade, currency depreciation and levels of growth. By the early 1970s this had changed to unemployment, and by the late 1970s and early 1980s to 'stagflation' – the unhappy and unexpected combination inflation and unemployment (Parsons, 1987). In the late 1980s and the 1990s the housing market and unprecedented levels of government borrowing have figured more prominently. Priming research demonstrates that (in all probability) the public are sensitive to these alterations in news output, and Gavin and Sanders 1996a, 1996b suggest that the public are influenced by the content of this shifting agenda. In this sort of context, then, we would actually *anticipate* that the formal models of government support that feature official statistics would be unstable over time – if, as can be argued, they really measure, not the 'objective' economy, but a media reflection of that economy.

In simplified terms, when the news focuses on, say, unemployment, the public's attitudes on the issue will become more salient in their political evaluations. This in turn will be reflected in government support. Moreover, the information embodied in the news will make an important contribution to the formation of their attitudes (towards unemployment and, perhaps, the economy generally). In this sort of context official figures on unemployment might well be strongly related to political support (although they do not necessarily do so only in their capacity as a surrogate measure of public *experience* of unemployment). On the other hand, if the agenda changes to a preoccupation with the housing market, priming research suggests that this ought to overtake or displace the issue of unemployment in public attitudes and evaluations. It is precisely at this point that we might anticipate that official statistics on housing transactions would show up as a important parameter in a formal model, while unemployment ceased to show up as statistically significant variable (even though it is trending in such a way that we might anticipate there being political implications). The instability is difficult to explain within the Downsian heuristic where the punishing/rewarding of governments is a function of people's direct economic experience. It is less difficult if we entertain the notion of the impact of the media (both informing and priming public opinion) and take seriously the implications of a shifting media agenda and the sort of informational content that forms the substance of economic reports.[5]

Of course this conceptualization of the underlying dynamics of the statistical relationship between economy and popularity is a simplification of an undoubtedly complicated set of interrelated processes. As a result, this notion of the importance of priming an explanation of model instability is necessarily tentative and speculative. But it does seem as if there is ample room here for theoretical cross-fertilization, and it is heartening to note that it looks likely that the issue of priming will receive sustained empirical attention at the forthcoming election.

Conclusions

It is very important to note that the preceding comments and observations do *not* simply add up to a reiteration of the old hypodermic models of strong media effects. It is fully appreciated and acknowledged that even when priming, consonance and dependency are salient features of the public's experience with the media, partisan predispositions will colour people's evaluation of the news they watch and read (Heath and McDonald, 1988). As such, the impact of these processes may well be at the margins. But as we are all aware, those margins (populated by those with weak or little partisan commitment) may be growing – they are certainly broader than they were twenty years ago. Moreover, the theoretical issues I have dealt with here are applicable beyond the limited sphere of economic news and economic voting. One example should suffice, although others are equally suitable. This example concerns the issue of crime. The media gives continuous, and perhaps disproportionate, attention to crime and criminal activity. In doing so it is capable of priming the British public on this highly controversial issue. There are a set of questions that immediately follows from this. Are people in low crime areas dependent on the media for an appreciation of the 'realities' of crime in the sphere beyond their direct experience? Moreover, to what extent are people with no contact with crime and criminals (other than as the occasional, casual victim) dependent on the media for information about the *causes* of crime (and, indeed, for the range of possible cures)? Finally, to what extent is there a degree of consonance across the media on the causes of crime, its general prevalence or trends in crime statistics?

This is a set of questions that might also be asked about the health or otherwise of the NHS or the educational system. With all these sets of questions in mind, it is clear that the 'margins' referred to above are relevant to a broad range of topics and can, indeed, overlap. If this is the case and the issues of dependency, consonance and priming are relevant in a variety of contexts, it seems likely that these sorts of theoretical developments can usefully inform interdisciplinary research. Although this may be difficult given the paucity of media content archives (Ludlam, 1995; Gavin, 1995), it is not impossible. To return to the area of economic news and public attitudes towards the economy, Gurevich and Levy (1986) and Furnham (1982) have tried to map public attitudes towards the causes of economic phenomena. But in neither case was their analysis married to an exhaustive inventory of *media* coverage of the phenomena derived from systematic content analysis. But at least this approach offers a potential means of determining the degree to which the media inform perceptions of the causes of economic phenomena. In addition, some time-series work has been done on the impact of economic news, but this needs to be extended to cover the *combined* output from those media that surveys suggest are the public's most important source of political information.

If we are to be in a position to effectively and fully assess the nature of impact of economic news (and the contingencies that arise from consonance or dissonance of output across media), we need to track the content of coverage of the most pervasive media over time. Only then will we begin to get a fully rounded and integrated appreciation of the dynamics of public opinion, economic news and political support.

NOTES

1. The numbers represent cell frequencies. The two attitudinal dimensions coincide in the diagonal cells. The top table from the Index takes the classical sociotropic and personal retrospective format. The lower table is drawn from a retrospective questions with the same year-long time frame. The General Retrospective question is very similar in format to its Gallup analogue (q.52a.). On the other hand, the personal question is based on a question that relates income to prices ('Looking back over the last year or so, would you say your household's income has...', q.52c.). However, this was considered to be of sufficiently similar structure to be worth consideration.
2. Noelle-Neumann argues convincingly that an explanation for consonance in coverage can be found in journalistic practice and routines.
3. See Gavin and Goddard (forthcoming) for details of the content analysis procedures and detailed examples relating to the categories. The data are derived from a project supported by the ESRC (Ref. R000221336), whose support the author gratefully acknowledges.
4. The problematic nature of the relationship between media presentation of the economy and its *actual* state, are touched upon in Gavin and Sanders (1996b).
5. It is important to note that this sort of process would also allow high profile (but non-economic) events, such as the Falklands crisis (or rather media representations of the crisis) to displace the economy completely as an important factor in the dynamics of political support – even if this were only temporary.

BIBLIOGRAPHY

Abramowitz, Alan I., David J. Lanoue and Subha Ramesh (1988) 'Economic Conditions, Causal Attribution and Political Evaluations in the 1984 Presidential Election', *Journal of Politics* 50: 848–63.
Alt, James E. (1979) *The Politics of Economic Decline: Economic Management and Political Behaviour in Britain Since 1964.* Cambridge: Cambridge University Press.
Ball-Rokeach, Sandra (1985) 'The Origins of Individual Media-System Dependency: A Sociological Framework', *Communication Research* 12: 485–510.

Ball-Rokeach, Sandra and Melvin L. DeFleur (1976) 'A Dependency Model of Mass Media Effects', *Communication Research* 3: 3–21.

Becker, L.B. and Whitney, D.C. (1980) 'Effects of Media Dependencies: Audience Assessment of Government', *Communication Reserch* 7/1: 95–120.

Benton, Marc and P. Jean Frazier (1976) 'The Agenda-Setting Function of the Mass Media at Three Levels of Information Holding', *Communication Research* 3: 261–74.

Blumler, Jay G., Dennis McQuail,and Tom J. Nossiter (1975) *Political Communication and the Young Voter*. London: Social Science Research Council.

Conover, Pamela J., Stanley Feldman, and Kathleen Knight (1987) 'The Personal and Political Underpinnings of Economic Forecasts', *American Journal of Political Science* 31: 559–83.

Curtice, John and Holli Sometko (1994) 'Does it Matter What the Papers Say? in Anthony Heath, Roger Jowell and John Curtice (eds) *Labour's Last Chance? The 1992 Election and Beyond*, pp.43–64. Aldershot: Dartmouth.

Denver, David (1989) *Elections and Voting Behaviour in Britain*. Oxford: Philip Allen.

Denver, David and Gordon Hands (1992) *Issues & Controversies in British Electoral Behaviour*. London: Harvester & Wheatsheaf.

Downs, Anthony (1957) *An Economic Theory of Democracy*. New York: Harper & Row.

Dunleavy, Patrick and Christopher T Husbands,. (1985) *Democracy at the Crossroads: Voting and Party Competition in the 1980s*. London: Allen & Unwin.

Entman, Robert M. (1993) 'Framing: Towards Clarification of a Fractured Paradigm', *Journal of Communication* 43: 51–8.

Furnham, Adrian (1982) 'Explanations for Unemployment in Britain', *European Journal of Social Psychology* 12: 335–52.

Gamson, William A. and Andre Modigliani (1989) 'Media Discourse and Public Opinion on Nuclear Power: A Constructivist Approach, *American Journal of Sociology* 95: 1–37.

Gavin, Neil T. (1995) 'Sources of Machine-Readable Text for the Analysis of Mass Media Output: The Case of Television', *SocInfo Journal* 1: 42–4.

Gavin, Neil T. and Peter Goddard (forthcoming) 'Television News and the Economy: Inflation in Britain, 1993–94', *Media, Culture and Society*.

Gavin, Neil T. and David Sanders (1995) 'The Impact of Televisual Economic News on Public Perception of the Economy and the Government, 1993–1994', *Paper Presented to a specialist PSA Conference on Parties Elections and Public Opinion*, London Guildhall University, September.

Gavin, Neil T. and David Sanders (1996a) 'The Impact of Televisual Economic News' in David Farrell, David Broughton, David Denver and Justin Fisher (eds) *British Elections and Parties Yearbook, 1995*, pp.68–84. London: Frank Cass.

Gavin, Neil T. and David Sanders (1996b) 'Economy, News and Public Opinion: Britain in the Mid-1990s', *Paper Presented to a British Politics Group at the APSA Conference*, San Francisco, September.

Glasgow University Media Group (1980) *More Bad News*. London: Routledge, Kegan and Paul.

Gurevich, Michael and Mark R. Levy (1986) 'Information and Meaning: Audience Explanations of Social Issues', in John P. Robinson and Mark R. Levy (eds), *The Main Source: Learning from Television News* pp.159–75. Beverley Hills: Sage.

Halloran, James, Philip Elliott, and Graham Murdock (1970) *Demonstrations and Communication: A Case Study*. Harmondsworth: Penguin Books.

Harrop, Martin (1987) 'Voters', in Jean Seaton and Ben Pimlot (eds) *The Media in British Politics*, pp.45–63. Aldershot: Avebury.

Heath, Anthony, Roger Jowell, and John Curtice (1985) *How Britain Votes*. Oxford: Pergamon Press.

Heath, Anthony, Roger Jowell, , John Curtice, , Geoffrey Evans, , Julia Field, and Sharon Witherspoon (1990) *Understanding Political Change*. Oxford: Pergamon Press.

Heath, Anthony and Sarah K. McDonald (1988) 'The Demise of Party Identification Theory?', *Electoral Studies* 7: 95–108.

Hibbs, Douglas A. (1982) 'Economic Outcomes and Political Support for the British Government Among Occupational Classes: A Dynamic Analysis', *American Political Science Review* 76: 259–279.

Husbands, Christopher T. (1985) 'Government Popularity and the Unemployment Issue, 1966–1983', *Sociology* 19: 1–18.

Iyengar, Shanto and Donald R. Kinder (1987) *News That Matters: Television and American Opinion.* Chicago: University of Chicago Press.

Iyengar, Shanto and Adam Simon (1993) 'New Coverage of the Gulf Crisis and Public Opinion: A Study of Agenda-Setting, Priming and Framing', *Communication Research,* 20: 365–83.

Johnston, Ron and Charles Pattie (1995) 'People, Place and the Economic Theory of Voting: The 1992 British General Election', *Politics* 15: 9–17.

Kinder, Donald R. and D. Roderick Kiewiet (1981) 'Sociotropic Politics: The American Case', *British Journal of Political Science* 11: 129–61

Klapper, Joseph (1960) *The Effects of Mass Communication.* New York: The Free Press.

Klapper, Joseph (1968) 'Mass Communication: Effects', in *International Encyclopedia of the Social Sciences* Vol. III pp.81–90. London: Crowell Collier and Macmillan.

Lazarsfeld, Paul F., Bernard Berelson, and Hazel Gaudet (1944) *The People's Choice.* New York: Columbia University Press.

Lewis-Beck, Michael S. (1986) 'Comparative Voting: Britain, France, Germany, Italy', *American Journal of Political Science* 30: 315–46.

Lockerbie, Brad (1991) 'The Influence of Levels of Information on the Use of Prospective Evaluations', *Political Behaviour* 13: 223–35.

Ludlam, Steve (1995) 'CD-ROMs for Political Scientists', *Political Studies* 43: 349–68.

Miller, William L. (1991) *Media and Voters: The Audience, Content and Influence of Press and Television at the 1987 General Election.* Oxford: Clarendon.

Miller, William L., Harold D., Clarke, Martin Harrop, , Lawrence Leduc, and Paul Whiteley (1990) *How Voters Change: The 1987 British Election Campaign in Perspective.* Oxford: Clarendon Press.

Mosley, Paul (1984) '"Popularity Function" and the Role of the Media: A Pilot Study of the Popular Press', *British Journal of Political Science* 14: 117–33.

Nannestad, Peter and Michael Paldam (1994) 'The VP-Function: A Survey of the Literature on Vote and Popularity Functions After 25 Years', *Public Choice* 79: 213–45.

Newton, Ken (1992) 'Do People Read Everything They Believe in the Papers? Newspapers and Voters in the 1983 and 1987 Election', in Ivor Crewe, Pippa Norris, David Denver and David Broughton (eds) *British Parties and Elections Yearbook, 1992,* pp.51–74. London: Simon and Schuster.

Newton, Ken (1993) 'Economic Voting in the 1992 General Election', in David Denver, Pippa Norris, David Broughton and Colin Rallings (eds) *British Elections and Parties Yearbook, 1993,* pp.158–76. London: Harvester Wheatsheaf.

Noelle-Neumann, Elisabeth (1981) 'Mass Media and Social Change in Developed Societies', in Elihu Katz and Tamas Szesco (eds) *Mass Media and Social Change,* pp.137–66. London: Sage.

Noelle-Neumann, Elisabeth and Rainer Mathes (1987) 'The "Event as Event" and the "Event as News": The Significance of "Consonance" for Media Effects Research', *European Journal of Communication* 2: 291–414.

Paldam, Martin (1981) 'A Preliminary Survey of the Theories and Findings on Vote and Popularity Function', *European Journal of Political Research* 9: 181–99.

Parsons, Wayne D. (1987) *The Power of the Financial Press: Journalism and Economic Opinion in Britain and America.* Aldershot: Edward Elgar.

Paulson, Bruno (1994) 'The Economy and the 1992 Election: Was 1992 Labour's Golden Chance?', in Anthony Heath, Roger Jowell and John Curtice (eds) *Labour's Last Chance? The 1992 Election and Beyond,* pp.85–106. Aldershot: Dartmouth.

Peffley, Mark (1984) 'The Voter as Juror: Attributing Responsibility for Economic Conditions', *Political Behaviour* 6: 275–294.

Peffley, Mark and John T. Williams (1985) 'Attributing Presidential Responsibility for National Economic Problems' *American Politics Quarterly* 13: 393–425.

Petrocik, John R. and Fredrick T Steeper,. (1986) 'The Midterm Referendum: The Importance of Attributions of Responsibility', *Political Behaviour* 8: 206–29.

Sanders, David (1991) 'Government Popularity and the Next General Election', *Political Quarterly* 62: 235–61.

Sanders, David, David Marsh, and David Ward (1993) 'The Electoral Impact of Press Coverage of the Economy, 1979–87', *British Journal of Political Science* 23: 175–210.

Sanders, David, David Ward, and David Marsh, with Tony Fletcher (1987) 'Government Popularity and the Falklands War: A Reassessment', *British Journal of Political Science* 17: 281–314.

Semetko, Holli, Margaret Scammell, and Tom Nossiter (1994) 'The Media's Coverage of the Campaign', in Anthony Heath, Roger Jowell and John Curtice (eds) *Labour's Last Chance? The 1992 Election and Beyond*, pp.25–42. Aldershot: Dartmouth.

Severin, W.J. (1988) *Communication Theories*. London: Longman.

Weaver, R. Kent (1986) 'The Politics of Blame Avoidance', *Journal of Public Policy* 6: 371–98.

Webber, Richard (1993) 'The 1992 General Election: Constituency Results and Local Patterns of National Newspaper Readership', in David Denver, Norris, Pippa, David Broughton and Colin Rallings (eds) *British Elections and Parties Yearbook 1993*, pp.205–15. London: Harvester Wheatsheaf.

Error-correction Models of Party Support: The Case of New Labour

Harold D. Clarke, Marianne C. Stewart and Paul Whiteley

The dynamics of public support for political parties fascinate students of politics in Britain and elsewhere. An important reason for this is that a party's standing with the electorate can vary markedly over short time periods. The massive reversals of fortune experienced by the Conservative and Labour Parties since the April 1992 British general election provide excellent examples of this phenomenon. Although some commentators speculated that the 1992 election might have been 'Labour's Last Chance' (Heath *et al.*, 1994), the party's sharp upward swing in popularity and the accompanying precipitous slide in Conservative approval in the months following that contest emphasize the need for theoretical models capable of explaining such short-term dynamics. Recently developed time-series analytic techniques can do much to facilitate the specification and testing of such models. In the present article we illustrate these techniques in analyses of forces driving Labour support since 1992. Unlike most previous studies which have relied heavily on macroeconomic indicators, especially inflation and unemployment rates, as principal explanatory variables (see Lewis-Beck, 1988; Miller 1989; Norpoth, 1992), we accord pride of place to two largely neglected variables – party leader performance evaluations and party identification. By incorporating these variables, our models are designed to bridge the longstanding theoretical gap between aggregate- and individual-level analyses of factors governing party support.

The article begins by reviewing three central controversies in the party support literature. This section is followed by a methodological discussion of how the important econometric concepts of cointegration and error correction and associated methods of analysing nonstationary time series can guide model development and testing. These methods are used to investigate the properties of monthly data on variations in Labour vote intentions, best prime minister perceptions and party identification over the January 1992–August 1996 period. The results of these analyses inform the specification and testing of alternative error-correction models of Labour vote intentions. Then, we construct and estimate models of voters' judgements that the Labour leader would make the best prime minister and Labour Party identification, and perform tests for the exogeneity of leader evaluations and party identification vis-à-vis Labour vote intentions. In the conclusion, we reprise major findings in the context of a brief discussion of how the models and methods presented in the article can facilitate understanding of the dynamics and determinants of the fortunes of British parties in the run-up to the 1997 general election.

What Drives Party Support? Three Continuing Controversies

One of the most interesting controversies in the party support literature is the multifaceted debate concerning the concept of party identification. In its original 'Michigan-school' definition, party identification is a stable psychological attachment that results from early-life socialization processes and acts as a strong long-term force on voting behavior in successive elections (for example, Campbell *et al.*, 1960: chs 6–7). After enjoying widespread acceptance during the 1950s and 1960s, this social-psychological conception was disputed in the 1970s by scholars influenced by the resurgent political economy tradition. These revisionists accepted the proposition that party identification informs electoral choice, but they argued that it should be conceptualized as a summary running tally of economically grounded party performance evaluations (for example, Fiorina, 1981: ch. 5; see also Franklin, 1992).[1] As economic conditions change, voters update their party performance evaluations, and they accord more weight to recent, as opposed to earlier, ones. *Pace* the social psychologists, these ongoing evaluations can fluctuate markedly over short time intervals, and this means that individual- and aggregate-level partisan change are recurrent possibilities.

In the 1990s, this controversy concerning the conceptualization and dynamics of party identification has become intertwined with methodological debates concerning its measurement. These latter debates were sparked by MacKuen *et al.* (1989) who demonstrated that aggregate level or 'macropartisanship' in the United States as measured by a party identification question in monthly Gallup surveys responds to voters' economic evaluations and their presidential approval ratings. However, Abramson and Ostrom (1991) argued that the Gallup party identification question is flawed, and that aggregate responses to the traditional party identification question used in the biennial American National Election Studies are affected only weakly by economic evaluations and not at all by presidential approval. Although the American macropartisanship debate now has raged for several years (for example, Bishop *et al.*, 1994; Box-Steffensmeier and Smith, 1996; Clarke and Suzuki, 1994; MacKuen *et al.*, 1992), in Britain, a lack of appropriate data has prevented scholars from using time-series analysis of party identification variables to address longstanding disagreements over the nature and extent of partisan (in)stability (for example, Budge *et al.*, 1976; Crewe, 1986; Crewe *et al.*, 1977; Heath *et al.*, 1985; Heath *et al.*, 1991; Heath and McDonald, 1988; Heath and Pierce, 1992; Sarlvik and Crewe, 1983). Data unavailability also has meant that party identification variables have not appeared in models of the interelection dynamics of support for British parties.

A second controversy in Britain concerns whether and how party leader images affect parties' standing with the electorate. In this regard, a venerable conventional wisdom certified by Butler and Stokes (1976: ch. 17; see also Crewe, 1985; Dunleavy and Husbands, 1985; Rose and McAllister, 1990) maintains that leader images matter little, if at all. However, several multivariate analyses of cross-sectional and panel survey data have clearly demonstrated that, controlling for a variety of other factors, voters' perceptions of the party leaders have strong effects on electoral choice (for example, Crewe and King, 1994; Miller *et al.*, 1990; Stewart and Clarke, 1992). Recently, these individual-level findings have been reinforced by the results of aggregate-level time-series analyses showing that prime ministerial approval ratings (Clarke and Stewart, 1995) and public perceptions of which leader would make the best prime minister (Nadeau *et al.*, 1996) have strong effects on governing party vote intentions in the interims between elections.

A third controversy involves the impact of economic conditions on parties' vote intention shares. As noted, models of the influence of these conditions traditionally have relied on inflation, unemployment and other objective measures of the state of the economy as major explanatory variables. Such unmediated economy-to-polity models were popularized in the British context by the pioneering work of Goodhart and Bhansali (1970), and they continue to be very influential. Recently, however, the inclusion of subjective economic evaluations, that is, public judgements of national and personal economic circumstances, has done much to improve model specification by including variables that form intermediate links between the objective economy and party support. Particularly important in this regard is the widely cited 'Essex model' developed by David Sanders and his colleagues. This model specifies that macroeconomic conditions, particularly interest rates, strongly influence voters' expectations about personal financial circumstances which, in turn, propel a governing party's support (Sanders, 1991, 1993, 1995; Sanders *et al.*, 1993). Although the Essex model's emphasis on the importance of personal economic expectations has been adopted by others (for example, Nadeau *et al.*, 1994), Clarke and Stewart (1995) have shown that other kinds of economic evaluations, including those that focus on national as opposed to individual economic conditions, perform well in analyses of the dynamics of Conservative support in the Thatcher and Major eras.

Although the controversies discussed above often have been viewed in isolation from one another, it is clear that progress towards resolving them requires the development of rival multivariate models of the dynamics of party support that include various combinations of explanatory variables at issue. Recognizing that the testing of such models requires suitable time-series data on all relevant variables and that such data were unavailable, we initiated a long-term data collection effort.[2] This study began in January 1992 and it involves adding the standard British Election Study (BES) party identification battery[3] and various other questions to British Gallup's monthly opinion polls. The inclusion of the BES party identification items avoids the controversy over question-wording that has bedevilled research on the aggregate dynamics of partisanship in the United States. The utility of the data we are gathering is enhanced by the fact that the Gallup surveys regularly ask a sizable number of questions concerning perceptions of party leader performance, vote intentions and evaluations of national and personal economic conditions.[4] Here, these monthly data are used to analyse alternative models of the determinants and dynamics of Labour over the January 1992–August 1996 period. We begin by outlining our methodological approach.

Non-stationarity, Cointegration and Error-correction Models of Party Support

Much of the early work on relationships between the economy and party support in Britain (for example, Goodhart and Bhansali, 1970) involved regression analyses which included nonstationary variables, that is, variables that do not fluctuate around a constant mean (see, for example, Mills, 1991: 64–5). Some nonstationary variables, such as the retail price index, increase continuously over time, whereas others, such as the number of unemployed persons, resemble a 'drunkard's walk', and may drift upwards or downwards for protracted periods. Economists (for example, Keynes, 1939; see also Hendry, 1980) and statisticians (for example, Yule, 1926) long had been suspicious of analyses of nonstationary variables, and research in the 1970s and 1980s demonstrated that indeed such analyses very often do produce spurious findings. In particular, Granger and Newbold's (1974, 1986) classic Monte Carlo studies showed that regression models involving nonstationary variables were quite often capable of demonstrating bogus statistically significant relationships between wholly unrelated variables. This is largely because of the fact that in time-series analysis, unlike cross-sectional analysis, theoretically unrelated variables can grow in a similar way, which gives the false impression that they are related.

Later work on the short-term dynamics of party support (for example, Whiteley, 1984; Clarke and Whiteley, 1990) solved this problem by modelling all of the relevant variables in the model in *first-differenced* form, that is, as a change over adjacent time periods ($\Delta X_t = X_t - X_{t-1}$). A variable such as the retail price index, for example, is very likely to fluctuate around a constant mean when modelled in first-differenced, instead of its original level, form. However, this strategy comes with a price, in that it ignores any long-term equilibrium relationships that might exist between variables, permitting the researcher the opportunity of capturing only short-term links between the economy and political support (see, for example, Beck, 1992).

Following pioneering theoretical work by Engle and Granger (1987), advances in the econometric analysis of time-series data (see, for example, Alogoskoufis and Smith, 1995; Harris, 1995; Hendry, 1995; Muscatelli and Hurn, 1995) make it possible to capture both short-term and long-term relationships between variables in a model containing nonstationary variables, provided that the latter *cointegrate*, or are in a type of equilibrium relationship with one another. As an example of this, Clarke and Stewart (1995) demonstrated that voting intentions and prime ministerial performance evaluations cointegrated for the Conservatives in Britain over the 1979–92 period. Clarke *et al.* (1997) extended this line of inquiry to include Conservative Party identification for the 1992–96 period. These results mean that, net of any factors that may have affected their short-term dynamics, these variables tend to travel together over the long run. Thus, any shock that reduced the percentage of persons intending to vote Conservative was eroded or 'reequilibriated' by the cointegrating relationship existing between Tory vote intentions, on the one hand, and prime ministerial approval and Tory party identification, on the other. Note that the notion of cointegration is quite general, and it is not necessary to invoke the powerful, but restrictive, theoretical machinery associated with the notion of equilibrium in microeconomic theory to conceptualize cointegrating variables as moving together through time in a type of symbiotic relationship.

If, as in the above example, two or more series are in equilibrium while they are increasing or decreasing over time, they will not drift apart from each other, but rather tend to fluctuate together in response to external shocks. In this situation, a series which represents the *difference* between some combination of the original series (that is, a linear combination of those series) will itself be stationary. In other words, although the original series may be mean nonstationary, the difference between the series will be a stationary variable, since otherwise the series of interest could not be in equilibrium with each other. The important theoretical advance of Engle and Granger (1987) was to demonstrate analytically via their 'representation' theorem that if after conducting appropriate tests the researcher concludes that two or more series are nonstationary and cointegrate, then these series may be modelled in error-correction form. Conversely, the use of an error-correction specification implies that the series cointegrate. The work of Engle and Granger thus demonstrated the theoretical attractiveness and potential analytic power of error-correction models for analysing factors affecting the short- and long-run dynamics of time-series data. In economics, the use of such models had been pioneered by Dennis Sargan in the 1960s (for example, Sargan, 1964), and subsequently popularized by David Hendry and other members of the 'LSE' school of econometrics in the 1970s and 1980s (see, for example, Alogoskoufis and Smith, 1995). However, until recently, error-correction models have been largely ignored by students of party support or other political scientists.

Since the 'spurious regressions' threat to inference arises when one attempts to model nonstationary series, the first stage in building an error-correction model is to test if the variables of interest are, in fact, nonstationary. This is most commonly done by means of a Dickey-Fuller unit-root test (see, for example, Harris, 1995: ch. 3; Muscatelli and Hurn, 1995: 174–8).[5] If a series has a unit-root, it is mean nonstationary. Assuming it is established that the dependent variable and one or more independent variables in the model are nonstationary, then the next step is to see if these nonstationary variables cointegrate. Engle and Granger (1987; see also Engle and Yoo, 1991) suggest that a simple procedure for doing this is to regress hypothesized dependent series on the hypothesized independent ones, and then determine if the residuals of this regression are stationary, which is done by means of another Dickey-Fuller test.[6] Clearly, the residuals of such a regression constitute a linear combination of the original variables. If the residuals fluctuate around a constant value, this implies that the variables tend to move together over time which, in turn, confirms that they cointegrate.[7]

If stationary, the residuals of this cointegrating regression can be subsequently incorporated into the full model of factors affecting the short- and long-term dynamics of party support. Operating with a lag in the model, the residuals from the cointegrating regression constitute a measure of the so-called *error-correction mechanism* (ECM) which controls the rapidity with which a shock to the equilibrium relationship among the cointegrating variables is eroded by that relationship. For example, if the Conservative vote intention share fell precipitously in a given month (say by 20 points) because of a political shock (for example, a widely publicized scandal involving a high-ranking cabinet member), this would disturb the long-run equilibrium relationship among party identification, prime ministerial approval and voting intentions in the popularity function model of Conservative support (see Clarke *et al.*, 1997). However, since these three variables are cointegrated, this equilibrium will be restored in due course, with the speed with which this occurs being determined by the coefficient on the error-correction mechanism variable in the model. As is implied by the notion of negative feedback that is naturally associated with the conception of *error-correction* mechanism (see, for example, Harris, 1995: 24), the ECM coefficient should carry a negative sign, and have an absolute value greater than 0 and less than 1.0. If, for example, the coefficient in the ECM for the Tory vote intention model was -0.75, this means that 75 per cent of the 20-point shock to the Conservative vote intention share occasioned by the aforementioned scandal would be eroded in the first period after the event occurred. This reequilibriation process continues at the same speed in subsequent periods.

Given this informal introduction to error-correction models, we next develop such models for Labour Party support over the 1992–96 period.

Error-correction Models of Support for New Labour

Although formal statistical tests are required to prove the point, the spectacular surge in Labour's vote intention share in public opinion polls since the party's defeat in the April 1992 general election provides *prima facie* evidence that variables measuring support for Labour and its leaders have been nonstationary since that time. In this regard, an ocular analysis of the data presented in Figure 1 is instructive. The figure shows that although 35% voted Labour in that contest, exactly four years later 55% of the respondents in our Gallup Poll survey claimed that they were prospective Labour voters. The party's vote intention percentage has remained impressive and circa August 1996 47% stated that they would cast a Labour ballot in the next general election. The surge in Labour vote intentions has been accompanied by large increases in the percentages of persons who think that the Labour leader would make the best prime minister and identify with Labour (Figure 1). Indeed, since the September 1992 currency crisis Labour's leaders have been consistently favoured over their Conservative counterpart, John Major, in public judgements concerning who would make the best prime minister. Labour's share of party identifiers has not varied to the same extent as vote intentions or best prime minister judgements[8] but, as Figure 1 also shows, it has displayed a substantial and continuing dynamic with the percentage of Labour partisans ranging from 30% in February 1992 to 47% in December 1994. Moreover, movements in Labour vote intentions, party identification and best prime minister judgements are closely interrelated. Although Labour's vote intention percentage has exceeded its partisan share virtually every month since January 1992, the two series have tracked each other closely, and their overall correlation is strong ($r = +0.66$). Judgements that the Labour leader would make the best prime minister have moved in tandem with these two series. Correlations between these judgements, on the one hand, and Labour vote intentions and party identification on the other are +0.88 and +0.70, respectively. These impressive correlations among the three series suggest that the possibility that they cointegrate and there are important causal connections among them.

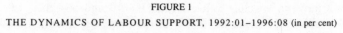

FIGURE 1

THE DYNAMICS OF LABOUR SUPPORT, 1992:01–1996:08 (in per cent)

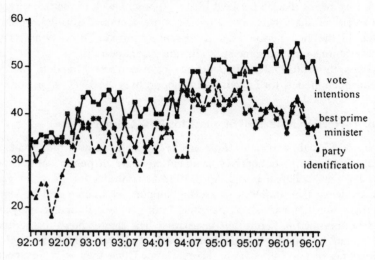

Following our discussion of the steps involved in developing error-correction models, we pursue the cointegration possibility by performing Dickey-Fuller unit-root tests to determine if Labour vote intentions, Labour leader as best prime minister, Labour Party identification are nonstationary. We also perform Dickey-Fuller tests for various economic variables that might be included in Labour support models. The analyses (Table 1) demonstrate that in every case but one (national economic expectations) these several variables are nonstationary but become stationary when (first) differenced. For example, the t-ratio for the Dickey-Fuller test for the stationarity Labour vote intentions is -2.19, well below the critical value of -2.92 required to reject the null hypothesis of *non*-stationarity at the 0.05 level. However, the t-ratio for the first differenced version of this series is fully -10.53, easily rejecting this null hypothesis.

Since the three Labour support series are nonstationary, we test if they cointegrate. Engle and Granger (1987) and Engle and Yoo (1991) procedures are employed for this purpose.[9] Following our earlier discussion, we first regress Labour vote intentions on Labour leader as best prime minister and Labour Party identification. Then, we use a Dickey-Fuller test if the residuals from this regression for non-stationarity. The regression indicates that the best prime minister and party identification variables have strong, statistically significant, and properly signed (that is, positive) effects on Labour vote intentions (Table 2). The adjusted Engle and Yoo estimates of the regression

TABLE 1

DICKEY-FULLER UNIT-ROOT TESTS FOR LABOUR VOTE INTENTIONS, LABOUR LEADER AS BEST PRIME MINISTER, LABOUR PARTY IDENTIFICATION AND ECONOMIC SERIES, 1992:02 – 1996:08

Series	Unit-Root Test‡
Labour vote intentions†	-2.19*
Δ Labour vote intentions	-10.53
Best prime minister	-2.39*
Δ Best prime minister	-8.81
Labour Party identification†	-2.62*
Δ Labour Party identification	-10.66
Economic Evaluations:	
Personal financial expectations	-2.64*
Δ Personal financial expectations	-8.73
Personal financial retrospections	-1.41*
Δ Personal financial retrospections	-8.89
National economic retrospections	-2.01*
Δ National economic retrospections	-6.51
National economic expectations	-3.36
Δ National economic expectations	-7.33
Most Important Problem:	
Inflation	-2.67*
Δ Inflation	-10.33
Unemployment†	-1.50*
Δ Unemployment	-11.60
Interest rates	-2.67*
Δ Interest rates	-5.11

Notes: Δ first-difference operator
* fails to reject null hypothesis of non-stationarity, critical value = -2.92, $p = .05$
† augmented Dickey-Fuller test, lag = 1.
‡ t-ratio

coefficients and their standard errors confirm this finding. Also, as should be the case if the series in question cointegrate, a unit-root test shows that the residuals from this regression (a linear combination of the nonstationary series) are a stationary variable. Since the three Labour series cointegrate, we may model the impact of the best prime minister and party identification variables on Labour vote intentions in error-correction form. We also note that additional tests for cointegration involving the three Labour series and various economic series (considered one at a time) demonstrate that none of the latter are involved in a cointegrating relationship with the former. This means that although these economic variables may affect short-term movements in Labour support, they are not part of any error-correction mechanism that drives the *long-term* dynamics of that support.

TABLE 2

COINTEGRATING REGRESSION:
LABOUR VOTE INTENTIONS, LABOUR LEADER AS BEST PRIME MINISTER AND
LABOUR PARTY IDENTIFICATION,
1992:01–1996:08

Regressor Variables	b	s.e.
Labour leader	.616	0.083
	.721	*0.232*
Labour Party identification	.592	0.078
	.423	*0.218*

$R^2 = .716$

Unit-root test for residuals = -3.41, rejects null hypothesis of non-stationarity at 0.05 level, critical value = -3.33

Note: Engle and Yoo 'three-step' estimates in *italics* .

The Labour vote intention error-correction model is:

$$\Delta LAB_t = \beta_0 + \beta_1 \Delta LBPM_{t-1} + \beta_2 \Delta LPID_{t-1} + \beta_3 ECM_{t-1} + \beta_4 \Delta ECEV_{t-1}$$
$$+ \beta_5 \Delta INTR_{t-1} + \beta_6 \Delta IMIP_{t-1} + \beta_7 \Delta UMIP_{t-1} + \Sigma\beta_{8-k} SHOCKS_{t-1} + \varepsilon_t \qquad (1)$$

where: LAB = Labour vote intentions, $LBPM$ = Labour leader as best prime minister, $LPID$ = Labour Party identification, ECM = error-correction mechanism, $ECEV$ = one of four subjective economic evaluations, INTR = interest rates, IMIP = inflation as most important problem, UMIP = unemployment as most important problem, SHOCKS = miscellaneous political and economic events, ε = stochastic error process ($\sim N(0,\sigma^2)$), Δ = difference operator, β_0 = constant, β_{1-k} = regression coefficients. The error-correction mechanism (ECM) is measured as the residuals from the cointegrating regression, that is, $ECM = LAB_t - \alpha_1 LBPM_t - \alpha_2 LPID_t$. As noted, these residuals are a stationary linear combination of the three series. Four types of. subjective economic evaluations (personal and national prospections, personal and national retrospections) are employed in four variants of the model. Theory does not specify the exact time lags at which the effects of these and other variables operate on Labour vote intentions, but it is plausible that delayed effects occur at short lags. Thus, alternative preliminary specifications are assessed at lags of 0, 1 and 2 periods. Model parameters are estimated via OLS regression.

Preliminary analyses indicate that one of the hypothesized shock variables, the September 1992 currency crisis, did not have a significant impact on Labour vote intentions net of other predictors. Reestimating the four variants of the model without this variable yields the results shown in Table 3. As hypothesized, both Labour leader as best prime minister and

TABLE 3

ERROR-CORRECTION MODELS OF LABOUR VOTE INTENTIONS, 1992:04–1996:08

Predictor Variables	Models			
	PE	PR	NR	NE
Constant	0.49c	0.50c	0.50	0.47
Best prime minister (t)	0.24a	0.28a	0.26a	0.27a
Labour Party identification (t-2)	0.25a	0.21c	0.21c	0.20c
Error-correction mechanism (t-1)	-0.18c	-0.16c	-0.16c	-0.17c
Economic evaluations:				
Personal expectations (t)	-0.09c	X	X	X
Personal retrospections (t)	X	-0.02	X	X
National retrospections (t)	X	X	-0.02	X
National expectations (t)	X	X	X	-0.02
Interest rates (t)	1.64c	1.66c	1.58d	1.53d
Most Important Problem:				
Inflation (t-1)	0.73a	0.57a	0.57a	0.56a
Unemployment (t-1)	0.17b	0.16b	0.16b	0.16b
Maastricht (t)	2.52c	2.83c	2.75c	2.80c
Local elections/Smith (t)	4.54a	4.43a	4.39a	4.36a
Major reselection (t)	-3.16c	-2.83c	-2.87c	-2.81c
Harman affair (t)	-3.02c	-2.78c	-2.81c	-2.83c
Mad Cow (t)	1.93d	1.43	1.48	1.44
Demon eyes/Shadow cabinet (t)	-3.37d	-3.35d	-3.28d	-3.22d
Model Diagostics				
R^2	0.69	0.67	0.67	0.67
Adjusted R^2	0.59	0.55	0.56	0.56
Standard error of estimate	1.80	1.88	1.87	1.87
Durbin-Watson	2.07	2.27	2.23	2.23
General serial correlation	14.58	14.35	14.81	15.06
Functional form	0.35	0.12	0.18	0.15
Normality	3.26	2.33	2.42	2.53
General heteroskedasticity	0.75	1.00	1.29	1.12
ARCH (1)	0.39	0.23	0.68	0.51

Notes: X – variable not included in model;
(a) $p \leq 0.001$, (b) $p \leq 0.01$, (c) $p \leq 0.05$, (d) $p \leq 0.10$ (one-tailed test).

Labour Party identification have significant, positive short-term effects on Labour vote intentions. Considering the personal expectations (PE) version of the model, parameter estimates indicate that a 1% increase in the percentage of persons believing a Labour leader would make the best prime minister increases the party's vote intention share by 0.24%, whereas a 1% increase in the cohort of Labour Party identifiers increases that share by 0.25%. Although these effects might seem small, recall that both the percentage of persons believing that the Labour leader would make the best prime minister and the percentage of Labour identifiers have grown substantially during the period under consideration.

Regarding other predictors, the economic variables in Model PE also operate as anticipated, with Labour voting support varying positively with interest rates and the percentages of persons mentioning inflation or unemployment as most important national problems, and inversely with the balance of positive versus negative personal economic expectations. As for various shocks, parameter estimates indicate that Major's reelection as party leader in July 1995 and the 'Harriet Hypocrite' affair in February 1996 temporarily lowered Labour support by approximately 3% in each case. The effects of the complex of August 1996 events concerning Labour's internecine bickering over its shadow cabinet elections and the Tory 'Demon Eyes' advertisements had a negative impact of similar magnitude. Not all shocks have been negative – the 1994 local elections/death of John Smith temporarily raised Labour support by more than 4%, and the spring 1996 'Mad Cow' revelations, by nearly 2%. Finally, net of these several effects, the error-correction mechanism has the expected negative parameter consistent with its underlying conception as a reequilibriating or negative feedback device. The estimated coefficient (-0.18) for the ECM in Model PE indicates that shocks (of whatever kind) affecting Labour voting support can have relatively long half-lives. *Ceteris paribus,* such influences are reequilibriated by the long-term cointegrating relationship involving voting support, best prime minister and party identification at a rate of slightly less than 20% in each subsequent period after they occur.

Viewed more generally, the personal expectations model (Model PE) performs quite well. As Table 3 shows, the model has a reasonably good fit (adjusted $R^2 = 0.59$, s.e.e. = 1.80), and it easily passes a standard battery of diagnostic tests for residual autocorrelation, heteroskedasticity, functional form and normality.[10] The attractiveness of PE is further enhanced by the finding that none of the other three types of subjective economic evaluations (personal retrospections, national retrospections, national prospections) has statistically significant effects (see Table 3, models PR, NR and NE). Moreover, although these rival specifications of the basic Labour voting intentions model perform well in terms of the behavior of most other individual predictors, overall fit and residual diagnostics, a battery of encompassing tests (Charemza and Deadman, 1992: 297–303) reveals that models PR, NR and NE are encompassed by PE, but do not encompass it. This means that the PE model is statistically superior to the PR, NR and NE models, and for that reason is to be preferred. Overall, and unlike the results of analyses of Conservative Party support (Clarke and Stewart, 1995; Clarke et al., 1997), these latter results are consonant with the Essex model specification that emphasizes the role of personal economic expectations in party support models.

To untangle the skein of forces affecting the short- and long-term dynamics of Labour voting intentions, we next consider the determinants of perceptions of the Labour leader as best prime minister and Labour Party identification. In these analyses we again investigate the effects of different kinds of economic evaluations in four alternative model specifications. Other predictor variables in the best prime minister models include party identification, interest rates, inflation and unemployment as most important problems, and several political and economic events. Since Labour has had three leaders during the period under consideration, two of these latter variables are designed to capture public reactions to the two leadership changes (from Kinnock to Smith in July 1992 and from Smith to Blair in July 1994). Other shocks in the best prime minister models include the 'Black Wednesday' currency crisis (permanent effect), John Major's reselection as Tory leader (permanent effect), a post-election 'anti-honeymoon' for Neil Kinnock (temporary effect), the 'Harriet Hypocrite' and 'Mad Cow' affairs (temporary effects), and the 'Demon Eyes/Shadow Cabinet' publicity (a necessarily permanent effect since our time series end in August 1996).

Preliminary analyses indicate that interest rates do not have significant effects in the best prime minister models. Restimated models that omit this variable perform well – they explain substantial amounts of the variance in the dependent variable (for example, adjusted R^2 ranges from 0.69 to 0.72) and they pass the extensive battery of residual diagnostic tests (Table 4). Several predictor variables perform as advertised. The effect of the Smith–Blair leadership change was particularly profound – net of all other considerations the selection of Mr Blair prompted a 14–15% upward shift in the percentage of persons believing the Labour leader would make the best prime minister. The currency, Maastricht and 'Mad Cow' crises all had smaller positive effects (3–5% in each case), with the former being permanent, and the latter two, temporary. Negative forces are in evidence as well – the party's 1992 election defeat and the 'Harriet Hypocrite' affair both prompted temporary (one-month) decreases (of 4–5%) in Labour's best prime minister percentage. Major's reelection and the Demon Eyes campaign/shadow cabinet election had a similarly sized, albeit permanent, negative impacts.

Finally, as anticipated, subjective economic evaluations also exerted negative influences – as these evaluations became more sanguine, the percentage of voters selecting the Labour leader as best prime minister declined. Unlike the Labour vote intention analyses, all four types of economic evaluations have significant effects on choice of best prime minister (Table 4) and, thus, the case for a personal expectations version of the best prime minister model is not immediately evident. In this regard, a battery of encompassing tests reveal that the personal expectations model encompasses its personal retrospections and national expectations rivals. These tests also show that the personal expectations model encompasses the national retrospections alternative. However, the encompassing test evidence for personal expectations vis-à-vis national retrospections in the best prime minister analyses is not as

TABLE 4

MODELS OF LABOUR LEADER AS BEST PRIME MINISTER, 1992:04–1996:08

Models

Predictor Variables	PE	PR	NR	NE
Constant	-0.08	0.04	0.06	-0.08
Labour Party identification (*t-2*)	0.20c	0.16	0.13	0.13
Economic Expectations:				
Personal expectations (*t*)	-0.16b	X	X	X
Personal retrospections (*t*)	X	-0.20c	X	X
National retrospections (*t*)	X	X	-0.13a	X
National expectations (*t*)	X	X	X	-0.06c
Most Important Problem:				
Inflation (*t-1*)	0.34c	0.29d	0.23	0.28d
Unemployment (*t-1*)	0.10d	0.08	0.10d	0.10
Post-election anti-honeymoon (*t*)	-5.29b	-5.89a	-4.07c	-5.21b
Currency crisis (*t*)	4.60c	4.93c	3.99c	5.35c
Maastricht (*t*)	2.68d	2.74d	2.34d	3.14c
Leadership changes:				
Kinnock—>Smith (*t*)	4.10c	2.51	2.98	3.99d
Smith—>Blair (*t*)	15.00a	14.14a	14.75a	14.11a
Major reselection (*t*)	-5.28c	-5.00c	-4.97c	-5.52c
Harman affair (*t*)	-5.03a	-5.23a	-4.92a	-5.06a
Mad Cow (*t*)	4.62b	3.99b	3.89b	3.93c
Demon Eyes/Shadow Cabinet (*t*)	-5.03c	-5.05c	-4.53c	-4.84c
Model Diagnostics				
R^2	0.72	0.70	0.73	0.69
Adjusted R^2	0.63	0.60	0.64	0.59
Standard error of estimate	2.26	2.34	2.22	2.37
Durbin-Watson	2.50	2.59	2.41	2.44
General serial correlation	16.08	18.72	14.41	16.25
Functional form	3.02	0.09	0.11	0.99
Normality	2.74	0.31	1.69	1.56
General heteroskedasticity	1.60	2.10	2.04	1.70
ARCH (1)	0.78	1.71	0.09	0.40

Notes: X – variable not included in model;
(a) – $p \leq 0.001$, (b) – $p \leq 0.01$, (c) – $p \leq 0.05$, (d) – $p \leq 0.10$ (one-tailed test)

strong as it was in the vote intention ones, since two of six tests suggest that the national retrospections also encompass personal expectations.

We next consider forces driving the dynamics of Labour Party identification. The set of predictors in the party identification models are similar to those used in the best prime minister models and, once more, we employ the four types of economic evaluations in separate analyses. Preliminary soundings indicate that perceptions of inflation as the most important problem and some political shocks do not have significant effects, and thus we omit these variables and reestimate the models. The analyses show that personal expectation is the only significant subjective economic evaluation and, as expected, its impact on the percentage of

Labour identifiers is negative (Table 5). In contrast, interest rates and perceptions of unemployment have positive influences on the Labour identification share; as rates increase and worries about joblessness grow, the size of Labour partisan cohort swells. Perhaps most noteworthy are the very large effects associated with the currency crisis – its immediate and lagged effects prompted a permanent 11–12% upward movement in Labour partisanship. The party also benefited from the Tories' continuing divisions over Europe, gaining another, permanent, 4+% in its identifier share as a result of the Maastricht crisis. Labour also enjoyed a sizable (3–4%), but temporary, increment in party identifiers as a result of the 1994 local elections and the untimely death of John Smith. Effects associated with the 'Mad Cow' affair also were temporary and positive, but smaller (2+%). Not all of the shocks have had positive influences on Labour partisanship; the party's widely publicized internecine bickering associated with the 'Harriet Hypocrite' affair prompted a temporary drop of 4–5%, and Major's reelection as Tory leader, a 3–4% permanent decrease.

TABLE 5

MODELS OF LABOUR PARTY IDENTIFICATION, 1992:04–1996:08

Models Predictor Variables	PE	PR	NR	NE
Constant	-0.01	0.04	0.04	0.01
Economic Evaluations:				
Personal expectations (*t*)	-0.13c	X	X	X
Personal retrospections (*t*)	X	-0.08	X	X
National retrospections (*t*)	X	X	-0.02	X
National expectations (t)	X	X	X	-0.01
Interest rates (t-2)	1.89c	1.85d	1.79d	1.70d
Most Important Problem:				
Unemployment (*t-1*)	0.13c	0.13c	0.13c	0.13c
Currency crisis (*t*)	7.49a	7.99a	7.93a	8.17a
Currency crisis (*t-3*)	5.20c	4.10d	4.04d	3.93d
Maastricht (*t-1*)	4.40c	4.45c	4.27c	4.20c
Major reselection (*t-1*)	-3.04d	-3.30d	-3.52c	-3.62d
Local elections/Smith (*t*)	3.35c	3.03c	2.93c	2.89d
Harman affair (*t*)	-4.77a	-4.68b	-4.52b	-4.55b
Mad Cow (*t*)	2.56d	2.20d	2.22d	2.23d
Model Diagnostics				
R^2	0.49	0.44	0.44	0.44
Adjusted R^2	0.37	0.31	0.30	0.30
Standard error of estimate	2.29	2.40	2.41	2.41
Durbin-Watson	2.42	2.47	2.48	2.47
General serial correlation	16.16	17.04	17.26	17.65
Functional form	0.24	0.53	0.32	0.39
Normality	1.95	4.54	3.62	4.53
General heteroskedasticity	1.90	1.02	1.26	1.15
ARCH (1)	0.15	0.04	0.05	0.02

Notes: X – variable not included in model ;
(a) – $p \leq 0.001$, (b) – $p \leq 0.01$, (c) – $p \leq 0.05$, (d) – $p \leq 0.10$ (one-tailed test)

Overall, the party identification models confirm the story conveyed visually by Figure 1 – the upward movements in the Labour partisan share in the electorate since the 1992 election have been both sizable and lumpy, with the biggest increases coming in the wake of highly publicized events (especially the currency and Maastricht crises) that severely damaged the credibility of the governing Conservatives in the public mind (Clarke *et al.*, 1997; see also Sanders, 1995). The Labour Party identification models also strengthen the case for the preeminence of personal economic expectations as determinants of party support. Personal prospections are the only type of economic evaluations to achieve statistical significance in these models, and the battery of encompassing tests indicates that the PE model encompasses its three rivals, without being encompassed by them.

The models presented above collectively tell a plausible and intriguing story about the dynamics of Labour support since 1992. The plot is simple and straightforward, focusing on the short- and long-term effects of party identification and party leader evaluations on vote intentions. But it is possible that there are simultaneous causal linkages among these variables. Such simultaneity will bias parameter estimates, making statistical inference unreliable. Stated technically, we need to demonstrate that Labour Party identifications and judgements that the Labour leader would make the best prime minister are weakly exogenous to Labour vote intentions (see Hendry, 1995: 162–4). This means that while these variables contemporaneously influence voting intentions, the latter does not contemporaneously influence them. Such a demonstration provides warrant for our causal inferences.[11]

As Charemza and Deadman (1992: 265–6) observe, the test for weak exogeneity in an error-correction model specification has two steps. In the present context, one must first show that the ECM term is statistically insignificant in the models for best prime minister and Labour Party identification. If weak exogeneity exists and these variables are not contemporaneously influenced by Labour voting intentions, then the coefficient of the error-correction mechanism, which it will be recalled contemporaneously links voting, party identification and prime ministerial popularity, will be zero. If this is not the case, then Labour voting intentions has an immediate impact on party identification and prime ministerial support, which in turn distorts the estimates in Table 3.

An additional requirement for weak exogeneity is to show that the residuals for the Labour Party identification and best prime minister models (with an analysis that omits the ECM term) are insignificant in the model for Labour vote intentions. If they are not, it implies that some unexplained component of both variables is influencing vote intentions, again with the potentiality of biasing the estimates. Empirically, both conditions are met. Testing at the 0.05 level of probability, we find that the t-ratios for the ECM term in the best prime minister and Labour Party identification models are -0.84, and 1.26, respectively. Coefficients for the residuals from these models in the Labour vote intention model have t-ratios of 0.92 and 1.52, respectively. Thus, we conclude that the best prime minister and party identification variables are weakly exogenous to vote intentions and the inferences drawn from our Labour support analyses are justified.

Error-correction Models for New Labour

In recent years, the standard model of macroeconomic effects on aggregate-level party support has been augmented with subjective assessments of national and personal economic circumstances. In this article, we have argued that other variables – party identification and assessments of which party leader would make the best prime minister – also have important effects. These arguments are buttressed by the results of analyses of recently available 1992–96 time-series data on public support for the Labour Party and its leaders. The analyses are conducted using econometric methods for modelling nonstationary, cointegrating variables, and the specification for such models in error-correction form. In addition to revealing the presence of a long-term cointegrating relationship among vote intentions, best prime minister perceptions and party identification, the new time-series data show that the short-term dynamics of Labour Party identification have been substantial. This finding, coupled with other investigations documenting sizable short-run movements in Conservative partisanship in Britain and Democratic and Republican Party identification in the United States, accords well with a conceptualization of party identification as a summary of party performance evaluations. Since these evaluations are updated over time and new evaluations may occasionally strongly contradict earlier ones, voters' partisan attachments are potentially mutable factors in the set of forces governing parties' electoral fortunes.

The dynamics of Labour partisanship also help to account for the changes in the party's vote intention share and public judgements of the Labour leader as making the best prime minister. Other variables have been influential as well. In analyses of Labour vote intentions and Labour Party identification, models incorporating personal economic expectations outperform rival models that utilize other types of economic evaluations. Additionally, although all four types of evaluations have significant influences on best prime minister perceptions, encompassing tests make the case for the superiority of the personal economic prospections model. Individual leaders clearly matter too – the shift to Tony Blair in the summer of 1994 did much to convince people that the leader of the Labour Party would make the best prime minister.

As part of their long campaign to win the 1997 general election, the Conservatives have argued strenuously that voters ought to 'feel good' about the British economy and their personal financial prospects. At the time of writing (1996), however, negative economic assessments have steered many people towards Labour partisanship and convinced them that Tony Blair has the right stuff to be prime minister. The Tories are also conducting a massive advertising blitz to frighten voters into believing that New Labour presents new dangers. As voters take a new look at New Labour and its rivals in the run-up to the election, models of party support that incorporate partisanship, politicians and evaluations, can help to understand what they see and the choices that they will make.

Error-correction Models of Party Support and the 1997 Election: A Brief Postscript

The massive Labour victory in the 1997 general election accords well with the analyses presented above. Our error-correction models give pride of place to party identification and party leader evaluations. Parameter estimates based on January 1992–August 1996 data show that these variables have sizable short- and long-term effects on Labour support. Reestimating the models using data through April 1997 confirms these findings. Together with information about the dynamics of party identification and party leader evaluations, these models enable one to comprehend the key forces propelling New Labour to power.

Our monthly Gallup surveys reveal that in April 1992 John Major enjoyed a wide margin of public approval over his Labour counterpart, Neil Kinnock. At that time 52% thought Mr Major was doing a good job in office, and 43% believed he would make the best prime minister. Kinnock's ratings were only 35% and 25%, respectively. However, Major's leadership advantage subsequently evaporated. In April 1997, only 28% judged he would be the best prime minister, and only 36%, that he was doing a good job. In contrast, Tony Blair's prime ministerial rating was 39%, and his leadership approval score was fully 69%. The Conservatives' partisan base also eroded. Although their cohort of identifiers did rebound as the election approached, in April 1997 it was 32%, 4% less than five years earlier. In contrast, Labour's partisan share rose by 6%, to 40%. Our models indicate that Labour would enjoy substantial electoral benefits if leadership and partisan factors were working in their favour on election day. Similar models for the Conservatives show that they would be in deep trouble if their leader became unpopular and their partisan share dropped (Clarke, Stewart and Whiteley, 1997). When the electorate went to the polls, all of these conditions obtained.

But, what about the economy? In their long campaign, the Tories emphasized that 'Britain was booming'. Many voters evidently agreed; personal economic expectations (the 'feel-good' factor) climbed smartly from -8.6 in December 1996 to +11.0 in April 1997, the latter figure being exactly the same as in April 1992. Such expectations had a significant, negative impact on Labour support. However, the effect was not especially large, perhaps because many people were unconvinced that the Tories should claim credit for the buoyant economy. Opinions about the government's economic acumen had shifted markedly since the last election when 49% judged that the Conservatives were best able to guide the economy, whereas 32% selected Labour. Five years later, the comparable numbers were 38% and 47%, respectively.

Does this mean that economic factors were unimportant in 1997? Our analyses suggest otherwise. The currency crisis came early, but it set the stage for Labour's long march to power. Its impact on party leader evaluations and party identification – key variables in our vote intention models – are abundantly evident. Combined with the Tories' subsequent, suicidal wrangling over the single currency, Black Wednesday markedly diminished confidence in Mr Major and his party, something they could ill afford when confronting an opponent as formidable as Tony Blair-led New Labour. As our election forecast scenarios (based on the error-correction models) presented at the last two EPOP meetings have suggested, this configuration of forces signalled electoral disaster for the Conservatives and a very big win for Labour. Accordingly, we were not at all surprised when Mr Blair and his New Labour legions trounced the Tories.

NOTES

1. Formally, $PID_t = \Sigma\beta_{t-i,k}EVAL_{t-i,k} + \varepsilon_t$, where PID_t is party identification at time t, $EVAL_{t-i,k}$ is a vector of current and past party performance evaluations, and ε_t is $\sim N(0, \sigma^2)$. Viewing party performance evaluations as an infinite distributed lag where the effects of prior ones decline at a geometric rate (λ) leads to a Koyck-type transformation, i.e., $PID_t = \alpha(1-\lambda) + \Sigma\beta_{t,k}EVAL_{t,k} + \lambda PID_{t-1} + v_t$. Empirical analyses of individual-level (BES) data using these types of models in the British context include Alt (1984) and Clarke and Stewart (1984).

2. The authors are the principal investigators of the British party support study that includes the party identification, emotional reaction and other variables. This study spans the January 1992–April 1997 period and is supported by National Science Foundation grant SES-9309018. Stewart is the principal investigator of the project which has continued the administration of the economic evaluation questions. This project covers the September 1995–April 1997 period and is supported by National Science Foundation grant SES-9600018. The fieldwork for both projects is being conducted with Gallup's generosity and Robert Wybrow's assistance. Neither NSF nor Gallup is responsible for the analyses and interpretations of the data presented in this article.

3. Party identification is measured in this article using responses to the first question in the standard BES sequence: 'Generally speaking, do you think of yourself as Conservative, Labour, Liberal Democrat, or what?' The SNP and Plaid Cymru also are mentioned in Scotland and Wales, respectively.

4. In the Gallup surveys, the best prime minister question is: 'Who would make the best Prime Minister, Mr Major, Mr Kinnock/Smith/Blair, or Mr Ashdown?' The vote intention questions are: (a) 'If there were a General Election tomorrow, which party would you support?'; (b) [If 'don't know'] 'Which party would you be most inclined to vote for?' Labour support is calculated as the sum of the percentages of persons responding 'Labour' to (a) or (b). The economic evaluation questions are: (a) 'How do you think the financial situation of your household will change over the next 12 months?' (personal prospections); (b) 'How does the financial situation of your household now compare with what it was 12 months ago?' (personal retrospections); (c) 'How do you think the general economic situation in this country will develop over the next 12 months?' (national prospections); (d) 'How do you think the general economic situation in this country has changed over the last 12 months?' (national retrospections). The response categories for these questions are: 'get a lot better', 'get a little better', 'stay the same', 'get a little worse', 'get a lot worse'. The economic evaluation variables are constructed by subtracting the percentage offering negative responses from the percentage offering positive ones.

5. If a variable has a unit root then an autoregression, in which contemporary values are modelled on past values, produces an autoregressive coefficient of 1.0. That is, in the model $z_t = \phi z_{t-1} + ut$, $\phi = 1.0$, which implies that an external shock which impacts the series at a given point of time will continue to influence the series indefinitely into the future. Clearly, if this is true the series will not return to a constant mean value if it is shocked in this way, which implies that it is nonstationary. More technically, a time series is (weakly) stationary if its mean and variance are time invariant, that is, $E(x_t) = \mu$ and $E(x^2_t) = \sigma^2$ for all t, and its autocovariances $E(x_{t-i}-\mu, x_{t-j}-\mu)(I \neq j)$ depend only on the length of the time lag, k, separating I and j (see Mills, 1991: 64–5). A stationary variable is said to be integrated of order zero ($I(0)$), whereas a nonstationary series which can be rendered stationary by differencing once is said to be integrated of order one (I(1)). The difference operator Δ, means: $\Delta X_t = X_t - X_{t-1}$. Note that, although Dickey-Fuller unit-root tests involve familiar t-ratio test statistics, the critical values for these tests are nonstandard. See, for example, Harris (1995: 28–9).

6. Like unit-root tests, the critical values for cointegration tests are nonstandard. However, the two sets of critical values differ. See, for example, Muscatelli and Hurn (1995: 176).

7. When one is analysing three or more variables, there is a possibility of multiple cointegrating vectors. Johansen procedures may be used to test for the number of cointegrating vectors. A good description of these procedures is Harris (1995: ch. 5).

8. The standard deviations (σ) for Labour vote intentions, perceptions of the Labour leader as making the best prime minister and Labour Party identification are 5.97, 7.04 and 3.90, respectively.

9. For a non-technical discussion of the Engle and Yoo procedure, see Harris (1995: 56).

10. Exhaustive diagnostic testing is one of the hallmarks of the LSE approach to econometric modelling. For a discussion of such tests and a guide to relevant literature, see McAleer (1995). See also Hendry (1995).

11. A variable X_t is weakly exogenous to another variable Y_t if the latter affects the former only with a lag of one or more periods (for example, Charemza and Deadman, 1992: ch. 7). If Y_t does not affect X_t either contemporaneously or with a lag, that is, if there is both weak exogeneity and Granger noncausality, then one can say that X_t is strongly exogenous to Y_t. Strong exogeneity is not required for inferences about the impact of Xt on Y_t.

BIBLIOGRAPHY

Abramson, Paul R. and Charles W. Ostrom (1991) 'Macropartisanship: An Empirical Assessment', *American Political Science Review* 85: 181–92.

Alogoskoufis, George and Ron Smith (1995) 'On Error Correction Models: Specification, Interpretation, Estimation', in Les Oxley, Donald A. R. George, Colin J. Roberts and Stuart Sayer (eds) *Surveys in Econometrics*, pp.139–70. Oxford: Basil Blackwell.

Alt, James E. (1984) 'Dealignment and the Dynamics of Partisanship in Britain', in Paul Allen Beck, Russell Dalton and Scott Flanagan (eds) *Electoral Change in Advanced Industrial*

Societies, pp.298–329. Princeton: Princeton University Press.

Beck, Nathaniel (1992) 'Comparing Dynamic Specifications: The Case of Presidential Approval', in James A. Stimson (ed) *Political Analysis*, volume 3, pp.51–88. Ann Arbor: University of Michigan Press.

Bishop, George F. *et al.* (1994) 'Question Form and Context Effects in the Measurement of Partisanship: Experimental Tests of the Artifact Hypothesis', *American Political Science Review* 88: 945–58.

Box-Steffensmeier, Janet M. and Renée Smith (1996) 'The Dynamics of Aggregate Partisanship', *American Political Science Review* 90: 567–80.

Budge, Ian, Ivor Crewe and Dennis Farlie (eds) (1976) *Party Identification and Beyond: Representations of Voting and Party Competition*. New York: John Wiley & Sons.

Butler, David and Donald E. Stokes (1976) *Political Change in Britain*, second college edition. New York: St. Martin's Press.

Campbell, Angus, Philip E. Converse, Warren E. Miller and Donald E. Stokes (1960) *The American Voter*. New York: John Wiley & Sons.

Charemza, Wojciech W. and Derek F. Deadman (1992) *New Directions in Econometric Practice*. Aldershot: Edward Elgar.

Clarke, Harold D. and Marianne C. Stewart (1984) 'Dealignment of Degree: Partisan Change in Britain, 1974–83', *Journal of Politics* 46: 689–718.

Clarke, Harold D. and Marianne C. Stewart (1995) 'Economic Evaluations, Prime Ministerial Approval and Governing Party Support: Rival Models Reconsidered', *British Journal of Political Science* 25: 597–622.

Clarke, Harold D., Marianne C. Stewart and Paul Whiteley (1997) 'Tory Trends: Party Identification and the Dynamics of Conservative Support Since 1992', *British Journal of Political Science* 27: forthcoming.

Clarke, Harold D. and Motoshi Suzuki (1994) 'Partisan Dealignment and the Dynamics of Independence in the American Electorate, 1953–88', *British Journal of Political Science* 24: 57–78.

Clarke, Harold D. and Paul F. Whiteley (1990) 'Perceptions of Macroeconomic Performance, Government Support and Conservative Party Strategy 1983–1987', *European Journal of Political Research* 18: 97–120.

Crewe, Ivor (1985) 'How to Win a Landslide Without Really Trying: Why the Conservatives Won in 1983', in Austin Ranney (ed.) *Britain at the Polls 1983*, pp.155–96. Durham, NC: Duke University Press.

Crewe, Ivor (1986) 'On the Death and Resurrection of Class Voting: Some Comments on *How Britain Votes*', *Political Studies* 35: 620–38.

Crewe, Ivor and Anthony King (1994) 'Did Major Win? Did Kinnock Lose?: Leadership Effects in the 1992 British General Election', in Anthony Heath, Roger Jowell and John Curtice (eds) *Labour's Last Chance? The 1992 Election and Beyond*, pp.125–48. Aldershot: Dartmouth.

Crewe, Ivor, Bo Sarlvik and James E. Alt (1977) 'Partisan Dealignment in Britain, 1964–1974', *British Journal of Political Science* 7: 129–90.

Dunleavy, Patrick and Christopher T. Husbands (1985) *British Democracy at the Crossroads: Voting and Party Competition in the 1980s*. London: Allen & Unwin.

Engle, Robert F. and Clive W. J. Granger (1987) 'Co-integration and Error Correction: Representation, Estimation and Testing', *Econometrica* 55: 251–76.

Engle, Robert F. and Sam Yoo (1991) 'Cointegrated Economic Time Series: An Overview with New Results', in Robert F. Engle and Clive W.J. Granger (eds) *Long-Run Economic Relationships*, pp.237–66. Oxford: Oxford University Press.

Fiorina, Morris P. (1981) *Retrospective Voting in American National Elections*. New Haven: Yale University Press.

Franklin, Charles H. (1992) 'Measurement and the Dynamics of Party Identification', *Political Behavior* 14: 297–310.

Goodhart, Charles A. and R.J. Bhansali (1970) 'Political Economy', *Political Studies* 18: 43–106.

Granger, Clive W.J. and Paul Newbold (1974) 'Spurious Regressions in Econometrics', *Journal of Econometrics* 2: 111–20.

Granger, Clive W.J. and P. Newbold (1986) *Forecasting Economic Time Series* (2nd edition). Orlando: Academic Press.

Harris, Richard (1995) *Cointegration Analysis in Econometric Modelling*. London: Harvester Wheatsheaf.

Heath, Anthony, Roger Jowell and John Curtice (eds) (1985) *How Britain Votes*. Oxford: Pergamon Press.

Heath, Anthony, Roger Jowell and John Curtice (eds) (1994) *Labour's Last Chance? The 1992 Election and Beyond*. Aldershot: Dartmouth.

Heath, Anthony and Sarah-K. MacDonald (1988) 'The Demise of Party Identification Theory?', *Electoral Studies* 7: 95–108.

Heath, Anthony and Roy Pierce (1992) 'It was Party Identification all Along: Question Order Effects on Reports of Party Identification in Britain', *Electoral Studies* 11: 93–105.

Heath, Anthony, John Curtice, Geoff Evans, Julie Field and Sharon Witherspoon (eds) (1991) *Understanding Political Change: The British Voter 1964–1987*. Oxford: Pergamon Press.

Hendry, David (1980) 'Econometrics – Alchemy or Science?', *Economica* 47: 387–406.

Hendry, David (1995) *Dynamic Econometrics*. Oxford: Oxford University Press.

Keynes, John Maynard (1939) 'Professor Tinbergen's Method', *Economic Journal* 44: 558–68.

Lewis-Beck, Michael S. (1988) *Economics and Elections: The Major Western Democracies*. Ann Arbor: University of Michigan Press.

MacKuen, Michael B., Robert S. Erikson and James A. Stimson (1989) 'Macropartisanship', *American Political Science Review* 83: 1125–42.

MacKuen, Michael B., Robert S. Erikson and James A. Stimson (1992) 'Controversy: Question Wording and Macropartisanship', *American Political Science Review* 86: 475–86.

McAleer, Michael (1995) 'Sherlock Holmes and the Search for Truth: A Diagnostic Tale', in Les Oxley, Donald A. R. George, Colin J. Roberts and Stuart Sayer (eds) *Surveys in Econometrics*, pp.91–138. Oxford: Basil Blackwell.

Miller, William L. (1989) 'Studying How the Economy Affects Public Attitudes and Behavior: Problems and Prospect', in Harold D. Clarke, Marianne C. Stewart and Gary Zuk (eds) *Economic Decline and Political Change: Canada, Great Britain, the United States*, pp.143–72. Pittsburgh: University of Pittsburgh Press.

Miller, William L., Harold D. Clarke, Martin Harrop, Lawrence LeDuc and Paul F. Whiteley (1990) *How Voters Change: The 1987 British Election Campaign in Perspective*. Oxford: Oxford University Press.

Mills, Terence C. (1991) *Time Series Techniques for Economists*. Cambridge: Cambridge University Press.

Muscatelli, Vito Antonio and Stan Hurn (1995) 'Econometric Modelling using Cointegrated Time Series', in Les Oxley, Donald A. R. George, Colin J. Roberts and Stuart Sayer (eds) *Surveys in Econometrics*, pp.171–214. Oxford: Basil Blackwell.

Nadeau, Richard, Richard G. Niemi and Timothy Amato (1994) 'Expectations and Preferences in British General Elections', *American Political Science Review* 88: 371–83.

Nadeau, Richard, Richard G. Niemi and Timothy Amato (1996) 'Prospective and Comparative or Retrospective and Individual? Party Leaders and Party Support in Great Britain', *British Journal of Political Science* 26: 245–58.

Norpoth, Helmut (1992) *Confidence Regained: Economics, Mrs. Thatcher, and the British Voter*. Ann Arbor: University of Michigan Press.

Rose, Richard and Ian McAllister (1990) *The Loyalties of Voters: A Lifetime Learning Model*. London: Sage Publications.

Sanders, David (1991) 'Government Popularity and the Next General Election', *Political Quarterly* 62: 235–61.

Sanders, David (1993) 'Why the Conservatives Won – Again', in Anthony King *et al.*, *Britain at the Polls 1992*, pp.171–222. Chatham, NJ: Chatham House Publishers.

Sanders, David (1995) 'The Economy and Support for the Conservative Party, 1979–96', paper presented at the Annual Conference of the Political Studies Association, University of York, 18–20 April.

Sanders, David, David Marsh and Hugh Ward (1993) 'The Electoral Impact of Press Coverage of the British Economy, 1979–87', *British Journal of Political Science* 23: 175–210.

Sargan, David (1964) 'Wages and Prices in the United Kingdom: A Study in Econometric Methodology', Reprinted in David Hendry and K. Wallis (eds) *Econometrics and Quantitative Economics*, pp.275–314. Oxford: Basil Blackwell, 1984.

Sarlvik, Bo and Ivor Crewe (1983) *Decade of Dealignment: The Conservative Victory of 1979 and Electoral Trends in the 1970s.* Cambridge: Cambridge University Press.

Stewart, Marianne C. and Harold D. Clarke (1992) 'The (Un)Importance of Party Leaders: Leader Images and Party Choice in the 1987 British Election', *Journal of Politics* 54: 447–70.

Whiteley, Paul F. (1984) 'Macroeconomic Performance and Government Popularity in Britain – the Short Run Dynamics', *European Journal of Political Research* 14: 45–61.

Yule, George Udny (1926) 'Why Do We Sometimes Get Nonsense-Correlations between Time Series', *Journal of the Royal Statistical Society.* 89: 1–64.

The Enhancement of Leadership Power: The Labour Party and the Impact of Political Communications

Richard Heffernan and James Stanyer

The Centrality of Party and Leadership in the Deployment of Political Communications Strategies

Although political communications are 'notoriously difficult to define with any precision' (McNair, 1995: 3) one broad working definition offered by Wolton (1990: 12), 'as the space in which contradictory discourse is exchanged between three actors with the legitimate right to express themselves in public on politics, namely politicians, journalists and public opinion by means of opinion polls' is a useful starting point. This illustrates the fact that politicians and media coincide in the construction of political communications. The media are the primary medium to which party strategies are directed while the activities of the politicians are public events of natural interest to the media.

Political actors increasingly address potential audiences through broadcast media and print journalism and political communications have significant consequences for the modern political party. A number of these are well attested: the establishment of a unified corporate party identity to control the way in which the party is perceived and the manner in which its appeal is evaluated; the importance of promoting a positive image in packaging the party as a product to be marketed and sold in electoral competition; the acceptance that the party leader is the primary feature of the identity of the party. The projection of the leader places him or her as the integral part of the overall promotion of the party (Harrop, 1990; Franklin, 1994; Scammell, 1995; Kavanagh, 1995).

From the perspective of the party the difference between political marketing and public relations must be established (McNair 1995: 6–7). Political marketing involves the long-term promotion of the party as product and need not necessarily involve the day-to-day media strategy which links the party to the outside world. Here, public relations forms of political communications enable parties to communicate with audiences through the news media by managing its broadcast and print journalist profile. The 'product' when 'packaged' has to be 'sold'; criticism of the 'product' has to be responded to rapidly. Political marketing allows the party to position itself in a political marketplace but public relations strategies enable parties to 'sell' their message and control its interpretation.

Public relations-based political communications result from a symbiotic association between political actors and media practitioners against the background of social, political and economic events. This interaction constructs political messages that promote and so help shape the public identity of the political party (these messages being subsequently decoded by the audiences to which they are addressed). Research into media and politics is often confined to media impacts upon the political preferences and electoral behaviour of citizens. Media does not simply affect what electors think and how they act but impacts upon what parties think about and how they act. Political communications and media impacts in general do not just concern the consumer side (the electors) of political activity but also affects the producer side (the parties); it affects what parties do, not just how voters act. Political communications are for the most part producer-led through the interaction of political actors and media practitioners. Public relations therefore involve parties in strategies to influence media reportage by attempting to regulate this interaction in their favour: an analysis of its influence focuses on the production of political outputs (the sender and carrier) rather than on the consumption of those outputs (the recipient).

Public relations strategies lie at the heart of electioneering efforts and certain producers (the leadership rather than the wider party) have advantages conferred upon them. The ability to influence political communications by the control of the media strategy deployed by the party is a tool in the hands of the leadership, a consequence of the centrality of the media in contemporary politics. Parties are therefore involved in producing the message they wish to promote at the same time as they attempt to control the manner in which it is presented by the media (and ultimately consumed by the identified audience). The supposed presidentialization of British politics is a (not so new) phenomena which has attracted much comment. The personification (if not the presidentialization) of politics has greatly encouraged this tendency and taken it to even greater heights than previously envisaged. The media access political actors enjoy and the control they can exercise over the party media strategy is highly dependent upon their location within the internal hierarchy. As Franklin (1994: 21) suggests, politicians have differential relations with the media and a prime minister or leader of the opposition, 'enjoys high status, considerable prestige and their published and broadcast comments are vested with an authority that reflects their office.' While media scrutiny focus public attention on leaders, this scrutiny also encourages political leaders to focus public attention on themselves. It is not so much that party leaders have the spotlight shone on them that they come to greater prominence; rather they come to greater prominence because they covet the attention of the spotlight. They do not simply bask in this public searchlight but use it aggressively for their own particular ends.

Public relations strategies impact upon party organization and its internal power structures. This is reflected in: the increasing control of the party hierarchy over the communications strategy employed; the increasing deployment of public relations strategies by this hierarchy to use presentation strategies to manipulate the party through the media to their own advantage; the encouragement of a growing professionalization on the part of this hierarchy (the use of electoral professional techniques rather than the employment of autonomous electoral professionals) to present the party to a wide range of potential audiences. In exploring this phenomena research should: narrate the process by which public relations strategies are formed to uncover; the purpose which lies behind them; the ends they serve; and, perhaps more importantly, the consequences they have for media and politics and the internal workings of the political party. The party's communications strategies enable a party élite to project a 'party identity' through the news media by attempting to 'manage' the party's journalist profile. Where media impacts in general affect what parties do and how voters react, distinguishing the impact of media on parties as 'producers' in addition to its effects of electors as 'consumers' is important in understanding and explaining the chronology, causes and, in terms of the internal workings of political parties, the consequences of political communications.

A Model of the Labour Elite

Modern political communications (both political marketing and public relations strategies) empower the party hierarchy over other party actors. Party leaders tend inevitably to devote themselves to consolidating their own positions of power; defending the party apparatus and maintaining this authority is therefore one lodestone of success (Michels, 1962). While the party may successfully impose some restrictions upon the leadership (their right to rebel, the leader's obligation to listen, to encourage followers and accept a meaningful veto exercised by a powerful player) the opportunities for non-leadership groups to exercise influence are heavily circumscribed within the contemporary political process.

Labour, as with most contemporary political parties, is effectively run by a small, tightly knit caucus or insider group, operating at and around the apex of the apparatus. Here, although subject to a number of constraints, the selection of policy and strategy is increasingly dominated by the party leadership. As a result, in combination with the centrality of political leaders within the contemporary political process, a modern Labour leader can enjoy significant opportunities to attempt to lead their party from the front in an manner of their own choosing. Final authority rests not merely with the parliamentary party but, more crucially, its parliamentary leadership (McKenzie, 1964).

In recent years the freedom of action of nominally autonomous Labour Party bodies such as the Shadow Cabinet, the National Executive Committee (NEC) and the annual party conference has been limited. Although *de facto* power was divested from these existing political institutions it was handed over by other political 'players' (members of the NEC and the Shadow Cabinet, power-broking trade union leaders at party conference) they chose to invest the leadership with the authority it demanded. Under Neil Kinnock and Tony Blair, theoretically sovereign institutions have ceded many of their powers and responsibilities as greater powers have been granted a core élite comprising the leader, his private office, trusted campaign professionals and those members of Labour's front bench considered by the leadership (to coin a phrase) to be 'one of us' (Shaw 1994; Heffernan and Marqusee, 1992; see also Kinnock, 1994; Smith, 1994).

A contemporary model of the organizational component structure of the Labour Party comprises six key elements: the Inner Core Elite comprising: the leader and his immediate entourage; personal advisers; and leadership insiders and selected members of the front bench, the NEC and party officials; the Outer Core Elite comprising: the Shadow Cabinet; other front bench spokespersons; the NEC; a Peripheral Elite comprising: the Parliamentary Party (backbench Labour MPs); party officials; External Power Brokers comprising: trade union élites; organized activists; Unorganized Activists; and Inactive Members and Supporters. This structure may be illustrated as a series of concentric circles at the heart of which lies the Inner Core Elite. It is a representation of power from the centre to the periphery; the closer to the centre the more powerful and influential the player. The Inner Core Elite is more inclusive than 'the leadership' and wider than 'the leader's office'. It comprises an extended court of chosen and favoured insiders, confidents, aides and advisers. Here lies the locum of power within the Labour Party. These components, while usually stable over time, are not fixed and unchanging but subject to fluctuations in membership.

The relationship of each party component to another is important in understanding the dynamic that underpins the party as an organization. Internal power structures determine who decides what the party does. The importance of leaders cannot be understated but must be qualified by the role that intra-party power relationships play in determining the location of authority. The leadership does not automatically have its own way. Its powers are necessarily constrained often by circumstance and its authority subject to the interaction that takes place between the Inner Core Elite, the Outer Core Elite and (to a lesser extent) the Peripheral Elite. The particular strength of the Inner Core Elite is dependent upon its ability to dominate other components of the party, an objective attained by the assertion of central executive authority and/or the construction of a internal party coalition that is supportive of the leadership.

As Labour leader since 1994, Tony Blair uses his authority as a potential prime minister to dominate his party and he is, as was his predecessor Neil Kinnock, quick to take every opportunity to convert such authority into executive power. The Blairite élite has regularly employed the media to map out Labour strategy in a remarkably successful attempt to determine their party's agenda (as is illustrated by the effective use of public relations and a political marketing strategy to essentially rename the party with the addition of the prefix New to the title Labour). These initiatives are organized around Blair as an individual and often take the form of public speeches and press statements and are intended to raise the public profile of the party and to present policy drawn up by the Inner Core Elite. These 'public events' (public speeches; media interviews; press releases and press conferences) help to set Labour's internal agenda and place the party leader at centre stage. Principal occasions in 1995–96 when Blair pursued this objective include speeches to the annual conference in October 1994; the Scottish Labour Party in March 1995; the Clause Four conference in April 1995; Labour's annual conference in October 1995; the Mais lecture at City University in May 1995; and speeches to News Corporation Leadership conference in July 1995; the CBI in November 1995; on the stakeholder society in Singapore in January 1996; to the British–US Chamber of Commerce in New York in April 1996.

In 'leading from the front', other elements of the party hierarchy (the Outer Core Elite, the Peripheral Elite, and External Power Brokers) to say nothing of Activists, Inactive Members and Supporters are all part of the audience the further away from the centre they are located. Blair is of course the beneficiary of historical developments. The emergence of an powerful executive leadership combines with 'the professionalization of campaigning' to provide a series of opportunities for the leadership to agenda set within the party. As Kavanagh (1995: 108) suggests: 'centralization of decision making and the adoption of public relations are interconnected.'

Identifying Labour's 'Strategic Community'

Recent developments witness the emergence of a new professional strata within the political party, one composed of a cadre of organizers versed in the techniques of political marketing and public relations strategies and accountable to the party leader. In the case of the Labour Party, 'the leader's office now houses an unprecedented proliferation of aides, assistants and advisers, with an overview of, and involvement in, all aspects of party activity' (Minkin, 1992: 630). Under first Kinnock and then Blair this 'executive office' forms the centre of the 'strategic community' (Shaw, 1994: 57), a grouping of 'campaign professionals' which work for the leadership (and not necessarily the party) in the form of the Inner Core Elite (Heffernan and Marqusee, 1992).

The emergence of this powerful strategy making community is the product of three factors which arose from Neil Kinnock's efforts to remake Labour in order to achieve freedom of manoeuvre for the party leadership: the creation of Labour's Campaigns and Communications Directorate under Peter Mandelson in 1985–90; the construction of the Shadow Communications Agency in 1985 and its post-1992 successors under Philip Gould and Mandelson; and, more significantly, the post-1983 expansion of the leader's office. The Communications Directorate and the Shadow Communications Agency were immediately drawn into an extended apparatus exclusively available to the party leader. Together these formal institutions and *ad hoc* groupings formed an interlocking network at the centre of which lay the party leader, the apex of a new emergent power structure, one that has been further entrenched in the wake of Tony Blair's succession to John Smith. While Labour's present media strategy is largely similar (if more powerful in scale) to that enacted in the key period of the Kinnock years during 1986 to 1990 (Heffernan and Marqusee, 1992), Blair has placed the projection of his party and himself in the media at the top of his agenda. He is determined to control the construction and dissemination of Labour's message as far as is practicable.

Some twenty individuals officially work in Blair's private office and five have responsibility for media liaison under the direction of Blair's Press Secretary, Alistair Campbell. Wider media operations (as co-ordinated from Blair's office) are enacted by personnel at Millbank, the party's new £2 million, 20,000 sq ft media centre under the direction of Labour Chief Election Strategist, Peter Mandelson and probably the figure with the most influence over the Labour leader. Blair's recent appointment of Mandelson as Chief Election Strategist testifies to the influence and significance of the 'strategic community'. This post subsumes that of director of campaigns and communications and is now, in the opinion of one senior Labour official, the equivalent of Chairman of the Conservative Party. Mandelson's occupancy of this key post despite the fact that he is neither a member of the Shadow Cabinet nor on the National Executive illustrates the power granted to key insiders within Labour's Inner Core Elite.

'Media advisers' (in essence leadership insiders) are an integral resource of the Inner Core Elite. Advertising agencies, public relations advisers,

pollsters and other technical experts all work to members of the party's Inner
Core Elite. Philip Gould is known as Blair's media adviser just as Maurice
Saatchi and Tim Bell were Thatcher's media advisers in 1987 and 1983 as was
Gordon Reece in 1979. They are part of an informal network which in essence
is the 'efficient' (as opposed to the 'dignified') part of Labour's constitution.
The so-called Gould Memorandum leaked to *Guardian* journalist Seamus
Milne in September 1995 is a striking illustration of the workings of the
'strategic community' (as distinct from media professionals) at the heart of
the Inner Core Elite. This private document, written by Blair's
communications adviser Philip Gould (former head of the Shadow
Communications Agency under Kinnock), called for a 'unitary command
structure leading directly to the party leader' which would install the leader as
'sole ultimate source of campaigning authority' heading up a 'cohesive,
integrated political party sharing the same political ideology' (*The Guardian*
12 September 1995).

Recommending that an 'operations/ war room should be established in the
leader's office... [which] should be the heart of our campaigning' the
document revealed that Jonathan Powell, head of Blair's Private Office,
should have responsibility for co-ordinating Labour's message: Alastair
Campbell should take the lead in disseminating the message; Joy Johnson,
then Labour's head of campaigns and communications, should have the task
of rebutting negative stories: and that Peter Mandelson be given charge of
implementing the overall *strategy* (*The Guardian* 12 September 1995).
Despite protests to the contrary at the time of the publication of the document
it would seem that these recommendations (save that of Johnson who has
departed the employ of the party) have all been acted upon according to a
number of Labour sources. One Labour frontbencher claimed that the
document illustrated the determination of the leadership to create a
centralized command structure: 'The conference, the NEC, and even the
parliamentary party are not even mentioned. What is being created is a small
group of unelected and unaccountable personnel around the leader
responsible for taking all decisions' (*The Guardian* 12 September 1995).

The process of organizational change has been documented by Panebianco
(1988) who presents a model of the 'electoral-professional' party. The
privileges (or otherwise) conferred upon political insiders is underlined by the
experience of a number of party officials in the recent past. Of the four heads
of Labour's Campaigns and Communications Directorate, Peter Mandelson,
John Underwood, David Hill and Joy Johnson, two – Underwood in June
1991 and Johnson in January 1996 – resigned the party's employ because they
did not enjoy the confidence of the leadership, although both were media
professionals who met the criteria established by Panebianco. Andrew Grice
of *The Sunday Times* wrote that the resignation of Joy Johnson was 'the

perfect illustration of how ruthlessly Blair's exclusion zone works: [she] fought with his key aides, Peter Mandelson and Alistair Campbell, and lost' (*The Sunday Times* 28 January 1996). Johnson effectively had the job she was appointed to reallocated to others (in essence Mandelson). An established media professional with considerable experience in television news production, Johnson, as competent an 'electoral-professional' as can be suggested by Panebianco's definition, was not given membership of the Inner Core Elite (neither had Underwood at the time of his resignation). Her influence over communications strategy was countermanded by others close to the leadership and, despite her official job description and the responsibility placed in her by the National Executive, Johnson found herself on the outside looking in. It is therefore the centrality of 'electoral-professionalism' as a method not necessarily 'electoral professionals' as an identifiable party grouping that explains the workings of the Labour élite. Access to the Inner Core Elite is not automatically granted the 'electoral-professional' however talented they may be (as a reading of Panebianco suggests). As one Labour insider suggests; the price of admission to the Blair circle is loyalty and total subservience, not just talent and professionalism. The individual wrongly identified as Labour's most important 'electoral-professional', Peter Mandelson, is first and foremost a politician, one working to the party leader, and emphatically not a media professional. Much of the comment on Mandelson makes a lot of his brief stint as a television producer on LWT's *Weekend World,* yet this role (or on another political magazine programme) calls for a degree of political expertise rather than media expertise; one has to know one's way around Whitehall, Westminster and the political parties rather than be familiar with the media.

'Electoral-professionalism' in the form of leadership insiders is a resource through which leaders enhance their power. Public relations political communication strengthens the party centre at the expense of the periphery. Pulling the party into line is one such feature. 'Unattributable briefings' by a 'close supporter', 'senior aide' or 'spokesperson' of the party leader delivered on a lobby basis are stock in trade of the spin doctor, the source of information about the thinking and opinions of the party élite. Using the media to control the party is an established art as perfected by Thatcher's Press Secretary Bernard Ingham. Cabinet Ministers such as Francis Pym, John Biffen, Geoffrey Howe and Michael Heseltine all felt the weight of prime ministerial disapproval conveyed to them over the airwaves and in their morning newspaper (Harris, 1991; Franklin, 1994). This process, one of bringing the Peripheral Elite to heel, has a Labour track record testified to, among many others, by Clare Short and John Prescott who have gone on record to suggest that people around Neil Kinnock had misused the media to attack and undermine senior figures of the party (such as Michael Meacher, Bryan Gould and John Prescott) with whom they were displeased. The use of public relations strategies to control political actors was tellingly illustrated in the leadership's reaction to Clare Short's suggestion in April 1996 that higher earners on her level of income should contribute more under a fairer tax system. Because Blair has abandoned Labour's commitment to raising tax thresholds journalists were told that Short had been 'infelicitous, unprofessional and incompetent' (*The Guardian* 16 April 1996). A similar anonymous charge was levelled against the TGWU General Secretary, Bill Morris, who was described in March 1995 by a 'leadership source' as being 'confused, muddled and pusillanimous' in wishing to retain the old Clause IV (Jones 1996: 185–6). The leadership could have suggested that Short's position on taxation was a 'personal opinion' and emphasized Labour's fiscal position. Instead strategists deliberately generated the issue into a major news story in order to publicly reprimand a member of the Shadow Cabinet and warn other members against stepping out of line, so limiting the autonomy of other Labour actors who held similar views. This process may occasionally work more than one way: news media reportage of political events may also enable peripheral élite actors to bring pressure to bear upon the Inner Core Elite in the case of, say, a frontbench or a backbench MP using the lobby to send a message to their party leadership.

The power of Labour's spin doctors has attracted much comment and criticism of their role has become almost a political pastime. Former deputy leader Roy Hattersley has launched a series of scathing attacks on Blair's spin-doctor-in-chief: 'The obvious example [of a spin doctor who has assumed a life of their own] is Peter Mandelson who seems to be in the paper far too often, who seems to be on television far too often, who seems to take himself, and be taken, far more seriously than I think is appropriate' (*The Guardian* 19 August 1996). Much of this criticism misconstrues senior spin doctors as media functionaries rather than the integral actors they are. Labour's 'chief election strategist' is no run-of-the-mill political communicator. Mandelson's centrality within the party derives entirely from his close personal association with the Labour leader and his membership of the Blairite inner circle; his prominence is a reflection of that fact and not his reputation as a spin doctor. One former BBC correspondent, Steve Richards, suggests that 'senior [Labour] spin doctors see themselves as much more powerful than most Shadow Cabinet members' (*The Guardian* May 8 1995). This may be because senior advisers within the Core Elite (through Blair) do have more power. Peter Mandelson, taking up his appointment as Labour's Communication supremo in 1985, defined his role as 'deciding what we say, how we say it, and which spokespersons and women we choose to say it' (*The Guardian* 25 November 1985). The ability to do so derives almost exclusively from the exercise of the prerogatives of the party leader.

Spin doctors are courtiers who serve leaders rather then the party. Many observers commonly underestimate the role that members of the Inner Core Elite play in the making of Labour strategy. Hattersley mistakenly suggests that, 'the people who have the responsibility of advancing the ideas are becoming more important, at least in their own mind, than the people who worked out the ideas in the first place' (*The Guardian* 19 August 1996). In reality there is often no distinction between those who have the responsibility of advancing ideas and those who work out the ideas. Labour's spin doctors have not taken on 'a life of their own' as Hattersley protests because no clear distinction between policy formation and policy representation exists. Within Labour's Inner Core Elite both Mandelson and (to a lesser extent) Alistair Campbell are not mere functional advisers but key political deciders. As part of the leader's inner circle they have both the power and the *de facto* authority to influence policy just as much as they have the task of publicly advocating that policy. The term 'spin doctor' is in many ways a misnomer: the ability of senior advisers (as opposed to functionary press officers) to discharge the functions of media spokesperson/ intermediary and to co-ordinate information (to say nothing of the task of advising on media strategy) confers very real powers.

Articulating Public Relations Media Strategies

Within communications literature authors divide media strategies into a series of dualities: promotion and restriction (Franklin, 1994), offensive and defensive (Ericson *et al..,* 1989), publicity and secrecy (Tunstall, 1970) and promotion and avoidance of risk (Schlesinger and Tumber ,1994). These strategies reflect the fact that parties have to minimize the impact of negative publicity at the same time as they positively promote themselves. As such the Labour Inner Core Elite seeks to exercise some 'control' over the media environment at the same time as the 'control' of other actors on this environment is restricted.

Labour's 'strategic community' attempts to act as 'news producer' to influence (if not determine) the media profile of the party. It encourages reportage that is considered desirable at the same time as it discourages that which is undesirable. Public relations strategies involve parties in news management and production (a very separate function from the marketing of an organization or product). As such they can be involved in news generation through one (or more) of three general ways: the provision of news items and issues; the regulation of the interpretation of such items and issues; and the management of the consumption of these items and issues.

This media strategy relates to the entire range of the public work of the party although a news-led strategy and party centric strategy can be distinguished. The Inner Core Elite is keen to showcase itself, jealous of its privileges, and keen to 'command' the news agenda by producing news rather than responding to it. This distinction is all too often a source of contention within the Inner Core Elite and the strategic community which works to it. Here, policy advocacy (or criticism of an opponent) is managed and presented to ensure 'maximum exposure on a continuous basis' (Jones, 1996: 126). Two distinctive types of public relations media strategies can be identified: Proactive Public Relations Strategies which involve the party actively initiating an event and producing a news story; while Reactive Public Relations Strategies are deployed in response to an issue or event not of the party's own making, one uninitiated by the leadership but to which it is obliged to react (McNair, 1995).

The starting point for a proactive strategy is the provision of primary news information to initiate a story or reinforce existing stories. Once news has been initiated the aim of the proactive strategy is to maximize the publicity it receives by trailing extracts of a speech or a policy launch prior to its delivery; designing a news event; and promoting a series of post-event initiatives (follow-up speeches and media interviews) to maintain the momentum of a story. The objective is to lengthen the media issue attention cycle. Labour's media strategy involves four distinctive types of proactive activity (although some have been applied with greater success than others): Trailing, Presentation, Follow-Up, and Maintaining Momentum.

Where a proactive strategy maximizes good publicity, reactive strategies are designed to minimize bad publicity. Reactive strategies are much more difficult to pull off because the Inner Core Elite have no way of predicting what unfavourable things will happen to them and how news media will report it. The deployment of reactive strategies to unfavourable news items is an essential response to an unfavourable news story originating outside of the Inner Core Elite. Essentially this involves a damage limitation exercise, its aim to kill off or otherwise reduce the life expectancy of the attention cycle of an unfavourable news story that casts the party in an non-advantageous position. The objective of the 'strategic community' is to react to such situations as and when they arise to diffuse a situation by utilizing the resources of the Inner Core Elite to maximum advantage. Here, the Inner Core Elite has to choose between non-intervention and intervention. All too often the initial response is one of panic followed by the hope that the issue will fizzle out if left to its own devices. If the party is forced to engage with the story the agreed 'line' is carefully made public. As an exercise in damage limitation attempts are made to persuade journalists to report the strategists' interpretation of events in a effort to damp down the story. A reactive strategy depends upon speed, the quicker the reaction the better. An analysis of Labour's media strategy uncovers four distinctive types of reactive activity to protect the Elite: Selective Intervention Damage Limitation, Actively Mobilizing Comment, Repudiation, and Opportunity Seeking.

Proactive and reactive media strategies are mechanical, almost automatic, and usually routine and standardized. Coverage is usually guaranteed and, should the occasion demand, often substantial. This involves 'spinning' in which journalists are briefed and provided with a plethora of information about the event in question. Press officers pound the telephone and endlessly parrot the line to any available political journalist. Targeting journalists as well as tailoring the message is a feature of both proactive and reactive strategies. Senior officials contact journalists at major news organizations to reinforce the established line. The 'strategic community' target favoured journalists and provide stories with insider information about a particular event. Key political journalists who have an inside track to Labour's Inner Core Elite have included Alistair Campbell (when at *The Daily Mirror* and *Today*), Patrick Wintour of *The Observer* and Andrew Grice of *The Sunday Times*. Other print journalists whose coverage is considered particularly significant by Labour strategists include Peter Riddell and Philip Webster of *The Times*, and Michael White of *The Guardian*. Here, the role played by the Parliamentary lobby is of central importance (Cockerell *et al.*, 1984; Harris, 1991; Ingham, 1994).

The relationship between media and political actors is not simply one of structured subordination (Hall *et al.*, 1978) nor are all journalists simply mouthpieces for political parties. The media exhibits a licensed autonomy, what Semetko *et al.* describe as a 'discretionary power', dependent upon the media's formative role in shaping the news agenda in conjunction with forces that facilitate or else prevent their ability to do so (Semetko *et al.*, 1991). While external agencies can structure the news debate journalistic reportage is far more than the sum of information obtained by news organizations: 'Journalists necessarily exercise value judgements in selecting the information they receive and in directing their news seeking [they] reframe and reinterpret the material they process and the events they witness' (Deacon, 1996: 193).

The news media display more autonomy when the party Inner Core Elite defensively deploy a reactive strategy and less autonomy when the Elite advance a proactive strategy. Here, perhaps unsurprisingly, the 'strategic community' working to the Inner Core Elite are more in control of the stories they initiate rather than those they do not originate and to which they must react. News media amplify the news event activated by the party when the media is obliged to act as a common carrier for its views and opinions rather than initiating stories of their own.

Should the media (or sources other than the party's Inner Core Elite) initiate a news event to which the strategic community is obliged to respond, the resultant news story illustrates the autonomy of the media and the efforts to which an Inner Core Elite goes to limit, restrict or otherwise restrain this autonomy in their own (quite natural) partisan interests. Media are spectators and participants in the framing of the news story. Political communications is therefore a symbiotic relationship between media and politicians (involving opposing parties eager to 'command' the news agenda) where both influence the prominence and attention of particular issues. The purposes of public relations strategies in both reactive and proactive form therefore involves five interrelated activities: establishing an agenda, influencing an agenda, altering an agenda, and reinforcing an agenda. The dissemination of spin involves political actors providing information and opinion to journalists in order to influence their interpretation of events. For journalists, 'communication [is] a tool of public enlightenment; to [political actors], a weapon in a two-way struggle against rival parties and professional journalists' (Blumler et al., 1989: 157): The degree to which actors are successful determines the party's ability to construct a story.

The objective of a party's public relations strategy is to reduce the media autonomy over the reportage of the political party while simultaneously strengthening the autonomy that the Inner Core Elite (not the party) has to project the 'public identity' they have chosen. While the Inner Core Elite are ever eager to promote the party in their chosen form they are not always successful. They have to deal with an autonomous news media capable of pursuing their own news agenda with regard to the Labour Party and as such are obliged to deploy both proactive and reactive public relations strategies. News stories are also generated by Labour sources outside the Inner Core Elite. Such party insiders, the Outer Core Elite; the Peripheral Elite or even the party periphery, often challenge (or merely privately question) the agenda of the Inner Core Elite and use an autonomous news media to pursue such a campaign (numerous examples of this may be cited foremost among them the spate of 'Blair is a dictator' stories generated by Labour MPs in 1995 and 1996). Political opponents such as the Conservatives also target their own negative campaign through the news media in an effort to discredit Labour's appeal (evidenced by the Tories 'double whammy' effort to paint Labour as the party of excessive taxation in 1992).

As such the power of the Inner Core Elite is necessarily constrained and its media strategies are a series of attempts to re-negotiate these constraints and limit the autonomy of other actors involved in the production of the news agenda. Its control over its party's political communications strategy does however strengthen its hand within the political party. Whereas Neil Kinnock was on the receiving end of a largely hostile press (his party the subject of effective negative campaigning) the 'strategic community' he led was none the less able to successfully promote his agenda within his party and strengthen the party centre at the expense of the periphery: where he led, Tony Blair has followed. While this command over political communications strengthens the Inner Core Elite within the party it does not guarantee that the Elite will be always able to determine (as opposed to influence) a news agenda generated by the interaction of Labour with opposing parties and the interplay of political events together with an autonomous news media able to shape a news agenda according to their own instrumental intentions. Despite the wish of the Inner Core Elite (and often their best endeavours) the media remains a forum for different interests and various points of view: the central objective of Labour's media strategists is to limit this autonomy as far as is possible in regard of publicity relating to their party.

Public Relations Media Strategies and the Enhancement of Leadership Power

That political leaders now use media strategies to enhance their power and autonomy is a clearly a recipe for centralization; it demands co-ordination from the centre. The media is not only the methods by which political actors communicate to the electorate but it also provides the means for élite political leaders to communicate to their supporters. Leaders always use their privileges; they constantly seek to establish themselves and the media provides an additional means of doing so.

The power enjoyed by the Inner Core Elite derives from its association with the personage of the party leader and the command that the leadership has over four primary power resources: authority and ability to command and discipline; control of appointment and patronage, reward and penalty; control over party organization; ability to generate expectations of electoral benefit to the party. Together these primary power resources strengthen the leadership's grip on two secondary power resources which are indispensable for executive leadership: influence over policy determination; influence over strategic planning. The first power resource, the authority and ability to command and discipline, is the most important. It is not a guaranteed resource nor is it finite. Rather it is indeterminate and fluid, affected by the play of political events and the success or otherwise of the political leader in meeting the objectives identified by the party he or she leads. Without the power resource of authority no other resource can come into play; from it all others follow. The control of appointment and patronage combined with command of the party organization confers the leadership (in the form of the Inner Core Elite) with the ability to exercise control over policy determination and strategic planning. These may be usefully described as interlocking power resources. To the above four primary power resources a fifth may be added: (5) control over public relations media strategies. This additional power resource (often deployed in tandem with political marketing strategies) is worthless without the contribution of the other three resources. It cannot compensate for their absence. Leaders have combined the media preoccupation with leadership with their powerful monopoly of the party's public relations and political marketing strategies to project their favoured public profile. This allows the Inner Core Elite to seek to 'lead from the front' and establish a public identity of which party colleagues are obliged to take note. The leader's public media utterances (or those delivered on their behalf by a favoured insider) play an important role in orienting the political direction of the party. In the case of Labour their contribution is all too often more significant than any meeting of the National Executive, the Shadow Cabinet or the annual conference.

Two-tier models of political communications presupposes that whereas parties communicate to electors through media, party élites can also communicate to their party through the media. Several objectives behind the political communications strategies of a party (in the two forms identified above) may be noted. Assuming that parties are office seekers (and acknowledge that policy-seeking is dependent upon successful office seeking) there are attempts to: (1) Communicate to Voters and Electoral Choice Shape; by (2) Defining an Ideological Appeal and Projecting a Political Image (or else attacking the appeal and image of their opponents). To do these things successfully the party leadership has to; (3) Influence the Media as Opinion Former and; (4) Stimulate the Interest and Support of the 'Political Community'. The ideal communication process will attempt to defining an ideological appeal and projecting a political image through influencing the media as opinion former in order to stimulate the interest and/or support of the 'political community' to communicate to voters and electoral choice shape.

Modern political communications (being at the centre of the party's electioneering efforts) will also (5) Enhance Leadership Power, Authority and Status. If electoral choice shaping in the pursuit of office seeking is a prime objective the enhancement of leadership power is a consequential spin-off of this phenomena. The party's political communications strategies will not necessarily make the weak leader strong: an army of spin doctors and campaign strategists would have made little or no difference, say, to the public persona and appeal of Michael Foot in 1981–83 but the impact of political communications in general offers an additional primary power resource to enable the party leadership to strengthen its grip on the secondary power resources of influence over policy determination and influence over strategic planning. This process is historically a consequence of the development of modern political communications; today it is possible to conceive of it as part of a deliberate strategy.

The task of Inner Core Elite strategists is to promote the party in the form of the leader. This has the dual function of attracting attention to the party, and directing the attention of the party. It serves to define 'legitimate opinion' within the party and influence the behaviour of other political actors. It creates leadership supporters and establishes the parameters that define insiders from outsiders. In a presidential age a party which openly repudiates its leader inevitably damages its public image and weakens its electoral standing. This phenomenon is exacerbated in a media age when journalistic searchlights combine with a willingness on the part of party figures to leak and brief. Public (as opposed to private unattributable) repudiation of the leader (or of initiatives taken in their name), while not impossible, are therefore extremely rare. Powerful party leaders are quick to turn this fact to their advantage.

When power is exercised by an Inner Core Elite party members are able only to ratify decisions taken elsewhere. As Eric Shaw (1994: 120–21) illustrates, 'the opportunities and incentives for institutional horizontal communications are being diminished and replaced by the growth of direct vertical communications between the centre and the rank and file' with the result that 'the individual member under direct democracy is more likely to be in a position where he or she can only respond to questions set and an agenda formed by the party's central'. This is increasingly enacted through a media strategy. It encourages atomized, disorganized, individual (i.e. non-collective) party members to accept decisions taken at the centre by a 'political executive' rather than the 'political legislature' involving a process of 'consultation' rather than 'empowerment'; 'ratification' rather than 'decision'. It is plebiscitary rather than democratic. In the case of Labour, this process is exacerbated by the downgrading of a trade union link which (whatever its faults) has historically been another constraint (as well as a source of leadership authority, see McKenzie, 1964; Minkin, 1978) of the Inner Core Elite.

Modern media politics increasingly result in the marketing and packaging of the party leadership, not the wider political party and empower political leaders to agenda set within their own party and in the wider political world. The Inner Core Elite is thus well placed to decide Labour's political appeal and make the greatest contribution to the 'public identity' of the party. The more likely the Inner Core Elite is to determine this identity, the more powerful the party leadership becomes and the more it decides party strategy, the method chosen to make present a public image in the minds of electors, political observers and also other party actors located within the Outer Core and Peripheral Elites and other various components of the party hierarchy.

BIBLIOGRAPHY

Blumler, Jay (1993) 'Elections, the Media and the Modern Publicity Process' in Marjorie Ferguson (ed.), *Public Communications: Themes and Perspectives*, 104–25. London: Sage.

Blumler, Jay Michael Gurevitch and T.J. Nossiter (1989) 'The Earnest Versus the Determined: A Study of Election News Making at the BBC' in Ivor Crewe and Martin Harrop (eds) *Political Communications: The 1987 General Election*, 157–174. Cambridge: Cambridge University Press.

Cockerell, Michael, Peter Hennessy and David Walker (1984) *Sources Close to the Prime Minister.* London: Macmillan.

Deacon, David (1996) 'The Voluntary Sector in the Changing Communication Environment', *European Journal of Communication* 11: 173–99.

Ericson, Richard, Patricia Baranek and Janet Chan (1989) *Negotiating Control.* Buckingham: Open University Press.

Franklin, Bob (1994) *Packaging Politics: Political Communications in Britain's Media Democracy,*London: Edward Arnold.

Hall, Stuart, Chas Critcher, Tony Jefferson, John Clarke and Brian Roberts (1978) *Policing the Crisis,* London: Macmillan.

Harris, Robert (1991) *Good and Faithful Messenger* London: Faber and Faber.

Harrop, Martin (1990) 'Political Marketing', *Parliamentary Affairs* 43: 277–91.

Heffernan, Richard and Mike Marqusee (1992) *Defeat from the Jaws of Victory: Inside Kinnock's Labour Party* London: Verso.

Ingham, Bernard (1994) The Lobby System: Lubricant or Spanner? *Parliamentary Affairs* 47: 549–65.

Jones, Nicholas (1996) *Soundbites and Spin Doctors.* London: Cassell.

Kavanagh, Dennis (1995) *Election Campaigning: The New Marketing of Politics.* Oxford: Basil Blackwell.

Kinnock, Neil (1994) 'Remaking the Labour Party' *Contemporary Record* 8: 535–54.

McKenzie, R.J. (1964) *British Political Parties: The Distribution of Power Within the Conservative and Labour Parties.* London: Heinemann.

McNair, Brian (1995) *An Introduction to Political Communications.* London: Routledge.

McQuail, Denis and Sven Windahl,(1993) *Communications Models* . London: Longman.

Michels, Robert (1962) *Political Parties.* New York: Free Press.

Minkin, Lewis (1978) *The Labour Party Conference* Manchester: Manchester University Press.

Minkin, Lewis (1992) *The Contentious Alliance: Trade Unions and the Labour Party* Edinburgh: Edinburgh University Press.

Panebianco, Angelo (1988) *Political Parties: Organisation and Power* Cambridge: Cambridge University Press.

Scammell, Margaret (1995) *Designer Politics: How Elections are Won.* London: Macmillan.

Schlesinger, Philip and Howard Tumber (1994) *Reporting Crime: The Media Politics of Criminal Justice.* Oxford: Clarendon Press.

Semetko, Holli, Jay Blumler, Michael Gurevitch and D. Weaver (1991) *The Formation of Campaign Agendas: A Comparative Analysis of Party and Media Roles in Recent American and British Elections.* New Jersey: LEA.

Shaw, Eric (1994) *The Labour Party Since 1979: Crisis and Transformation.* London: Routledge.

Shaw, Eric (1996) *The Labour Party Since 1945.* Oxford: Basil Blackwell.

Smith, Martin J. (1994) 'Neil Kinnock and the Modernisation of the Labour Party' *Contemporary Record* 8: 555–66.

Tunstall, Jeremy (1970) *The Westminster Lobby Correspondents.* London: Routledge.

Webb, Paul (1992) 'Election Campaigning, Organisational Transformation and the Professionalism of the British Labour Party', *European Journal of Political Research* 21: 267–88.

Wolton, Dominique (1990) 'Political Communications: The Construction of a Model', *European Journal of Communications* 5: 9–28.

Wring, Dominic (1996) 'From Mass Propaganda to Political Marketing: The Transformation of the Labour Party's Election Campaigning' in Colin Rallings, David Farrell, David Denver and David Broughton (eds) *British Elections and Parties Yearbook 1995*, pp.105–24. London: Frank Cass.

From the Europe of Nations to the European Nation? Attitudes of French Gaullist and Centrist Parliamentarians

Agnès Alexandre and Xavier Jardin

With the prospect of the single currency, the French right-wing parliamentary party is haunted by its past. Europe remains at the heart of internal divisions, in spite of President Chirac's efforts to unite his members in the old Gaullist tradition. The current parliamentary majority in France is organizationally and politically fractured. The two elements of the coalition, the Rally for the Republic (RPR) and the Union for the French Democracy (UDF) are openly divided on certain issues including European integration. And each of these two parties faces internal ideological divisions.

The RPR was founded by Jacques Chirac in 1976, as the direct heir of de Gaulle's doctrine. It defends a national and voluntarist conception of the state viewed as the guarantor of national independence and sovereignty. However, from 1981, Chirac's main aim was to create a powerful instrument for the presidential election. The Socialist victory in 1981 compelled the Gaullist Movement to ally with the UDF. In opposition to the new government, the RPR became more liberal. Chirac's leadership was not challenged until the 1988 presidential defeat. In 1989, the Reformers' movement, led by Michel Noir, called for the renewal of the Gaullist Party. The following year, Charles Pasqua and Philippe Seguin tried to found a new *Rassemblement* within the party, and in 1992, the referendum on the Maastricht Treaty highlighted the dissidence of Philippe Seguin and Charles Pasqua who campaigned for a 'no' vote. A new cleavage occurred with the 1993 legislative election victory when Edouard Balladur became Prime Minister and decided to run for president. Nowadays the RPR is divided between *Chiraquiens*, such as Alain Juppé and Jacques Toubon, who remain faithful to Jacques Chirac, *neo-Gaullists*, such as Philippe Seguin and Charles Pasqua, who call for a new 'Rassemblement' in the Gaullist tradition, and *Balladuriens* who stand for more liberal positions closer to the UDF

The UDF was founded in 1978 by President V. Giscard d'Estaing in order to balance Gaullist Party domination. The UDF is a federation of parties, mainly the Republican Party (PR) which prevails within the Union in terms of influence, and Democratic Force (FD) which was formerly called the

Social Democrats Centre (CDS). From the beginning, the UDF had to face external competition with the RPR and internal competition between the PR and the CDS. PR gathers together people favourable to a modern liberalism based on the European integration process and the liberalization of world trade. CDS represents the Social Democrat tradition. Its members are much more favourable to state interventionism on social issues than PR liberals. Moreover they keep faith in the idea of the United States of Europe based on a purely federal model, whereas PR members are advocates of a confederal Europe. In 1995, these internal divisions prevented the UDF from entering a candidate in the presidential election. The defeat of Edouard Balladur, who was supported by the UDF, and the election of a new UDF president reinforced the rivalries between leaders within the Union.

It has become more and more common to identify increasing dissent within moderate right-wing parties in the EU. The French RPR and UDF, like the British Conservatives are no exceptions to this rule. Only an accurate assessment of parliamentary individual attitudes towards the present evolution of the EU can measure the extent of these divisions. In 1992, an academic team from the University of Sheffield carried out a survey (Baker *et al.*, 1995, see also Baker *et al.*, 1993a, 1993b, 1994) on the attitudes of the Conservative Members of Parliament towards European integration. They demonstrated that the Eurorebellion in the parliamentary Conservative Party was far wider than the numbers of MPs prepared to defy the Whips would have suggested. Following this research, the survey on RPR and UDF parliamentary attitudes starts from the same hypotheses. The results presented here compare French and British attitudes and give further detail on French attitudes to Europe.

Comparing French and British Right-wing attitudes towards European Integration

Franco–British Agreements

The survey first revealed a strong consensus on economic policy, especially on liberal measures, such as reducing social costs on employers or making European labour markets more flexible, which is not surprising given the liberal identity of the parties concerned (Table 1a). In terms of institutional issues, the Sheffield survey already underlined the Tory backbenchers' neo-Gaullism, which is mainly illustrated by their common opposition to further supranationalism. However, in the field of subsidiarity, Conservative MPs proved more radical than French parliamentarians because, as was mentioned in the Sheffield survey, about three-quarters of them wished to see most policy areas being handled at the national level, whereas UDF and RPR

TABLE 1
PARLIAMENTARIANS' VIEWS OF EUROPE: ANGLO-FRENCH COMPARISONS

a. Franco-British Agreements

	Strongly agree or agree (%)		Difference (F–UK)
	France	UK	
Reduction of the burden of social costs placed on employers is necessary to job creation in the EU.	85.7	88	-2.3
Inflexibility in European labour markets is the principal cause of unemployement.	73.4	71	+2.4
A single European army would underpin the security of France (UK).	46.8	15	+31.8
The 1996 IGC should abolish QMV.	33.8	20	+13.8
France should block the use of QMV in the areas of foreign and defence policy.	54.5	87	-32.5
The key to closing the 'democratic deficit' is strengthening scrutiny by national parliaments of the EU legislative process.	83.1	82	+1.1
There should be a common policy on training.	40.9	16	+24.9
There should be a common policy on deregulation.	72.7	54	+18.7
There should be a common policy on privatizations.	41.6	26	+15.6
Border controls would be better handled at the national level.	56.5	74	-17.4
Terrorism would be better handled at the national level.	54.5	57	-2.5
Immigration would be better handled at the national level.	61.7	81	-19.3
Drugs would be better handled at the national level.	51.3	47	+4.3
Health would be better handled at the national level.	51.3	71	-19.7

b. European Monetary Union

	Strongly agree or agree (%)		Difference (F–UK)
	France	UK	
EMU is realizable by the end of the 20th century.	73.4	35	+38.4
A single currency is necessary to maintain the single market.	87.0	14	+73.0
It could damage the national economy if the country didn't join the European single currency.	81.8	26	+55.8
There should be a national referendum before the country enters a single currency.	39.6	55	-15.4

c. Bones of Contention

	Strongly agree or agree (%)		Difference (F–UK)
	France	UK	
Company taxation should be harmonized within the EU.	83.1	15	+68.5
VAT should be harmonized within the EU.	87.7	20	+67.7
Income taxation should be harmonized within the EU.	49.4	2	+47.4
Customs tariffs should be harmonized within the EU.	92.9	35	+57.9
Subsidiarity reinforces the federalist tendency the EU.	61.0	31	+30.0
A federal Europe could be ruled by Germany.	47.4	58	-10.6
There should be a common policy on infrastructure.	81.2	38	+43.2
There should be a common policy on investment.	61.7	16	+45.7
Agriculture would be better handled at the national level.	34.4	72	-37.6
Environmental protection would be better handled at the national level.	41.6	48	-6.4

repondents proved to be more divided on those matters. There is a strong consensus on the idea of handling terrorism at the national level probably because France and Britain both went through such painful experiences owing to the difficult relationships between the French government and Algeria on the one hand, and the British government and Northern Ireland on the other hand.

On training and immigration both French and British right-wing parliamentarians are more in favour of adopting measures at the national level, even if more Conservative MPs seem to take a tougher line on those issues. On certain issues British Conservatives seemed more radical than their French counterparts. On a single European army, which was supported by a majority of UDF parliamentarians, neither French RPR nor British Conservative respondents proved willing to accept the prospect of dissolving national armed forces into a Euro-army, and this may in consequence turn out to be as difficult for the Conservative Party leadership as for the RPR's.

On blocking the use of Qualified Majority Voting (QMV) in the areas of foreign and defence policy, there also seems to be a loose consensus between British and French parliamentarians, which illustrates their common wish to promote intergovernmentalism in the decision-making process.[1]

Bones of Contention

On many issues, French and British right-wing parliamentarians would justify divergent stances by asserting national peculiarities. Often, British Conservative and French right-wing backbenchers were in complete opposition and revealed fundamental differences of attitudes which proved to be strongly related to the historical positions of the two countries in Europe.

The key issue on which this opposition was focused was Economic and Monetary Union (EMU). French parliamentarians seemed as favourable as British parliamentarians were hostile to the creation of a European single currency. For instance, on the four statements on EMU, responses were clearly opposite (Table 1b).

These results underline the existence of two specific visions of EMU. The British one is mainly pessimistic. Backbench attitudes to a single currency reveal fears and reservations. At present, EMU is indeed the focal point of Euroscepticism among Conservative backbenchers, who fear that entering the single currency could be disastrous for British national sovereignty. To some extent, the French stance is more optimistic. More than three-quarters of French respondents chose to support the idea of a single currency despite its possible consequences for the national economy and sovereignty. But French enthusiasm remains ambivalent. Since the Maastricht Treaty was actually ratified, this issue has not been mentioned very often, probably because of the enormous support – either by conviction or by loyalty – of the present parliamentary majority for Jacques Chirac's European policy and Prime Minister Alain Juppé's economic policy. However, there is still an important minority of French Eurosceptics who remain opposed to EMU, in spite of Jacques Chirac's ability to appeal to the loyalty of his members. This minority certainly jeopardizes the cohesion of the RPR–UDF majority two years before the next general election.

On the whole, British Conservative MPs appeared much more radical on certain issues which arouse national collective fears, such as the fear of German domination and the idea of federalism which is still associated in the minds of some Eurosceptics with the fear of a unitary centralized state (Table 1c).

The French Right and Europe : A Marriage of Convenience

The Gaullist Party under President de Gaulle was as European as de Gaulle could be. De Gaulle was deeply attached to the idea of the nation-state as the only legitimate source of political sovereignty and authority and was clearly opposed to a supranational and federal model of European integration. De Gaulle was rather favourable to a Europe of nations in which France would be likely to play a major part. His successor, George Pompidou, kept faith in de Gaulle's beliefs on Europe but he accepted the entry of Great Britain into the European Community and gave his support to the project of the Economic and Monetary Union shaped by the 'Werner plan'. The unity and cohesion of the Gaullists on the European issue was not challenged until the election of President Valéry Giscard d'Estaing in 1974. Valéry Giscard d'Estaing was more favourable to a confederal Europe. In 1977, he tabled a bill on direct elections to the European Assembly. Gaullists proved openly divided on this issue: 'ultras' such as Michel Debré and Jacques Chirac himself were against the project whereas Europeanists such as Jacques Chaban-Delmas were much more in favour of an active participation in the European process. The 1979 European election reinforced the divisions within the Gaullist Party. Jacques Chirac was then utterly opposed to the EC as being a large free-trade zone which could endanger French jobs and interests. Moreover, the opposition between the RPR and the newborn UDF reached a critical point the same year. Chirac refused to form a joint list with the UDF for the European elections, and he finally lost the elections. This defeat highlighted the need for the Gaullists to rethink their position on Europe.

The 1981 presidential election and the socialist victory forced the RPR and the UDF to form an alliance, and their lines on Europe converged. In 1983, the RPR defined a new position on Europe, which advocated more active French involvement in the EC. This U-turn was motivated by pragmatic considerations rather than ideological reasons. Thus, the RPR and UDF presenteded joint lists of candidates at the 1984, 1989 and 1994

European elections. But on the 1992 Maastricht Referendum, as new controversial issues were raised, the RPR shifted to a more nationalist position.

After the revision of the Constitution in the National Assembly and in the Senate, the Maastricht Treaty was actually ratified on 20 September 1992 by means of a referendum which was won by a very narrow majority of 51% of the people (see Appleton, 1992, Blumann, 1994, Criddle, 1993). Consequently, opinion polls were not particularly interested in parliamentary attitudes although some politicians expressed their views publicly. On the following question: 'Did you vote for or against the ratification of the Maastricht Treaty?', 65.5% answered that they voted in favour, 30.5% against and 1.3% abstained. The results reflected and confirmed the official positions held by the RPR and UDF during the referendum campaign. The UDF was indeed almost unanimously (93%) in favour of Maastricht and most members campaigned for a 'yes' vote with their leader, Valéry Giscard d'Estaing and with the European Movement. The RPR was so openly divided on the question that the leader, Jacques Chirac, decided to allow the members to make their own decision but announced that he would personally cast an affirmative vote in September.

Actually, RPR parliamentary attitudes have changed a lot since Maastricht, particularly since the 1993 parliamentary election (for a historical overview see Shields 1996). A poll conducted for the French daily newspaper *Libération* on the 28 March 1993, just after new members were elected at the National Assembly, revealed that only 38.8% of the RPR deputies answered that they voted in favour of Maastricht, whereas 58% said that they opposed it.

Two events can be considered as the starting points of this evolution : the 1993 legislative election and the 1995 presidential election. It is true that the strong loyalty of RPR parliamentarians to President Chirac mainly accounts for this change. Indeed, the Gaullist Party has always been characterized by the internal discipline of the group and the authority of a leader who encountered no particular difficulty in imposing his personal views on parliamentarians. From the famous *appel de Cochin*, a speech delivered by Jacques Chirac in 1978 in which he violently opposed the 'foreign' nature of the EEC, to his present attempt to promote a more conciliatory policy towards his European partners, most deputies and senators have remained faithful to their charismatic leader.

In an attempt to assess the degree of emotional attitudes to the Maastricht Treaty, respondents were provided with a scale of five increasing feelings ranging from complete hostility to Maastricht to absolute enthusiasm for the Treaty: one-third of respondents placed themselves on the rather pro-Maastricht fourth position on the scale (Figure 1).

FIGURE 1
GENERAL FEELINGS TOWARDS EUROPEAN INTEGRATION DEFINED BY THE
MAASTRICHT TREATY

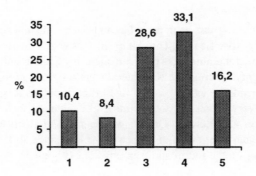

Cross-tabulated with party membership, the result highlighted deep differences between the two parties, since more than three-quarters of the UDF respondents placed themselves on positions four and five on the scale, whereas almost three-quarters of the RPR placed themselves on the first three positions (Figure 2).

FIGURE 2
RPR AND UDF FEELINGS TOWARDS EUROPEAN INTEGRATION DEFINED BY THE
MAASTRICHT TREATY

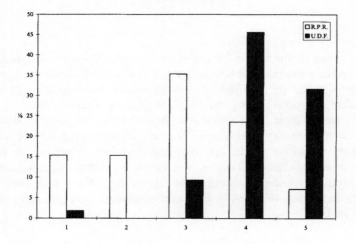

Apart from broad emotional questions on Maastricht, all statements dealt with the most debated European matters at the moment, which were directly and indirectly related to the idea of national sovereignty.

Nation and Sovereignty

From a historical viewpoint, each party has approached the question of national sovereignty very specifically. The UDF has always openly advocated a confederal Europe tightening links between countries without undermining their national sovereignty, whereas the RPR has always sought to promote the notion of national independence as the basis of its European policy. Respondents were thus faced with very broad questions aiming at evaluating their main feelings about their nation and Europe. On the whole, most of them appeared quite favourable to greater integration of France to the EU, since almost half of them placed themselves on the fourth and fifth positions (Figure 3).

FIGURE 3
GENERAL FEELINGS ABOUT FRANCE AND EUROPE

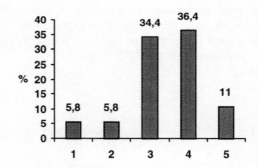

However when respondents were asked the type of European configuration they wished to see develop, almost half of them (46.8 %) declared themselves in favour of a Europe of nations following the Gaullist tradition (26% in favour of a Confederal Europe and 18.2% of a Federal Europe.

As for the different geographical units they said they felt close to, such as their town, their *département* (one of France's administrative subdivisions), their region, the nation and Europe, they expressed their attachment to their nation very strongly (almost 91%) and apart from this undeniable nationalism, their attachments varied according to the size of the political unit: they felt closest to their town, followed by their *département*, their region and finally Europe (Table 2).

TABLE 2
ATTACHMENT TO GEOGRAPHICAL AREA

Do you feel:	very close	rather close	not very close	not close at all
to	%	%	%	%
your town	79.2	13.0	1.9	0.6
your *département*	56.5	27.3	9.7	1.3
your Region	.24.0	41.6	23.4	4.5
your Nation	76.0	14.9	3.9	2.6
Europe	19.5	37.7	29.9	8.4

Cross-tabulated with party membership, the data underlined deep differences between the two parties. As a matter of fact, the UDF appeared much more in favour of France being more integrated to the EU – half of them clustered at the fourth position, whereas half of RPR respondents gathered at the average, third position (Figure 4).

FIGURE 4
RPR AND UDF FEELINGS ABOUT FRANCE AND EUROPE

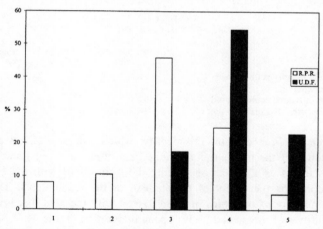

The question of the type of Europe configuration cross-tabulated with party membership confirmed the Gaullist attachment to a Europe of nations (69.4 %: Table 3). As far as the UDF was concerned, respondents quite surprisingly declared themselves rather federalist (40.4 %). As a matter of fact, during the 1994 European election, when they campaigned with the RPR in the same coalition, they all agreed to avoid reference to a federal in their manifesto, and even proved reluctant to pronounce the 'F-word' in public. Nevertheless, their

Maastricht campaign was sponsored by the European Movement and most UDF members happened to belong to it. If the UDF appeared slightly closer to France (94.7%) than the RPR (89.4%), they also proved much closer to Europe (73.7%) than their Gaullist counterparts (44.7%). And more than a half of the RPR respondents admitted that they felt not very or not close at all to Europe.

TABLE 3
ATTITUDES TOWARDS EUROPE BY PARTY

	RPR (%)	UDF (%)
Type of Europe (by party membership)		
A Europe of Nations	69.4	14.0
A Confederal Europe	16.5	36.8
A Federal Europe	5.9	40.4
Feeling of closeness (by party membership)		
to Nation:		
Very and rather close	89.4	94.7
Not very and not at all close	8.2	5.3
to Europe:		
Very and rather close	44.7	73.7
Not very and not at all close	50.5	24.6

TABLE 4
CULTURAL IDENTITY AND THE EU

	Strongly agree or agree (%)	Disagree or strongly disagree (%)
France's Cultural Identity is threatened by European integration.	31.2	66.9
French concept of *Laïcité* could be used as an example by other EU member-states.	62.3	33.8

The threat to France's cultural identity, which can be defined as the common values of the national community, has often been put forward by some Eurosceptics as a means of striking the right chord with the French people. It confirms the extent of nationalism of the respondents. Thus, a significant minority of one-third of them agreed with the idea that France's cultural identity was threatened by European integration (Table 4).

As for the very French notion of *laïcité* – the approximate equivalent to secularism – it is considered as one of the most important and controversial republican values based on the principle of the complete separation between the state and the various churches. This principle is often presented as one of the major characteristics of French Republican identity and raised controversy by opposing people who were in favour of forbidding pupils to display any religious sign and those who considered that this ban would pave the way for intolerance. Therefore, the possibility of exporting this example to other European countries was sometimes put forward and still seemed to be considered by some RPR and UDF parliamentarians as a good idea; 62.3% of respondents agreed with it.

Nevertheless, the fact that only 50.9% of UDF respondents agree with the idea of secularism – compared with 74.1% of the RPR – could be explained by the existence of a strong Christian-democratic tradition within the UDF (Table 5). This tradition is mainly represented by a party called *Forces démocrates* gathering two former parties, the *Parti Social Démocrate* and the *Centre des Démocrates Sociaux*, which is particularly faithful to the Catholic Church on various religious or moral matters.

TABLE 5
CULTURAL IDENTITY AND THE EU, BY PARTY

	RPR (%)	UDF (%)
France's Cultural Identity is threatened by European integration.		
Strongly agree or agree	40.0	19.3
Disagree or strongly disagree	57.6	80.7
French concept of *Laïcité* could be used as an example by other EU member states.		
Strongly agree or agree	74.1	50.9
Disagree or strongly disagree	21.2	45.7

Some deep differences also occurred between the RPR and the UDF parliamentarians as related to their attitudes towards other countries. The idea that a federal Europe could be ruled by Germany in the future remained a very divisive issue (Table 6a): 47.4% of the respondents agreed with it, mainly belonging to the RPR (60%) and only 28% of UDF respondents. The fact that the RPR parliamentarians broadly reject a federal Europe is associated with the fear of German domination. However, it should be noted that, during the Maastricht episode, this argument was very ambivalent. It was not only used by opponents to the Treaty as a means of stirring up aversion to Maastricht and fostering the underlying xenophobic feelings of some voters. It was also exploited by pro-Maastricht activists in terms of preventing Germany from becoming too powerful. As a result, both pro- and anti-Maastricht politicians perceived their own stand as the best way to prevent German domination.

The question of enlargement of the EU, especially in relation to its impact on the role of France, also led to a high degree of division (Table 6b): only 44.2% of respondents agreed with it. Among UDF respondents, 50.9% thought that the membership of new states could weaken France's role, a position that can be explained that the fact that many parliamentarians in this party argue that enlargement could hinder further integration and that it requires preliminary institutional reform.

TABLE 6
THE IMPACT OF OTHER STATES IN THE EU

a. Germany

	RPR (%)	UDF (%)	Total
Germany could be dominant in a federal Europe.			
Strongly agree or agree	60.0	28.1	47.4
Disagree or strongly disagree	37.6	68.4	49.4

b. New states

	RPR (%)	UDF (%)	Total
New states' membership of the EU could weaken the role played by France.			
Strongly agree or agree	42.4	50.9	44.2
Disagree or strongly disagree	54.2	47.4	52.6

On the very sensitive issue of subsidiarity, several statements were gathered concerning the idea of handling certain policy areas at the national or the European level (Table 7). Following the Sheffield survey statements, all the policy areas that we proposed were issues on which parliamentary opinion proved to be almost equally divided. The specific areas which respondents were rather in favour of handling at the national level happened to be controversial issues in France, such as terrorism, immigration and border controls which the French government has great difficulties in tackling. They also included areas, such as culture and training, which are often said to contribute to the definition of a nation's identity.

TABLE 7
SUBSIDIARITY

	Strongly agree or agree (%)	Disagree or strongly disagree (%)
Subsidiarity reinforces the federalist tendency the EU.	61.0	37.6
Agriculture would be better handled at the national level.	34.4	61.7
Environmental protection would be better handled at the national level.	41.6	53.2
Border controls would be better handled at the national level.	56.5	38.3
Terrorism would be better handled at the national level.	54.5	41.6
Immigration would be better handled at the national level.	61.7	33.1
Trade would be better handled at the national level.	45.5	48.1
Drugs would be better handled at the national level.	51.3	44.8
Health would be better handled at the national level.	51.3	44.8
Technology would be better handled at the national level.	42.9	52.6
Culture would be better handled at the national level.	57.1	38.9
There should be a common policy on infrastructure.	81.2	11.7
There should be a common policy on training.	40.9	50.7
There should be a common policy on investment.	61.7	28.5
There should be a common policy on deregulation.	72.7	19.4
There should be a common policy on privatizations.	41.6	50.6
There should be a common policy on *aménagement du territoire*.	59.7	35.0
There should be a common policy on immigration controls.	83.1	11.0

The various fields where the two parties adopted quite different lines mainly concerned agriculture, border controls, immigration and privatization (Table 8). On agriculture, three-quarters of the UDF respondents disagreed with the claim that it would be better handled at the national level, whereas this question almost equally divided the RPR respondents because one of the major electoral bases of the Gaullist Party is provided by French farmers. As for statements on law and order, on which the Gaullists are said to be generally tougher than their Centrist counterparts, the two parties held different views. Unlike the UDF, almost three-quarters of the RPR (63.5% and 75.3%) respondents agreed with the idea of handling border controls and immigration at the national level. On the statement about privatizations, the result reflected the official positions held by the two parties on economic policy, since the UDF is traditionally more liberal and therefore more reluctant to let the privatization of national companies being handled by a supranational authority.

TABLE 8
SUBSIDIARITY BY PARTY

	RPR (%)	UDF (%)
Agriculture should be better handled at the national level.		
Strongly agree or agree	44.7	22.8
Disagree or strongly disagree	50.6	75.4
Border controls should be better handled at the national level.		
Strongly agree or agree	63.5	43.9
Disagree or strongly disagree	29.4	52.7
Immigration should be better handled at the national level.		
Strongly agree or agree	75.3	42.1
Disagree or strongly disagree	8.8	52.7
There should be a common policy on privatizations.		
Strongly agree or agree	47.0	36.8
Disagree or strongly disagree	44.7	56.1

As a procedure for overriding national vetoes, QMV is considered a direct threat to national sovereignty (Table 9). Hence 54.5% of respondents agreed with the idea of blocking the use of QMV in the areas of foreign and defence policy, although only a third (33.8%) of them thought that the 1996 IGC should abolish it (Table 9). And on this result, the RPR proved more ambivalent than the UDF: 64.7% disagreed with abolishing QMV at the 1996 IGC compared with 57.9% of the UDF, but 57.6% of the Gaullists said to be in favour of blocking the use of QMV in foreign and defence policy, compared with 50.9% of their Centrist counterparts.

TABLE 9
QUALIFIED MAJORITY VOTING

	RPR (%)	UDF (%)	Total
The 1996 IGC should abolish QMV.			
Strongly agree or agree	31.8	33.3	33.8
Disagree or strongly disagree	64.7	57.9	61.1
France should block the use of QMV in the areas of foreign and defence policy.			
Strongly agree or agree	57.6	50.9	54.5
Disagree or strongly disagree	38.8	36.9	38.9

Economic and Social Questions

Questions on economic and social issues played a major part in the definition of RPR and UDF attitudes towards European integration. However, unlike European political union, economic issues did not arouse similar fears or reservations. Indeed, both political parties fully supported economic integration, mainly because they share liberal principles. UDF members have been advocates of liberalism for years and appear to be the French Euro-enthusiasts, whereas Gaullists have shifted to neo-liberalism more recently – from the first half of the 1980s – and a large minority of them still adopt a nationalist stance. However, the difference on economic questions between the two right-wing parties is not really significant today, except on the EMU issue.

The liberalism of French right-wing parliamentarians was illustrated by their positions on the opinion scale on the economic role of the state which reflected the desire shared by 37% (positions 1 and 2) of respondents for a minimal government (Figure 5). Only 15.5% (positions 4 and 5) were in favour of further interventionism, the others (41.6%) placed themselves in the middle (position 3).

FIGURE 5
GENERAL FEELINGS ABOUT THE ECONOMIC ROLE OF THE STATE

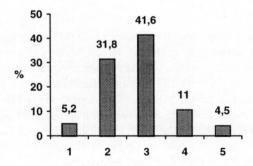

Gaullists were less liberal than UDF respondents – 30.6% of Gaullist respondents stand on positions 1 and 2, and nearly 50% of UDF members – and appeared to be a little more in favour of state interventionism (18.8% against 14%). This divergence may be explained by the interventionist tradition of Gaullist practice of power since 1958. From the Gaullist point of view, the state should be strong, respected and independent from the liberal point of view of UDF Centrists, it is necessary to reduce the state's prerogatives.

The union between the two parties during the socialist era – from 1981 to 1986, and again from 1988 to 1993 – has nevertheless led Gaullists to a more liberal position. Nowadays, Gaullists share liberal principles, such as minimal government, free trade, privatization and reduction of social costs placed on employers, but remain deeply attached to the idea that the state is the guarantor of national independence and sovereignty (Baudouin, 1990).

As for the questions on free trade, they unsurprisingly produced large majorities of agreement. 80.5% of respondents were opposed to the adoption of any protectionist measures (Table 10a), and almost 66% agreed with the idea that free trade is the mainspring of economic growth in the EU.

According to the survey results, the Gaullist and Centrist positions were very similar on these issues, which confirms the fact that, since the beginning of the 1980s, the Gaullist Party has definitely shifted to a strong liberal position.

In France, EMU is not really a focal point for dissidence, and our survey revealed great approval on this issue (Table 10b). Nearly three-quarters of respondents see EMU as realizable by the end of the twentieth century. More than 80% thought that it could damage France's economy if the country did not join the European single currency. Almost 90% agreed with the idea that a single currency is necessary to maintain the single market. Moreover, three-quarters of respondents were in favour of the creation of a European Central Bank. And nearly three-quarters accepted the idea of transferring sovereignty to create the single currency.

Although Gaullists and UDF members were favourable rather than hostile to a European single currency, 40% supported a referendum on this issue. These reservations can be explained by the conservative and the nationalist principles that still define the French right. They basically accept the idea of a European single currency, but still fear that monetary union subjects the French economy to EU control. The paradox is that French right-wing backenchers are strong advocates of liberalism but remain simultaneously supporters of a protected national economy.

However, cross-tabulated with party membership, the data on EMU highlighted significant differences. Strong oppositional minorities emerged in the Gaullist Party: more than a third of Gaullist respondents thought that

TABLE 10
ATTITUDES TOWARDS THE EU

a. Free Trade	Strongly agree or agree (%)	Disagree or strongly disagree (%)
France should adopt protectionist measures to prevent itself from excessive economic competition.	16.2	80.5
Free trade is the incentive to economic growth in Europe.	66.2	29.2

b. Single Currency	Strongly agree or agree (%)	Disagree or strongly disagree (%)
EMU is realizable by the end of the 20th century.	73.4	25.3
It could damage France's economy if the country didn't join the European single currency.	81.8	16.8
A single currency is necessary to maintain the single market.	87.0	12.3
Transferring sovereignty so as to create a single currency can not be accepted.	24.7	72.7
There should be a national referendum before France enters a single currency.	39.6	59.1

c. Jobs and Unemployment	Strongly agree or agree (%)	Disagree or strongly disagree (%)
Reduction of the burden of social costs placed on employers is necessary to job creation in the EU.	85.7	12.3
Inflexibility in European labour markets is the principal cause of unemployement.	73.4	25.3
Unemployment could only be prevented by a common policy.	77.3	20.7

d. Tax Harmonization	Strongly agree or agree (%)	Disagree or strongly disagree (%)
Rates should be harmonized within the EU.	26.0	70.8
Company taxation should be harmonized within the EU.	83.1	14.9
VAT should be harmonized within the EU.	87.7	8.4
Income taxation should be harmonized within the EU.	49.4	48.1
Customs tariffs should be harmonized within the EU.	92.9	4.5

e. Political Power in the EU	Strongly agree or agree (%)	Disagree or strongly disagree (%)
The powers of the Council of Ministers should be extended so that the Commission could be better controlled.	93.5	5.2
The right to initiate legislation should be balanced between the Commission and the European Parliament.	70.8	25.3
The need to maintain the democratic legitimacy of the EU requires efforts to arrest centralization of European institutions.	85.7	12.9
The key to closing the 'democratic deficit' is strengthening the scrutiny by national parliaments of the EU legislative process.	83.1	16.2

EMU is not achievable by the end of the century, while only 7% of UDF members shared the same view. Nearly 26% of Gaullists disagreed with the idea that France's economy could be damaged if the country did not join the European single currency, but only 3.5% of UDF members. Nearly 20% of Gaullists disagreed or strongly disagreed with the idea that a single currency is necessary to maintain the single market, compared to only 1.8% of UDF members. Moreover, a third of Gaullists agreed with the idea that transferring sovereignty is not acceptable, but only 10.6% of UDF members shared the same opinion. And, 28% were opposed to the creation of an European central bank (see Balleix, 1993, Banerjee 1995), while 8.8% of UDF members took the same view. Finally, 47% of Gaullists asked for a referendum and only 28% of UDF members. On these issues, the RPR appeared to be deeply divided. Although Gaullists have adopted a less nationalist stance, a large minority of them still defend national integrity and the independence of the state.

Survey statements on the social dimension – social costs, labour market flexibility and common policy against unemployment – produced large agreement (Table 10c). Ironically, as the Sheffield paper (Baker *et al.*, 1995) noted, those statements 'reflect the stance of Jacques Delors's white paper on growth'. Unsurprisingly, more than 85% agreed with the idea that social costs placed on employers have to be reduced so as to create jobs. And nearly 75% thought that labour inflexibility is the principal cause of unemployment in the EU.

Cross-tabulated with party membership, the results revealed that the Gaullists answers are very similar to the Centrists' – 89.4% of Gaullists agree with reducing social costs, 85.9% of Centrists respondents concur; 70.6% of Gaullists thought that inflexibility is the main cause of unemployment, 78.9% of Centrists. For Gaullists and Centrists, the European Union has to be a liberal organization. There was considerable approval in both parties for a European common policy on unemployment. This may be mainly explained by the fact that Gaullists and Centrists believe that unemployment affects all members of the EU and that it has to be eradicated at the European level through a common and liberal policy.

There was great ambivalence on the tax harmonization issue (Table 10d). On the one hand, respondents strongly agreed with the harmonization of indirect taxation, such as company taxation (83%), VAT (88%) and customs tariffs (93%). On the other hand, they were opposed to the harmonization of direct personal taxation such as local taxation (70.8%), and they were openly divided on the income tax issue (49.4% agree, 48% disagree). Local taxation and income tax are sometimes both considered as symbols of the direct relationship between citizens and the state, and are consequently part of the sovereignty of the state.

The division on income taxation was reflected within each of the two political parties. French right-wing parliamentarians remain, to a large extent, reluctant to accept any fiscal intervention from the European Community which would jeopardize national independence.

It appears, then, that the attitudes of French right-wing parliamentarians on economic issues reveal strong similarities between the two parties. Nevertheless, linked to the European integration issue, these attitudes may be more often explained by political strategies than by a strong commitment to European principles. A single, but striking, example of this is the consensus of the respondents on the idea of a common policy against unemployment. This problem is viewed as an international one and could not be tackled without a common strategy. Therefore, the Gaullist and Centrist agreement on the economic European Union is not really unconditional.

The Constitution of the EU

We included in the survey several institutional statements dealing with reform of EU institutions, the electoral systems, enlarging the EU and handling foreign and defence policy (Table 10e). On the issue of institutional reform, there was a very strong consensus between the UDF and the RPR respondents, mainly illustrated by common opposition to further supranationalism, in particular a common preference for the Council of Ministers as the supreme institution, and a common wish to strengthen the role of national parliaments in the making of EU legislation. Respondents almost unanimously (93.5 %) agreed with extending the powers of the Council of Ministers. This idea was included in Jacques Chirac's manifesto for the 1995 presidential election. As he said, 'it is the only institution whose legitimacy is derived from the sovereignty of the states'. Almost three-quarters of respondents also proved in favour of a better balance of the right to initiate legislation. The idea of strengthening the scrutiny by national parliaments of the EU legislative process was put forward by some members of the National Assembly during the Maastricht debates, and as a way to solve the problem of the democratic deficit this proposal was also endorsed by Jacques Chirac in his manifesto; 83.1% of respondents supported this view. In a speech he delivered two months before the May 1995 election, he explicitly said that national parliaments had to be more closely associated to the European legislative process because 'nothing good will be achieved without the involvement of peoples. And parliamentarians in Europe are precisely the voice of democracy'.

The idea of introducing a single electoral system for European elections was supported by 79.2% of respondents and on this point, there was no strong difference between the two parties (Table 11). However, the right to vote and run for office given to Europeans inspired a spirited debate in France. Indeed, during the debates on the constitutional revision, Charles Pasqua, President of the RPR group in the Senate, introduced an amendment specifying that only

EU citizens could vote and run for office, and that this right could only become effective through an Act of Parliament. So asking parliamentarians if they would be willing to help Europeans living in France to register on electoral rolls led to a high degree of division: 53.2% agreed with this idea. However, when cross-tabulated with party membership this issue revealed the specific position of the RPR: 48.2% of them disagreed against 44.7%, whereas 64.9% of the UDF respondents agreed with it.

TABLE 11
ATTITUDES TOWARDS EUROPEAN ELECTIONS

	Strongly agree or agree (%)	Disagree or strongly disagree (%)	
A single electoral system for European elections should be introduced	79.2	19.5	

	RPR (%)	UDF (%)	Total
Would you help Europeans living in France to register on electoral rolls?			
yes	44.7	64.9	53.2
no	48.2	31.6	40.9

The issue of enlargement proved to be highly divisive between the two parties (Table 12). It was often raised by RPR parliamentarians as the best means to arrest centralization of the political power of the EU Thus a great majority (92.9%) of respondents agreed with the necessary acceptance of European law and institutions as a condition of entry of new states into the EU. For almost three-quarters of them, enlargement was not considered to be the best way to change the balance of institutional powers in the EU. Actually, 63.5% of the RPR respondents shared this idea, compared with 84.3% of the UDF. Moreover, 87% of respondents thought that deepening European institutions was a prerequisite to widening the EU. The question of accession of the new states from Eastern Europe was really a bone of contention between both parties. On the whole, only 48.1% of the respondents agreed with it and 50% disagreed but, on this point, we found that 58.8% of the RPR respondents agreed against 38.8% opposed, whereas only 35.1% of the UDF agreed against 64.9%. As noted above, this confirmed the fact that, for most UDF parliamentarians, enlargement needs preliminary institutional reform because the present EU institutions are not appropriate for the entry of too many states.

The area of foreign and defence policy is also controversial. Almost all respondents agreed that the war in Bosnia requires strengthening the common security and foreign policy (96.8%) and that a common defence policy necessarily underlines the political identity of the EU (95.5%). However, only 46.8% of respondents agreed with the fact that a single European army would underpin the security of France and cross-tabulated with party membership, this result proved that the RPR feared that a Euro-army could threaten the very existence of the national army as one of the symbols of French sovereignty. Only 42.4% of the Gaullists would support the creation of a single European army, compared to 59.7% of the Centrists.

TABLE 12
ENLARGEMENT OF THE EU

	RPR (%)	U.D.F (%)	Total
Acceptance of European law and institutions must be a condition of entry of new states into the EU.			
Strongly agree or agree	89.4	98.3	92.9
Disagree or strongly disagree	10.6	1.8	7.1
Enlargement is the best means to change the balance of institutional powers in the EU.			
Strongly agree or agree	33.0	14.0	25.9
Disagree or strongly disagree	63.5	50.0	71.4
The entry of new states from Eastern Europe into the EU is desirable in the short term.			
Strongly agree or agree	58.8	35.1	48.0
Disagree or strongly disagree	38.8	64.9	50.0
Deepening European institutions is a prerequisite to widening the EU.			
Strongly agree or agree	82.4	96.5	87.0
Disagree or strongly disagree	14.1	3.5	10.3

Some of the questions addressed by this article remain open. However, two major points can be raised. On the one hand, those results confirmed parliamentarians' support for the official views held by the parties, such as the 'closed federalism' of the Centrists which turned out to be incompatible with the views of an ardent Eurosceptic like Philippe de Villiers. The creation of his own party in 1994, called the *Mouvement pour la France*, therefore remained the only solution he could face. As for the Gaullists, the results suggested the extent of parliamentary support to Jacques Chirac's European policy, so much that even a dissident leader like Philippe Séguin declared last year (Séguin, 1996) that 'the creation of a European single currency was based upon a political union initiated by France and Germany'. On the other hand, the survey disclosed some significant divergences between the two parties. For example, the massive Centrist objection to enlarging the EU was hardly mentioned in their manifesto. Moreover, despite the fact that President Chirac recently dropped his electoral promise of a referendum on the single currency, a significant minority of Gaullists remains in favour of such a vote, like their British counterparts on this issue. Therefore, 'in the foreseeable future', the issue of a single currency is bound to become as problematic for the management of the Gaullist Party as it is for the leaders of the British Conservative Party.

APPENDIX

For comparative purposes, we kept some original statements from the Sheffield survey, but on certain issues we had to find new questions that were specific to the French situation. Finally the survey questionnaire contained 62 questions or statements, including 9 on personal information. The survey was conducted by three mailings between January and June 1996.

Our sample was composed of 116 deputies, 28 senators and 10 Members of the European Parliament, giving an overall response rate of 21.3 %. Among these 116 deputies, 67 belong to the party of President Chirac, the Gaullist RPR, 42 to the UDF and 7 who belong to neither of them or failed to respond. There are also 14 RPR senators and 12 UDF senators as well as 4 members of the European Parliament belonging to the RPR, 3 MEPs from the UDF, and one from the *Mouvement pour la France* led by Sir James Goldsmith and the famous Eurosceptic Philippe de Villiers.

Among all respondents, there were 92.9% of men and only 5.2% of women, which precisely reflects the female minority in the French Parliament: 31.2% aged between 35 and 49 years old, 35.7% between 50 and 59 and 33% more than 60 years old.

	Members	%	Survey (members)	Survey (%)
National Assembly :	461	63.9	116	75.3
Senate :	221	30.4	28	18.2
European Parliament :	41	5.7	10	6.5
Total	723	100.0	159	100.0

ACKNOWLEDGEMENT

We are particularly grateful to Andrew Gamble and Steve Ludlam who gave us assistance and encouragement.

NOTES

1. For the original wording of the French questions, refer to the authors; for the wording of the British questions, see Baker *et al.* (1995) or the British team's Web site at http://www.shef.ac.uk/uni/academic/N-Q/pol/EUROTORY.HTML

BIBLIOGRAPHY

Appleton, Andrew (1992) 'Maastricht and the French Party System : Domestic Implications of the Treaty Referendum', *French Politics and Society* 10: 1–18.

Baker, David, Andrew Gamble and Steve Ludlam (1993a) 'Whips or Scorpions ? Conservative MPs and the Maastricht Paving Motion Vote', *Parliamentary Affairs* 46: 151–66.

Baker, David, Andrew Gamble and Steve Ludlam (1993b) '1846...1906...1996 ? Conservative Splits and European Integration', *Political Quarterly* 64: 420–34.

Baker, David, Andrew Gamble and Steve Ludlam (1994) 'The Parliamentary Siege of Maastricht 1993: Conservative Divisions and British Ratification of the Treaty on European Union', *Parliamentary Affairs* 47: 37–60.

Baker, David, Imogen Fountain, Andrew Gamble and Steve Ludlam (1995) 'Conservative Attitudes to European Integration', *Political Quarterly* 66: 221–33.

Balleix, Corinne (1993) 'Discours politique et intégration européenne : les gaullistes face au projet de banque centrale européenne ', *Revue d'Intégration Européenne* 17: 7–52.

Banerjee, Corinne (1995), 'Libéraux et Centristes face au projet de banque centrale européenne', *Revue du Marché Commun et de l'Union Européenne* 387: 228–37.

Baudouin, Jean (1990) 'Le "moment néo-libéral" du RPR: essai d'interprétation ', *Revue Française de Science Politique* 40: 830–43.

Blumann, Claude (1994) 'La ratification par la France du Traité de Maastricht', *Revue du Marché Commun et de l'Union Européenne*, 379: 393–406.

Chirac, Jacques (1995) 'Mon projet international: une ambition pour l'Europe', *La Lettre de la Nation Magazine*, 292: 6–13.

Criddle, Byron (1993) 'The French Referendum on the Maastricht Treaty September 1992', *Parliamentary Affairs* 46: 228–38.

Séguin, Philippe (1996) 'Colloque Charlemagne' opening speech, Aachen.

Shields, James (1996) 'The French Gaullists', in J. Gaffney (ed.) *Political Parties and the European Union*, pp.86–109. London: Routledge.

The Conservative Party, Electoral Strategy and Public Opinion Polling, 1945–64

Andrew Taylor

This article examines the Conservative Party's adoption and use of opinion research from its defeat in 1945 to the general election of 1964 and seeks to answer two questions: why was polling adopted and what was the influence of polling on party strategy in these years?

The Conservatives were the first British party to adopt opinion research. This continued the party's practice of adopting the most up-to-date electioneering and campaigning techniques in order to bolster its political dominance (Cockett, 1994). Defeat in the 1945 and 1950 general elections and their small parliamentary majority (and minority of votes) in 1951 indicated suspicion of the Conservatives and considerable stability in mass support for Labour. Despite the Conservative victory in 1955, party strategists were puzzled by the electorate's increased volatility in the late 1950s and the consequences of affluence in creating an increasingly instrumental electorate. The instability of the party's support seemed confirmed by its rapid decline after the triumph of 1959, culminating in a narrow defeat in the 1964 general election.

In this increasingly complex and unstable environment, opinion research offered a scientific method of understanding the electorate. Polling was also seen as enabling the party to better target policy and propaganda on those sections of the electorate which were crucial to Conservative victory at the polls.

Opinion Polling and the Post-war Electoral Environment

Defeat in 1945 stimulated Conservative interest in opinion research. The British Institute of Public Opinion (BIPO, later Gallup) had identified the leftward shift in British politics during the war and predicted Labour's landslide in 1945 (Sibley, 1990). Churchill was astonished to learn of the BIPO/*News Chronicle* polls but by the 1950 election he was an avid consumer of polls (Moran, 1966: 335). Conservative interest in opinion research increased further when discontent with the Labour government failed to translate into resounding Conservative victories in 1950 and 1951 (Taylor, 1996). Mark Abrams, one of the founding fathers of opinion research in

Britain, dates the Conservative interest in polling from 1948 when Conservative Central Office (CCO) approached the Colman, Prentis and Varley (CPV) advertising agency for advice on a poster campaign and CPV's research department suggested that market research should be carried out to explore the posters' effect. Abrams claims that the Conservative Party 'was interested only at a dilettante level, and remained uninterested, at least until 1951' (Abrams, 1963: 11). However, the Public Opinion Research Department (PORD) was created in 1947 and despite its short life (it was merged with the Publicity Department in 1952) it made several important contributions to party strategy. Most importantly, it placed polling and opinion research firmly in the Conservative electoral armoury and emphasized the importance of the lower-middle/skilled working-class electorate.

PORD argued strongly that the closeness of the gap between Labour and Conservative meant that ex-Labour and floating voters held the key to victory (CRD, 1949a). Floating voters had decided the outcome of the 1948 presidential election in the United States, and 'If we are to avoid that happening here, most of our methods of approach to the Electorate will surely have to be shaped from now onwards to fit the particular condition of this all-important group'. Polls could penetrate 'this all-important group' and help in formulating an effective appeal (CRD, 1949b).

In the late 1940s the Conservatives identified a large floating vote of affluent, upwardly mobile, politically pragmatic ex-Labour voters who were drawn to Conservatism. These voters were concentrated at the higher paid end of the working class, tended to be married, had steady jobs, did not fear unemployment, had a slightly higher than average level of car ownership, 30% were home owners and one-third were trade unionists. The typical floating voter identified by the survey was 'a fairly well-established individual near the prime of life, standing somewhere about the level where the working class merges into the middle class, a citizen with a degree of responsibility, intelligence, and general interests above the average': 23% identified the Liberals as closest to their way of thinking but only 2.5% had voted Liberal in 1945, consequently, 'One is tempted to draw the conclusion that the label "Liberal" is being used as a convenient cover for many who are really standing at the crossroads'. PORD estimated that 3.5 to 4 million voters had drifted away from Labour since 1945 but only one-third had come over to the Conservatives in 1950 and 1951 (CRD, 1949c).

Conservative electoral strategists were fascinated by the embourgeoisement thesis (the process whereby manual workers adopted middle class consumption patterns and thereby middle class social and political values) and the rise of instrumental voting (Goldthorpe et al.,1968) and the affluent working class became the focal point of Conservative strategy. The logic of instrumentalism pointed to the emergence of a substantial group of voters who felt a basic loyalty to Labour but whose current support was conditional on Labour satisfying their material desires (or offering a persuasive commitment to do so). Labour support was, therefore, less secure. The dissipation of class solidarity from the mid-1950s opened the working class to further penetration by the Conservatives but, paradoxically, also rendered them vulnerable to instrumental evaluations. These developments had been discerned by PORD in the late-1940s and were precisely the sort of electoral developments that polling could explore.

It has been suggested that the Conservative Party was not seriously interested in polling between 1951 and 1955 (Abrams, 1963: 11). This is not so. Close attention was paid to the Gallup polls which indicated that 'there seems to have been little long-term trend' towards the Conservatives among the electorate (CRD, 1954). A subsequent analysis identified a long-run tendency for Labour to be negatively evaluated when voters were asked 'Which party is best...' questions by pollsters, but this was balanced by an indifference to politics generally (CRD 1955a).

From the mid-1950s the political consequences of developing mass affluence became a staple of Conservative electoral thinking and it was in this context that the Conservatives won the Sunderland South by-election (13 May 1953). Labour appealed to memories of the 1930s; the Conservatives to the steady abolition of rationing, increasing prosperity, its housing programme, and the maintenance of full employment and welfare spending. Conservatives won considerable support among affluent young married couples on new housing estates and their majority of 1,175 was described as a 'striking success', signalling the emergence of 'The New Conservatism'. This was the first time since 1924 that a government had won an opposition seat in a by-election and marked a reversal of the normal swing of the pendulum (*The Times* 14 May 1953). Growing working-class Conservatism, Crossman argued, was 'partly owing to the Labour government's success in removing the necessity which drove people into the solidarity of the Labour Movement. If you give people a bourgeois sense of security, the type of working-class movement we had forty years ago will no longer appeal to them. The younger people don't feel the same significance in the slogans.' (Morgan, 1981: 247).

CRD ascribed the Conservative victory in the 1955 general election to Labour abstentions produced by prosperity, its left–right divisions, and lack of an inspirational appeal rather than viewing it as a positive endorsement of Conservatism. None the less, 'Successful post-war Conservative administrations, plus the growing distance of time, rendered the pre-war myths about the Conservatives irrelevant to the mass of voters' (CRD, 1955b). Sir Stephen Pierssene, Central Office General Director, warned Prime Minister Eden that his increased majority and the 2.4% swing 'should not be ascribed so much to a movement of opinion in our favour as to a greater number of abstentions' by Labour supporters. Pierssene had no doubt that the political environment was moving against Labour and growing affluence had left Labour with no programme, 'Conservatives just said that people were better off and left it at that'. Substantial numbers of electors still retrospectively evaluated the party negatively and the period of Conservative rule after 1951 'was too short politically to dispel that feeling'. Labour 'had little or no positive policy of their own and crusading fervour of past days was gone' (CRD, 1955c).

Given the absence of any major ideological controversy dividing the parties, the electorate's evaluation of the relative competence of the government and opposition was of crucial importance (CRD, 1955d). Michael Fraser, deputy CRD director, argued that 'With the Welfare State established and with nationalisation...a non-runner electorally, they [Labour] had run out of ideas' and his conclusion was straightforward: 'After three and a half years of Conservative Government the nation felt on the whole satisfied and in no mood for a change' (CRD, 1955e).

Polling, Instability, Affluence and Conservative Strategy

A key figure in promoting opinion research in the Conservative Party was Oliver Poole (Party Chairman, July 1955–September 1957, and deputy chairman until October 1959). Polling was not used to determine policy or propaganda but to establish how the impact of policy and propaganda could be maximized by identifying and targeting key electoral groups, rather than by blanket appeals to the electorate as a whole. Poole's 'greatest achievement', it has been argued, was 'his single-mindedness in picking out and sticking to one target for Party propaganda', in particular younger affluent working-class voters to whom the appeal of a working-class party calling for working-class solidarity was not strong (Hennessy, 1961: 249). Poole's conviction was confirmed anecdotally by his observation of Saturday morning shoppers in Watford.

In the spring of 1957 he commissioned CPV to begin preparatory work on the next general election campaign and CPV conducted surveys to establish the effect of their poster campaign. Poll evidence underpinned the autumn 1957 poster campaign, *You're Looking at a Conservative*, which used photographs of blue- and white-collar workers, housewives, and so on to reaffirm the notion of the Conservatives as the party of 'One Nation'. Poole also used Neilsen's and the newly formed National Opinion Polls Ltd (NOP), the polling arm of the *Daily Mail*, but Gallup remained the main source of poll data. Despite this activity, Abrams argues that 'in the early part of the 1957 to 1959 period, Conservative headquarters' attitude towards polling was distant and uninterested' and he dates the party's shift in attitude from the publication of *Marginal Seat* in 1958. R.A. Butler (who was the chairman of CRD) wrote the preface to the book in which he acknowledged the importance of behavioural research in Conservative political strategy and said that this was the direct result of the Rochdale by-election (12 February 1958). The seat was captured by Labour because of Liberal intervention and from this point Conservative 'interest in public opinion became almost continuous' (Abrams, 1963: 11; Milne and Mackenzie, 1958: xvii).

Rochdale was pivotal in the party's use of polling. NOP was asked to identify which Conservative voters had defected to the Liberals, and why they had done so (CRD, 1958a). The survey confirmed a substantial (and worrying) loss of support among the lower middle/skilled working class which was the source of 45% of Conservative defectors. The main reason for defection was not the attractiveness of Liberal policies (cited by only 8% of defectors) but general dissatisfaction with government (36%) and the Conservative candidate (24%) (CRD, 1958b).

This pattern was repeated at Torrington (March 1958), a Conservative seat taken by the Liberals. Here, the Labour vote fell by 10.3%, the Conservative by 27.7%, and the Liberals came from nowhere to 38%. Torrington was, however, lost by only 200 votes (polls had predicted a Liberal majority of 2–3,000). This was a marked improvement on Rochdale and the improvement was also reflected in the five by-elections held on 12 June 1958. The Liberal vote worried party strategists who feared initially that by-election success would encourage the Liberal Party to field more candidates, risking a split in the anti-Labour vote. This was soon discounted as there were only six seats with majorities of less than 3,000 where Liberals had stood in 1955, although it was noted that no Liberal had stood in either Rochdale or Torrington in 1955 (CRD, 1958d and 1958c).

January 1957 to October 1959 was a difficult period for the Conservatives. Disaffection was concentrated in two groups: the affluent, upwardly mobile skilled/semi-skilled working class, who were not Conservative partisans, and core lower-middle class Conservative voters. Both groups perceived themselves to be the victims of inflation and expressed hostility to trade union militancy. Controlling inflation in a way that did not jeopardize the Conservative Party's cross-class appeal went to the heart of party and government strategy. After the Ipswich by-election (September 1957), at which the Conservative share of the vote fell by 14.4%, Michael Fraser warned that the party's greatest asset was Labour's unelectability. However, a 'middle-class revolt' – the 'main public expression takes the form of demands from the hard core of the Party for 'more Conservative policies' and for a 'show-down' with the trade unions' – was brewing. Fraser believed that 1955–58 had been wasted so 'our political aim in this second period of office should have been to achieve some rehabilitation of the middle class in the widest sense of that word, while not in the process alienating that wider measure of manual-working [class] support which we had gained by 1955 and upon which we depend for a reasonable majority' (PRO, 1958). These uncertainties required that very close attention be paid to public opinion as 'The days when policy could be framed with complete disregard for public opinion are long past and if we have to take account of public opinion, we might as well take account of a correct measure of public opinion rather than a biased one. Moreover, though policy should perhaps disregard opinion propaganda cannot' (CRD, 1958d: 4).

The Conservative recovery after the summer of 1958 remained fragile. Surveys found that 'Macmillan's popularity has vastly increased [and] Tory voters are drifting back to voting Tory in sufficient numbers to give the Conservatives a small majority' (*The Times* 14 June 1958). The government was also overcoming the perception that it was not in control of events, fostering an image of competence and determination in domestic and foreign affairs. Macmillan's image was crucial to this perception: 'he is prepared to take action, that he is firm and unruffled, that he is sincerely trying to solve our problems had undoubtedly had a considerable effect'. These positive evaluations reinforced the perception of Labour as a divided party without a coherent policy. Future Conservative prospects hinged on prosperity to reinforce this image of competence but events could erode this (CRD, 1958e). To avoid this, Conservative strategists wanted better data on the various electoral sub-groups so as to be better able to target the party's appeal (CCO, 1958).

During the run-up to the 1959 campaign and during the campaign itself, Conservative politicians and strategists detected a climate very different to that of 1951 and 1955, indicating a sea-change in mass political loyalties (Evans and Taylor, 1996: 118–19). Lancashire Conservatives emphasized the importance of affluence, coupled with doubts about Labour's tax policies. Home Counties Conservatives stressed the importance of the government's record and the electorate's belief that prosperity would continue under a Conservative government. They concluded that the party was 'right to exploit the feeling that things were going well: that so many "never had it so good"'. Although Essex Conservatives reported that 'large numbers of Socialists have undergone a complete change and are going to vote Conservative', they also sounded a note of caution. These converts were 'still Socialist at heart, but at the moment their head warns them of the dangers of Socialist Government', the party's hold on these votes was tenuous as 'It might still be possible for the Labour Party to win them back with a powerful emotional appeal' (CCO, 1959a, 1959b and 1959c). The skilled and semi-skilled working class were crucial to the Conservative victory. These constituted two-thirds of the electorate so 'The Conservatives cannot rule unless they succeed in obtaining considerable support within this group'. In 1955 the Conservatives won about one-third, so any losses in this group could deny the Conservatives office (CCO, 1959d: 5). Surveys had now clearly established that discontented supporters tended to abstain or vote Liberal. Liberal by-election surges showed Conservatives registering their disquiet by voting Liberal but then voting Conservative in the subsequent general election.

By the end of the 1950s, the Conservative Party had considerable experience with polling and there was a perception that Conservative electoral success was related to opinion research (Crosland, 1960: 24 n.1).

The party had made extensive use of polls for some time and the decision not to call an election in May 1959 had been based, in part, on poll evidence. Polls were now influencing important decisions so the party had to be assured of their reliability. No assessment or consideration of the contribution of opinion research to party strategy had been made and for this purpose the CRD established the Psephology Group in March 1960.

A digest of the NOP and Gallup evidence was sent to David Butler, who advised the Group that on questions of gathering data pollsters were undoubtedly expert, but on interpreting the data and making political judgements 'there was no reason to believe that pollsters were any more reliable than academics, political journalists or the staffs of political parties'. Butler pointed out that the constant refining of methodology was itself an important source of potential error as this vitiated comparison between surveys. From a party's point of view, comparison over time was more valuable than the snapshot provided by an individual poll. Polls had little predictive value, nor could they accurately detect absolute levels of support for a party; their value lay in discerning broad trends over time. A political party which used polls as forecasts or as a substitute for political judgement was taking a grave risk, Butler argued, but polls could provide useful information on, for example, which social groups voted for which party and what issues concerned the electorate. Polls, he concluded, had an important but limited contribution to make to the formulation of a party's electoral strategy (CRD, 1960a).

James Douglas (the Group's secretary and CRD's in-house psephologist) wrote a critical analysis of Rita Hinden's *Socialist Commentary* survey. Douglas stressed the resilience of the belief that Labour was the 'protector of the underdog' so current patterns of support were, in part, a historical residuum balanced by dislike of aspects of Labour's image (see Table 1). In contrast the Conservative image was of a united party with good leaders which had delivered prosperity; this suggested that a large proportion of Labour's support was retained only by a 'fragile bond'. One-third of Labour's supporters considered themselves not to be working class and one-quarter rejected the description of lower working class; these traits were even more

TABLE 1

PARTY IMAGE AND CLASS APPEAL OF THE LABOUR AND CONSERVATIVE PARTIES, 1960

a. *Perception of the Labour and Conservative parties by Non-Labour and Labour Supporters*

	Net Agree
Statements about each party:	(- = Labour Lead)
Has a united team of top leaders	47
Would make country more prosperous	34
Really respects British traditions	32
Most satisfying for a man with ideals	24
Has a clear-cut policy	24
Out for nation as a whole	13
Would give more chances to person to better self	7
Stands mainly for middle class	6
Would do most for world peace	-4
Believes in fair treatment for all races	-15
Raise standards of living of ordinary people	-20
Would really work to prevent nuclear war	-23
Would try to abolish class differences	-38
Would extend welfare services	-43
Is out to help underdog	-58
Stands mainly for the working class	-74

b. *Types thought most likely to support the Labour and Conservative parties*

	Net Difference
Social Types:	(- = Labour lead).
Middle class people	41
Ambitious people	39
Scientists	38
Office workers	32
Forward looking people	17
Wants stronger laws on crime	17
Young people	10
Practical people	6
Selfish people	6
Optimists	4
People who fiddle	4
Women	-2
Skilled craftsmen	-6
People interested in justice and fair play	-14
Housewives	-14
Parents of schoolchildren	-24
Old-age pensioners	-63
People interested in the underdog	-64
Factory workers	-75
Poor people	-82

Source: Calculated from data in M. Abrams, 'Why Labour has Lost Elections. Part One: Party
          Images', in *Socialist Commentary* (May) 1960, Table 1 (p.5), Table 3(p.7), Table 5 (p.8)
          and Table 6 (p.9).

marked among the non-Labour working class, half of whom described themselves as middle class.

In terms of the Conservative electoral strategy none of this was original and Douglas was careful not to argue that social change would inevitably produce a more Conservative electorate. He wrote, 'It is tempting to conclude that as material prosperity grows, as people become less attached to the working class label, as the lot of underdogs is improved, the Labour Party will disappear. This seems to me to be putting altogether too little weight on the recent inanity of Labour policy'. Labour's electoral weakness was political, not socio-structural, and could be remedied by resolute leadership; equally, many of the economic conditions underpinning the current Conservative dominance could fade 'if [Labour] ever got to the position where it was capable of offering the electorate a clear cut alternative to Conservatism' (CRD, 1960b). From a political strategy perspective, voters already had sharply differentiated images of the Labour and Conservative parties but discounted these images when voting.

Douglas thought that Crosland's *Can Labour Win?* was overly determinist: voting behaviour was a result of social class balanced by current party image. The Conservatives had shed 'many of the repulsive features of our image while the Labour Party has tended to lose the attractive features of their image, partly because we have been able to appropriate them, while they have tended to preserve their repulsive features and indeed add to them'. Crosland's argument was that the shrinkage of the traditional working class coupled with prosperity had eroded working-class solidarity and, if Labour was to recover, it must modernize to appeal to new voters and attitudes. If Labour adopted Crosland's prescriptions, Douglas concluded, it would be hard to differentiate it from the Conservative Party. Social class was important but so was the fact in 1959 'it was never sufficiently clear what you were voting for if you voted Labour' (CRD, 1960 c).

The Psephology Group discussed these issues with Mark Abrams who agreed that social change favoured the Conservatives although this could be swamped by short-term shocks or even a general election campaign. Abrams also stressed the impact of affluence on post-war voters, in particular the importance of home ownership (rather than consumer durables) among the working class, as surveys had shown that about three-quarters of working-class home owners/buyers were Conservative. Voters were marrying and taking on family responsibilities much earlier; they enjoyed better working conditions and were better educated than their parents (Conservative-supporting traits) but they supported high public spending (especially on medical services), favoured greater equality of incomes, and were willing to join trade unions (Labour-supporting traits) (CRD, 1960d). The evidence pointed to an increasingly instrumental, and volatile, electorate in the 1960s.

The Psephology Group's Report was submitted to the Party Chairman in September 1960. It argued that the greater tendency of Conservative supporters to vote was not a function of superior Conservative organisation but of the fact that the middle class were more likely to turn out, while Labour failed to mobilize its support. Thus Labour non-voters were a crucial swing segment of the electorate which

> if ever it was to be activated [would] sweep us far into opposition. They thus represent a danger, but they also represent an opportunity. People do not normally change over immediately from being Socialist to being Conservative. They first get disgruntled with the Labour Party and not bother to vote or vote Liberal, and then only gradually change later [sic] their political allegiance. The non-voting Socialist is thus a potential recruit for the Conservative Party. (CRD, 1960e: para 22)

Despite their importance, the Conservatives had inadequate information on this group and without information it was difficult to formulate an effective strategy. Only polling could elicit this information.

The Psephology Group were especially interested in the behaviour of the youngest age groups who had been particularly influenced by the Conservative image of competence. This effect was complicated, however, by historic class identification, society's changing occupational balance, the growth of middle-class consumption patterns, and home ownership. The conclusion drawn from this was, 'We must keep bright our "image" – competence, opportunity, home ownership, etc.' (CRD, 1960f).

Between 1951 and 1959 the Conservatives had made considerable gains in the 21–30 age group (CRD, 1960e: paras 47 and 51). These voters were drawn to the Conservatives for instrumental reasons, however. They identified themselves as middle class and were optimistic about their future but

> this age group even more than its elders wants to see more money spent on hospitals, houses, roads and...schools...housing...is a much more important issue for them than for their elders. They are prepared to see higher taxation to pay for these things...This is perhaps another indication that what attracts them to the Conservative Party is the 'competence' image rather than the traditional policy distinctions. (CRD, 1960e: paras 52–3)

Crude embourgeoisement theories implied that mass affluence would cause large numbers of Labour working-class voters to defect to the Conservatives, so eroding the class basis of politics: 'that when a working man [sic] has a television set, a refrigerator or a car he is more likely to vote Conservative' (CRD, 1960e: para. 62). However, growing electoral instability, underlying economic weakness, and the polls' demonstration of a solid residuum of 'class' sentiment suggested a much more complex electorate than that implied by crude theories of embourgeoisement. The Psephology Group believed that deferential working-class Conservative voters would decline in numbers (they were concentrated among older voters) in favour of instrumental voters. These were less securely tied to a party but their social background and attitudes inclined them to Labour, and although many voted Conservative they could drift away. The 1959 election had emphasized the importance of these voters: 'The Conservatives cannot rule unless they succeed in obtaining considerable support within this group' (CCO, 1959d: 5). In general, the working class voted Conservative because they saw them as competent and responsible for their affluence and this led the Psephology Group to reject crude affluence theories of political change. Society was changing and becoming wealthier, and the Conservatives had benefited from these changes, but the Group identified no unambiguous causal link between social change and electoral behaviour. Paradoxically, while barriers between the classes were far lower than in the 1930s, the class basis of electoral behaviour was stronger. 'The connection between social class and voting intention...seems fairly well established' and despite social change there had been only a 1% swing to the Conservatives among the manual working class between 1951 and 1959 which meant that Britain was a long way from being a middle-class society (CRD, 1960e: paras 58–9). Acquiring consumer goods, the Group concluded, did not noticeably affect voting, except for home ownership. Of working-class adults who did not vote Labour, one-third were owners or were in the process of buying their house, so 'It would seem that so far as a property owning democracy is concerned "l'appétit vient en mangeant".' (CRD, 1960e: para. 63).

The Psephology Group's analysis reinforced the convergence of the Conservative appeal on the median voter while seeking to maximize the turnout of their core electorate (Abrams, 1964: 14–16 and CRD, 1960e: para 30). Electoral behaviour, in both by-elections and general elections, suggested that the most damaging losses came not from 'core' voters but from 'movements in the centre of the political spectrum'. This was the lesson of Rochdale, where 'it was the loss of the lower middle-class and upper-working class votes...that proved decisive' and by extension it was their retention in 1959 which gave the Conservatives their third consecutive election victory (CRD, 1960e: para 31). The implications for party electoral strategy were clear; 'The critical class lies, so to speak, at the juncture of the lower middle class and working class' and although this was a difficult group to isolate, winning its support was the key to electoral victory (CRD 1960e: para 60).

Polling and the Conservative Decline 1961–64

By the early 1960s fieldwork in Conservative marginals was emphasising the importance of mass prosperity in electoral behaviour. In Hemel Hempstead, for example, a Conservative seat believed vulnerable to the Liberals, a survey found:

> a change of attitude on the part of the general public. A survey such as this conducted before the war, would have invariably drawn a high percentage of comments on the low prosperity the informant was enjoying…Today, we find a much wider field of concern than purely feeding one's family, and from this we can deduct [sic] that people really are enjoying the benefits of a healthy standard of living.

The effect of this was to undermine the social bases (especially class) of party loyalty and over 26% of those polled reported 'an acceptance of the non-class political approach' (CCO 1961: 3).

Between the autumn of 1960 and the general election in October 1964 the Conservative government endured a series of major disasters. These were the collapse of public confidence in Macmillan as Prime Minister, the Liberal revival and the problem of an out-dated party image, symbolized by Sir Alec Douglas Home as Prime Minister (Cockerell 1988: 96–112). These problems were interconnected and all focused on the outdatedness of the Conservative image, a growing perception of boredom with the Conservatives and receptivity to the idea that it was time for a change. Assessing these problems and formulating a strategy was a task for which opinion polls (the doubts of the Psephology Group notwithstanding) were ideally suited.

In March 1963 the dormant Psephology Group returned to its 1960 report and reassessed its conclusions in the light of current politics. It found that 'the new middle classes' had become estranged from the Conservative cause and this underpinned the Liberal resurgence. The C1/C2s gave most cause for concern. They were a large part of the electorate and it had been established in post-by-election surveys that they accounted for 70% to 80% of Conservative defectors. Liberal voting indicated a loss of confidence in the government as many 'Liberal' voters knew nothing about Liberal policies. CRD focused on the key question of the perceived competence of Conservative governments in delivering prosperity. This factor had been crucial in weakening Labour's grip on the working-class electorate. The report stressed the dangers of an instrumental electorate. 'This', the report noted, 'has a bearing on strategy. They are not the sort of people for whom Socialism is a bogey. For most of them a Labour government would be a perfectly normal choice approved by most of their fellows'. The report went on to raise the intangible, but none the less vital electoral factor of the 'climate of the times'; 'In voting Conservative in 1955 and 1959 they were probably conscious of being rather daring, emancipated and smart. They no longer think it smart' (CRD, 1963: para. 10).

The difficulty lay with the young voter who had no political memory of any government other than a Conservative one or of economic conditions other than full employment and prosperity. The 1955 and 1959 victories had been built upon the votes of a prosperous but traditional working class which had not been converted to Conservatism. This electorate's 'political movements have been influenced by nothing much more deep seated than a change of mood, fashion tinged with self-interest and a fairly shrewd, though superficial, assessment of their rulers'. Principles or ideologies were irrelevant compared to 'bread and butter' issues. These voters were weakly committed to parties but evaluated how they affected (or might affect) their day-to-day existence and were disaffected from government (CRD 1963: para 11–12). The Conservative victories of 1955 and 1959 had been based on the delivery of prosperity and their current problems could not be ascribed simply to current economic (and other) difficulties but to a change of mood generated by that prosperity; 'To-day what has been achieved still seems good but it is no longer seen as in danger and it is no longer sufficient. The record of the 1950s is irrelevant'. The party might not benefit even if the economy recovered as attention had now focused on the question of the government's competence; 'Above all, the present image of ineffectualness and indecisiveness needs to be attacked...an impression of vacillation and half-hearted policies' (CRD, 1963: para. 15–16).

In their study of electoral change between 1959 and 1964 Butler and Stokes (1969: 350) found that barely one-fifth of Labour's lead in 1964 was due to the conversion of Conservative voters, indicating the solidity of the core Conservative vote. The Conservative defeat in 1964 was the product of a small shift of opinion within the electorate based on dissatisfaction with the performance and image of the Macmillan and Home governments. The political turbulence of this period underpinned the Conservative Party's acceptance of polling: 'the polls came in from the cold, the study of electoral behaviour became almost acceptable, psephology changed into a pseudo-scientific subject from being considered witchcraft and mumbo-jumbo' (Teer and Spence, 1973: 159). Making increased use of polls did not make the task of dealing with the party's slump in popularity any easier, indeed there is evidence of 'information overload'. That the government and party's image had collapsed after July 1961 was incontrovertible but the poll data gave no clear hint of how to respond, especially as some of the key problems (for example, boredom) were very difficult to deal with politically (Evans, 1981: 191).

These problems led to an increase in opinion research which was accompanied by considerable scepticism within Central Office and from senior politicians. Interestingly, Butler and King report that the Conservative's use of opinion research in this period was less effective than Labour's, which is significant given Crosland's earlier strictures (1965: 91). NOP's post-mortem on the Orpington by-election disaster had found the same factors at work as at Torrington, but of greater significance was the NOP survey of 10,000 voters conducted in 1963. This remains the largest single survey ever conducted by a political party in Britain and the hope was that it would provide the basis for a challenge to the slump in popularity. The NOP 10,000 focused on the hardy perennials of Conservative strategy: Conservative defectors, new voters, floating voters and those who did not intend to vote. The survey produced a huge amount (four volumes) of data but added little to the party's knowledge about the electorate. Its conclusions were, first, that the post-1959 swing away from the Conservatives had been heaviest among the young, the lower-middle class, and the affluent working class. Second, the party was perceived to be too close to big business and too middle class in orientation; and third, Home's leadership was a source of electoral weakness whereas Wilson was attractive to large number of voters (CCO, 1964). There was nothing here that could not be gleaned from by-election results, published polls, or by following Poole's example in Watford and listening to what people were saying.

The Conservatives had a clear picture of what was wrong but found it difficult to formulate a response at a time when opinion was hostile and when the party had a leader who was difficult to 'package'. The NOP 10,000 is sometimes portrayed as a lost opportunity for the Conservatives, and it has been suggested that had they acted upon its message the 1964 election could have been won. This is doubtful as the survey confirmed what was already known but did not clarify how things might be changed. The conventional wisdom was (and remains) that the poor Conservative image relative to Labour in this period led the Conservatives to adopt a modernisation strategy. In fact, modernisation had been pushed strongly by Macmillan as early as 1961 and, despite a renewed publicity effort in the winter of 1964, modernisation did not influence opinion, largely because it was not convincing. Modernisation became the dominant appeal only after Heath's election as leader in 1965. Party strategists were suspicious of calls by publicity specialists for a 'big idea' (such as modernisation) with which to appeal to the voter. One critic wrote in early 1959, 'I am convinced and always have been that people want to keep more of their own money and the first party that lets them will gain the day' (CCO, 1959e). This is why the party returned to the themes of the 1959 election, concentrating on what had been achieved and warning of the threat posed by Labour. This strategy (and Home's stumping the country) proved very successful as the Conservative lost the 1964 election narrowly, Labour having a majority of only four seats.

A post-election survey of 1964 voters, which measured party image, came to clear and worrying conclusions about the Conservative Party. The survey found that the party was 'considered *less* honest, good, wise, united, exciting, young and modern than either of the other two parties' (CCO, 1965: 43). All three parties had improved their image but the relative positions had remained unchanged with one important exception. The Conservatives were 'seen as a little less powerful, expert and strong-minded than Labour'. This testified to the party's failure 'to project itself as capable of dealing with the problems people consider important', which had been the core of its appeal in the late 1950s and early 1960s. But the image problem went deeper as:

> the Party is still seen as potentially expert and forceful, but not in touch with modern, exciting ideas. Its failure to attract young people supports this suggestion, as well as in general augering [sic] badly for the future. Policy makers might well conclude that to give the Party a younger image is extremely important.

The survey also found the Conservative vote to be 'softer' than Labour's. Intending Conservative voters, for example, 'share[d] the general feeling about the Conservative Party's modernity [and] they are less wholehearted about their own party than Labour voters'. Leader image was an important aspect of the party image. Home had regained a considerable amount of public esteem before and during the 1964 election. His image ('honest, good and wise') was an asset but Home was also perceived to be 'slightly less powerful, expert and strong-minded' than the Conservative Party and this was of concern. It was believed that in modern electioneering, with its emphasis on television, the media inevitably concentrated on the party leader. So, it was considered essential that the leader should be more popular than his party. The weakest aspect of the party's image was its perceived lack of modernity. On the other hand it was seen as 'reasonably expert' but at the same time was perceived to be increasingly ineffective. Home's personal character compensated for this to some degree but he was also seen as ineffective compared to Wilson, while Labour was perceived as modern, expert and able to get things done (CCO, 1965: 43–7).

Home was disdainful of the polls and could not understand why they attracted so much political and media attention but he was very interested in how a picture of party and leadership image was built up using poll data. In an attempt to assess the polls' utility he paid a secret and private visit to NOP in July 1965 where he was very impressed by the speed with which computers translated punch-cards into results (indicating a fall in Labour's lead). Despite attempts to keep the character profiles secret, Home insisted on seeing them, which was unfortunate as they showed that the public believed Wilson to be more sincere and trustworthy than Home. This crystallized Home's doubts about the wisdom of continuing as party leader (Margach, 1978: 134–5).

Thus, polls attained 'a new level of prominence during the 1959–64 parliament and they had an unquestionable impact on the style in which the 1964 election was fought and on the morale of the protagonists' (Butler and King, 1965: 204). After the 1964 election defeat and Home's resignation in 1965, the Conservative Party moved rapidly to embrace polling as a central weapon in its attempts to regain office from Labour and to project a new, modern image under its new leader, Edward Heath (Campbell, 1993: 170–71). Defeat in 1964 and 1966 was seen as the result of both poor communications and a failure to remain in intimate contact with public opinion. Both could be addressed by more and better polling (Kavanagh, 1995: 51).

Conclusion

Electoral behaviour from 1945 to 1964 was far more complex than is usually allowed, as Liberal revivals and growing mass affluence pointed to an increasingly instrumental and volatile electorate. Opinion polling and opinion research offered a way of increasing the Conservative Party's understanding of electoral change. Traditionally, the Conservative approach to mass democracy has involved four pillars. First, election campaigns are the culmination of a long-term propaganda effort. Popular opinion had to be monitored constantly and propaganda adjusted accordingly. Second, party policy had to be presented in an easily understood way and be directly relevant to the voters' every-day experience. Third, professional expertise was indispensable in opinion politics and, finally, public opinion should never supplant party policy but be used to improve the attractiveness of the latter. In this sense the Conservative Party's growing interest in the politics of public opinion and opinion research was part of a tradition central to Conservative statecraft. Opinion polling was the latest in a long succession of techniques used by the Conservatives.

The lesson of the mid-to-late 1950s was that party (and government) image was an increasingly important determinant of party choice at a time when voters appeared to be abandoning their historical loyalties. These trends were all the more important because central to the Conservatives' image was their reputation as the party of affluence which itself was identified a major solvent of long-term loyalties. The Psephology Group recognized the value of the polls in exploring broad trends and divining the issues which concerned voters, so influencing the presentation of the party's image. As Michael Fraser commented, polls had little role in policy but much to offer propaganda.

Polls did not, however, significantly enhance the party's control over the electorate. Up to 1965 and Heath's election as leader, the party's use of polls was reactive and diagnostic, explaining which groups had defected (and why) from the party, and the evidence they produced largely confirmed what was already known. So in this sense polls were of limited value to the party in the period covered by this article but they were to play a crucial role in rebuilding the party's image after 1965.

The direct effect of the polls on Conservative political and electoral strategy is not easy to discern. From the late-1940s, however, polls led to a closer consideration of the nature of the floating voter and offered the possibility of targeting sub-groups of voters. Elections were decided by weak partisans, abstainers, and don't knows whose unpredictability was exacerbated by a perception that policy differences between Labour and Conservative were narrowing, despite the continued strength of the class base and a clear perception that the two parties had very different images and social appeal. This was a consequence of affluence and social change which encouraged voters unattached or weakly attached to a party to vote instrumentally. If these voters had been won to Conservatism because Conservative governments were perceived to be both competent and delivering prosperity, they could be lost with a change of perception. This made the task of government and party far more complex.

By the early 1960s groups which had benefited from the prosperity of the 1950s were precisely those which were defecting, as their perception of the Conservative government's competence changed. The party's use of polls helps to explain the direction of Conservative politics in the early 1960s and why they embraced modernisation. The Psephology Group's report, by-election post-mortems and the NOP 10,000 survey created an appreciation of what polls could and could not achieve. By 1961–62, however, the Conservative image of competence had been undermined and this, coupled with economic and political difficulties fuelled the government's adoption of a modernisation strategy to win back the affluent upwardly mobile. This lacked credibility under Sir Alec Douglas Home whereas Labour's revival under Harold Wilson, whose modernisation theme contrasted sharply with the Conservatives' poor image, was sufficient to put Labour in government. The lesson learned (or, more accurately, re-learned) by the Conservative Party, was the oldest in liberal democratic politics: the party which loses contact with public opinion loses elections.

ACKNOWLEDGEMENT

The author would like to thank the Conservative Party chairman for permission to consult and quote from this material and Dr Martin Maw (the party archivist) for his help in finding the relevant information.

BIBLIOGRAPHY

Abbreviations used in the references: CCO is Conservative Central Office and CRD is Conservative Research Department. All CCO and CRD files are held in the Conservative Party Archive at the Bodleian Library, Oxford.

Abrams, Mark (1963) 'Public Opinion Polls and Political Parties', *Public Opinion Quarterly* 27: 9–18.

Abrams, Mark (1964) 'Opinion Polls and Party Propaganda', *Public Opinion Quarterly,* 28: 13–20.

Butler, David and Anthony King, (1965) *The British General Election of 1964.* London: Macmillan.

Butler, David and Donald Stokes, (1969) *Political Change in Britain. Forces Shaping Electoral Choice.* Harmondsworth: Penguin Books.

Campbell, John (1993) *Edward Heath. A Biography,* London: Jonathan Cape.

CCO (1958) *4/8/36 James Douglas to Ronald Simms,* 13 August.

CCO (1959a) *4/8/113 Fourth Intelligence Report,* 16 September.

CCO (1959b) *4/8/107 North West Area Report on the General Election Campaign,* 20 October.

CCO (1959c) *4/8/107 Home Counties North/Home Counties South East Report on the General Election,* October.

CCO (1959d) *4/8/104 The General Election of 1959,* no date.

CCO (1959e) *4/8/36 Public Opinion Polls,* 19 January.

CCO (1961) *4/8/36 Field Survey (Autumn 1960) of Hemel Hempstead Constituency,* February 1961.

CCO (1964) *180/11/1/1 The NOP 10,000 Survey.*

CCO (1965) *180/11/2/1 Voters in the 1964 General Election, Volume 1.*

Cockerell, Richard (1988) *Live From Number 10. The Inside Story of Prime Ministers and Television,* new edition. London: Faber and Faber.

Cockett, Richard (1994) 'The Party, Publicity, and the Media', in Anthony Seldon and Stuart Ball (eds.), *Conservative Century. The Conservative Party Since 1900,* pp.547–77. Oxford: Oxford University Press.

CRD (1949a) *2/21/1 Brigadier Clarke to Chief Publicity Officer,* 22 November.

CRD (1949b) *2/21/1 The Approach to the Ex-Socialist Floating Voter,* 30 December.

CRD (1949c) *2/21/1 The Floating Vote,* 28 November.

CRD (1954) *2/21/5 Gallup Polls,* 14 June.

CRD (1955a) *2/21/5 Gallup Polls,* 2 December.

CRD (1955b) *2/28/54 The General Election,* 8 June.

CRD (1955c) *2/28/54 General Director's Report to the Prime Minister,* 22 June.

CRD (1955d) *2/28/54 The British General Election 1955. Appendix: Personal Observations.* (P.B. Bunyan).

CRD (1955e) *2/28/4 Report on the General Election of 1955. Policy and Administration: General Assessment of the Campaign,* 17 June. (M. Fraser).

CRD (1958a) *2/21/5 Abstract of National Opinion Polls Ltd. Rochdale By-Election,* 27 February.

CRD (1958b) *2/21/5 Rochdale By-Election,* 27 February.

CRD (1958c) *2/21/5 Notes on National Opinion Poll Reports,* 27 February.

CRD (1958d) *2/21/5 Public Opinion,* 21 February.

CRD (1958e) *2/21/5 Report on Public Opinion,* 9 October.

CRD (1960a) *2/21/6 Psephology Group 6/11 Minutes of 5th Meeting,* 13 June.

CRD (1960b) *2/21/6 Psephology Group 60/2 Comments on Dr. M. Abrams, Why Labour Has Lost Elections.* (James Douglas).

CRD (1960c) *2/21/6 Psephology Group, 'Can Labour Win?' by Anthony Crosland,* 15 May. (James Douglas).

CRD (1960d) *2/21/6 Psephology Group 60/13 7th Meeting,* 18 July.

CRD (1960e) *2/21/6 First Report of the Psephology Group to the Chairman of the Conservative Party,* 15 October.

CRD (1960f) *2/21/6 Psephology Report: Political Lessons which Emerge.* (no date, but 1960).

CRD (1963) *2/21/6 PG 63/19 Psephology Report Reviewed in the Light of Current (March 1963) Conditions*, 10 April.

Crosland, Anthony (1960) *Can Labour Win?* Fabian Tract 234. London: Fabian Society.

Evans, Brendan and Andrew Taylor (1996) *From Salisbury to Major: Continuity and Change in Conservative Politics*, Manchester: Manchester University Press.

Evans Harold (1981) *Downing Street Diary*. London: Hutchinson.

Goldthorpe, John, David Lockwood, Frank Bechhofer and Jennifer Platt (1968) *The Affluent Worker: Political Attitudes and Behaviour*, Cambridge: Cambridge University Press.

Hennessy, David (1961) 'The Communication of Conservative Policy, 1957–1959', *Political Quarterly* 32: 238–56.

Kavanagh, Dennis (1995) *Election Campaigning. The New Marketing of Politics*, Oxford: Blackwells.

Lamb, Richard (1995) *The Macmillan Years 1957–63. The Emerging Truth* , London: John Murray.

Margach, James (1978) *The Abuse of Power. The War between Downing Street and the Media from Lloyd George to Callaghan*, London: W.H. Allen.

Milne, A. and R. Mackenzie (1958) *Marginal Seat*. London: The Hansard Society.

Moran, Lord (1966) *Winston Churchill: The Struggle for Survival, 1940–1965*. London: Sphere Books.

Morgan, Janet (ed.) (1981) *The Backbench Diaries of Richard Crossman*. London: Jonathan Cape.

Public Record Office (1958) *PREM 11/2248 Some Thoughts of the Present Situation*, 20 September.

Sibley, R (1990) 'The Swing to Labour During the Second World War: When and Why?', *Labour History Review* 55: 23–34.

Taylor, Andrew (1996) 'Public Opinion, Party Strategy and the Emergence of the New Conservatism, 1945–1955', Working Paper 9, Department of Politics: University of Huddersfield.

Teer, Fred and Jack Spence (1973) *Political Opinion Polls*. London: Hutchinson.

Reference Section

To a large extent the range and nature of material covered in this section are now well established. As in previous volumes in the series, we begin with the handy chronology of important events in 1996 prepared, as usual, by David Broughton; anyone who has had to survey the period since the last election will know that Broughton's annual chronologies are invaluable.

The next three sections are also regular features – detailed results of the three parliamentary by-elections held during the year, summaries of opinion poll results on voting intentions and other relevant matters, and a summary of the May local election results together with information on local by-elections. The latter formerly concerned hardly anyone outside a small circle of enthusiasts but during 1996 they began to be cited by the Conservatives as evidence of a recovery in their popularity.

Section 5 re-introduces a topic which we covered in earlier editions of *British Elections & Parties* – details of various economic indicators in summary form, which might save readers some research time if they are looking for this sort of material.

The section on political parties contains material updated from previous editions and finally we include an updated and substantially expanded list of Web sites of interest to teachers, researchers and students working on parties, elections and public opinion.

We would like to express our thanks to those who have helped in the gathering and checking of the material contained in this section, including David Broughton, David Cowling, Colin Rallings, Michael Thrasher, Nick Moon of NOP and Bob Wybrow of Gallup.

David Denver
Justin Fisher

1. Chronology of Events 1996

JANUARY

1. A man was shot dead in Lurgan in Northern Ireland by the *Direct Action Against Drugs* organization, the seventh such killing since April 1995.

3. An order was issued for the deportation of a Saudi Arabian dissident, Mohammed al-Mas'ari, following complaints by the Saudi Arabian government over his activities in London.

5. It was officially confirmed that there was no intention to sell Admiralty Arch in central London.

8. An industrial tribunal ruled that the Labour Party's policy, requiring selection of prospective parliamentary candidates in certain constituencies to be from women-only short lists, contravened the Sex Discrimination Act of 1975.
   Labour Party leader, Tony Blair, made a speech in Singapore in which he set out his vision of a 'stakeholder economy'.
   François Mitterrand, President of France 1981–95, died aged 79.

9. Sir Christopher Bland was appointed chairman of the BBC in place of Marmaduke Hussey.

11. The former Prime Minister, Baroness Thatcher, delivered the Keith Joseph Memorial Lecture in which she called for radical expenditure cuts and derided what she termed 'no-nation Conservatism'.

17. Sir Richard Body resumed the Conservative whip in the House of Commons which he had voluntarily resigned in November 1994 over the European Communities (Finance) Bill. The overall Conservative majority in the Commons was thereby restored to five, with two by-elections pending.

18. The Prime Minister, John Major, announced that the government would issue a White Paper setting out its position on Europe prior to the opening of the European Union's Inter-Governmental Conference (IGC) in March.

The Home Secretary, Michael Howard, announced that the practice of shackling pregnant prisoners who were about to give birth would be discontinued.

19.   At the end of a trial lasting nearly eight months, Kevin and Ian Maxwell were cleared by a jury of conspiracy charges in connection with the collapse of the companies controlled by their father, the late Robert Maxwell.
         The House of Commons narrowly failed to give a second reading to the British Time (Extra Daylight) Bill, a private member's measure to align time in the United Kingdom with that on the continent of Europe.

21.   Sharp differences over education policy emerged in the Labour Party when it was revealed that Shadow Cabinet member Harriet Harman was to send her son to a selective grammar school in Kent.

22.   The ruling faction of Walsall Metropolitan District Council was displaced by another faction of the Labour Group.

23.   The House of Commons privileges committee issued a report critical of the former editor of the *Guardian* (Peter Preston) for using House of Commons headed paper in a fax purporting to come from the then Chief Secretary to the Treasury, Jonathan Aitken. The committee declined to take any further action.

24.   The Prime Minister announced proposals for elections to a Northern Ireland assembly.

26.   Kevin Maxwell was ordered to stand trial on further charges of conspiracy to defraud, in connection with the collapse of companies controlled by his late father.
         The House of Commons gave an unopposed second reading to the Offensive Weapons Bill, a private member's bill designed to forbid the carrying of dangerous knives.

30.   Nicholas Soames, Minister for the Armed Forces, announced that a series of epidemiological studies would be undertaken arising from allegations of the effects of Gulf War syndrome.
         Gino Gallagher, an alleged leader of the banned Irish National Liberation Army, was shot dead in Belfast.
         A large cross-party grouping of MPs called for the issue of parliamentary salaries to be referred to the Nolan Committee.

31.   The Labour Party announced that it would not be appealing against the ruling that its policy on all-women short lists was illegal.

FEBRUARY

1.   The Labour Party retained the Hemsworth parliamentary seat in a by-election. A Socialist Labour Party candidate saved her deposit.

The Conservative backbench 1922 committee agreed new procedures whereby it would not be possible to launch a direct challenge to John Major's leadership of the Conservative Party before the next general election.

Gerry Adams, the President of Sinn Féin, held a meeting with President Bill Clinton in Washington.

5.   The first privatized rail services began running on South West Trains and Great Western routes.

7.   Tony Blair, the Labour Party leader, announced his party's proposals for removing from hereditary peers their right to participate in the work of the House of Lords.

8.   United News and Media (publishers of the *Daily Express* and other newspapers) and MAI (a television and financial services group) announced their intention to merge.

The National Health Service prescription charge was increased from £5.25 to £5.50 with effect from 1 April.

The Roman Catholic Archbishop of Liverpool since 1976, Derek Worlock, died aged 76.

9.   A huge bomb exploded on the Isle of Dogs in east London, apparently having been placed by the IRA, thus effectively ending the IRA ceasefire.

12.   John Townend was elected chairman of the Conservative 92 Group of right-wing MPs in succession to Sir George Gardiner who did not stand for re-election.

15.   The report of Sir Richard Scott's inquiry into the export of defence equipment to Iraq was published. The interpretation of the report's contents differed markedly between the government and the opposition, in particular over whether the report had exonerated the Cabinet ministers concerned.

18.   A bomb exploded on a bus in central London, killing the alleged IRA member who was carrying it.

19.   Gillian Shepherd, the Education and Employment Secretary, announced a far-reaching national committee of inquiry into higher education, to be chaired by Sir Ron Dearing.

22.   Sir Richard Scott made known his disapproval of what he called the selectivity on the part of ministers in quoting his report on the export of defence equipment to Iraq.
        Peter Thurnham announced his resignation of the Conservative whip over the party's attitude to the report of the Nolan Committee and Sir Richard Scott's report on defence exports to Iraq. He intended to sit in the House of Commons as an independent. The Conservative Party's majority was thereby reduced to two.

26.   At the end of a debate on the Scott report, the government had a majority of one. The issue was also debated in the House of Lords.

27.   It was confirmed that Labour MP Geoffrey Robinson had acquired the ownership of the *New Statesman and Society* which had recently gone into receivership.

28.   The Prime Minister and his Irish counterpart, John Bruton, announced detailed plans for progress on Northern Ireland, including elections to a forum for all-party talks and a fixed date for the start of such talks.
        The Princess of Wales announced that she had agreed to a divorce from the Prince of Wales
        The Labour Party's national executive committee decided to review the selection of prospective parliamentary candidates in three constituencies.

MARCH

1.   Ron Davies, Labour's Shadow Welsh secretary, voiced doubts in a television interview about the fitness of the Prince of Wales to become king. He later apologized and withdrew the remarks.

4.   The first session of the revised peace talks in Northern Ireland were boycotted by most of the potential participants, while Sinn Féin delegates were refused entry.

5. The European Court of Justice ruled that the UK was liable to pay damages to owners of Spanish fishing vessels which were excluded from British waters for a period between 1989 and 1990.
    The Chief Immigration Appeal Adjudicator ruled that the Home Secretary, Michael Howard, should reconsider his decision to deport the Saudi Arabian dissident, Mohammed al-Mas'ari.

12. The government issued a White Paper on its approach to the forthcoming European Union Inter-Governmental Conference.
    An Advocate General of the European Court of Justice delivered the preliminary opinion that the UK must adhere to a maximum of a 48-hour working week as laid down in a 1993 directive on the grounds that this was a health and safety measure rather than a social measure.

13. Sixteen young children and their teacher were shot dead at their school in Dunblane in Scotland by a man (Thomas Hamilton) who then killed himself. The following day, Lord Cullen, a senior Scottish judge, was appointed to undertake an inquiry into the shootings.

14. A total of 23 Labour MPs opposed the regular continuation of the Prevention of Terrorism Act even though the Labour Party was not opposing the renewal.

20. Stephen Dorrell, Secretary of State for Health and Douglas Hogg, Minister for Agriculture, both made statements to the House of Commons on a report that there was a link between Creutzfeld-Jakob disease (CJD) and BSE (mad cow disease).

21. John Major announced the arrangements for elections to take place in Northern Ireland on 30 May to the new peace forum.
    France, Belgium and the Netherlands were among the countries to ban the import of British beef in the light of the report linking CJD in humans with BSE in cattle.

22. Ron Hayward, general secretary of the Labour Party 1972–82, died aged 78.

27. The European Commission imposed a total ban on exports of British cattle, beef and beef products to other EU member states and elsewhere in the world.
    The Labour Party national executive committee announced that the party's draft manifesto for the next general election would be put to

all party members for endorsement later in the year, after its submission to the party's annual conference.

29.   Heads of Government from the 15 EU member states met in Turin in Italy to launch the Inter-Governmental Conference.

The Home Office agreed to settle the unfair dismissal claim of the former director-general of the Prison Service, Derek Lewis, who had been sacked in October 1995.

Will Hutton, assistant editor of the *Guardian* was appointed editor of the *Observer* in place of Andrew Jaspan.

APRIL

3.   A meeting of European Union Agriculture Ministers ended without any agreement on lifting the EU ban on exports of British beef.

The Home Secretary, Michael Howard, published a White Paper (*Protecting the Public*) which set out a strategy for tackling crime which included radical reforms to sentencing.

8.   The first march of the 'marching season' in Northern Ireland was marked by confrontation between the police and loyalist marchers.

11.   In a by-election, the Labour Party won the Staffordshire South East seat, with a 22 per cent swing from the Conservatives, whose parliamentary majority was thereby reduced to one.

12   Mirror Group Newspapers and Irish Independent Newspapers provided further funding for Newspaper Publishing (publisher of the *Independent* and the *Independent on Sunday*) of which they were the dominant shareholders.

15.   Sir George Young, the Transport Secretary, confirmed that the whole of Railtrack would be sold in a privatization planned for May.

16.   The government said it would challenge the EU ban on the export of British beef in the European Court of Justice.

17.   A bomb apparently placed by the IRA exploded in South Kensington in London.

18.   Mohammad al-Mas'ari, the Saudi Arabian dissident, was given permission to remain in the UK for four years.

23. The House of Commons rejected, by 83 votes to 77, leave for the introduction of the European Communities (European Court) Bill proposed by Conservative MP, Iain Duncan Smith, which sought to 'disapply' judgements, rulings and doctrines propounded by the European Court of Justice.

24. A large bomb believed to have been placed by the IRA was discovered and disarmed on Hammersmith Bridge in London.
The Home Secretary, Michael Howard and the Scottish Secretary, Michael Forsyth, announced a firearms amnesty to run 3–30 June.

26. Andrew Marr was appointed editor of the *Independent*.

MAY

1. It was announced in the Defence White Paper that the last RAF base in Germany would be closed in the year 2002.
Arthur Scargill, the President of the National Union of Mineworkers, formally launched the Socialist Labour Party.

2. In local elections in many parts of England, the Conservatives suffered net losses of more than 500 seats, while the Labour Party and the Liberal Democrats made net gains of over 400 and nearly 150 seats respectively. Labour secured control of 10 of the 13 new unitary authorities and the Liberal Democrats gained control of one.
It was announced that Lord Taylor of Gosforth was to retire prematurely as Lord Chief Justice on health grounds.
The High Court ruled that the Home Secretary, Michael Howard, had been wrong to impose 15-year prison sentences on the two juveniles convicted of the murder of two-year old James Bulger in 1993.

7. A revised register of MPs' interests was published, although a number of Conservative MPs had declined to state their earnings from consultancy work.

9. Dame Shirley Porter, a former Conservative leader of Westminster City Council, was surcharged, along with two of her former colleagues, with the sum of £31 million for the role she had played in implementing housing policy in marginal wards in Westminster designed to secure a Conservative majority on the council.

10.   The government blocked the passage in the House of Commons of the Stalking Bill introduced by Labour MP Janet Anderson, which would have made stalking a criminal offence.

16.   The Nolan Committee published its second main report on local spending bodies such as further and higher education bodies, grant-maintained schools and housing associations.

20.   The privatization of Railtrack was completed with the allocation of shares within the oversubscribed UK public offer.

21.   The Prime Minister announced that, in the light of the EU's failure to lift the ban on exports of British beef, the UK government would block decisions requiring a unanimous decision of EU member states.

24.   Sir Thomas Bingham was appointed Lord Chief Justice in place of Lord Taylor of Gosforth. Bingham was succeeded as Master of the Rolls by Lord Woolf, hitherto a Law Lord.

28.   Two ministers (Baroness Chalker, the Minister for Overseas Development and Roger Freeman, the Chancellor of the Duchy of Lancaster) implemented the government's policy of blocking decisions within the EU.

29.   The inquiry led by Lord Cullen into the murder of 16 children and their teacher in Dunblane opened in Stirling.

30.   In elections to the new 110-member constitutional forum in Northern Ireland, the Official Unionists won 30 seats, the Democratic Unionist Party won 24, the SDLP won 21, Sinn Féin won 17 and six other parties won 18 seats between them.

JUNE

2.   Rod Richards resigned as Under-Secretary of State at the Welsh Office after press allegations of an extra-marital affair.

4–7.   The Irish President, Mary Robinson, began a four-day visit to the UK, the first official visit by an Irish President, during which she held talks with the Prime Minister and met the Queen.

5. The European Commission agreed to ease the ban on the export from the UK of certain beef products (gelatine, tallow and semen).
    The Nolan Committee announced that its next study would cover standards in public life in local government.
    The second Severn Crossing road bridge was opened linking England and Wales across the River Severn.

6. Former US Senator, George Mitchell, was named as the co-chair of the forum to consider the future of Northern Ireland.

7. John Birt, the director general of the BBC, announced widespread changes to the internal structure of the corporation

10. The new peace forum opened in Northern Ireland amid controversy over the role of George Mitchell as co-chair. Sinn Féin was not allowed to participate in view of the absence of an IRA ceasefire.

11. The House of Commons approved the introduction of the Referendum Bill, proposed by Conservative MP William Cash, to provide for the holding of a referendum on the need for changes to the Maastricht Treaty. A key provider of funds to the 'pro-referendum' European Foundation was Sir James Goldsmith, a French MEP.

13. Two Conservative MPs, Sir John Gorst and Hugh Dykes, threatened to withdraw their support from the government over the provision of casualty services at a hospital in Edgware in north London.

15. The IRA exploded a huge bomb in the centre of Manchester which caused massive damage and injuries to nearly 200 people.

20. Former Chief Secretary to the Treasury, Jonathan Aitken, was cleared by the House of Commons select committee on trade and industry of complicity in the sale of arms to Iran while he was a director of BMARC.

20–21. Royal Mail members of the Union of Communication Workers staged a 24-hour strike in support of their claim for better pay and work conditions. A second strike was held on 27–28 June.

21. Violence occurred in Belfast as republicans sought to prevent an Orange Order march passing through a nationalist area.

21–22. At a meeting of the European Council in Florence, heads of state and government reached agreement on an eventual relaxation of the ban on the export of British beef and on increased assistance to British farmers.

25.   The House of Commons rejected a motion by the Liberal Democrats to reduce by a nominal amount the salary of Douglas Hogg, the Minister for Agriculture, in criticism of his role in the dispute with the European Union over the export of British beef.

28.   The IRA was suspected of responsibility for a mortar attack on a British Army base in Osnabruck in Germany.

30.   The Royal Ulster Constabulary prevented an Orange Order march passing through a nationalist area in Belfast.

JULY

3.   The Prime Minister announced that the Stone of Destiny (Stone of Scone) would be returned to Scotland from Westminster Abbey after 700 years.

4.   The Labour Party launched its 10,000 word pre-manifesto statement entitled *New Labour, New Life for Britain* which would be discussed at all levels of the party prior to becoming the manifesto for the next general election. The document contained five main pledges for early fulfilment by a Labour government.

7.   The Royal Ulster Constabulary (RUC) halted an Orange Order march at Drumcree on the approaches to Portadown in County Armagh.

9.   The government announced that it was sending 1,000 more troops to Northern Ireland in view of the security situation there.
        President Mandela of South Africa began a five-day state visit to the UK.
        The government published proposals to make stalking and other acts of harassment or intimidation a criminal offence.

10.   The House of Commons voted for recommendations of the Senior Salaries Review Body for a 26 per cent increase in the pay of MPs and large increases for ministers.

The South Korean LG conglomerate announced a £1,700 million investment project in South Wales.

11.   The RUC finally allowed an Orange Order march to pass through Catholic areas to the centre of Portadown in County Armagh. The decision was followed by violence on the part of Republicans.
President Mandela addressed both Houses of Parliament in Westminster Hall.

12.   The European Court of Justice upheld the European Commission's decision to ban the export of British beef on health grounds.

13.   A large bomb believed to have been planted by a Republican group destroyed a hotel in Enniskillen and injured 17 people.

22.   David Heathcoat-Amory resigned as Paymaster-General in disagreement over the government's 'disastrous' failure to refuse to join the European Union's future single currency.

23.   The Prime Minister carried out a minor government reshuffle following the resignation of David Heathcoat-Amory and the decision of two other ministers (Tim Eggar and Steve Norris) not to seek re-election at the next general election.

24.   Elections to Labour's Shadow Cabinet resulted in only one change, with Jack Cunningham replacing Joan Lestor who did not stand for re-election.
John Major announced the establishment of an Academy of Sport with assistance from National Lottery funds.

25.   The governors of the BBC approved a restructuring of the World Service.

31.   Peter North, Vice-Chancellor of Oxford University, was named as the chair of an independent review of sectarian parades in Northern Ireland and the policing of them.
The House of Commons select committee on home affairs completed a report which said that a ban on the private holding of handguns would be impractical. Labour members of the committee planned to issue a separate report supporting such a ban.

AUGUST

1.   Tony Blair completed the allocation of junior parliamentary
      responsibilities outside the Shadow Cabinet.

5.   Ian Lang, the President of the Board of Trade, announced that the Post
      Office's monopoly on the delivery of letters costing less than £1 was
      suspended for a month following the decision by the Union of
      Communication Workers to continue with its programme of one-day
      strikes at the Royal Mail.
      Peter Lilley, the Social Security Secretary, launched a 'beat a cheat'
      campaign to encourage people to inform on those suspected of
      carrying out social security fraud.

7.   Sir Patrick Mayhew, the Northern Ireland Secretary, made an order
      prohibiting the proposed annual Apprentice Boys march in
      Londonderry due on 10 August from passing alongside the strongly
      Catholic Bogside area of the city.

13.   The House of Commons select committee on home affairs published
      a report rejecting the prohibition of the private possession of
      handguns but proposing more stringent conditions generally for
      firearms licences.

20.   Fourteen 'working' life peers were created, six of whom were
      nominated by Tony Blair and two by Paddy Ashdown.

22.   It was disclosed that, due to interpretation of rules relating to time
      spent in prison on remand before sentencing to consecutive terms of
      imprisonment, a number of prisoners were being released earlier than
      had been expected. The following day, the Home Secretary suspended
      any further releases. This decision was later upheld by the High Court.
      The Home Secretary, Michael Howard, announced proposals for a
      new, voluntary identity card.

30.   Ronnie Flanagan, a Deputy Chief Constable of the RUC, was named
      to succeed Sir Hugh Annesley as Chief Constable with effect from
      November.
      A report commissioned by the Scottish National Party was published
      which set out the plans for a transition of Scotland to independence.

31.   The executive of the Scottish Labour Party agreed that a Labour

government should hold two referendums in Scotland: first, on whether voters wanted a separate Scottish parliament and whether such a parliament should have the powers to raise extra taxes and second, if a parliament had been created, before it could exercise its tax-raising powers.

SEPTEMBER

6. The Labour Party's main spokesman on Scottish affairs, George Robertson, announced that the party, if in office, would not conduct two separate referendums on the establishment of a Scottish parliament and on its tax-raising powers.

9. The Trades Union Congress (TUC) opened its annual conference in Blackpool.
The multi-party talks on the future of Northern Ireland re-opened at Stormont.

10. The Labour Party lost control of Hackney Borough Council in London after 16 Labour councillors left to form a separate group after disciplinary action had been taken against them.

11. The TUC Congress voted to call for a national minimum wage of £4.26 an hour.

12. The TUC Congress approved a package of employment rights which it would ask a future Labour government to enact.

16–17. Douglas Hogg, Minister for Agriculture, began talks with other agriculture ministers over the EU ban on exports of British beef.

19. The Anglican Church in Wales voted in favour of the ordination of women priests.

20. The Green Party, at its annual conference in Hastings, decided to field a limited number of candidates at the next general election.

23. The Liberal Democrats' annual conference opened in Brighton.

24. Paddy Ashdown, the leader of the Liberal Democrats, told his party's annual conference that the Conservatives had demonstrated 'false

patriotism' and fear as their only weapons, while Labour had chosen to be timid on issues of constitutional reform. If Labour won the forthcoming general election, the country would see a change of government but not a change of direction.

25.   The Scottish National Party's annual conference opened in Inverness.

30.   The Labour Party's annual conference opened in Blackpool when a largely unchanged national executive committee was elected.
Former junior minister Neil Hamilton and public relations lobbyist Ian Greer withdrew their libel action against the *Guardian* relating to the House of Commons 'cash for questions' affair.
Prisoners belonging to the Northern Ireland Ulster Defence Association withdrew their support for the two-year old loyalist ceasefire.

OCTOBER

1.   Tony Blair set out the policies for a future Labour government at the party's annual conference, a government which he claimed would bring 'an age of achievement' to the country. His government would make education a priority; there would be 'fairness not favours' for employers and employees alike; Labour would be tough on public spending; it would build a new and constructive relationship in Europe and would attempt to realize the potential of information technology in creating a 'national grid for learning'.

3.   Baroness Turner of Camden was forced to resign as a Labour frontbench spokesperson in the House of Lords after she had publicly defended Ian Greer who was involved in the 'cash for questions' allegations.

5.   John Major attended a special meeting in Dublin of heads of government to discuss progress in respect of the EU's Intergovernmental Conference.

6.   Lord McAlpine of West Green, a former Treasurer of the Conservative Party, announced that he was defecting to the Referendum Party.

7.   Two bombs exploded within the Army's Northern Ireland headquarters in Lisburn, County Antrim. It was the first major attack

in Northern Ireland itself for more than two years. On 11 October, one soldier died of injuries caused by the explosion.

8. The Conservative Party's annual conference opened in Bournemouth.

9. Ian Lang, the President of the Board of Trade, told the Conservative Party conference that the government planned to make trade unions which called strikes in monopoly public services liable for damages.

11. John Major told the Conservative Party conference that if they won the next general election, his government would extend 'opportunity for all' by helping more people to save for retirement, reducing taxes and moving towards the abolition of capital gains and inheritance taxes. He also pledged that the National Health Service would receive more money over and above inflation year on year throughout the lifetime of the next Conservative government.
    The death of Terry Patchett, a Labour MP since 1983, caused a by-election vacancy in his Barnsley East constituency.
    It was announced that Rosie Boycott would succeed Peter Wilby as editor of the *Independent on Sunday*.

12. Peter Thurnham, the MP for Bolton North East who had resigned the Conservative Whip in February, formally joined the Liberal Democrats.

14. The House of Commons select committee on standards and privileges launched a full-scale inquiry into 'cash for questions' allegations made against Neil Hamilton, a former Conservative junior minister.

15. Agreement was reached on an agenda for the all-party talks on the future of Northern Ireland within the elected forum between the Ulster Unionist Party (UUP) and the Social Democratic and Labour Party (SDLP).

16. The report of Lord Cullen's inquiry into the shooting of 16 children and their teacher at Dunblane primary school in March recommended restrictions on the holding of self-loading pistols and revolvers.

19. The Referendum Party held its inaugural conference in Brighton.

21. Michael Forsyth, the Scottish Secretary, announced that the Stone of Destiny (Stone of Scone) would be housed in Edinburgh Castle.

23.   The new session of parliament opened, with 13 main pieces of legislation. Two other items dealing with stalking and sexual offences against children were to be government bills rather than private members' bills.

       The Director of the Office of the National Lottery (OFLOT) announced that Camelot would hold a second weekly draw from early 1997.

25.   United News and Media bought from Scottish Television the latter's almost 20 per cent holding in HTV.

29.   The Labour Party and the Liberal Democrats announced that they were to hold joint talks on constitutional reform.

       The Education and Employment Secretary, Gillian Shepherd, said that there was a great deal of support for the use of corporal punishment in schools. The Prime Minister later confirmed that the re-introduction of caning was not part of government policy.

NOVEMBER

3.   The death of Barry Porter, Conservative MP since 1983, caused a by-election vacancy in his Wirral South constituency.

4.   It was announced that individual Labour Party members had by a majority of 218,023 to 11,285 (in a turnout of 61 per cent) endorsed the party's draft manifesto.

6.   The Home Secretary, Michael Howard, announced that the police would be given greater powers to stop people whom they suspected of carrying knives.

       Electors in Dwyfor in north-west Wales voted by 24,325 to 9,829 to allow the sale and consumption of alcohol on Sundays; in Rhondda Cynon Taff in south Wales, there was a 24,863 to 3,424 vote in favour.

11.   David Willetts, the Paymaster General, appearing before the House of Commons select committee on standards and privileges, ascribed to his inexperience any interpretation that he was seeking to reduce the level of scrutiny given to issues surrounding the 'cash for questions' affair.

12.   The European Court of Justice told the UK government that, as a

health and safety measure, it had to implement the 1993 EU Working Time Directive and a minimum of four weeks paid holiday a year.

13.   The government had a majority of one in the House of Commons at the end of a debate critical of its handling of the BSE crisis.

18.   A fire broke out on a freight shuttle train on the UK-bound line of the Channel Tunnel. Two people were seriously injured and there was extensive damage to the tunnel itself.

19.   Staff at all levels in universities and other institutions of higher education carried out a one-day strike over a pay dispute.

22.   The government announced a high-level 'leak' inquiry into the circumstances surrounding the 'leak' on 21 November of most of the details of the budget to the *Daily Mirror*. The paper returned the documents to the government without publishing them.

25.   The Chancellor of the Exchequer, Kenneth Clarke, came under close questioning in the House of Commons over the issue of any UK participation in a single European currency.

26.   The Chancellor of the Exchequer, Kenneth Clarke, presented his budget, which included a 1p reduction in basic income tax from 24p to 23p but also a number of tax increases and cuts in public expenditure.

27.   The Referendum Party set out the questions which it called to be put to the voters on membership of the European Union. The precise wording however should be decided by Parliament.

DECEMBER

2.   Sir Nicholas Scott was formally 'de-selected' as the parliamentary candidate for the next general election by his Kensington and Chelsea Conservative Association.

4.   The Firearms (Amendment) Bill completed its third reading in the House of Commons without a vote. The bill proposed a ban on handguns above .22 calibre and to impose tight security on gun clubs and more rigorous vetting of individuals. A campaign to ban all types

of handgun was supported by the Labour Party who said that it would legislate for a total ban if it formed the next government 'at the first reasonable opportunity'.

Eurostar passenger services resumed through the Channel Tunnel after more than two weeks' suspension following a freight service fire.

6.   Conservative MP Sir John Gorst announced that he was withdrawing support from the government in protest at its policy over his local hospital although he was not actually resigning the Conservative whip.

11.   David Willetts resigned as Paymaster General following publication of a House of Commons report which criticized him for seeking to reduce the political impact of the 'cash for questions' issue. He had 'dissembled' in his testimony to the select committee on standards and privileges. Willetts was replaced by Michael Bates.

12.   The Labour Party retained the Barnsley East seat in a parliamentary by-election thereby eliminating the government's majority in the House of Commons. The Conservative candidate came third.

13.   The Labour Party retained the Merseyside West seat at a by-election for a seat in the European Parliament.

13–14. John Major attended a meeting of the European Council in Dublin when progress was made in discussions surrounding the introduction of a single European currency. Details were made known of the format of the 'euro' bank notes.

16.   The government had a majority of 11 at the end of a debate in the House of Commons on the EU's fisheries policy. The next day, controversy flared over the 'pairing' of MPs in the vote.

19.   It was announced that Ian Greer Associates whose founder Ian Greer was involved in the 'cash for questions' affair was being placed in voluntary liquidation.

2. Parliamentary By-elections 1996

Note: There were three parliamentary by-elections during 1996 – at Hemsworth, Staffordshire South East and Barnsley East, making only eighteen in the course of this Parliament so far, compared with 24 between 1987 and 1992. One seat remains vacant (Wirral South) with a by-election scheduled for 27 February 1997. The by-elections reported here are numbered consecutively from the general election of 1992.

15. HEMSWORTH 2 February 1996 (Death of Mr D. Enright)

Result

Candidate	Description	Votes
J. Trickett	Labour	15,817
N. Hazell	Conservative	1,942
D. Ridgway	Liberal Democrat	1,516
B. Nixon	Socialist Labour	1,193
Lord Sutch	Official Monster Raving Loony	652
P. Davies	UK Independence	455
P. Alexander	Green	157
M. Thomas	Mark Thomas Friday Nights Channel 4	122
M. Cooper	National Democrat	111
D. Leighton	Natural Law Party	28

Labour Hold: Majority 13,875

Turnout and Major Party Vote Shares (%)

	By-election	General Election	Change
Turnout	39.5	75.9	-36.4
Con	8.8	18.6	-9.8
Lab	71.9	70.8	+1.1
Lib Dem	6.9	10.5	-3.6

16. STAFFORDSHIRE SOUTH EAST 11 April 1996 (Death of Mr D. Lightbown)

Result

Candidate	Description	Votes
B. Jenkins	Labour	26,155
J. James	Conservative	12,393
J. Davey	Liberal Democrat	2,042
A. Smith	UK Independence	1,272
Lord D. Sutch	Monster Raving Loony	506
S. Edwards	National Democrats	358
S. Mountford	Liberal	332
L. Taylor	Churchill Conservative	123
N. Bunny	Official Bunny News Party	85
N. Samuelson	Daily Loonylugs Earring	80
D. Lucas	Natural Law Party	53
F. Sandy	Action Against Crime Life Means Life	53
A. Wood	Restoration of Death Penalty	45

Labour Gain: Majority 13,762

Turnout and Major Party Vote Shares (%)

	By-election	General Election	Change
Turnout	60.3	82.0	-21.7
Con	28.5	50.7	-22.2
Lab	60.1	38.2	+21.9
Lib Dem	4.7	9.6	-4.9

17. BARNSLEY EAST 12 December 1996 (Death of Mr T. Patchett)

Result

Candidate	Description	Votes
J. Ennis	Labour	13,683
D. Willis	Liberal Democrat	1,502
J. Ellison	Conservative	1,299
K. Capstick	Socialist Labour	949
N. Tolstoy	UK Independence Party	378
J. Hyland	Social Equality	89

Labour Hold: Majority 12,181

Turnout and Major Party Vote Shares (%)

	By-election	General Election	Change
Turnout	33.7	72.7	-39.0
Con	7.3	14.2	-6.9
Lab	76.4	77.2	-0.8
Lib Dem	8.4	8.6	-0.2

TABLE 2.1 *Summary of By-election Results 1992–96*

Constituency	Turnout Change	Change in Share of Vote			
		Con	Lab	Lib Dem	SNP/PC
Newbury	-11.5	-29.0	-4.1	+27.8	
Christchurch	-6.5	-31.5	-9.3	+39.7	
Rotherham	-27.6	-13.9	-8.4	+17.4	
Barking	-31.5	-23.5	+20.5	-2.5	
Bradford South	-31.6	-20.6	+7.7	+10.2	
Dagenham	-33.5	-26.4	+19.7	-3.1	
Eastleigh	-24.0	-26.6	+6.9	+16.3	
Newham North East	-24.9	-15.9	+16.6	-7.0	
Monklands East	-4.9	-13.8	-11.5	-2.0	+26.9
Dudley West	-34.8	-30.1	+28.1	-2.9	
Islwyn	-35.8	-10.9	-5.1	+4.9	+8.8
Perth and Kinross	-14.9	-18.8	+9.7	+0.4	+4.4
North Down	-26.7	-	-	-	
Littleborough & Saddleworth	-17.1	-20.9	+13.6	+2.2	
Hemsworth	-36.4	-9.8	+1.1	-3.6	
Staffordshire South East	-21.7	-22.2	+21.9	-4.9	
Barnsley East	-39.0	-6.9	-0.8	-0.2	

3. Public Opinion Polls 1996

TABLE 3.1 *Voting Intentions (unadjusted) in Major Polls 1996 (%)*

Fieldwork	Company	Sample Size	Con	Lab	Lib Dem	Other
Jan						
3–8	Gallup	1135	21	61	15	4
18–19	NOP	1549	25	54	18	3
19–22	MORI	1770	29	55	13	2
na	ICM	na	22	53	17	4
Feb						
1–5	Gallup	1020	28	55	15	3
2–4	ICM	1200	27	52	17	4
15–16	NOP	1569	25	54	16	5
23–26	MORI	1877	26	57	14	3
Mar						
29/4–4/3	Gallup	1060	23	58	16	4
2–4	ICM	1200	26	51	20	4
14	NOP	1500	27	55	14	4
22–25	MORI	1910	28	57	13	2
27–1/4	Gallup	1119	26	56	16	3
Apr						
12–13	ICM	1200	25	56	16	4
19–22	MORI	1947	28	54	14	4
25	NOP	1592	28	52	16	4
27	MORI	1068	29	54	13	4
May						
1–3	ICM	1000	26	52	15	6
1–6	Gallup	1095	25	56	16	5
3–5	ICM	1200	26	50	20	5
10–13	MORI	1931	27	56	13	5
16	NOP	1563	26	53	17	4
23–26	MORI	1610	27	54	15	4
June						
30/5–3/6	Gallup	1042	25	56	16	5
31/5–2/6	ICM	1200	25	51	18	5
7–10	MORI	1970	27	56	13	3
20	NOP	1580	31	50	15	4
21–24	MORI	1846	31	52	12	5
27/6–1/7	Gallup	1010	26	55	15	5
28/6–1/7	MORI	1969	32	52	12	3
July						
5–6	ICM	1200	25	50	20	5
25	NOP	1565	31	48	16	5
23–28	MORI	1928	29	53	12	6

TABLE 3.1 *(contd.)*

Fieldwork		Company	Sample Size	Con	Lab	Lib Dem	Other
Aug							
	31/7–5/8	Gallup	1021	25	59	11	5
	2–3	ICM	1200	30	50	18	3
	9–12	MORI	1893	30	52	13	4
	15	NOP	1592	28	54	14	4
	20–25	MORI	1708	30	51	13	6
Sept							
	28/8–3/9	Gallup	1024	26	59	11	5
	6–7	ICM	1200	28	51	15	5
	6–9	MORI	1928	28	56	12	3
	18–24	Gallup	1033	27	54	14	5
	na	NOP	1546	28	55	13	4
	20–23	MORI	1800	29	52	14	5
	29–1/10	Gallup	1047	28	52	15	6
Oct							
	3	NOP	1543	25	57	13	5
	3–4	Gallup	587	24	57	15	4
	4–5	ICM	1200	27	54	15	3
	4–7	MORI	1879	29	54	13	5
	11–14	MORI	1990	30	53	12	5
	17	NOP	1579	33	47	14	5
	18–21	MORI	1027	27	54	12	7
	25–28	MORI	1747	28	56	12	4
Nov							
	30/10–1/11	MORI	1002	30	54	12	4
	30/10–5/11	Gallup	1055	28	55	11	6
	1–2	ICM	1202	33	48	15	4
	8–11	MORI	1515	33	50	12	5
	14	NOP	1547	26	56	13	5
	27–29	MORI	1025	30	52	13	5
Dec							
	27/11–2/12	Gallup	1072	22	59	12	7
	29/11–1/12	ICM	1200	27	53	16	4
	6–9	MORI	1872	30	51	13	6
	na	NOP	1541	29	52	13	6

Notes: The figures shown are unadjusted voting intention percentages after the exclusion of respondents who did not indicate a party preference. Gallup results are normally reported to the nearest 0.5 but all such cases here have been rounded up.

TABLE 3.2 *Voting Intentions (adjusted) in Major Polls 1996 (%)*

Fieldwork	Company	Sample Size	Con	Lab	Lib Dem	Other
Jan						
na	ICM	na	26	48	22	4
18–19	NOP	1549	27	53	17	3
Feb						
2–4	ICM	1200	31	47	19	3
15–16	NOP	1569	28	50	17	5
Mar						
2–4	ICM	1200	31	45	20	4
14	NOP	1500	29	53	14	4
Apr						
12–13	ICM	1200	29	50	17	4
25	NOP	1592	29	51	16	4
May						
3–5	ICM	1200	28	45	21 ·	5
16	NOP	1563	27	52	17	4
June						
31/5–2/6	ICM	1200	30	46	19	5
20	NOP	1580	31	50	15	4
July						
5–6	ICM	1200	30	45	21	4
25	NOP	1565	31	48	16	5
Aug						
2–3	ICM	1200	33	45	19	3
15	NOP	1592	30	51	15	4
Sept						
6–7	ICM	1200	32	47	16	5
na	NOP	1546	31	50	14	5
Oct						
3	NOP	1543	29	52	13	6
4–5	ICM	1200	31	49	16	3
17	NOP	1579	33	47	14	5
Nov						
1–2	ICM	1202	34	47	15	4
14	NOP	1547	30	50	15	5
Dec						
29/11–1/12	ICM	1200	31	50	15	4
13–14	ICM	1412	30	50	14	5
na	NOP	1541	31	50	14	5

Note: Following criticism of the polls after the 1992 general election, NOP and ICM began to adjust their voting intention figures, publishing the resulting scores as their 'headline' figures. In both cases the adjustment partly involves taking account of past voting.

TABLE 3.3 *Voting Intentions in Scotland 1996 (%)*

	Con	Lab	Lib Dem	SNP
Jan	12	53	11	23
Feb	12	54	9	23
Mar	13	54	10	23
Apr	13	53	9	23
May	12	54	8	24
Jun	15	54	9	25
Jul	15	51	10	23
Aug	15	48	7	29
Sep	13	49	12	24
Oct	11	55	8	23
Nov	12	53	10	24

Note: System Three do not poll in December but have separate polls in early and late January. The January figure shown is the average of the two January polls. Rows do not total 100 because 'others' are not shown.

Source: System Three Scotland polls, published monthly in *The Herald* (Glasgow).

TABLE 3.4 *Monthly Averages for Voting Intentions 1996 (%)*

	Con	Lab	Lib Dem		Con	Lab	Lib Dem
Jan	24	56	16	Jul	28	50	16
Feb	27	55	16	Aug	29	53	14
Mar	26	55	16	Sep	28	54	13
Apr	28	54	15	Oct	28	54	13
May	26	54	16	Nov	30	53	13
Jun	28	53	14	Dec	27	54	14

Note: These are the simple means of unadjusted voting intentions.

TABLE 3.5 *Ratings of Party Leaders 1996*

	Major			Blair			Ashdown		
	Pos	Neg	Net	Pos	Neg	Net	Pos	Neg	Net
Jan	24	68	-44	61	22	+39	55	22	+33
Feb	25	68	-43	59	24	+35	57	21	+36
Mar	25	67	-42	62	21	+41	57	22	+35
Apr	24	68	-44	62	21	+41	58	21	+37
May	24	68	-44	60	22	+38	59	20	+39
Jun	25	67	-42	60	23	+37	57	22	+35
Jul	26	66	-40	57	25	+32	57	22	+35
Aug	27	66	-39	53	29	+24	55	23	+32
Sep	28	64	-36	56	25	+31	56	22	+34
Oct	28	63	-35	59	22	+37	58	20	+38
Nov	28	63	-35	61	23	+38	57	21	+36
Dec	27	65	-38	58	25	+33	54	23	+31

Notes: The figures are based on responses to the following questions:
'Are you satisfied or dissatisfied with Mr Major as Prime Minister?'; 'Do you think that Mr Blair is or is not proving a good leader of the Opposition?'; 'Do you think that Mr Ashdown is or is not proving a good leader of the Liberal Democratic Party?'

The data are derived from the 'Gallup 9,000', which is an aggregation of all Gallup's polls in the month concerned. The difference between 100 and the sum of positive and negative responses is the percentage of respondents who replied 'Don't know'.

Source: Gallup Political and Economic Index.

TABLE 3.6 *Best Person for Prime Minister 1996 (%)*

	Major	Blair	Ashdown	Don't Know
Jan	17	41	14	28
Feb	18	38	15	29
Mar	18	42	14	27
Apr	17	42	14	27
May	18	39	16	28
Jun	19	38	15	28
Jul	18	38	15	29
Aug	19	36	15	30
Sep	21	38	14	27
Oct	21	38	14	27
Nov	21	39	13	27
Dec	21	39	14	27

Source: Gallup Political and Economic Index. The data are derived from the 'Gallup 9,000'.

TABLE 3.7 *Approval/Disapproval of Government Record 1996 (%)*

	Approve	Disapprove	Don't Know	Approve–Disapprove
Jan	14	75	12	-61
Feb	14	75	11	-61
Mar	13	75	12	-62
Apr	14	74	12	-60
May	14	74	13	-60
Jun	15	72	13	-57
Jul	15	72	14	-57
Aug	16	71	13	-55
Sep	17	70	13	-53
Oct	17	69	14	-52
Nov	18	68	14	-50
Dec	17	70	13	-53

Notes: These are answers to the question 'Do you approve or disapprove of the government's record to date?'. The data are derived from the 'Gallup 9,000'.

Source: Gallup Political and Economic Index.

TABLE 3.8 *National and Personal Economic Evaluations 1996*

	National Retrospective	National Prospective	Personal Retrospective	Personal Prospective
Jan	-31	-13	-13	-2
Feb	-35	-14	-16	-6
Mar	-36	-14	-13	-3
Apr	-31	-14	-12	-5
May	-29	-10	-11	0
Jun	-28	-10	-10	+5
Jul	-20	-2	-10	+4
Aug	-22	-9	-13	-3
Sep	-11	-4	-4	+3
Oct	-27	+2	-11	+4
Nov	-17	+3	-8	+2
Dec	-21	-9	-18	-8

Notes: These data derive from the '1974 series' of economic indicators used by Gallup and are based on answers to the following questions:
'Do you consider that the general economic situation in this country in the last 12 months has improved a lot, improved slightly, remained the same, deteriorated slightly or deteriorated a lot?';
'Do you think that the general economic situation in the next 12 months is likely to improve a lot, improve slightly, remain the same, deteriorate slightly or deteriorate a lot?';
'In the last 12 months has the financial situation of your household improved a lot, improved slightly, remained the same, become a little worse or become a lot worse?';
'Do you consider the financial situation of your household in the next 12 months will improve a lot, improve slightly, remain the same, deteriorate slightly or deteriorate a lot?'.
In each case, entries are the percentage of respondents saying things have deteriorated/will deteriorate subtracted from the percentage saying things have improved/will improve.

Source: Gallup Political and Economic Index.

TABLE 3.9 *Best Party to Handle Economic Difficulties 1996*

	Conservative	Labour	No Difference	Don't Know
Jan	23	45	19	13
Feb	24	45	19	12
Mar	23	47	18	12
Apr	23	47	18	12
May	25	46	18	12
Jun	25	45	18	11
Jul	26	42	20	12
Aug	26	42	20	12
Sep	27	43	18	12
Oct	26	44	18	13
Nov	27	44	17	12
Dec	26	44	18	12

Note: These are answers to the question 'With Britain in economic difficulties, which party do you think could handle the problem best – the Conservatives under Mr Major or Labour under Mr Blair?'. The figures are derived from the 'Gallup 9,000'.

Source: Gallup Political and Economic Index.

4. Local Elections 1996

Local elections in Britain are valuable indicators of the state of public opinion, have important effects on the morale of party workers and determine political control of local authorities. For these reasons the annual rounds of local elections attract increasing attention in the media, but interpretation of the results is complicated by the fact that the various authorities have different election cycles. Indeed, even keeping track of election cycles is currently not an easy task as piecemeal changes are being made to the structure of local government in England. A summary of the different types of authority that now make up the British local government system and their electoral cycles is as follows:

England
1. *Counties* (35)
   All members are elected every four years and next elections are due in 1997.

2. *Metropolitan Boroughs* (36)
   One third of members are elected annually except in those years when there are county elections. Next elections are due in 1998.

3. *Shire Districts with 'annual' elections* (100)
   Approximately one-third of members are elected annually except in those years when there are county elections. Next elections are due in 1998.

4. *Shire Districts with 'all in' elections* (160)
   All members are elected every four years mid-way between County elections. Next elections are due in 1999.

5. *London Boroughs* (32)
   All members are elected in another four-year cycle. Next elections are due in 1998.

6. *Unitary Authorities* (27)
   'Shadow' authorities elected in 1995 and 1996. Subsequent election cycle varies.

Scotland
  1. *Unitary Councils* (32)
     All members were elected in 1995 and the next elections will be in
     1999.

Wales
  1. *Unitary Authorities* (22)
     All members were elected in 1995 and the next elections will be in
     1999.

In 1996 there were no local elections in Scotland, Wales or London. Elections
were held, as normal, in the 36 metropolitan boroughs and in 100 shire
districts with 'annual' elections. In addition, one established unitary authority
(Hartlepool) had its first round of annual elections and in 13 areas there were
elections for 'shadow' unitary authorities which would assume responsibility
in April 1997. These were Bournemouth, Brighton and Hove, Darlington,
Derby, Leicester, Luton, Milton Keynes, Poole, Portsmouth, Rutland,
Southampton, Stoke on Trent and Thamesdown.

In the past, little attention has been paid to the results of local by-elections,
although Rallings and Thrasher have argued that the steady stream of these
contests provides a valuable resource for charting trends in the popularity of
the parties. During 1996 the Conservatives claimed that local by-elections
indicated some recovery in their popularity and the data provided here gives
some support for that claim.

Election watchers in Britain owe a debt of gratitude to Colin Rallings and
Michael Thrasher whose indefatigable work in collecting and publishing
authoritative local election results has smoothed the paths of many others.
They have supplied the data presented in Table 4.1. Full details of the 1996
results, including individual ward results and commentary, can be found in
their *Local Elections Handbook 1996* (Local Government Chronicle Elections
Centre, University of Plymouth), obtainable from LGC Communications,
33–39 Bowling Green Lane, London EC1R 0DA.

TABLE 4.1 *Summary of 1996 Local Election Results*

	Candidates	Seats Won	Gains/ Losses	% Share of Vote
Metropolitan Districts (36)				
Turnout 30.5%				
Con	726	72	-196	22.7
Lab	836	624	+173	53.1
Lib Dem	640	126	+25	20.1
Other	187	14	-2	4.2
'Annual' Shire Districts (100)				
Turnout 37.2%				
Con	1394	347	-435	29.7
Lab	1442	712	+299	40.4
Lib Dem	1177	375	+135	25.2
Other	258	94	+1	4.7
English Unitary Authorities (14)				
Turnout 34.6%				
Con	600	96	–	26.2
Lab	637	411	–	46.0
Lib Dem	513	131	–	21.8
Other	132	20	–	6.0
All English Authorities (150)				
Turnout 33.6%				
Con	2720	515	-683	26.1
Lab	2915	1747	+512	46.8
Lib Dem	2330	632	+173	22.5
Other	577	128	-2	4.6

Note: Gains and losses are as compared with seats won in the same authorities in 1992 and cannot be calculated for new authorities. The figures for all English authorities are, therefore, estimates.

Source: C. Rallings and M. Thrasher.

TABLE 4.2 *Monthly Party Vote Shares in Local Government By-elections 1996 (%)*

	Con	Lab	Lib Dem	Oths	N of Wards
Jan	38.6	33.8	25.1	2.5	6
Feb	35.0	31.1	30.3	3.5	20
Mar	26.7	39.2	28.9	5.1	19
Apr	23.1	42.6	22.2	12.3	11
May	35.2	31.5	29.3	4.0	29
Jun	25.7	41.7	30.2	5.2	21
Jul	34.7	36.4	26.2	2.7	13
Aug	29.8	36.3	26.4	7.5	8
Sep	34.0	39.6	22.5	3.9	24
Oct	33.2	39.4	19.4	8.0	26
Nov	28.4	36.3	28.6	6.7	38
Dec	33.3	33.3	30.8	2.9	14

Note: These figures relate to the results of local government by-elections in wards and electoral divisions contested by all three major parties.

Source: David Cowling, ITN.

TABLE 4.3 *Seats Won and Lost in Local Government By-elections 1996*

	Con	Lab	Lib Dem	Others
Held	53	115	51	13
Lost	10	29	32	21
Gained	38	16	23	15
Net	+28	-13	-9	-6

Source: David Cowling, ITN.

TABLE 4.4 *Projected National Share of Votes in Local Elections 1993–96 (%)*

	1993	1994	1995	1996
Con	31	28	25	28
Lab	41	40	47	44
Lib Dem	24	27	23	23

Source: C. Rallings and M. Thrasher

5. Economic Indicators

TABLE 5.1 *Unemployment, Retail Price Index, Inflation, Tax & Price Index, Interest Rates, Sterling Exchange Rate Index, Balance of Payments (Goods), Terms of Trade Index*

	UN	RPI	INF	TPI	%TPI	IR	SI	BP	TOFT
1993	10.3	140.7	1.6	131.4	1.2	5.50	88.9	-13,460	103.5
1994	9.3	144.1	2.4	135.2	2.9	6.25	89.2	-10,831	102.2
1995	8.2	149.1	3.5	140.4	3.8	6.50	84.2	-11,628	98.9
1996									
Jan	7.9	150.2	2.9	141.6	3.2	6.25	83.2	-1,327	99.5
Feb	7.9	150.9	2.7	142.3	3.0	6.25	83.8	-1,376	99.8
Mar	7.8	151.5	2.7	143.0	3.0	6.00	83.5	-924	99.6
Apr	7.8	152.6	2.4	141.7	1.0	6.00	83.8	-1,289	99.5
May	7.7	152.9	2.2	142.0	0.7	6.00	84.6	-1,030	99.5
Jun	7.7	153.0	2.1	142.1	0.6	5.75	86.0	-852	99.3
Jul	7.6	152.4	2.2	141.5	0.8	5.75	85.7	-1,249	99.8
Aug	7.5	153.1	2.1	142.2	0.6	5.75	84.7	-620	99.9
Sep	7.4	153.8	2.1	143.0	0.7	5.75	86.1	-1,059	99.8
Oct	7.2	153.8	2.7	143.0	1.3	6.00	88.4	-454	99.5
Nov	6.9	153.9	2.7	143.1	1.3	6.00	92.0	-1017	101.5
Dec	6.7	154.4	2.5	143.6	1.1	6.00	93.8	-825	101.5

Notes:

UN = Unemployment. Seasonly adjusted percentage of the workforce defined as unemployed. The current definition is used to estimate the whole series.

RPI = Retail Price Index. All Items. January 1987=100.

INF = Inflation rate and is the percentage increase in the RPI compared with the same month in the previous year.

TPI = Tax & Price Index. 1987=100.

%TPI = Percentage increase in the TPI compared with the same month in the previous year.

IR = Interest rates based upon selected retail banks' base rates.

SI = Sterling Exchange Rate Index. Compares the value of sterling with a range of other currencies. 1990=100.

BP = Balance of Payments (goods) in £millions.

TOFT = Terms of Trade Index. Price Index of exports as a percentage of the price index of imports.

Sources: Office for National Statistics – *Economic Trends, Monthly Digest of Statistics*.

TABLE 5.2 *Gross Domestic Product, Balance of Payments (All), Real Personal Disposible Income Index, House Price Index*

	GDP	BPCP	RPDI	HOUSE
1993	99.6	-10,756	103.8	100.0
1994	103.5	-2,419	105.1	102.5
1995	106.2	-3,914	108.5	103.2
1996				
Q1	107.6	-1,111	110.9	104.3
Q2	108.2	344	111.8	104.4
Q3	108.9	-71	112.7	108.5
Q4	109.7	837	113.6	108.6

Notes: **GDP** = Gross Domestic Product at factor cost. 1990=100. **BPCP** = Balance of Payments Current Balance which includes all goods, services and invisibles. £millions. **RPDI** = Real Personal Disposable Income. 1990=100. **HOUSE** = Index of House Prices for all dwellings. 1993=100.

Source: Office for National Statistics – *Economic Trends*.

6. Political Parties

PARTY MEMBERSHIP

The table below shows individual membership levels UK parties, as declared by the political parties themselves. Some of these figures carry a strong 'health warning', however, since they are estimates. There is a variety of reasons accounting for this, not least the fact that the parties themselves are unable (or unwilling) to give precise figures where membership records are not held centrally. These figures should, therefore, be treated as indicative levels of membership and readers should take account of the footnotes to the table.

Party	Declared Individual Membership
Conservative Party [1]	na
Labour Party	400,000
Liberal Democrats	103,000
Scottish National Party [2]	*
Plaid Cymru	10,000
Green Party	4,000
Liberal Party [3]	na
Ulster Unionist Party	10,000–12,000
Democratic Unionist Party	5,000
SDLP	*
Alliance Party	4,000
Sinn Féin	na

Notes: * Party policy not to reveal membership figures.

1. There is a considerable discrepancy in membership figures for the Conservative Party. The last figure released from Conservative Central Office was an estimated 750,000 members in 1996. However, in *True Blues: The Politics of Conservative Party Membership*, Whiteley, Seyd and Richardson calculate that the Conservative Party is losing on average 64,000 members per year. On that basis, given that their estimate of 750,000 was calculated in 1992, this would suggest an estimated membership figure of 430,000 in 1997.

2. Estimated membership of the Scottish National Party ranges between 10,000 and 20,000

3. National membership figure for the Liberal Party is not available as records are kept at a local level.

Data collected January 1997.

THE CONSERVATIVE PARTY

Main Addresses
Conservative and Unionist Central Office
32 Smith Square
Westminster
London SW1P 3HH
Tel: 0171-222-9000
Fax: 0171-222-1135

Scottish Conservative and Unionist Central Office
Suite 1/1
14 Links Place
Edinburgh EH6 7EZ
Tel: 0131-555-2900
Fax: 0131-555-2869

Other Addresses
Conservative Research Department
32 Smith Square
Westminster
London SW1P 3HH
Tel: 0171-222-9000
Fax: 0171-233-2065
Director: Daniel Finkelstein
Deputy Directors: Alistair Cooke, Andrew Cooper

Conservative Political Centre
32 Smith Square
Westminster
London SW1P 3HH
Tel: 0171-222-9000
Fax: 0171-233-2065
Director: Alistair Cooke

National Union of Conservative and Unionist Associations
32 Smith Square
Westminster
London SW1P 3HH
Secretary: Chris Poole
Tel: 0171-222-9000
Fax: 0171-222-1135

One Nation Forum
32 Smith Square
Westminster
London SW1P 3HH
Tel: 0171-222-9000
Fax: 0171-222-1135
Chairman: Sir Geoffrey Pattie
Secretary: Tom Peet

Board of Management

Brian Mawhinney	Sir Marcus Fox
Lord Bowness	John Taylor
Dame Hazel Byford	Hon. Michael Trend
Sir Malcolm Chaplin	Lord Sheppard of Didgemere
Robin Hodgson	Tom Spencer
Tony Garrett	Martin Saunders (Secretary to the Board)

Officers

Party Chairman	Brian Mawhinney
Deputy Chairman	Michael Trend
Vice Chairmen	Dame Angela Rumbold (Candidates)
	Sir Graham Bright (Campaigns, One Nation Forum)
	Charles Hendry (Communications)
	Eric Pickles (Local Government)
	The Baroness Seccombe (Women)
Chairman of the Party in Scotland	Sir Michael Hirst

Staff

Directors

Research	Daniel Finkelstein
Communications	Charles Lewington
Fundraising/Treasurer's	Tim Cowell
Campaigning	Tony Garrett
Finance	Martin Saunders

Deputy Directors

Research Department	Alistair Cooke, Andrew Cooper

Departmental Heads

Local Government	David Trowbridge
Speakers	Penny Brook

Conservatives Abroad   David Smith
Chief Press Officer   Alex Aiken
Training   Geoffrey Harper
Elections Unit   Stephen Gilbert
Legal Officer   Paul Gribble

Regional Directors   *Telephone*
London and Eastern   John Earl   0171-222-9000
Yorkshire & North East   Peter Smith   01532-450731
North West   Ron Bell   0161-7971231
Midlands   Rachael Dyche   01455-239556
Southern   David Simpson   01932-866477
Western   Bill Henderson   01392-58231
Wales   Martin Perry   01222-616031
Scotland   Roger Pratt   0131-5552900

Board of Treasurers
Lord Hambro (Chairman)   David Davies
Lord Harris of Peckham   Sir Nigel Mobbs
 (Deputy Chairman)   Sir Geoffrey Leigh
Sir Malcolm Chaplin   Alan Lewis
William Hughes   Leonard Steinberg
Lord Feldman   David Evans

National Union Advisory Committees
Conservative Women's National Committee
Chairman: Dame Joyce Anelay
Secretary: Mary Shaw

Young Conservatives' National Advisory Committee
Chairman: Jason Hollands
Secretary: Hugh O'Brien

Conservative Trade Unionists' National Committee
Chairman: Derek Beard
Secretary: Hugh O'Brien

National Local Government Advisory Committee
Chairman: David Heslop
Secretary: David Trowbridge

Conservative Political Centre National Advisory Committee

Chairman: Ross Coates
Secretary: Alistair Cooke

Association of Conservative Clubs
Chairman: Sir Marcus Fox
Secretary: Ken Hargreaves

THE LABOUR PARTY

Address
The Labour Party
John Smith House
150 Walworth Road
London SE17 1JT
Tel: 0171-701-1234
Fax: 0171-277-3300

Information
Tel: 0171-277-3346
Fax: 0171-277-3555

Regional Secretaries		*Telephone*
Northern & Yorkshire	Andrew Sharp	01924-291221
North West	David Evans	01925-574913
Central	Roy Maddox	0115-9462195
West Midlands	Fiona Gordon	0121-553-6601
South East	George Catchpole	01473-255668
Greater London	Terry Ashton	0171-490-4904
South West	Graham Manuel	0117-9298018
Wales	Anita Gale	01222-398567
Scotland	Jack McConnell	0141-332-8946

Officers and Staff

Leader	Tony Blair
Deputy Leader	John Prescott
General Secretary	Tom Sawyer
European Coordinator	Larry Whitty
Chief Party Spokesperson	David Hill
Election Campaigning	Peter Mandelson
Organization and Development	David Gardner

Policy	Matthew Taylor
Finance	Paul Blagborough
Parliamentary Labour	
Party Secretary	Alan Haworth
Computers	Roger Hough
Women's Officer	Meg Russell
Youth Officer	Salli Randi
Senior Development	
Officer	Nick Smith

National Executive Committee 1996–97

Chair	Robin Cook
Vice-Chair	Richard Rosser
Treasurer	Margaret Prosser
Ex Officio Members	Tony Blair, John Prescott

Division 1: Trade Unions

John Allen (AEEU)	Bill Connor (USDAW)
Vernon Hince (RMT)	Diana Holland (TGWU)
Alan Johnson (CWU)	Maggie Jones (UNISON)
John Mitchell (GPMU)	Steve Pickering (GMP)
Richard Rosser (TSSA)	Mary Turner (GMB)
Margaret Wall (MSF)	Christine Wilde (UNISON)

Division 2: Socialist, Co-operative and Other Organizations
Ian McCartney (Labour Clubs)

Division 3: Constituency Labour Parties

Diane Abbott	Robin Cook
David Blunkett	Harriet Harman
Gordon Brown	Mo Mowlem
	Dennis Skinner

Division 4: Women Members

Margaret Beckett	Diana Jeuda
Brenda Etchells	Hilary Armstrong
Clare Short	

Youth Representative
Catherine Taylor

Result of Elections to National Executive Committee 1996-7
Names asterisked were elected. Figures for 1995 are shown in brackets if applicable.

Trade Unions (12 places of which 4 must be women.)

• John Allen	3,489,000	
• Bill Connor	3,506,000	(3,594,000)
• Vernon Hince	3,199,000	(3,685,000)
• Diana Holland	3,578,000	(3,685,000)
• Alan Johnson	3,522,000	(3,607,000)
• Maggie Jones	3,556,000	(3,639,000)
• John Mitchell	3,577,000	(3,683,000)
• Steve Pickering	3,454,000	
• Richard Rosser	2,842,000	(2,955,000)
• Mary Turner	3,599,000	(3,659,000)
• Margaret Wall	3,519,000	(3,611,000)
• Christine Wilde	2,588,000	(1,488,000)
Mike Leahy	1,413,000	(1,447,000)
Steve Kemp	175,000	

Socialist, Co-operative and Other Organizations (One place.)

• Ian McCartney	35,000
Alun Mitchell	24,000

Constituency Labour Parties (Seven places of which three must be women.)

• Robin Cook	109,801	(85,670)	Tam Dalyell	35,790	(30,705)
• David Blunkett	94,096	(75,984)	Alice Mahon	32,462	(29,212)
• Gordon Brown	93,679	(79,371)	Lynette Jones	31,353	
• Dennis Skinner	73,390	(64,288)	Joyce Quinn	28,407	(21,903)
• Mo Mowlem	68,271	(53,578)	Jeremy Corbyn	25,529	(22,457)
• Harriet Harman	58,112	(69,092)	Angela Eagle	22,431	(21,857)
• Diane Abbott	54,800	(45,653)	Jean Bishop	21,160	
Jack Straw	64,547	(58,486)	Alan Simpson	18,125	(12,409)
Ken Livingstone	58,593	(53,423)	Suzanne L'Estrange	9,737	(7,787)
Peter Hain	42,169	(32,394)	Kevin Cluskey	5,815	

Women Members (5 places. Result announced in percentage terms.)

• Margaret Beckett	20.82%	(18.73%)
• Clare Short	18.64%	(17.15%)
• Diana Jeuda	16.73%	(17.84%)
• Hilary Armstrong	16.49%	(9.75%)

• Brenda Etchells 15.67% (14.68%)
Christine Shawcroft 6.61% (3.57%)
Julie Gibson 5.04%

THE LIBERAL DEMOCRATS

Addresses
The Liberal Democrats
Party Headquarters
4 Cowley Street
London SW1P 3NB
Tel: 0171-222-7999
Fax: 0171-799-2170

Scottish Liberal Democrats
4 Clifton Terrace
Edinburgh EH12 5DR
Tel: 0131-337-2314
Fax: 0131-337-3556

Welsh Liberal Democrats
57 St Mary Street
Cardiff CF1 1FE
Tel: 01222-382210
Fax: 01222-222864

Associated Organizations
Association of Liberal Democrat Councillors
President: William Le Bretton
Chair: Sarah Boad
Tel: 01422-843785
Fax: 01422-843036

Association of Liberal Democrat Trade Unionists
President: Tudor Gates
Chair: Michael Smart
Tel: 01375-850881

Youth and Student Liberal Democrats
Chair: Ruth Berry
Tel: 0171-222-7999 ext. 587/8

Women Liberal Democrats
President: Hilary Campbell
Chair: Jo Hayes
Tel: 0171-222-7999 ext. 408

Ethnic Minority Liberal Democrats
Chair: To be elected
Tel: 0181-870-5348

Liberal International (British Group)
President: Sir David Steel

Federation of European Liberal Democrat and Reform Parties
97 Rue Belliard
1047 Brussels
Belgium
Tel: (00)-322-284-2207
Fax: (00)-322-231-1907
President: Willy de Clerq
Secretary-General: Christian Ehlers

Regional Contacts		*Telephone*
Chilterns	Dave Hodgson	01908-503001
Devon and Cornwall	Noel Thomson	01803-842246
East Midlands	Richard Lustig	0116-2543833
Eastern	Nina Stimson	01223-460795
Hampshire and Isle of Wight	Gerald Vernon-Jackson	01703-848484
London	Paul Farthing	0171-2220134
Northern	Philip Appleby	01388-601341
North West	Flo Clucas	0161-2365799
South East	Dave Manning	01273-202300
West Midlands	Jim Gosling	01384-872296
Western	Gill Pardy	01202-516329
Yorkshire and Humberside	Andrew Meadowcroft	01709-816601

Party Officers

Party Leader	Paddy Ashdown
President	Robert Maclennan
Vice-Presidents	Andrew Duff (England)
	Marilyne MacLaren (Scotland)
	Rev. Roger Roberts (Wales)

Chair of Finance	Tim Clement-Jones
Treasurer	Tim Razzall

Scottish Party

Leader	Jim Wallace
President	Roy Thomson
Convenor	Marilyne Maclaren
Chief Executive	Andy Myles

Welsh Party

Leader	Alex Carlile
President	Martin Thomas
Administrator	Judi Lewis

Federal Party Staff

General Secretary	Graham Elson
Press Officer	Elizabeth Johnson
Campaigns and Elections Director	Chris Rennard
Campaign Department	Paul Rainger, Candy Piercy, Mel ab Owain, Derek Barrie, Willie Rennie, David Loxton, Paul Schofield Frances Tattersfield, Paul Bensilum
Candidates Officers	Sandra Dunk, Garry White
Policy Director	Neil Stockley
Policy Officers	Emma Leeds, Iain King, Candida Goulden
International Officer	Kishwer Khan
Finance	Ken Loughlin, Steve Sollitt
Head of Membership Services	Keith House
Membership Finance Co-ordinator	Helen Sharman
Conference Organizer	Penny McCormack
Director of Strategy and Planning	Alan Leaman
General Election Planning Manager	Alison Holmes
Liberal Democrat News Editor	David Boyle

Periodicals

Liberal Democrat News	Weekly party newspaper
Liberator	Eight times a year, independent forum for debate
The Reformer	Quarterly, independent journal of policy and strategy

OTHER PARTIES

Scottish National Party (SNP)
6 North Charlotte Street
Edinburgh EH2 4JH
Tel: 0131-226-3661
Fax: 0131-226-7373
President: Winifred Ewing
National Convenor: Alex Salmond
Parliamentary Leader: Margaret Ewing
National Secretary: Alasdair Morgan
Director of Organization: Alison Hunter
Communications and Research: Kevin Pringle

Plaid Cymru (PC)
51 Cathedral Road
Cardiff CF1 9HD
Tel: 01222-231944
Fax: 01222-222506
President: Dafydd Wigley
General Secretary:Karl Davies

Green Party
1a Waterlow Road
Archway
London N19 5NJ
Tel: 0171-2724474
Fax: 0171-2726653
Chair: Jenny Jones
Press Officer: Peter Barnett

The Liberal Party
Gayfere House
22 Gayfere Street
London SW1P 3HP
Tel: 0171-233-2124
Fax: 01704-539315
email libparty@libparty.demon.co.uk
President: Michael Meadowcroft
Chair of National Exec.: Rob Wheway

NORTHERN IRELAND

Ulster Unionist Party
3 Glengall Street
Belfast BT12 5AE
Tel: 01232-324601
Fax: 01232-246738
Leader: David Trimble
Party Chairman: Dennis Rogan
Party Secretary: Jim Wilson

Democratic Unionist Party
91 Dundela Avenue
Belfast BT4 3BU
Tel: 01232-471155
Fax: 01232-471797
Leader: Ian Paisley
Deputy Leader: Peter Robinson
Party Chairman: James McClure
Party Secretary: Nigel Dodds
Press Officer: Samuel Wilson
General Secretary: Allan Ewart
Treasurer: Gregory Campbell

Social Democratic and Labour Party (SDLP)
Cranmore House
611c Lisburn Road
Belfast BT9 7GT
Tel: 01232-668100
Fax: 01232-669009
Leader: John Hume
Deputy Leader: Seamus Mallon
Party Chairman: Jonathan Stephenson
General Secretary: Gerry Cosgrove

Alliance Party
88 University Street
Belfast BT7 1HE
Tel: 01232-324274
Fax: 01232-333147
Leader: Lord John Alderdice
Party Chairman: Stephen McBride

General Secretary: David Ford
President: Addie Morrow

Sinn Féin
Belfast Headquarters
147 Andersontown Road
Belfast BT11 9BW
Tel 01232 301719

Press Office
51-55 Falls Road
Belfast BT13
Tel: 01232-323214
Fax: 01232-231723

Dublin Office
44 Cearnóg Pharnell (Parnell Square)
Dublin 1
Republic of Ireland
Tel: (00) 3531-8726932/ 8726100
Fax: (00) 3531-8733441
President: Gerry Adams
Vice-President: Pat Doherty
General Secretary: Lucilita Bhreatnach
National Chairman: Mitchel McLaughlin
Six County Chairman: Gearóid O hÉara
Director of Publicity: Rita O'Hare

7. National Newspapers

TABLE 7.1 *Circulation of National Newspapers (Average Net Circulation)*

Newspaper	Jul 96– Dec 96	Oct 95– Mar 96	Jul 95– Dec 95
Sun	3,980,808	4,072,971	4,027,850
Daily Mirror/Daily Record	3,124,454	3,240,354	3,281,620
Daily Mail	2,090,803	1,981,707	1,876,011
Daily Express	1,195,069	1,262,920	1,261,977
Daily Telegraph	1,084,440	1,044,281	1,052,928
Times	790,857	672,292	668,756
Daily Star	671,494	667,207	663,048
Guardian	396,800	401,988	395,135
Financial Times	296,834	304,854	295,740
Independent	265,037	288,364	292,827
London Evening Standard	425,028	463,146	441,287
News of the World	4,505,632	4,646,791	4,690,563
Sunday Mirror	2,437,662	2,454,204	2,534,566
Mail on Sunday	2,105,566	2,083,384	2,040,758
The People	2,049,509	2,066,608	2,092,056
Sunday Times	1,325,021	1,285,919	1,252,774
Sunday Express	1,177,094	1,309,301	1,362,974
Sunday Telegraph	776,231	663,196	674,031
Observer	453,353	465,538	463,301
Independent on Sunday	287,282	316,794	326,675
Sunday Sport	259,366	275,049	289,702

Source: Audit Bureau of Circulations

8. World Wide Web Sites

The Internet and World Wide Web have become important tools for political scientists. Beyond the common usage of electronic mail, the Internet is increasingly an important research and teaching resource. This year, we list an updated selection of World Wide Web sites which may be of interest to readers. Of course, listing such sites in 'hard-copy' might run counter to the ethos of the Web, but this guide is intended to simply highlight the availability of information. For those who use the Web regularly, the best route for political scientists is the Political Studies Association Home Page which provides a gateway to numerous sites. This can be found at **http://www.lgu. ac.uk/psa/psa.html** We hope that readers will also visit the EPOP Home Page at **http://www.lgu.ac.uk/psa/epop.html**

UK Government

http://www.Parliament.uk	Parliament
http://www.parliament.the-stationery-office.co.uk/ pa/ld/ldhome.htm	House of Lords
http://www.number-10.gov.uk/	No. 10 Downing Street
http://www.parlchan.co.uk/	Parliamentary Channel
http://www.pamis.gov.uk	Parliamentary Monitoring and Information Service
http://www.gchq.gov.uk	Government Communications Headquarters
http://www.open.gov.uk	HM Government: Main UK Open Government home page
http://www.coi.gov.uk/coi/depts/deptlist.html	Government Press Releases
http://www.coi.gov.uk/coi/	Central Office of Information
http://www.open.gov.uk/index/../dfee/dfeehome.htm	Department for Education and Employment
http://www.open.gov.uk/doe/doehome.htm	Department of the Environment
http://www.open.gov.uk/index/../doh/dhhome.htm	Department of Health

http://www.dti.gov.uk/	Department of Trade and Industry
http://www.open.gov.uk/index/../dot/dothome.htm	Department of Transport
http://www.fco.gov.uk	Foreign and Commonwealth Office
http://www.open.gov.uk/index/../customs/ c&ehome.htm	Her Majesty's Customs & Excise
http://www.open.gov.uk/index/../prison/prisonhm.htm	Her Majesty's Prison Service
http://www.hmso.gov.uk/	HM Stationery Office
http://www.hm-treasury.gov.uk	HM Treasury
http://www.open.gov.uk/index/../inrev/irhome.htm	Inland Revenue
http://www.open.gov.uk/maff/pages/maffhome.htm	Ministry of Agriculture, Fisheries and Food, UK.
http://www.mod.uk	Ministry of Defence
http://www.open.gov.uk/index/../nao/home.htm	National Audit Office
http://www.ons.gov.uk	Office for National Statistics (ONS)
http://www.nics.gov.uk/	Northern Ireland Office
http://www.nics.gov.uk/proni/pro_home.htm	Public Record Office of Northern Ireland
http://www.open.gov.uk/index/../scotoff/scofhom.htm	Scottish Office
http://www.open.gov.uk/woffice/whome.htm	Welsh Office
http://www.open.gov.uk/index/orghome.htm	UK Government Pages Organization Index
http://www.soton.ac.uk/~nukop/index.html	New Official Publications (University of Southampton)

Political Parties

http://www.albion-party.org.uk	Albion Party
http://ngwwmall.com/frontier/bnp/	British National Party

http://ourworld.compuserve.com/homepages/redweb/	Communist Party of Britain Greater London East Branch
http://www.conservative-party.org.uk/	Conservative Party
http://www.pncl.co.uk/~pwhite/CHARTER1.HTML	Conservative Party Charter Movement
http://www.conwayfor.org/	Conservative Way Forward
http://gnew.gn.apc.org/greenparty/	Green Party of England and Wales
http://www.prudhs.demon.co.uk/localgroups.html	Green Parties in North East England
http://www.connect.ie/labour/index.html	Irish Labour Party
http://www.poptel.org.uk/labour-party/	Labour Party
http://www.labour.org.uk/	Labour Party Conference
http://www.gpl.net/customers/labour/	Labour's Manifesto: 30 May 1996 Elections
http://www.u-net.com/~natlaw/	Natural Law Party of the United Kingdom
http://www.libparty.demon.co.uk/	Liberal Party
http://www.libdems.org.uk/	Liberal Democratic Party
http://www.powernet.co.uk/html/userwebs/ hack/ldlinx.html	Liberal Democrat Party in the UK: directory of UK Liberal Democrat web sites
http://www.compulink.co.uk/libdems/reformer.htm	The Reformer: Liberal-Democrat Party journal
http://www.digiweb.com/igeldard/LA/	Libertarian Alliance
http://www.netlink.co.uk/users/natdems/	National Democrats
http://www.wales.com/political-party/plaid-cymru/ englishindex.html	Plaid Cymru
http://www.pup.org/	Progressive Unionist Party (PUP)

http://www.conservative-party.org.uk/scottish/	Scottish Conservative and Unionist Party
http://www.scotlibdems.org.uk/	Scottish Liberal Democrat Party
http://www.tardis.ed.ac.uk/~alba/snp/	Scottish National Party
http://www.serve.com/rm/sinnfein/index.html	Sinn Féin
http://www.indigo.ie/sdlp/	Social Democratic and Labour Party (SDLP)
http://ourworld.compuserve.com/homepages/ GamesTheory/	Whig Party
http://www.workers-party.org/	Workers' Party
http://www.udp.org/	Ulster Democratic Party
http://www.dup.org.uk/	Ulster Democratic Unionist Party
http://www.btinternet.com/~ukip/	UK Independence Party

Elections

http://www.universal.nl/users/derksen/election/ home.htm	Parliamentary Elections World-Wide
http://www.klipsan.com/elecnews.htm	Daily World-Wide Election News
http://www.strath.ac.uk/Other/CREST/	CREST: Centre for Research into Elections and Social trends
http://ssdc.ucsd.edu/	Lijphart Election Data Archive at University of California
http://world.std.com/~nvri	National Voting Rights Institute
http://ssdc.ucsd.edu/	The Social Sciences Data Collection at the University of California San Diego
http://www.umich.edu/~nes/	The National Election Studies

http://www.klipsan.com/#results	Recent Election Results
http://www.ge97.co.uk/	1997 UK General Election
http://ourworld.compuserve.com/homepages/timb/	UK Elect: UK Election Resources (including UK-Elect Software)
http://www.warwick.ac.uk/~esrhi/vote/ukRes.html	Votes in General Elections since 1945.
http://www.qmw.ac.uk/~laws/election/index.html	British Parliamentary Elections since 1983
http://www.unite.net/customers/alliance/elfull.html	Election results in Northern Ireland since 1972
http://www.niweb.com/nielection/	Northern Ireland Elections 1996
http://www.niweb.com/nielection/wster.html	A Brief History of Northern Ireland Westminster Elections

Mass Media

http://www.yahoo.co.uk/headlines	Current UK and Ireland Headlines
http://www.tardis.ed.ac.uk/~ajh/politics.html	UK News and Politics
http://www.bbc.co.uk/westonline	BBC Westminster On-Line
http://www.irlnet.com/aprn/index.htmlAn Phoblacht /	Republican News
http://www.gallup.com	Gallup Polls
http://go2.guardian.co.uk	The Guardian
http://www.ajcunet.edu/her.htm	Higher Education Report
http://www.cix.co.uk/~ecotrend/LR/Review	Labour Review
http://www.gn.apc.org/labournet/llb	Labour Left Briefing
http://www.standard.co.uk	London Evening Standard
http://www.poptel.org.uk/morning-star	Morning Star
http://www.cleanroom.co.uk/nss/NSSHome.htm	New Statesman and Society

http://www.intervid.co.uk/intervid/eye/gateway.html	Private Eye
http://www.scotsman.com	Scotsman, The
http://www.the-times.co.uk	The Times Newpaper Group
http://www.timeshigher.newsint.co.uk	Times Higher: THES
http://www.cnn.com/POLITICS/index.html	CNN Political News Index

Academic Resource Sites

http://govinfo.kerr.orst.edu/stateis.html	United States of America 1990 Census of Population and Housing
http://ssda.anu.edu.au/cgi-bin/waiscensus	Australian Social Science Data Archives
http://www.cgs.niu.edu	Business and Industry Data Center, De Kalb, Ill.
gopher://gopher.sfu.ca/11/library/computer/rdl1/cnd.census	Canadian Census data (gopher)
http://dawww.essex.ac.uk/	The Data Archive
http://www.psych.ut.ee/esta/essda.html	Estonian Social Science Data Archive
http://www.sowi.uni-mannheim.de/eurodata/eurodata.html	Eurodata Research Archive
http://www.uni-mannheim.de/users/ddz/edz/edz.html	European Documentation Centre
http://www.social-science-gesis.de	GESIS (German Social Science Infrastructure Service)
http://www.uib.no/nsd/	Norwegian Social Science Data Archive (NSD)
http://ssdc.ucsd.edu/	Social Science Data Collection at UCSD
http://www.ssrc.org	Social Science Research Council
http://www.sosig.ac.uk/	SOSIG (UK Social Science Information Gateway)

http://www.ssd.gu.se/kid/sweind.html#census   Swedish Social Science
                                                     DataService

Libraries

http://www.ex.ac.uk/~ijtilsed/lib/uklibs.html   Index: UK Higher Education
                                                     and Research Libraries

http://www.nara.gov/nara/nail.html   NARA Archival Information
                                                     Locator

http://www.aa.gov.au/   Archives of Australia

http://www.c2.net/~brad/doc/index.html   Archive of US Historical
                                                     Documents

http://www.bodley.ox.ac.uk/   Bodleian Library

http://www.rsl.ox.ac.uk/imacat.html   Bodleian Library Image
                                                     Catalog

http://www.cpac.ca/english/resources/hist.html   CPAC Online Archive of
                                                     Historical Documents

http://www.lse.ac.uk/blpes/   British Library of Political &
                                                     Economic Science (BLPES)

http://www.ipt.com/city/cs/bush.htm   George Bush Presidential
                                                     Library

http://www.hometown.on.ca/clintonlibrary/index.html Clinton Library

http://www.niss.ac.uk/reference/opacs.html   Index: Higher Education &
                                                     Research Library Catalogues
                                                     – UK OPACs arranged by
                                                     region

http://www.iisg.nl/ialhiuk.html   International Association of
                                                     Labour History Institutions

http://www.interaxis.com/carter/   Jimmy Carter Library

http://web.calstatela.edu/library/index.htm   JFK Library

http://www.nara.gov/   National Archives and
                                                     Records Administration
http://147.252.133.152/nat-arch/   National Archives of Ireland

http://sunsite.unc.edu/lia/president/reagan.html   Ronald W. Reagan
                                                     Presidential Library

http://www.churchill.org/ — Winston Churchill Memorial and Library

Political Science Journals

http://www.sevenbridgespress.com/cr/crindex.html — *Critical Review: interdisciplinary journal of politics and society.*

http://www.frankcass.com/jnls/dem.htm — *Democratization*

http://www.psci.unt.edu/es/ — *Electoral Studies*

http://www.frankcass.com/jnls/ep.htm — *Environmental Politics*

http://www.ssn.flinders.edu.au/Politics/Journals/fjhp.html — *Flinders Journal Of History And Politics*

http://www.tau.ac.il/ijgt/index.html — *International Journal of Games Theory*

http://silver.ucs.indiana.edu/~isq/ — *International Studies Quarterly*

http://www.frankcass.com/jnls/ccp.htm — *Journal of Commonwealth and Comparative Politics*

http://www.frankcass.com/jnls/jls.htm — *Journal of Legislative Studies*

http://www.frankcass.com/jnls/lgs.htm — *Local Government Studies*

http://www.frankcass.com/jnls/mp.htm — *Mediterranean Politics*

http://www.shef.ac.uk/uni/academic/N-Q/perc/npe/ — *New Political Economy*

http://www.polisci.nwu.edu:8000/ — *Party Politics*

http://epn.org/psq.html — *Political Science Quarterly*

http://weber.u.washington.edu/~socmeth2/ — *Sociological Methodology* (American Sociological Association)

http://www.frankcass.com/jnls/wep.htm — *West European Politics*

http://www.wws.princeton.edu/world_politics/ — *World Politics*: contains abstracts of current articles

European Union

http://www.yahoo.co.uk/headlines/european/	Yahoo Current European Headlines
http://ibase139.eunet.be/clubdebruxelles/	Club de Bruxelles
http://www.ispo.cec.be/	Europa: European Commission
http://europa.eu.int/	Europa
http://www.ecu-notes.org/	ECU Notes
http://www.unicc.org/unece/Welcome.html	Economic Commission for Europe
http://www.echo.lu	I'M EUROPE
http://www.cec.lu/europarl/europarl.htm	EUROPARL: European Parliament Server
http://www.cec.lu/en/comm/opoce/wel.html	EUR-OP: Office of Official Publications of the European Communities
http://www.cec.lu/en/comm/eurostat/eurostat.html	EUROSTAT: Statistical Office of the European Communities
http://edms.esrin.esa.it/ecsl/index.html	European Centre for Space Law (ECSL)
http://www.inform.dk/edn/	Europe of Nations Group in the EU-Parliament
http://www.eea.dk	European Environment Agency
http://www.euro.centre.org/causa/ec/	European Centre for Social Welfare Policy and Research
http://www.axl.be/green/	Green Group in the European Parliament
http://wwwarc.iue.it/	Historical Archives of the European Communities
http://law.gonzaga.edu/library/ceeurope.htm	Index: Central and East European Legal, Political, Business and Economics

WWW Resources
– organized by country

http://www.paneuropa.org

International Paneurope
Union

http://www.fu-berlin.de/NewEurope/

Political Institutions and the
New Europe

http://www.ping.be/~ping0656/

Resource Link to European
Political Parties

http://ezinfo.ucs.indiana.edu/~amgrose/ceepg.html

Political Science Resources:
Central and Eastern Europe

NOTES TO CONTRIBUTORS

The manuscripts (referred to throughout as an 'article') should be submitted in duplicate, typewritten on one side only, unjustified on the right margin and double-spaced throughout (including notes, but not including tables/figures). Pages should be numbered consecutively, including those containing tables, illustrations and diagrams. A disk should accompany the manuscript. It should be labeled with the name of the article, the author's name and the software system used (ideally IBM compatible).

All tables, figures, maps, etc. must conform to the type area 108mm x 175mm. A clear hard copy of figures and maps must be provided. Sources should be given in each case. The article should be accompanied by a brief abstract (c. 150 words) and notes on the contributors, each in separate files.

STYLE
Font: Times New Roman 12pt. Headings: (1) Bold; (2) Italics (not underlined); (3) Italics, no new paragraph.

Quotation marks: single in text throughout; double within single; single within indented quotations.

Dates and Numbers: 12 July 1994. Abbreviate years: 1983–84; 1908–9; 1920–21; the 1930s *(not* 'the thirties').

Spelling: use the -z- alternative (recognize) except where -yse (analyse); -our rather than -or (favour) except in proper names, e.g. Labor Party, if that is its formal title.

Capitalization: Use capitals sparingly, for titles (the Secretary-General; President Mitterrand) and for unique or central institutions (the European Commission, the International Atomic Energy Authority) but not for general or local organizations and offices (a government minister, the mayor, Brigham parish council). Capitalize Party in a title (the British Green Party), otherwise lower case. Lower case for the state and for the left and the right (but the New Left, the New Right). Capitalize -isms from names (Marxism), elsewhere lower case (ecologism). In general, lower case for conferences and congresses (the party's tenth congress was held in 1995).

Notes and References: Essential notes should be indicated by superscript numbers in the text and collected on a single page at the end of the text. References cited in the text should read thus: Denver (1990: 63–4), Denver and Hands (1985, 1990). Use *'et al.'* when citing a work by more than two authors, e.g. Brown *et al.* (1991). The letters a, b, c, etc., should be used to distinguish citations of different works by the same author in the same year, e.g. Brown (1975a, b).

All references cited in the text should be listed alphabetically and presented in full after the notes, using the following style:

Articles in journals: Anker, Hans (1990) 'Drawing Aggregate Inferences from Individual Level Data: The Utility of the Notion of a Normal Vote', *European Journal of Political Research* 18: 373–87.

Books: Heath, Anthony, Roger Jowell and John Curtice (1985) *How Britain Votes.* Oxford: Pergamon.

Articles in books: Webb, Paul D. (1994) 'Party Organizational Change in Britain: The Iron Law of Centralization?', in Richard S. Katz and Peter Mair (eds) *How Parties Organize: Change and Adaptation in Party Organizations in Western Democracies,* pp.109–34. London: Sage.

Tables: set page width to 108mm (for wider tables, use landscape with maximum width 175mm). Place table in the text approximate position, placing a page break at the top and tall: there is no need to include such guidance as '[INSERT TABLE 2 ABOUT HERE]'. Do not use the 'Table function' in the word processing package as this causes difficulties at production stage. Instead, use the tab function, as follows: Set tabs for columns; align by decimal point; centre the headings. The font size of the Table is not so important; what matters is that the Table should fit within type area 108mm x 175mm.

Figures: try to avoid tints. If they are necessary, send a hard copy with tint, and a disk version without tint.

Maps: keep number of tints gradations to a minimum (if possible no more than 3). Provide a bromide and disk version.